# CHARLES BROCKDEN BROWN

CHARLES BROCKDEN BROWN

at about the age of twenty-eight, from a portrait by the English-
American painter, James Sharples (1751-1811)

DAVID LEE CLARK

# CHARLES BROCKDEN BROWN

## PIONEER VOICE OF AMERICA

1952

DUKE UNIVERSITY PRESS

DURHAM, NORTH CAROLINA

PRINTED IN THE UNITED STATES OF AMERICA
BY THE SEEMAN PRINTERY, INC., DURHAM, N. C.

This biography is respectfully
dedicated to the memory of the late

WILLIAM LINN BROWN
*grandson*

AND TO

MRS. EMILIE B. REIFF
*great granddaughter*

of Charles Brockden Brown

# PREFACE

*Charles Brockden Brown: Pioneer Voice of America* is an interpretation of Brockden Brown's place in American life and literature. Into the colorful field of fictionalized biography, though tempted, I have not strayed. Facts, tyrannous though they be, have ever been before me in my portrayal of the author's life. The emphasis on Brown as interpreter of American life has, I hope, not overshadowed Brown the man, the lover, and the friend, and has not lent credence to the fatuous fable that Brown was a consummate prig. In his manifold activities as lover, friend, editor, schoolmaster, merchant, literary critic, and novelist, Brown has been presented in this biography in as much fulness as the known facts would warrant.

The chief purpose of this biography has been to stress the varied interests and accomplishments of an American who, unfortunately, has been known merely as a novelist or as the first professional man of letters in America. In this volume Brown is for the first time presented in his full dimensions.

Several years ago William Linn Brown, grandson of Charles Brockden Brown, placed in my hands, for my exclusive use, a large body of unpublished manuscripts of his grandfather—letters, journals, and fragments of novels. This material—listed in detail in the bibliography—has enabled me to present a fuller and more accurate account of Brown's varied activities than would have otherwise been possible. Many previously obscure details of his life are now clarified.

In the preparation of this biography I have incurred more obligations than I can readily enumerate. Many little acts of kindness and of love must, I fear, go unacknowledged. To the late Carl Van Doren I am indebted for the suggestion that I undertake the work and for his encouragement when the going was difficult and the goal indistinct.

To the Graduate Research Institute of the University of Texas I am indebted for funds for the materials of research and for a research assistant, and for a semester's research leave from my official duties at the University.

Grateful acknowledgments are hereby made to the librarians of the following public institutions for valuable assistance: the Historical Society of Pennsylvania for permission to publish four manuscript letters and fragments of a novel, and to consult the Elijah Brown Diaries; the Library Company of Philadelphia for the use of a manuscript letter; Haverford College for permission to publish four manuscript letters; the New York Public Library for the use of one manuscript letter and for a photostatic copy of the original edition of *Alcuin;* the Library of the New York Historical Society for permis-

sion to quote from Dunlap's manuscript Diaries (Vols. XIV and XV);
the Library of Congress for photostatic copies of four political pamphlets, one manuscript letter of Brown's, and one of Thomas Jefferson's to Brown, and for permission to publish them; Yale University
for permission to consult and quote from the manuscript Diaries of
William Dunlap; Columbia University for unfailing assistance in the
early stages of the work; and the University of Texas for photostating
or borrowing rare Brown and collateral materials.

I hereby express my deep gratitude to my colleague Truman Guy
Steffan for reading large portions of the manuscript and making many
constructive suggestions.

To my research assistant, Miss Gladys Louise Maddocks, I owe a
debt which it would be difficult to express in full. But for her constructive work this biography might still be dormant. In blazing a
trail through the wilderness of material Miss Maddocks has made
my journey pleasant by making it less laborious.

My debt of gratitude to the late William Linn Brown and to his
niece, Mrs. Emilie B. Reiff, has been more than mere words can express. By putting rare Brown manuscripts at my exclusive disposition they have given to this work the status of an authorized biography.

My thanks are due especially to my wife for having read the entire
manuscript, from its nascent to its mature state, and for having offered
many valuable suggestions for its improvement. But for her untiring
effort in all phases of the work this biography would never have been
brought to its final conclusion.

Austin, Texas
September 18, 1952

# CONTENTS

# CHARLES BROCKDEN BROWN

# I

# INTRODUCTION

### THE CLIMATE OF IDEAS

THE STUDENT of American life and literature should feel vitally interested in the decades of the early National period, in which was laid the foundation of our political state and our cultural heritage.[1] The texture of the population of hardly three million people—English, German, Dutch, French, and Scandinavian stock—is even more significant than the number. With the Negro slaves and white indentured servants comprising almost a third of the population, there were few free wage earners. The planters, rich merchants, and ship-builders—the socially privileged classes—constituted the ruling elements; but class distinctions were less rigid than in Europe, for all except slaves might (theoretically) rise in the social scale.[2]

Each of the three sections of the new nation developed its own distinctive economic and cultural ideas: the middle and northern coastal region was largely mercantile and as a rule conservative; the smaller tradesmen—among whom were members of Charles Brockden Brown's family—artisans, and yeomen were democratic (republican); the Tidewater region was based on the plantation economy of slavery; the backcountry, or frontier, was decidedly agrarian and democratic. Diverse as these sections were before the Revolution, they had in common one desire—to be free from British interference. Once free, they were jealous of their own sectional rights and at first opposed establishing a national government; only when bitter experience proved that they were interdependent were they willing to surrender some of their individual rights for general welfare and protection.[3]

To understand the arguments for and against independence and the subsequent adoption of the Constitution, it is necessary to recall the winds of European doctrine, blowing across the Atlantic. The Tories drew heavily on Hobbes for their theories of absolute monarchy;

[1] "Factors to Be Investigated in American Literary History from 1787 to 1800," *English Journal* (College Edition), XXIII. (June, 1934), 481.

[2] Evart Boutell Greene, *The Revolutionary Generation* (New York, 1943), pp. 68-80.

[3] Vernon Louis Parrington, *Main Currents in American Thought* (New York, 1927), I, 180-182.

the Federalists found the *Leviathan* a valuable source of argument for a strongly centralized government; weighty were the political writings of Hume;[4] most influential for both sides was Locke, whose theories of natural rights, the state of nature, the social contract, and the right of revolution summed up definitively seventeenth-century political thought and passed it on to the eighteenth.[5] Price, Priestley, Paine, Jefferson, Brockden Brown, and others put a construction on Locke's theory of state—that government existed solely for the good of the people—that embraced all the current radicalism in France, England, and America.

Thomas Paine—an Anglo-American, American in spirit—was perhaps more than any other one person responsible for the American revolt. With characteristic impatience at temporizing, Paine threw himself headlong into the tense situation and wrote his famous *Common Sense* (1776) and raised the demand for a Declaration of Independence.[6] As editor of the *Pennsylvania Magazine*, Paine showed himself a pioneer in social reform. He vigorously advocated the abolition of slavery and helped organize the first American antislavery society. He pleaded for the arbitration of international disputes; he showed the necessity for rational divorce laws; and he demanded justice for women, anticipating by only a few months Brockden Brown's similar ideas. Beginning with *Agrarian Justice* (1796) Paine became the spokesman for social justice. To insure prosperity to the masses, to make life and limb more secure, to give all an equal chance at the goods and services of the nation, to aid the general welfare by social service and free public education were propositions which scarcely entered the mind of the average man.[7] The French political and social philosophers—Montesquieu, Helvétius, Holbach, and notably Rousseau—advocated an actual revolution to establish the majority will; Rousseau became the spiritual father of the French

[4] *Ibid.*, p. 280.

[5] See Merle Curti's excellent article in the Huntington Library *Bulletin* called "The Great Mr. Locke, America's Philosopher, 1765-1865," II (April, 1934), 107-151.

[6] James S. Allen, ed., *Selections from Thomas Paine* (New York, 1937), Introduction, p. 8.

[7] American independence won, Paine cast his lot with the British workers against their dictatorial government. In their behalf he composed one of the most popular and persuasive books of all times—*The Rights of Man*. This book led to his eventual exile from England and roused the hostility of ultra-conservative Americans. Driven from his native land, he took refuge in France and was made a member of the Assembly, where he exercised a mild and salutary influence in that often chaotic body. His active co-operation with the French government and his attack on orthodox religious systems in *The Age of Reason*, composed in part behind the bars of the Luxembourg prison, confirmed the hostility of unthinking Americans; and even Thomas Jefferson's influence was not enough to protect him from vilification on his return from France in 1802.

Revolution as well as the father of modern totalitarian democracy.[8] Montesquieu developed the system of separation of powers, with corresponding checks and balances.[9] Helvétius denounced positive institutions, particularly of government, as the source of all errors and prejudices of mankind. Wandering from nature's laws, contended Holbach, brought calamity upon mankind—man had always been a slave to natural law.[10] These French philosophies sooner or later found their way to America and influenced the growth of our incipient republic; be it noted that young Brockden Brown was an eager reader of these French philosophers. American thinkers, whether they espoused the English or the French philosophy, adapted it to their particular needs—and with varying results. The American Declaration of Independence with its lofty political philosophy of equality and justice committed the Congress to the establishment of a republic— not a democracy, for the conservative leaders looked upon the word *democracy* much as the conservatives today regard the word *communism*. The Founding Fathers feared democracy: political democracy they would grant to a degree, but economic and social democracy, never! In spite of the unsatisfactory state of the nation incident to the war, the revolutionary movement, instead of continuing to a more democratic and probably tragic end, as the French Revolution was to do, was checked, and a conservative reaction set in.[11] We shall see that Brockden Brown tried to drive a middle course in the liberal-conservative conflict.

Probably the most disturbing and disruptive element in the national scene was the bitter conflict between those who favored a government by the aristocracy of wealth and privilege and those who demanded a representative democracy responsible to the people. Jefferson and the agrarian democrats, ranged against the believers in the English constitutional theory, advocated a republic, a government by representation, and warned against any one branch gaining undue power. Jefferson was interested in both the political and the economic prosperity of America. In the long and acrimonious fight between the followers of Jefferson and of Hamilton, Brockden Brown contributed many valuable pamphlets, taking at first a disinterested point of view, but finally bowing discreetly to the Hamiltonian concept.

The story of the late Colonial and early National thought is the history of the Enlightenment—the general name given to the philo-

[8] John Herman Randall, Jr., *The Making of the Modern Mind* (Boston, 1940), p. 355.

[9] *Ibid.*, p. 345.

[10] *Système de la nature* (1770).

[11] James Truslow Adams, *The Epic of America* (Boston, 1932), p. 76; cf. William Dunlap, *Life of Brown*, II, 45; also see Carter Goodrich and Sol Davison, "The Wage-Earner in the Westward Movement," *Political Science Quarterly*, L (1935), 161-185, LI (1936), 61-116; Joseph Shafer, "Some Facts Bearing on the Safety Valve Theory," *Wisconsin Magazine of History*, XX (1936), 216-232.

sophical theories which attacked established authority and attempted to arrive at knowledge empirically—and its adaptation to American conditions.[12] It was concerned with the humanitarian movement, a natural outgrowth of the doctrine of perfectibility, sympathy for the oppressed, deistic faith in the natural goodness of man, Christian piety, and the doctrine of infinite progress of the human mind.[13] Many prominent Americans insisted that their countrymen had almost unlimited fields ahead of them: Thomas Paine believed that poverty and war could be abolished; Franklin and Rush declared that science would lead mankind to the promised land; most Americans, by virtue of their expansive, adventurous, scientific spirit, were perfectibilians. While Franklin and Jefferson and Brockden Brown had doubts as to the absolute perfectibility of human nature, they did believe that infinite progress could be made through the application of the truths of the social sciences. Another outgrowth of the Enlightenment was interest in education for women, strongly advocated in America in the writings of Brockden Brown.

Closely associated with the Enlightenment was the new philosophy of deism, which had a profoundly modifying influence on Puritanism.[14] The spread of deism, adopted by such leading thinkers as Franklin and Jefferson, was aided by the increasing secularization of thought, the growth of anticlericalism, and the agitation for complete separation of church and state. Many of Brockden Brown's closest friends were deists, and the philosophy of deism was examined in Brown's magazines and pamphlets.

Even more important than deism in framing the course of the new nation were the economic ideas fostered by the Enlightenment. According to Locke, wealth was based on and created by labor; Adam Smith in *The Wealth of Nations* (1776) pointed out the fallacies of the mercantile theory.

All these problems—political, social, literary, and religious—were, as we shall see, discussed at great length in the works of Charles Brockden Brown. His essays, his political pamphlets, his extended works on the rights of women, his magazine articles, and even his novels bear witness to Brown's deep concern about the issues facing the new nation.

Even before the Revolution the colonies were developing a cultural life of their own. With the unique environment of the New World and the mingling of various languages and cultures acting on the

[12] Howard Mumford Jones, "European Ideas in America," *American Literature*, VII (Nov., 1935), 253-254.

[13] Curti, *op. cit.*, p. 117.

[14] "The Puritan Way of Life," in Miller and Johnson, *The Puritans* (New York, 1938), is an excellent interpretation of the intellectual, cultural, and religious character of the Puritans.

predominantly British cultural pattern, a distinctive American type of thought was evolving.[15]

The idea of universal, free, public education as a necessary concomitant of the good life slowly gained ground. For a long time Southern planters sent their sons to England for their college careers.[16] In the East merchants encouraged their sons to study not only the classics but also useful subjects such as mathematics and navigation; the lower middle class did not trouble themselves with Latin and Greek, but learned the "practical" subjects. With the growing political ferment, artisans formed clubs and libraries and read newspapers.[17] Progress in education was slow indeed, for social and economic conditions following the Revolutionary War were chaotic.[18] Intellectually the evil effects of the war were numerous: men deserted scholarship for practical pursuits; many schools closed, never to reopen; libraries were ruined, and new books were almost unobtainable. But after the war there was a strong sentiment in favor of universal education. The mass of the people began to read pamphlets and newspapers, and the feeling that a self-governing people must be educated in order to enjoy democracy was as genuine as it was general. Colleges that reopened after the war modernized their courses of study; emphasis on language and literature was noted for the first time; literary societies were formed to study contemporary writers; professional schools were established; the American Philosophical Society, an outgrowth of Franklin's Academy (1744), encouraged all branches of learning, particularly science; an interest in geography and travel was stimulated; many maps and books appeared; trade with China fostered knowledge of the world;[19] research in geology, natural history, and chemistry spread. With their utilitarian bent, Americans proceeded to make practical application of their scientific knowledge, and men like Franklin and Jefferson praised inventors and encouraged ingenuity, with the result that between 1790 and 1800 a total of 276 patents were granted.[20]

Everywhere the spirit of nationalism was manifest. Both radicals and conservatives advocated cultural independence as well as political. No longer did Americans think of themselves as citizens of the British Empire, but rather as members of a new and separate nationality. Speakers and writers reiterated that arts and sciences, nourished by freedom, must flourish, and that scholarship must devote itself to the national welfare. We shall see that Charles Brockden Brown was a vigorous pioneer voice among those who advocated complete intellectual independence from Europe.

[15] Curti, *op. cit.*, p. 3.
[16] *Ibid.*, p. 29.
[17] See Carl Van Doren's *Benjamin Franklin* (New York, 1938).
[18] Greene, *op. cit.*, p. 289; Curti, *op. cit.*, p. 22.
[19] Curti, *op. cit.*, pp. 175-178.
[20] Jones, *op. cit.*, p. 254.

The Revolution also had had far-reaching social and political conse-quences. Industry and commerce flourished; the wealthy middle class, which had taken the place of the old aristocracy, yearned for the pomp, glitter, and special privileges of the pre-Revolutionary days. Only the untiring efforts of men like Paine and Jefferson prevented this faction from utterly destroying the young democracy. In the end a strong democratic national state prevailed.[21] Despite the far-reaching changes incident to the Revolution, European thought-patterns re-mained dominant, though modified to fit the American scene.[22]

Although the ideal of a national literature was not to be realized for nearly one hundred years, the American people began to be con-scious of their identity as a nation. But imitating British models prevented the early National period from developing any native litera-ture of the first rank.

Intensely preoccupied as the American people were with building a republic in the face of a watching and somewhat hostile world, they could hardly be expected to concern themselves, to any great extent, with "pure" literature.[23] Until Charles Brockden Brown's coura-geous attempt to live by writing, there were no professional authors in the United States, and few emulated him during the early National period. Fewer than one hundred books of native origin were pub-lished between 1776 and 1792.[24] Native genius was absorbed in po-litical issues (as in the cases of Barlow and Freneau), and there was almost no financial encouragement.

With the Colonial tendency toward the strictly practical, belles-lettres, native or imported, were not generally popular until well into the Revolutionary period. The colonists read to improve their souls and bodies; reading for enjoyment did not appeal until the arduous task of building a country had been completed and a leisure class had emerged. Finally, however, literature began to take hold, and the novels of the eighteenth-century masters—Fielding, Sterne, Smollett, and especially Richardson—were widely read. But the Puritan atti-tude toward all worldly joys, including novel reading, greatly ham-pered the spread of fiction reading until well into the nineteenth cen-tury. To this objection to reading "licentious" literature must be ascribed, at least in part, the delay in the appearance of an American novel. Finally the Gothic, didactic, and sentimental novels[25] became popular and stimulated the spread of lending and circulating libraries.

Magazines flourished.[26] The idea of an American magazine origi-

[21] Parrington, *op. cit.*, I, 193.

[22] Curti, *op. cit.*, pp. ix-x.

[23] "Prospectus," *Port Folio*, I (1801), i.

[24] Candidus, "On American Literature," *Monthly Magazine*, I (Aug., 1799), 340.

[25] For a full discussion of the novel of this period, see Herbert Ross Brown, *The Sentimental Novel in America* (Durham, N. C., 1940).

[26] Frank Luther Mott, *History of American Magazines*, I.

nated with Benjamin Franklin, who published his proposals on November 13, 1740; but Andrew Bradford, anticipating Franklin by three days, in January, 1741, published the first American monthly— the *American Magazine;* Bradford's magazine expired with the third issue, and Franklin's with the sixth. During the Revolution such publications ceased, but from 1783 till the close of the century the new republic was flooded with patriotic effusions, which created a demand for periodical publication. More than forty monthlies alone appeared during these seventeen years, of which four were really successful. Two of these, the *Columbian Magazine* (1786-1792) and the *American Museum* (1787-1792), were published in Philadelphia; the *Massachusetts Magazine* (1789-1796), in Boston; and the *New-York Magazine* (1790-1797), in New York City. For the first time one finds in these a native product. The new century produced the most successful American magazine of its time—the *Port Folio* (1801-1827). Under the brilliant editorship (1801-1809) of Joseph Dennie, it became the only literary magazine with national circulation.[27] But America was unable to sustain an array of magazines; the people were primarily materialists and could not rise to higher reaches of culture; imperfect communication, meager circulation, inadequate postal laws —all caused the failure of early American magazines.

New and powerful literary impulses having been awakened by the War for Independence, demands for literary independence were heard with increasing frequency. At first the publications were imitative of British magazines, but there arose a conscious effort to produce and encourage a native literature. Yet so long as there was no international copyright law, the cultivation of a native literature was practically impossible.

However, many of the contributors to these magazines were important figures whose literary reputation, though dimmed by time and by their absorption in political and practical matters, still warrants our attention. Probably the best known of these is Benjamin Franklin, whose *Autobiography* is admittedly one of the chief books of its kind;[28] his earlier *Poor Richard* appealed to the practical qualities of the Colonists. Philip Freneau, our first important poet, dedicated his talent to the Revolution and later to the fight against the conservatism of the economic royalists whose influence was dangerously threatening American democracy; he wrote more than sixty satires, odes, and elegies on the war, and later composed most of the lyrics which have won for him a small but lasting place in American literature. In defending America by spending his strength on bitter poetic satire and vigorous prose, Freneau sacrificed much of the name he

[27] H. M. Ellis, *Joseph Dennie and His Circle*, University of Texas *Studies in English*, no. 40 (1915).

[28] Carl Van Doren, ed., *Selections from Benjamin Franklin and Jonathan Edwards* (New York, 1920), Introduction, p. ix; also see *Benjamin Franklin*.

might have made as a lyric poet.[29]   In direct contrast to Paine and
Freneau was Francis Hopkinson, whose name, though bright in his
own day, has been almost forgotten; prominent in cultured circles,
he played amiably with art, literature, and music;[30] although Hopkinson's literary gift was a minor one, his good-natured, clever satire
was in welcome contrast to the general run of invective that disgraced
the pages of most of the American newspapers and magazines.   Far
more influential because of their unity were the group known as the
Connecticut (or Hartford) Wits, who, though more vigorous than
talented, deserve fame as the first real school of poetry in the
early republic; at first considered radical, they gradually became
conservative;[31] their political writings consisted of biting satire against
populism, Jeffersonian democracy, and anything that savored of the
French;[32] the three most important figures of the group were John
Trumbull, Timothy Dwight, and Joel Barlow.[33]   Trumbull is chiefly
remembered for *The Progress of Dulness*, a satire on college education, and *M'Fingal*, a Revolutionary satire on the Tories.   Timothy
Dwight—president of Yale, minister, and poet—was a steadfast champion of orthodoxy, and was abusive and intolerant as a satirist.[34]
Joel Barlow, after a sojourn abroad, broke completely with his former
ideas and aligned himself with the liberal thinkers; though radical in
politics, he was conservative in literature; his very readable prose
is generally neglected in the glare of *The Columbiad* (1807), his
"grand style" epic, which glorified America and American democracy.
But America, struggling for her political existence and demanding
the talents of her gifted men, was not yet ready to take her place in
literature among the great nations of the world.

The cause of democracy everywhere suffered a severe setback with
the failure of the French Revolution to live up to its early promises.
Conservative forces everywhere gained recruits while the liberals,
though hopeful, were daunted.   Mechanics, artisans, farmers deserted the liberal ranks and accepted the religious orthodoxy and
political conservatism that flooded the press.[35]   Brockden Brown,
though generally aligned with the liberal forces, had by 1803 found
himself thrown with the influential conservative elements of the nation, which reached into the whole political, social, and intellectual
fabric.   The new democratic doctrines of sex and race equality were

[29] Parrington, *op. cit.*, II, 380. For a full estimate of Freneau, see Harry H.
Clark, *Poems of Freneau* (New York, 1929); Lewis Leary, *That Rascal Freneau*
(New Brunswick, N. J. 1941).

[30] He was our first native composer (Marble, *Heralds of American Literature*,
Chicago, 1907, p. 43).

[31] Parrington, *The Connecticut Wits*, pp. 247-248.

[32] *Ibid.*, p. xxv.

[33] *Ibid.*, pp. xxxv-xxxvi.

[34] *Ibid.*, p. xl.

[35] Curti, *op. cit.*, pp. 188-189.

attacked; the idea that women could equal men was ridiculed, and some, like Hamilton, wanted to put women and children in factories to keep them out of mischief and teach them to be useful.[36] Literature showed the reaction when Charles Brockden Brown's democratic feminist novels yielded popularity to the writings of Hannah More and Susanna Rowson.[37] There was a waning of the antislavery sentiment. The churches, alarmed at what they considered infidelity, and having successfully attacked deism, now leveled their darts at "French Ideas"; revivalism akin to the Great Awakening struck the country and found its chief support in rural sections, and put into effect every sensational device to combat worldliness. The bounds of natural science were restricted, for the religionists believed the new scientific theories savored of deism and French "atheism." So in many spheres and levels of thought the conservative reaction made its deadening effect felt; and although the contending forces of progress and reaction had left their scars on the face of America, fortunately they were not so deep or malignant that time could not heal them. Eventually the forces of compromise and sanity prevailed, and by the end of the first quarter of the new century the country moved into the Era of Good Feeling.

Into this period of vital and stimulating changes and violently opposed currents of thought Charles Brockden Brown was born in 1771. A child during the Revolutionary War, he was an impressionable youth when the liberal-conservative controversy was at its height. Growing up in Philadelphia, the political and cultural center of the United States until well past 1800, Brown was exposed to all the currents of thought, European and American, that were molding a new country and a new people. As editor of three different magazines in that stirring first decade of the nineteenth century, Brown had a rare opportunity for observing, experiencing, and expressing its stirring life. As America's first considerable novelist he was fortunately situated in time and place to be the leader of those writers who labored for a national literature.

To show how Charles Brockden Brown, our first man of letters, was influenced by this turbulent and colorful background, how and to what extent these contending currents of thought shaped his life and personality, and how the national scene is reflected in the pages of his journals, private letters, magazines and novels, is the purpose of this biography.

[36] *Ibid.,* pp. 196-197.
[37] *Ibid.,* p. 197.

# II

# ANCESTRY, EARLY LIFE, SCHOOLING, AND APPRENTICESHIP

## PHILADELPHIA IN THE EIGHTEENTH CENTURY

IT IS ADVISABLE to re-create in some degree the general picture of the city where Charles Brockden Brown was born and reared, and in which he spent the first twenty and the last nine years of his brief but feverish life. Philadelphia, founded by William Penn in 1682, was settled by refugees from Old World tyrannies and oppressions— from England, Wales, Germany, and later France; being favorably situated on trade routes and being kind and generous to foreigners, within a century it had become one of the leading cities of the New World. Despite Quaker insistence upon a frugal, simple, democratic life, the city became the gayest and wealthiest city in America, teeming with the pomp and chivalry of Colonial days and leading the intellectual life of the nation; here were the foremost schools, newspapers, magazines, and libraries, and here scientific research and philosophical speculation reached new heights; here was the center of trade and commerce with Europe as well as the meeting place of Western fur traders; here met the most advanced ideas in government, in science, and in religion. It was thus no accident that the Continental Congress should meet here, that the proclamation of the Declaration of Independence should echo first in its halls, and that it should become the seat of government of the new nation. It was logical for Philadelphia to succeed New York as the capital, for here the monarchical tradition was weaker; the interests of the population were more varied; here lived more small tradesmen and artisans, more schoolmasters, music teachers, lawyers, physicians, surgeons, scientists, and philosophers; here long had been the home of religious dissidence, and here was greater political, social, and intellectual ferment and the freest thinking on all matters, human or divine.[1]

To this city in the closing decade of the eighteenth century came refugees in great numbers from France. Though they came as *émigrés,* many of them never returned to their native land, but settled down and added new blood and new thought to this melting pot. They

[1] Charles A. and Mary R. Beard, *A Basic History of the United States*, pp. 143-144.

had brought with them the culture of an older civilization to mingle with the many strains of the New World. Among those who came were Charles de Talleyrand, the Duc de Périgord; Louis Marie de Noailles—to be followed later by the Du Pont de Nemours, and others as distinguished. Their influence was potent in helping to shape the educational, philosophical, and economic course of the nation.[2]

### BROWN'S ANCESTORS

It was in this city, the meeting place of divergent and hetero-geneous ideas, and at a time when one world was dying and another struggling to be born, that Charles Brockden Brown was born, Jan-uary 17, 1771. It is no wonder, then, that as a youth he strayed from the narrowing Quaker fold to struggle in dark ways and to follow after strange gods. The ferment of a new life in a new nation stirred deep in his young soul and for a time drove him from the bosom of family and friends. In the struggle which ensued he wrestled long and mightily with himself and arose from that struggle a dedicated spirit, the voice of a native literature, and the first signer of America's declaration of literary independence.

Brockden Brown once remarked that he had been many times mor-tified in looking over the catalogue of heroes, sages, and saints to find not a single *Brown* among them. A careful and vigorous shaking of the Brown genealogical tree gives sad but eloquent confirmation of the grounds for his chagrin. Yet Charles Brockden Brown could number among his progenitors some very capable and talented men and women. Natives of England and professed Quakers, his ancestors settled in America and trusted to the savages and the wilderness rather than to the justice of their countrymen.[3]

According to the Quaker Records in the Library of the Pennsyl-vania Historical Society, Charles Brockden Brown's father, Elijah, was the son of James Brown of East Nottingham, Chester County, Pennsylvania. James was the son of William Brown of Maryland, and William the son of the James Brown, the novelist's great-great-grandfather, who with a number of other Englishmen left the mother-land in the good ship *Kent* to escape persecution at the hands of the "infamous Charles" the Second. On arrival in the New World they laid out the town of Burlington, New Jersey, in 1677, five years before the coming of Penn. A number of the Browns later settled in what is now known as Chester County, Pennsylvania. This county borders the state of Maryland and was for many years a bone of contention between Pennsylvania and that state. The Browns, apparently,

[2] *Ibid.*, pp. 144-145.
[3] William Dunlap, *The Life of Charles Brockden Brown* (Philadelphia, 1815), I, 11. (Hereinafter referred to as Dunlap.).

founded the town of East Nottingham, and here for some generations stuck close to the soil and the countinghouse, becoming small but prosperous farmers and merchants.

William Brown had moved over the line into Maryland, where was born Charles Brockden Brown's grandfather, James Brown. But it appears that James returned to the ancestral abode at East Nottingham, for here on October 4, 1734, he married Miriam Churchman. To them were born Edward, 1735; Hannah, 1737; Elijah, 1740; Estor, 1742; and William, 1746. Elijah at about the age of twelve was sent up to Philadelphia, sixty miles away, to attend the Friends Grammar School. What progress he made in his studies or how long he remained there, no reliable records are available to show. We know, however, that after his school days were over, he was apprenticed to a merchant of the city of Philadelphia.

All that we know of the character of young Elijah Brown is found in the church certificate of removal from East Nottingham to Philadelphia, dated February 19, 1757, which reads in part as follows:

Our certificate being requested of *Elijah Brown,* son of Jas. Brown of East Nottingham, who hath been sometime at school in your city, but now put as an apprentice to a Friend therein. We therefore after the usual enquiry certify that nothing appears but that he has been a dutiful child to his parents, soberly inclined, and of a good repute amongst us according to his age. We therefore recommend him to your Christian care and particular regard, sincerely desiring his farther growth and Establishment in the Truth in which we remain your Friends and Brethren.

In the meantime Elijah had met, wooed, and won the heart of Mary Armitt, daughter of Joseph Armitt of Philadelphia. The Armitts were prosperous merchants and appear to have had a better social standing than the Browns. They were numbered among the original followers of William Penn and helped to lay out the city of Philadelphia.

Elijah Brown and Mary Armitt were married on July 9, 1761, in the Arch Street Meeting House, Philadelphia. The marriage is there recorded: "*Brown, Elijah,* of Phil., son of James of Whiteland township, Chester Co., and Mary Armitt, Jr., of Phil., dr. of Joseph, of said city, deceased, at Phila. Meeting House. Wits.: William, Susanna, Sarah, William, Jr., and Susanna Brown, Elizabeth and Sarah Armitt,'' and fifty-five others. To them were born Joseph, who died in infancy, James, Joseph, Armitt, Charles Brockden,[4] Elijah, and Jane Elizabeth.

[4] The novelist was named for Charles Brockden (1683-1769), who came to America in his youth and became Philadelphia's first city Recorder, a position he held for half a century. His second wife was Mary Lisle, a sister of Elizabeth Armitt. Through this marriage Brockden became the great uncle of the novelist. For a somewhat fanciful account of his life, see the Dunlap *Life,* I, 12-13.

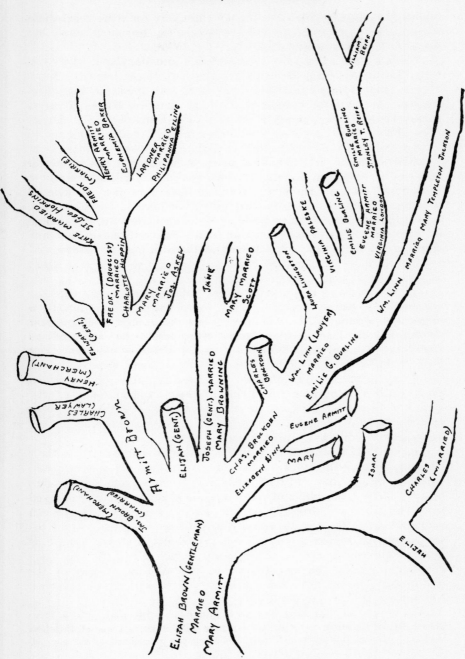

THE BROWN FAMILY TREE

(By permission of the late William Linn Brown of Philadelphia)

The unpublished journal of Elijah Brown (1794-1797), consisting for the most part of commonplace entries, does contain a list of his reading. Here are mentioned Godwin's *Political Justice*, Mary Wollstonecraft's *View of the French Revolution*, and Robert Bage's *Man As He Is*—all revolutionary works.

As Elijah Brown's family were reared in a liberal atmosphere, it is no wonder that the children broke with the more narrowing tenets of Quakerism. All apparently married outside the Quaker fold.

### PRINCIPLES OF QUAKERISM

Charles Brockden Brown's ancestors, both paternal and maternal, were devout followers of the sect known as Friends or Quakers, whose chief tenets were the right of private judgment and the rejection of sectarian beliefs—baptism, the doctrine of the Trinity, all sacraments, forms, and ceremonies; they made an effort to return to the spirituality and simplicity of the early Christians, with emphasis on humane ideas and philanthropic actions, such as the abolition of slavery and prison reform, which in time came to be accepted as fundamental, practical, social principles.[5]

The Browns and the Armitts were typical Quakers in their earnestness, devoutness, uprightness of character, and devotion to a simple but strenuous life. They were active in church affairs, and correspondingly inactive in matters pertaining to the larger affairs of society. None of them apparently sought to rise or did rise to any considerable station in political or civic life. They were contented merely to go their ways, unruffled by passing events and concerned chiefly with winning an honest living by their own individual efforts. Here was "free enterprise" in its pristine purity. Nor did the Browns seek wealth; for them a comfortable living with a modicum of the necessities of life constituted the end of labor.

During the Revolutionary War the Quakers remained true to their tradition in objecting to war; the conviction, however sincerely and honestly felt, did not entirely shield the Friends from slander and insult. There was complaint on every side that the Quakers enjoyed security of life and property without paying the price. If one can judge them by the Armitts and Browns, there was some ground for complaint, for so far as the records reveal not a single Armitt or Brown enlisted for service in the field, though Elijah Brown, merchant, had signed the nonimportation resolution in protest of the Stamp Act. This, then, is the most heroic deed of which a Brown could boast, if boast he would.

We have seen that Elijah Brown had been apprenticed to a merchant in Philadelphia. But soon after his marriage he established

[5] Sidney B. Fisher, *The Quaker Colonies* (New Haven, 1919), pp. 2-3; Howard H. Brinton, *Quaker Education in Theory and Practice* (Wellingford, Pa., 1940), pp. 26-27, 29-30.

himself in the mercantile business on his own account, in which he remained and prospered until adverse conditions incident to the Revolutionary War closed the doors of his shop. One can understand readily enough how the honest, hardworking Quakers resented the ruthless plundering of their homes and stores by the Colonial troops. There are many contemporary records of the hardships and burdens which were heaped upon them, largely because they refused to bear arms and to slay their fellow men. There is little wonder, then, that Charles Brockden Brown, whose most impressionable years were spent in a Quaker home, saddened by war without and humiliation within, should have been an early and lifelong enemy of war. He was what is now familiarly and vulgarly known as a pacifist or a conscientious objector.

How his father maintained a family of eight and kept the wolf from the door after his mercantile business had been ruined by the war has not been ascertained, but apparently he dabbled in real estate, for in 1785, when we have definite information, he was, according to the Philadelphia City Directory, "a conveyancer and landbroker." This pursuit he followed steadily for the next thirteen years.

### BROWN'S BOYHOOD INTERESTS

Of Charles Brockden Brown's boyhood days little can be said, for reliable records are extremely scant. Tradition has it that he was precocious and, judging from what he later accomplished against many odds, that tradition may well have been fact; for Brown was certainly a man of uncommon talent in expression, and he was a keen if not a profound or original thinker. Apparently he had an early and compelling passion for geography—a passion that clung to him throughout life.

Brown's unpublished manuscript Journal reflects the variety of his interests during this period when the energy of his teeming brain was searching for its true outlet. Besides the Ellendale letters (which, as will be seen in a later chapter, were philosophical disquisitions to imaginary correspondents), this Journal contains notes on a Utopian commonwealth of Brown's own imagining; a long description of a religion—its peculiar mode of worship and its essential philosophy; thirty-two pages of architectural drawings and designs, ranging from simple geometrical patterns to elaborate floor plans and sketches of completed structures and a "Rejang" alphabet, partly worked out, consisting of symbols representing sound combinations rather than single letters. This alphabet, no doubt, represents Brown's early interest in shorthand—an interest which grew with the years.

His letters and journals bear witness that curiosity ran high in him in his early days and that it found a natural outlet through the pages of books. His friends and companions were "folios," and they were as replete with life, as full of knowledge and amusement for him,

as the choicest sports and companions could have been to the average
American boy. It is related of him that when he was only an infant,
his father and mother would leave him at home poring over some
book with the gravity of a scholar, while they were bent on errands;
or later, when he had reached school age, they would likely find him,
shoes off, mounted on some chair or table, gazing with a wild surmise
upon a map suspended on the wall. No wonder, then, that at the age
of ten he was insulted when a visitor referred to him as a *boy*. When
the gentleman had departed, the youth burst out: "Why does he call
me boy? Does he not know that it is neither size nor age, but understanding that makes the man? I could ask him an hundred questions,
none of which he could answer."[6]

### BROWN'S QUAKER SCHOOLING

Obviously a youth of Brown's mentality was thoroughly qualified
to derive pleasure and knowledge from a course of schooling. There
is no positive evidence that Charles Brockden Brown ever attended
the elementary schools, though it is quite likely that he did. All that
we know is that he entered the Friends Latin School in his eleventh
year, presumably in March, 1781, for the school year was from March
to November. This period of Brown's life, therefore, one is compelled
to reconstruct from general sources and conditions, and trust that the
picture would answer to the experiences of Brockden Brown himself.
The gist of what the Allen-Dunlap biography says concerning these
years may be put in one sentence: Brown was very precocious, was
enamored of books, was exposed to the rudiments of Latin and Greek,
and by his too diligent application to his studies endangered his health.

Fortunately we know considerable about early Quaker ideas and
ideals of education, but unfortunately all too little about those principles as they may have been practiced in the particular school which
young Charles attended. Because the Friends established as many
schools as they did, it cannot be said that the Society opposed education as such; however, the acceptance of the doctrine of the "inner
light" might lead to a general disbelief in education, and recorded
statements show that educational accomplishments were not what they
might have been.[7] Fox fervently commended a practical education,
gained through a system of apprenticeship, and as fervently condemned general or classical education.

William Penn in a letter to his wife in regard to the education of
their children stated that their learning must be liberal, useful, consistent with truth and godliness; he believed that ingenuity and
industry were good for the body and the mind; he recommended the
useful parts of mathematics, such as that needed in building houses

[6] Dunlap, I, 13.

[7] Thomas Woody, *Quaker Education in the Colony and State of New Jersey*
(Philadelphia, 1923), p. 15.

or ships, measuring, surveying, dialing, navigation; in addition to learning reading, writing, languages, useful arts, and sciences, he believed the welfare of any people depended in a good measure on early instruction in the principles of true religion and virtue.[8] Such too was the opinion of prominent Quakers like Anthony Benezet, John Woolman, William Crouch, and Robert Proud. The Browns also must have been in favor of formal schooling; for Elijah Brown was sent to Philadelphia for his schooling, and Brockden Brown received the best education, short of a college course, then obtainable.

Charles Brockden Brown remained in the Friends Latin School until his sixteenth year. We are told that he applied himself so diligently to his studies that his already frail constitution was much impaired; and that as an antidote to overwork, the Master advised long walks into the country and allowed him to be absent from school for such purpose. During these five years the Latin School had in attendance, on the average, thirty boys under the guidance of the distinguished pedagogue, Robert Proud. Of the course of study little is known, but there is reason to think that the work was of a high order and the tasks set of an exacting nature.

Brown's evaluation of his schooling is given in some detail in the Journal some half-dozen years later when he had had time to sit in judgment. From an unpublished letter to Henrietta[9] in the Journal we learn of his knowledge of French, the rudiments of which he had apparently acquired in the school, and of his dissatisfaction with his classical education:

I received some knowledge of the Greek and Latin at a Grammar school, but this knowledge will by no means qualify me to instruct others. . . .[10]

Are you really desirous of wading through the crudities, obscurities, and discords of the grammatical chaos, of conning old Lillie's rule, and talking with colloquial Cordier and Erasmus? . . . But what is there, ambitious fair One, in the Latin language that can reasonably excite your curiosity? The ancient poetry is bare and despicable. You will perhaps be astonished at this assertion, but it is nevertheless true. There is scarcely any that can be read with patience by a man whose morals are yet untainted. . . .

There is nothing, however valuable, for which too great a price may not be paid. Before you engage in any study it is to be considered whether the labor of pursuit and the pleasure of acquisition be proportionate to each other, and whether the time which is thus consumed might not be more profitably employed. . . .

It is of more importance to you to become an adept in your native language than in any other. It is sometimes said that this knowledge cannot be obtained without a previous acquaintance with the classic tongues, but of this objection I shall always consider the example of my Harriet as an un-

[8] Thomas Woody, *Early Quaker Education in Pennsylvania*, pp. 29-30.
[9] "Love Among the Ruins," section 21.
[10] *Ibid.*, section 26.

answerable confutation. That the knowledge of Greek and Roman literature may be, in some degree, conducive to the attainment of skill in English, is needless to deny, but this motive only is not sufficient to justify our application to those studies, since it is indisputable that the improvement would be still greater if the time which is thus spent were devoted to British authors.

I cannot admit that the knowledge of ancient languages is otherwise to be esteemed than as they humanize the heart and polish the understanding, and though I am sincerely of opinion that it does not merit even this encomium, which indeed I must confess to be extremely high. Yet I am willing to bestow it, but must ask whether the study of British, French, or Italian literature is not equally conductive to the same end?[11]

Perhaps there never was a better illustration of the old adage that as is the teacher so is the school. During his nineteen years as master of the leading Friends school, Robert Proud succeeded, as no other master had done, in impressing high ideals upon the youth of Philadelphia. He was versed in the classics as well as in the sciences. He had no superior as teacher and was equaled only by Anthony Benezet. There is also more than one testimonial from his numerous pupils that he was more than a teacher—he was a friend and companion. As a master, Robert Proud was revered by all his pupils, for he was kind and generous to all. Much of the Master's character, the ideals of his school, and the daily routine of the workshop may be inferred from a reading of the rules which the Master pinned to the door. Heading the list was "Reverentia Jehovae Caput Scientiae," and then followed precepts on prompt and regular attendance, "clean and decent" conduct during the school day, "silent and orderly behavior"; obedience to the Master and respect and modesty toward any visitor to the school; pupils were exhorted to be submissive and kind toward their fellows and to acknowledge with proper gratitude any kindness received and ever to be forgiving; each should provide himself with all necessary books, etc., and avoid borrowing; the common language, Latin, was to be used with propriety and grammatical accuracy; transactions passed in school were not to be divulged, particularly if such pertained to the reputation of anyone in the school; instead of a place of punishment, reproof, or fear, the school should be a place of pleasure and delight.[12]

But admirable rules, friendly relations between Master and pupil, and the high quality of the recitation do not tell the whole story; for Robert Proud's greatest influence could not be expressed in terms of the daily mark, but was rather to be seen in the zeal for disinterested service to mankind with which he filled the hearts of the most promising of his disciples—Brown, Bringhurst, and Wilkins among them. The relation of the Master to these three brilliant boys was of the most intimate nature, and his influence in shaping the course of their

[11] *Ibid.*, sections 23, 24.

[12] Thomas Woody, *Early Quaker Education in Pennsylvania*, pp. 183-185.

lives cannot be measured by rule of thumb. That it was considerable, a careful reading of Brown's Journal and the letters that passed among the three friends, and also between them and the Master, is evidence sufficient. The numerous Proud manuscripts show him to have been a man of wide and varied interests and a student of the larger problems of life. It was precisely this catholicity of interests and tastes that had the most abiding influence upon Brockden Brown's ideals. The speculative passages from the ancient and modern philosophers and scientists and similar ones from the poets which Proud copied into his Journal contain the very heart of Brown's own speculations as seen in the Journal to which he was soon to commit his most intimate thoughts—and who would say that the connection is not significant?

During his school days Brown is said to have written many speculative essays, both in prose and verse, aping the Master, but none of these has been identified. It is likely that he contributed to some of the various student publications, such as the *Examiner,* the *Universal Magazine, Students' Gazette, Latonia,* the *Public School Gazette,* and the *Students' Magazine,* which, along with school news and foreign and domestic intelligence, contained the cream of student jests and many of their "burnt" offerings.[13] An innocent little item like the following gives a vivid glimpse into the life of the students: "From a certain expression which lately drop'd from one of the overseers, we would have the greatest reason to believe that Mr. Webster's gay appearance is rather disagreeable."

Brown's school exercises and his known ventures into the field of composition are not to be found in these numerous manuscripts, or if there, they are buried in anonymity.

When Brown quitted—for graduation there was none—the Latin School in November, 1786, he did not entirely cut communications with his Master, and the relation which subsisted between them even unto Brown's premature death was most cordial, as extant letters reveal. But, however considerable the influence of Proud on Brown's thoughts and actions, it was not powerful enough to break down the barriers of Quaker prejudices against higher education and send him to the University of Pennsylvania, only a few blocks away. Friends, having an inimical regard to classical and scientific knowledge, generally appeared hostile to all colleges and seminaries where the advanced branches were thoroughly taught.[14]

This does not, as has been pointed out, represent the attitude of the more enlightened Quakers, but there can be little doubt that the average Friend frowned upon college education, and we are quite

[13] Copies of these student magazines are now in the *Norris and Shippen* manuscripts in the Pennsylvania Historical Society's Library (Philadelphia).
[14] Samuel Hanson Cox, *Quakerism Not Christianity* (1833), pp. 56-57.

certain that no further ground need be sought for Brockden Brown's failure to attend college. There is reason to believe that, at this period of his life, Brown was outwardly a typical Quaker, and that, as late as 1797, he apparently gave voice in his *Alcuin; or the Rights of Women* to his own convictions in regard to the worthlessness, or at least the inadequacy for complete living, of a college education.

Whatever may have been Brown's actual attitude toward college, he was beyond doubt in moral sympathy with the spirit of investigation. As a member of various scientific and philosophical societies, he openly encouraged what the colleges were endeavoring to accomplish. What objection he entertained to the system of colleges did not flow from any fear of the undermining of the Christian or any other religion, but rather from the conviction that colleges were too often the arena of frivolity and of political and social immorality. Like his beloved William Cowper, he preferred the tutorial system for higher education.

It may be affirmed with confidence, however, that Charles Brockden Brown, with a turn of mind essentially collegiate, would have profited much by the systemizing influence of a good college education. As it was, he could not be restrained in his desire for education of a wider variety. Whatever were his convictions in regard to colleges, the one outstanding fact is that he did not go to college, but instead, and against his will, in 1787 entered the law office of Alexander Wilcocks—and thus began a new chapter in his brief career.

### AVERSION TO THE LAW

Charles Brockden Brown had not yet attained his sixteenth birthday when he left the Friends Latin School, with less than five years of classical education, to seek his living in a very practical world. For ordinary pursuits such an education was not exactly a hindrance, but it was of little practical value. Brown realized this fact, for a few years later he advised his correspondent Henrietta to eschew Greek and Latin because of both their impracticality and their indecency; and later yet, when he was editor of the *Literary Magazine,* he urged parents not to "require their sons to pore over Greek and Latin, during six or seven of the best years of their lives, without any specific object in view." Indeed, he declared:

If a boy be intended for trade or business, a classical education will be injurious to him. It is a common observation in England that men who have been educated at the university seldom make as active, expert, and successful merchants or tradesmen as those who have served an early apprenticeship and have been regularly bred to business. Instances of this nature have occurred in our own country. Habits of indolence, or of studious industry, are formed at college which are inimical to the mechanical processes of trade and to the activity and bustle of a man of business. If young men of a liberal education have a propensity for science or literature, they often neglect their necessary business to gratify their taste for learning. The dull uniformity and confinement of a shop or accounting room are irksome to men of genius and studious minds.[15]

The very sort of education Brown here decries was what he had actually received. And while at school Brown did dream and plan and question and debate, and such a state of mind led naturally to self-expression in writing. His application to his books and his pen was so constant and persistent and the intellectual stimulus which he gained was so abiding and so inspiriting that they changed the course of his future from law to literature. As the law was not of his choice, there is no need for surprise that his entrance into law proved the greatest mistake of his life; but at that time a legal career was the surest road to wealth and fame. The principles of humanism which stirred in him and the bustle and artifice of the lawyer's office were mutually antagonistic, and we feel that Brown entered the profession of law with a conscious knowledge of this conflict. He did not shrink from the hard work which he knew was in store for him, for he had already shown himself capable of serious, sustained mental labor, but his ardent enthusiasm was at complete variance with the dry-as-dust volumes of English and American law; and his clean, honest mind rebelled at the idea of the sordid scenes, the chicanery, and the humbuggery of the law; not only his mind but also his feelings were in revolt at the prospect. Resolving, however, to make the best of an untoward situation, he finally entered the law office of Alexander Wilcocks, a prominent and influential lawyer of Philadelphia. In the office of the first recorder, then, Brown observed the bickering and hairsplitting of the lawyer's profession, against which he was soon to recoil with an intensity that set all other considerations at naught.

But not all of Brown's business in the law was boring and unprofitable. He early became a member of a law society whose object it was to conduct moot courts on interesting cases, and he soon rose to be one of the leading members of this society. Later, he sat as judge in important cases in the Moot Court, and his decisions from the bench reveal his sense of justice as well as his heavy and laborious style when he was caught in the involutions and jargon of the law.[16]

### THE FRIENDS THOU HAST

Among the members of the law society was William Wood Wilkins, one of Brown's earliest and closest friends, who though a kindred spirit was cast in a slightly different mold. The correspondence be-

[15] "On Classical Learning," *Literary Magazine and American Register*, III (April, 1805), 256-257.

[16] Dunlap, I, 34-36.

tween Brown and Wilkins during their legal apprenticeship presents
a vivid picture of their friendship and their lack of progress in the
study of law.[17] The first of these letters indicates that the two had
known each other for a long time—perhaps at the Friends Latin
School. At the time of the early apprenticeship they were so intimate
that Wilkins, whose home was in Woodbury (often spelled Woodberry
by Wilkins), New Jersey, had induced his parents to allow him to
live in Brown's home in the city. This letter also shows the solid,
simple character of Wilkins's father and the high esteem in which
Charles was held by his elders. Near Brown's home the two ensconced
themselves in an old dwelling which they refer to as their lodge or
retreat; here they read, wrote, and played games. The law which they
ostensibly followed was far from their interests. The Wilkins letters
of the correspondence reveal his playful disposition and his poetic
temper as well as his tendency to moralize about God and nature, all
of which reveals the mental and moral kinship between him and
Brown. It is through this correspondence that we first learn of Henrietta. Throughout we find Brown's dissatisfaction with the legal
profession and his unwillingness to prostitute his powers to the practice of law; and here is ample evidence of Brown's tendency to question, to doubt, to moralize, and to see the dark side of life as well
as the speculative, consoling bent of his mind. Through the letters
we are introduced to Joseph Bringhurst, of whose choice spirit we
know very little. After Wilkins's removal to Trenton, New Jersey,
in October, 1792, to finish his legal education we find him attempting
to wrest Brown from his melancholy:

I love not the haughty aspect of advice or the stern feature of wisdom,
yet I must vivaciously wish that Charles would arise like Samson from his
slumbers before the bewitching art of Delilah withered his rivalled strength.[18]

Through all the letters runs the story of Brown's reflections on
the legal profession during the period of his vacillation and of Wilkins's determination to enter the legal profession, never wavering in
his ambition to become a successful lawyer.[19] Unable to understand
the indecision and turmoil in Brown, Wilkins incorrectly ascribed
Brown's trouble to indolence and despondency. Wilkins persisted
in the pursuit of his law studies and was admitted to the bar in the
spring of 1793. He promptly returned to Woodbury, New Jersey,
where he is next heard from bewailing his scanty practice. These
delightful letters give us perhaps our best opportunity to enjoy Wilkins's airy wit and bubbling good humor in the face of adversity.
His optimistic and scintillating personality most have fascinated the

[17] For the extant correspondence, see David Lee Clark, University of Texas
*Studies in English*, XXVII (1948), 75-107.

[18] Wilkins here probably referred specifically to Henrietta G.

[19] Clark, *op. cit.*, p. 95.

more somber Brown, and probably helped him to keep his balance during this trying period. Though Brown's refusal to practice law greatly disappointed Wilkins, it did not destroy their friendship, and the premature death of Wilkins in 1795 was a great blow to Brown. Although the letters do not strike the reader as coming from a pen "saddened . . . with its austerity, or melted . . . with its pathos," Wilkins's formal writings were doubtless as moralizing and sentimental as Brown thought them. On the sad occasion of Wilkins's death Brown drew a delightful portrait of his young friend:

He had no small portion of wit, and this power was in part exercised in company; but the moment he took up his pen to write a letter or an essay, he forgot all his mirth, became pensive, sentimental, and poetical. To hear him talk one would think that he never had a serious moment in his life. He literally sung himself to sleep, and awakened in a burst of laughter. To see the effusions of his pen, one would imagine that he was a stranger to smiles, that he was forever steeped in tears and wrapped in melancholy. In this there was nothing that deserved to be called affectation and hypocrisy, since he corresponded only with those with whom he was occasionally in the habit of conversing; and his tongue regaled them with unceasing jests, with just as much sincerity as his pen saddened them with its austerity, or melted them with its pathos. *His sonnets and letters talk almost altogether of love, and on this topic no Petrarch was ever more tender, refined, and pathetic. The youth was forever in love, and was all impassioned eloquence at the feet of an adored fair one; but his love was merely the exuberance of health and an ardent constitution. Consequently his love was always bestowed upon the present object, and never stood in the way of the most licentious indulgences.* After receiving a letter full of the most doleful eulogies of some divine but refractory creature and hinting his resolution to shake off the yoke of his inauspicious stars, I have hastened to his chamber to console him, and found him at a table presiding with marks of infinite satisfaction, and keeping the worthy crew that surrounded him in a constant roar. Such was my friend, and such were his letters. His tongue and his pen, his actions and his written speculations were as opposite to each other as the poles.[20]

An early letter of Brown's to Wilkins throws considerable light on the state of Brown's mind. His melancholy and his relations to that little congenial knot of friends of whom Wilkins and Bringhurst were the chief are vividly revealed. The letter makes first mention by Brown himself of a girl named Henrietta, with whom he was infatuated and around whom a few months later one of the most significant episodes in Brown's life was to center. The letter, without date or salutation, begins with a thoughtful three lines of poetry and ends with a charming, playful bit of original verse:

> O soul, in whom my thoughts find all repose
> My glory, my perfection, glad I see
> Thy face and Morn returned.

[20] Dunlap, I, 47-48.

Why is my inclination not attended with ability? Why do I find myself disposed to write without experiencing that rigor of conviction and facility of utterance of which I have at other times been sensible? Unseasonable langors take possession of me. Joyless slumbers weigh down my eye-lids. Not even the idea of my beloved friend, for whom, notwithstanding an impatient and capricious disposition, I entertain the most ardent and sincere affection, of which my heart is at this waning era of my existence susceptible, can banish this oppressive listlessness and rouse me into watchfulness or activity. What expedient shall I practice to restore me to the empire of my thoughts? How the curtain of each eye gradually falls, how the objects vanish by degrees "remote and small"! My pen moves with difficulty through the line. Each letter is at least a league in length, in traversing a third of which I grow unsufferably weary. I must sleep—doze, I mean; pos-itively I—m—m—ust sl—sle—sleep—.

What! have I lost the dominion of myself? Cannot I resist, when I will, the approach of that unseasonable and impertinent intruder sleep? What tranquillity is there in my lassitude! My heart is equally dead to the voice of sorrow and of joy. Let me as this moment of vacancy consider what is the idea which shall dwell the longest on my mind, which shall leave my intellects the last, for that it will be the ideal representation of what, whether thing or person, is the dearest to my heart, may justly be imagined. My eyes are closed, my head reposes on my arm, my thoughts are scattered, my attention dissipated. I linger for a moment on the verge of sleep; I just retain discernment to discover what it is that hovers over the threshold of my imagination, and is the only one of all the throng which has just retired from the penetralia that is visible. A sound reaches me that is, with difficulty, audible. Some spirit whispers in my ear the name of Wilkins, but before its last faint echoes are departed, my slumber is disturbed by that of Henrietta, but which, after it has vanished, none is found worthy to succeed, and sleep is at length permitted to ascend in silence and security her throne. Thus, a friend! thou seest in what relation thou standest to the *Sleeper*. That thy image is excluded only to admit the luminous idea of a gracious beauty, with whom if thou wast acquainted thou wouldst join me in adoring her, and in looking with contempt or indignation on the Dolls or Lucys that daily flutter in thy sight. Those toys! Those gildings, those baubles to amuse a thoughtless hour, those eye deluders; who, when absent, are invisible, and never visit the beholder in his solitude, nor fill his bosom with untractable enthusiasm or an agonizing softness. Where is that superiority of understanding, that sublimity of sentiment, that sanctity of virtue, that union of grace and dignity! Where are those features, mind-irradiated, and those eyes each glance of which appears to be an emanation of divinity? Ah, my friend, in the image at which my solitary hours are employed in gazing, all those attributes and more than I can number are comprised. What! my friend, are thou a lover? Yes, vain, pragmatical, and ignorant pretender, so thou audaciously pretendest, but let me tell thee that thou art able to describe its effects with just as much skill as an elephant can finger an harpsichord.

Be not angry at Sir Oracle, nor offended at his sincerity; he is conscious of his own defects, that he has read but few pages in the book of human nature and those with which he is acquainted were perused without attention or sagacity. The temple of science he has not yet visited. The tracts of literature he began, in resemblance of Barretier [?] and Haller, to treat in infancy, but untoward accidents retarded his career, ere it had scarcely been begun, and put a period to his progress, long before his entrance into manhood. Humble are therefore his pretensions, and few his claims. His prospect is confined to the surfaces of things and even to a narrow portion of the surface. He will, therefore, never aspire to conduct thee to the shrine of literary glory, or lead thee to the summits of ethereal science, or guide thee through the mazes of the human heart and teach thee the knowledge of thyself, of nature, or of God; but in whatever respect or in whatever degree, his weakness and ignorance be manifest, he is at least a proficient in Love. In an experimental knowledge of the motives, circumstances, and consequences of love, he will not scruple to esteem himself immeasurably superior to the reptiles that surround him, and on this superiority then my friend shouldst rely with beseeming deference and question not the truth of my assertion that thou art yet a stranger to the raptures and the agonies of love.

Monday afternoon

I have slept. How long I know not. Let me reconsider my dream. It has more correctness and vehemence than my dreams generally possess. The subjects, I perceive, are love and beauty: fertile topics, themes in which my friend takes greatest pleasure, in expatiating on which he thinks himself peculiarly qualified by long and melting experiences to pronounce decisively, and in which I will not deny that he is an adept. This conception may, perhaps, be contradictory to the tenor of my dream, but a visionary is not answerable for his sentiments or actions. I shall abide only by the decisions of my waking hours. Let me not therefore be accused of arrogance and presumption, because my arrogance was a dream and my presumption a shadow, and because, now that I am awake, I declare myself of a different opinion.

I will willingly become a pupil to you and be taught, by my amorous friend, the art and mystery of a Lover. His precepts will be highly useful, the result of infinite sagacity and long experience. With what nervous arguments and opposite instances will [thou] not prove that love is the same in brute and men, that true chastity is utterly unknown in the world, that every woman is a rake at heart, and that reputation is the only god of womankind. Vile, detestable, degrading maxims! Engendered in the corrupted heart and nourished by the perverted understanding of a prostitute! That forms the creed of the profligate and gains the approbation of fools! Ye are unworthy of the lips of virtue! But how shall I apologize for imputing opinions like these to my friend? For insinuating that he whose virtues and talents have engaged my love and admiration and induced me to aspire to his friendship, is capable of espousing tenets so base and despicable? I hope he will forgive me and impute my fault to inattention and negligence rather than to any inexcusable motive? I will endeavor to scotch his resentment with a song.

When Bringhurst and Wilkins are here
Diffusing the smiles of content
My bosom shall vanish its fear
My sorrow shall quickly relent.

No longer be moistened the eye
    The hours no longer in weeping
Be spent, nor the eloquent sigh
    No longer prevent me from sleeping.

No longer embellish the page
    With emblems of gloomy despair
Or struggle to temper its rage
    Or lighten the burthen of care.

With accents of musical woe
    Attuned to the voice of the flute
In teaching Aeolus to blow
    Or vocalizing the lute.

But sitting securely together
    We order the door to be shut
We pass from the news and the weather
    To shuffle, to deal, and to cut.

In tale of fictitious distress
    In study or converse the day—
In ombre or chequers or chess
    The even shall vanish away.

    I cannot write any more at present. This is written in the midst of difficulty and embarrassment, with disturbed intellects and lethargic stupor. I am, my dearest William, ever and faithfully yours[21]

*C. B. B.*

    A letter to Wilkins, headed "Cuilli Pays de Vaud," would give one the impression that Brown was at the time of writing in Geneva, Switzerland. No doubt, however, this is one of our author's endeavors to be playful. Although richly embroidered by Brown's colorful imagination, the letter was probably based on fact. It is quite likely that young Brown was engaged in teaching the English language to the daughter of one of those Frenchmen who, with the coming of the French Revolution, had fled to America. We learn from one of his Journal letters to Henrietta that Brown associated with some of them.[22]

    The letter, without date, was probably written from a village near Philadelphia, the meeting place of a group of *émigrés* in the early 1790's. It reads:

CUILLI PAYS DE VAUD<br>Wednesday morn.

    Write to me, my friend, I beseech you, in a less melancholy style. I would set you an example but that, I fear, in my present situation is impossible, but I shall always be prepared to smile at the elegant vivacities of my dearest

[21] Clark, *op. cit.*, p. 79.
[22] *Ibid.*, pp. 79-82.

William, and to applaud the effusions of his wit and gayety. They are rays which illume the gloomy atmosphere by which I am frequently surrounded; whose approach I hail with the utmost pleasure, and whose departure I observe with the utmost regret. I wish thou wouldest teach me to be witty, to tell, with suitable gravity, a mirthful tale, and give to the threadbare jest its original texture and the gloss of novelty. These accomplishments are of wonderful advantage; they will render him who in other respects is incorrigibly obstinate or stupid, an agreeable companion, and without them the man of real genius and sagacity will scarcely be able to find an hearer. Set yourself seriously to work, my friend. Take me under your tuition, and, thou man of infinite jest, endow with a small portion of that exhaustless, overflowing, and superabundant gayety, which renders thee so pleasing and vexatious a companion, thy teachable and humble scholar. Shall I not, thinkest thou, listen to thy lectures with the most uninterrupted attention and indefatigable patience? Shall I not in my progress to excellence, to word-dissecting, pun-contriving excellence, speedily outstrip my master, and degrade him, in his turn, to the station of a pupil? Ah! that a slight acquaintance with my friend will show to be impossible, and as, in the scale of the Universe, on which he, with so much subtlety, expatiated on Tuesday evening, the Soul of man will be to all eternity approaching, without ever reaching the divinity, so I, to compare small things with great, shall doubtless be continually winging nearer the perfection of my master without ever arriving at an absolute equality with him.

I am fearful that you were displeased with my last letter, and that my stupid raillery was not perfectly acceptable to you. In your intercourse with me you will find me liable to numberless faults, but I shall never scruple to repair them, as soon as they are discovered; my friend shall never be angry with me longer than while I am ignorant of his anger, and I shall always make use of the most compendious process to oust resentment from his bosom.

I am now in the midst of a delightful country, which the purity of manners and the political and domestic felicity of the inhabitants, the fertility of the soil and the beauties of the landscape have combined to render a paradise. Here am I immured in pleasing and enchanting solitude, banqueting on classical literature, or conversing with rural simplicity. I will not give you a minute description of my dwelling nor an account of the character of those with whom I am a fellow-tenant. I shall only mention that I live with an honest and thrifty husbandman, riot daily in the innocent and healthful luxury of wine, cheese, and butter, and am, (would you think it?) preceptor to my landlord's youngest daughter, who, possessing a fine understanding, a taste for reading, and a delicate constitution, her father is determined shall become a woman of importance. I am afraid, my friend, that my destiny is fixed, my matrimonial destiny, I mean, and that I shall live and die at the feet of Jacquelette. I will not attempt to describe this innocent and fascinating creature. It will be sufficient to observe that her age is no more than fourteen, that there is a mature dignity and gracefulness in her manner, that her shape though small almost to diminutiveness is the model of elegance and symmetry, and that her face has charms to the task of describing which my pen is inadequate. I have frequently accompanied her on a visit to her relations in Franche Compte, for her father places so implicit a reliance on the honor of his guest that he willingly intrusts her to my care. O my friend! What charms have innocence and beauty on a susceptible heart! I have taught her the Parisian French. The dialect of this country, as you very easily imagine, is extremely remote from the standard of purity, but my beauteous scholar prattles French and Italian, with the justest and most polished accent. Her voice, to which the softest and most delicious music is incomparably inferior, gives new graces to those languages, and her idiom is truly classical. How easily, my dearest friend, are our best concerted schemes defeated! I have almost entirely forgotten the purpose that brought me hither, and spend almost all my hours, sitting on the banks of the lake with *ma petite epouse,* for thus I always distinguish her from her equally beautiful but less accomplished sisters, relating to her my travels and adventures, and tracing my journeys on a map of Europe or America before me, or in reading and explaining to her some entertaining author.

On my last visit to Geneva, I became acquainted with a young English gentleman, between whom and myself there is such a conformity of disposition as naturally produces friendship. He is a beautiful and graceful youth, of an opulent and respectable family, who have placed so much confidence in his discretion that though no more than eighteen he is suffered to ramble over Europe without a conductor. He has resided in Italy and notwithstanding a fiery constitution and imperious passions he has escaped with impunity. His opinions are somewhat peculiar to himself, for instead of changing Eton for Oxford, in imitation of others, he is determined to finish his education in this country, and to be his own preceptor in philosophy and politics. For this purpose I have procured him a lodging in this village, and he will, in a short time, come hither with his books and devote his whole time to study and to me, his friend and only associate. He is a young man of great talents, capacious memory, and lofty ambition. He designs to qualify himself for an orator and politician, and for a seat in the British legislature, to which his rank and fortune will advance him as soon as he becomes of age. His elocution is rich, rapid, and harmonious, his probity remarkably great, and his powers of reasoning wonderful. We are scarcely ever of the same opinion and our life when together is one continual controversy, but our disputes never weaken or interrupt our friendship, and are rather exercises of the understanding than investigations of truth. I never fail to urge every objection against his scheme which my imagination suggests and am at length so accustomed to contradict him that as soon as his sentiments are known, I instantly and by a kind of involuntary impulse espouse and defend an opposite opinion. I have exhausted every topic of argument and ridicule, to show the absurdity of the method which he pursues for acquiring knowledge. He is a great admirer of antiquity and spends many hours in reading and translating the political and rhetorical performances of Greece and Rome. He despises the French and Italian manners and literature, and defends all his doctrines with surprising energy and subtlety. This is sufficient to make me of a different opinion, and I incessantly assail his strictures with every kind of argument and every engine of dispute; our debates are, in consequence, in the highest degree warm and animated, but never clamourous nor acrimonious nor irregular. Each entertains the utmost good will for the other, and notwithstanding our perpetual altercations, our friendship is daily increasing. As soon as he comes hither I am daily to accompany him and his book into the most retired recesses, where we are to read and converse with each other, for our mutual improvement. He is to read to me his translations and imitations of the Greek and Roman orators, and to recite them with suitable tones and attitudes, and I am to point out defects in his style, pronunciation, and delivery. But he shall not engross the whole of my time; a considerable part of it must be devoted to Jacquelette—and not the smallest portion to meditation and composition on subjects more congenial to my disposition and taste than those which *Stanton* (my friend) honors with his attention and regard.

I wish you could furnish me with a subject to write and think upon, but suffer me, I entreat you, to hear often from you, and convince me by the only means which the spacious interval between us renders practicable that you have not forgotten that there exists such a person as

C. B. B.

### CHOICE OF PROFESSION: LAW OR LITERATURE

The decision to forgo the practice of law and to espouse the hazardous profession of letters was the turning point in Brown's life, and as such it demands as full treatment as the meager firsthand details will warrant. It was maintained by his family and friends that, in order to justify his actions, Charles resorted to the meanest kind of quibbling; that he found comfort in "all the sophisms and paradoxes with which ignorance and ingenious prejudice had assailed the science or the practice of the law."[23]

The following excerpts from the Allen-Dunlap biography record one of the main reasons for Brown's failure to practice the law:

He professed that he could not reconcile it with his ideas of morality to become indiscriminately the defender of right or wrong; thereby intimating, if not asserting, that a man must, in the practice of the law, not only deviate from morality, but become the champion of injustice. . . .

They [friends of Brown] represented to him that men of irreproachable characters, who stood in the front ranks of honor, had acquired all their celebrity at the bar. His answer was that the opinion of the world was always equivocal, sometimes suspicious, and often beyond all question wrong. The favorable regards of the world were conferred indiscriminately on virtue or vice, innocence or guilt, as all history evinces. . . . In the present case he denied the validity of the evidence produced and contended that whether these men were justly entitled to such celebrity could only be known by themselves. Their motives to conceal their real characters from the world were obvious and palpable, and if they were monopolizers of the fame of better and more deserving men, this was of itself an argument why he should not add another name to their list.[24]

[23] This quotation has not been identified.
[24] Dunlap, I, 40-43.

That this represents the considered views of his family and friends it would be impossible to determine, but for sure Brown's decision was one of the most momentous of his life. After a careful study of his letters and early known writings touching upon his ideals and his opinions of mankind, one must conclude that there was a real lack of agreement between those ideals and the generally accepted ethics of the lawyer; and one feels that throughout Brown's study of the law and his observations of the indiscriminate defense of the right and the wrong, his mind and heart were alike in arms against the practice. That Brown loved the company of books is beyond dispute, that he delighted in society is equally certain; and that he shrank from the vulgar mass of men and from the advertisement of self needs no apology or extenuation. The truth of Brown's opinion of the law is found in one of his letters, perhaps to Wilkins. "Do you," Brown wrote, "read the books which you mention? Is your reading altogether legal? Surely such constant and invariable legality is not indispensably necessary. I indeed am inclined to think that, so far from being necessary to adhere so strictly to the case, it is absolutely necessary sometimes to deviate from it; but it is likely that I am mistaken. If my own experience were to determine my opinion, I should rather think that he only can derive pleasure, and consequently improvement, from the study of law, *who knows and wishes to know nothing else.*"[25] In the italicized words is to be found one of the chief reasons for Brown's disgust with the profession of the law—its narrowing effect upon the mind.

In the Brown-Wilkins correspondence Brown condemns his friend for following the profession of law for the sole purpose of gaining wealth. If he could regain his former ambition, if he could shake off his slumbers, Brown asserts that he would go to England and devote himself to the pursuit of law to his dying day, for in England a lawyer sought service and glory—not gold as in America.

Friday, November 3, 1792

W. Wood Wilkins
Trenton.
[no salutation]

I have, this moment, received my friend's letter. I suppose I ought to have gone to the packet. It may not be usual to leave letters at the houses of those to whom they were directed. If you purpose to maintain a regular correspondence, you shall never have reason to charge me with indolence or negligence.

But thou art sick, it seems, and very formally apologizest for telling me so, but with how little reason? Whatever affliction, whether of mind or person, happens to you, it is of importance to me to know it, because there is no one, whether connected with you by the tie of blood or friendship, who

[25] *Ibid.*, I, pp. 53-54.

is more deeply interested in your welfare. My hopes are transferred from myself to my friends, and as there is nothing in the contemplation of my own destiny that can afford me satisfaction, I naturally seek for consolation in surveying the prosperity of those whom I love. The rays of ambition are extinct to me, but the darkness of my fate is somewhat illumined by the reflection of them from another.

Unless you speak of your own affairs, of what will you speak? No topic can be so interesting to yourself, none more acceptable to me. Your friend is not a subject of entertaining disquisition. You are embarked on a sea where the breezes of prosperity are continually playing, and where nothing salutes the eye but verdant isles and woody shores, peaceful valleys and aspiring summits, but my vessel is entangled amidst lurking rocks and boiling eddies.

Let thyself and thy affairs, therefore, be the subject of thy conversation, for the happiness of my friend cannot be presented to my view in too great a variety of attitudes. I can never be weary of surveying it. The precept by which you revived me is by no means applicable to the intercourse of friends, for what are the purposes of friendship but the alleviation of sorrow and the increase of happiness by participating them with another? And if we are never suffered to speak of ourselves, how will those purposes be effected?

Had you followed our advice in staying till the next day, you would probably [have] avoided this disaster. There are few persons, I believe, whose health would not be affected by a nocturnal expedition of that kind.

I did not imagine that a momentary disorder would damp your gayety and involve your prospects in the clouds of melancholy. How fearful does my friend seem of appearing arrogant and dictatorial, and how unnecessary are those apprehensions! Have you not a right to dictate? I am well convinced that my conduct [in forgoing the practice of law] meets with your strongest disapprobation. I am convinced that it deserves to be treated with severity. If I condemn myself, why should I expect not to be condemned by you? Advice is only irksome and unacceptable when it implies the existence of faults which we do not acknowledge.

I look forward with pleasure to the time when my friend will step forth on the theatre of the world, and yet my satisfaction is much less than it would have been at an earlier age, when the purpose of your labors would have appeared not so much the acquisition of wealth as the attainment of glory. Our intellectual ore is apparently of no value but as it is capable of being transmuted into gold, and learning and eloquence are desirable only as the means of more expeditiously filling our coffers. In England the profession of the law is indeed the road to glory, and genius and application may derive new vigor from the contemplation of a double object, wealth and reputation.

O my friend! how peculiarly disastrous—hold! It is not my province to complain. I want not thy animating example nor thy friendly admonitions to incite me. There are other motives far more powerful, and which if any motives could be effectual, would quickly manifest their prevalence. What would I do were [I] at liberty to act? "I am a man, am in full possession of my faculties and organs, organs and faculties to the possible perfection of which there are no limits. Glory is my idol. The road to her temple passes through the field of law, and eloquence is the guide which conducts the pilgrim to it. No one idolizes knowledge more than I. No one is so thoroughly persuaded of the practicability of reaching its highest summits. I will hie as soon as possible to Europe and persist, to my dying day, in pursuit of legal and literary reputation." These would be my reflections should I once more awaken from my slumbers, but that will never be.

I hope speedily to hear from you again. I would be more copious were I not fearful, from the information which accompanied the delivery of your letter, that I shall be too late for the stage. Believe me, my dearest William,

Unalterably yours,

C. B. BROWN

And through all the letters runs the story of Brown's misery and unrest. Completely alone, misunderstood by his family and friends in his growing dissatisfaction with the law, Brown became melancholy, and even his closest friend, Wilkins, was apparently unable to understand the cause of the gloom which settled on him. Wilkins's reply to the above letter indicates that in spite of his own ill health and his apparently gay, irresponsible nature, he possessed immense capacity for hard work.

In answer to an urgent appeal to Brown from Wilkins to shake off his indifference to his friends and his hostility to the law, Brown, on January 22, 1793, replied in a Hamlet-like tone:

Never did I stand in as much need of a friend as at present. Bringhurst is indeed such an one to me. I have utterly forgotten the occasions of indifference or discontent between us and value you not more than you deserve; no, that is impossible, but, it may give credit to the dictates of this melting heart, as this spiritless and melancholy moment, as much as you deserve.

We are strange, unreasonable creatures; at least such am I. I utterly despise myself. I am the object of my most unbounded pity, the slave of a gloomy and distressful musing. The fair forms of social dignity and happiness still continue to diminish to my sight. I lift up my languid eyes and gaze after them without effect; they still mingle and are lost in dim obscurity and grey confusion, and nothing but a wide vacuity presents itself.

Was I born for nothing? Surely not. What consolation, then, can be hoped from dying, by one who is conscious that none of his duties are discharged; that he has not yet accomplished the purpose of his being? But no more of this. In spite of all my defects, I am of some use in the world; friendship is the sweetener of life; and while I live, W. W. W. can congratulate himself that there is at least one soul who cherishes his image and breathes the warmest and sincerest aspirations for his welfare.

You trifle in a manner worthy of you. You have done me the highest favor by sending those specimens to me. I thank you most ardently for them.

Cannot I discover in the manuscript essay an intended compliment to me? Pardon the vanity of this discovery. You must indeed pardon and allow that I have not erred in my conjecture. Praises are indeed of small importance to me, which do not receive the concurrence of my own heart, but there is not a little merit in the art and delicacy with which a compliment is insinuated, and this merit certainly belongs to my friend on this occasion, if any personal allusions were meant by the concluding observations of this essay.

And are you happy in your present situation? Doubtless you are. With such prospects before you, how can you be otherwise; O my friend! How truly happy; how greatly fortunate are you! To murmur would surely be impiety. I think you told me, but in a manner that left me in doubt whether you were in earnest in your tellings, that a gentle spouse, the soft endearing companion of your future life, was already selected. May every benignant star unite to shed felicity and honor on your union. She must be a sweet and amiable creature. I know she must. Your choice is an unquestionable proof of it.

Away! Ye idle phantoms of depraved ambition! Ye chimerical goods! Glory and fortune! In the soft bosom of domestic peace, in the worship of the household deities, true wisdom and genuine piety consist. A wife and children, though my destiny deny me those inestimable blessings, may they be the portion of my friend. Friendship cannot form a more affectionate wish.

If when you gave me this information you were only sporting with me, as I sometimes suspect, hasten, I beseech you, to make a choice. You do not despise women. Contempt of this kind renders equally questionable the rectitude of the heart and the soundness of the understanding; he must be, in this respect, an idiot or a brute, or both.

You have a strange mixture of passion and prudence in your character. Did you ever suffer the former to predominate? I shrewdly suspect not. Shall I be sincere with you? I will. Know, then, that the last sentence was far from being accompanied with a sentiment of approbation. Would you believe that in ascribing prudence to you I am far from intending a compliment, but rather censure?

Pity my depravity; excuse that sordid spirit that delights to level others with itself, that dotes on kindred faults, that is inclined to extenuate the merit of *youthful* prudence, and to censure rather than applaud the wisdom of age on juvenile shoulders and to ascribe it rather to superabundant insensibility than to superabundant discretion. We seldom acquire accession of wisdom but by diminutions of our sensibilities. The passions are not *subdued* in manhood and old age; they are *extinguished,* and they triumph only because they have no adversary. But what is a being without passion? What is that cold, sapless, and inanimate virtue founded only on principle, and not on sentiment?

There, my friend, is sincerity for you. But do not do me injustice. So far as those remarks have relation to your character, they incite only a momentary disapprobation, and the folly of these opinions instantly glares upon me in the strangest light, and when this temporary cloud has passed (you must ascribe it only to a distempered mind), your character shines out upon me, with more conspicuous and transcendant brightness.

Have I made you amends? In what? I am afraid you will not understand me. I do not understand what I have written on this page myself. Excuse it, therefore, in your most affectionate C. B. B.

If any doubt about Brown's antipathy to the law still lingers in the reader's mind, that doubt should be dispelled by a series of eight "Original Letters," published in the Philadelphia *Weekly Magazine,* between April 21 and June 2, 1798, but probably composed by Brown in 1794 shortly after his forsaking the law. They are dated as of March 3 to June 3, 1794. The letters purport to have been interchanged between a sister and her disappointed law-student brother in Philadelphia. There is no doubt that they are autobiographical. The following are pertinent passages.

The sister had written to her brother:

Lawyers . . . are merely the coiners of iniquitous subtleties and plotters against the majesty of truth. To puzzle the sagacity and contaminate the rectitude of mankind is, it seems, the scope of all their labors. . . .

And the brother replied:

I cannot as yet appeal to my own experience. A fortnight's reading can give me no information as to the merits or demerits of the *trade* [law]. It shows me, in a slight degree, of what materials the *science* is composed. They are sufficiently refractory and rugged, wrapt up in barbarous jargon, a spurious and motley compound of obsolete French and Latinized English. My poor head has been honored by you, with the epithet of metaphysical; but as skilful a dissector as I am of complex ideas, and as nice a weigher of abstruse distinctions, I fear I shall never untie legal knots or disinvolve from this maze my already bewildered understanding.

The sister in answer struck at the very roots of the legal profession, its pretentious nonsense and its unconcern with the principles of justice:

The question I am now called upon to discuss is a very important one, and requires to be considered in a two-fold point of view. Absolutely speaking, nothing is more true than that justice is due from every human being to his fellows; and that it ought to be spontaneously rendered. That this opinion should universally regulate the actions of mankind would argue the most perfect state of society, and its prevalence would, in most cases, supersede the necessity of permanent institutions for the protection of life, liberty, or property. The exertions of every individual would tend to secure these enjoyments and to promote every accession to the great mass of wisdom and happiness. If in any case the voice of the majority were requisite to define peculiar modes of justice and to explain the conduct which was necessary in particular emergencies, its decisions would always be expressed in terms simple, perspicuous, and adapted to the most tender capacity. You are aware that this state of things among us would render the profession of a lawyer useless, and of course contemptible. How would the members of such a community be affected if they were told that at a certain period of time, and in certain countries, it was customary for men to devote a large portion of their lives to the study of what is *justice,* and a still greater portion in explaining it to others; from which employment they derived large pecuniary rewards? Surely they would smile at the tale and consider it as the wildest of Utopian dreams. You are sensible that, viewed in this way, the profession of the law is neither liberal nor respectable. But there is another way in which it may be considered; which is in its relation to things as they are.

. . . . . . . . . . . . . .

Thus, my dear Harry, in the case before us I deem it *wrong* that laws should be multifarious or unintelligible; nevertheless I perceive they are so. The conduct of individuals is regulated by institutions whose written language is, to a large majority, without a meaning. It is therefore unquestionably *right* that some one should be capable of interpreting it to them. To those who undertake this office, talents and integrity are eminently necessary. If men *must* rely upon others for the knowledge of their rights and duties, it is momentous, in a high degree, that the expositor should be a sage rather than an idiot; that he should be a man of principle rather than a knave. You, my brother, possess splendid talents, and your integrity is founded on a broad basis. You excel in those graces of person and address which are so peculiarly advantageous to the orator. The emoluments arising from this exercise of your talents will, I trust, in your hands, be employed in the promotion of beneficial purposes. For you, therefore, and such as you, the profession of the law is eligible.

Brown was not alone in his day in holding the lawyer in contempt. Jefferson was equally averse to the profession, believing that the lawyer was primarily a quibbler, and should stand in society no higher than the grave digger.[26] This idea of the profession, to a certain extent, persists to this day.[27]

During the summer of 1793 Brown left the office of Alexander Wilcocks determined not to be a lawyer. The next half-dozen years were the most trying of his life. His friends and his family were keenly disappointed, and Brown was deeply grieved that his action should have brought so much sorrow to them. While he never for a moment was persuaded that he had taken the wrong course, his friends' disapproval almost unbalanced his mind. He was undoubtedly concerned about his immediate future and the disappointment of his friends, but he wrote nothing then or later to indicate regret at quitting the law. Indeed, at almost every opportunity Brown took occasion to express this antipathy. The few letters that have been preserved show that Brown was convinced that he was right in his decision.

Brown had made the inevitable decision to give up a law career not only because he detested the profession but also because of an increasingly insistent desire for authorship. This desire had shown itself in every period of his life: in his childhood, in his earliest school days, and during his law apprenticeship, when a choice had to be

[26] Edward Boykin, ed., *The Wisdom of Thomas Jefferson* (New York, 1941), p. 41.

[27] Fred Rodell, "The Law Is the Bunk," in *Prose Annual*, no. 3, ed. Gay, Boatright, and Wycoff (Boston, 1942), p. 57.

made between authorship and the law. Just why his friends and his family failed to see this is curious. The whole trend of Brown's life was, in fact, in this direction, and no amount of legal dalliance could have thwarted his desire to do what he really wanted to do.

We have seen that while Brown was poring over the dreary pages of Blackstone, he was in reality dreaming by day and by night of those grandiose epics of which in his early teens he imagined himself the proud author. That the poetical bent in him was strong is evidenced in a letter—here printed for the first time—to Wilkins, written during his period of indecision, and at a time when Brown and his coterie had inchoate plans for many literary projects. It can be seen from this letter that this aspiring group of literati drew heavily on Milton and his eighteenth-century imitators for both form and substance. The exact date of this letter cannot be determined, but it was evidently written between 1790 and 1793.

Thursday, Morn. 10 o'clock

Here am I seated at my desk—with pen and the writing implements at hand; and shall I not employ them? Yes, in good sooth I will, and they shall, for the present, be devoted to the pious use of showing my friend that his absence does not annihilate him—his local absence, for he's always intellectually present; and as he stands almost single in the writer's catalogue of friends my soul principally converses with his kindred spirit. Lend me your wings, I pray you; lend me your wings.

What wantest thou with my wings, thou most audacious and importunate of [MS mutilated] cannot share them. But, fond youth, thou knowest not what thou askest. My pinions, whose hues, as the poet says of my celestial friend Raphael, *are dipped in heaven,* are of finer texture than thou unwisely imaginest. They are fitted only to accelerate the speed of angels and to enable the airy messenger, who at thy divine command wanders through eternity, to perform more quickly the behests of God. They would be insufficient to support thy weight or bear thee from the spot whereon thou standst. Thou shall not have them.

I beseech thee, kind, propitious, amiable, gracious, bountiful divinity, I beseech thee, deny not the gift which I solicit. Thy present shall be momentaneously returned. Deny me not, I most eloquently entreat thee.

And what thinkest thou shall I do in the meantime? How shall I employ myself without my plumes?

Thou shalt be inactive but for a moment.

A moment, thou child of men, is a moment to thee, but an age to me. A spirit can traverse half the universe within a moment; can hover over the throne of Chaos, mingle with the infernal audience that throngs the hall of Pandemonium, and join the choral band that nightly circles the sacred *Mount,* that lifts its head in the midst of heaven and supports, with Atlantean shoulders, the weight of incumbent deity all in the compass of a moment. [It] can build and demolish worlds, can perform all that thy imagination can conceive, should she enjoy the leisure of a thousand years to form and execute her purposes, before the moment which thou mentionest could arrive at its period.

Well, my friend, I thought that my better angel, who used so frequently to answer me with propitious intimation my impetuous vows, and to bear me sometimes, though rarely, "beyond the visible diurnal sphere," could deny me nothing. But you see she deserts me "at my utmost need" and refuses me the loan of her pinions for a single moment, by whose assistance I meant to have paid a visit "to the heaven of invention" and to have thrown a little incense on the altar of the presiding deity, whoever may at this time have possessed the sovereignty of that enchanted region, that paradise of poets, that blest asylum of anxious and bewildered thought, in which your friend has always, by means of his spiritual auxiliaries, found a refuge from "Adversity's wild, cold wind and beating hail."

The poetical fervor is upon me. The magician whose friendship and [MS mutilated] is now standing at the threshold of his cell and waving his potent wand at my command. Do you not see him? He is present to my sight. A grave and venerable personage he is. I wish I could introduce you to his acquaintance. You have seen, in the tapestry of description, the metropolis of the fairy queen Panthea and the bridge of brass. He would show it to you, delineated by a bolder, life-diffusing, truth-mocking pencil, with brighter hues, on more commodious canvas. But unless I break his wand or make it motionless and drive the enchanter into his gloomy dwelling I shall be seduced to a greater distance from the tract of common sense than I am at present desirous of being.

What more shall I say to thee on this occasion? Wilt thou honor me with thy company this afternoon, if no more agreeable occupation and no previous engagement shall unluckily withhold thee? Shall I share my nectar and manna, my bread and coffee, with thee? If thou wilt walk, I will, with thy permission, accompany thee, and we will return together and will drink the potion and eat the morsel which shall be provided for us, and thou shalt be the loved associate of my solitude, until "the bell strike ten and thou take note of time." I shall infallibly expect thee, as soon as thou hast furnished nature with materials to work up on in her laboratory, and give employment to her active ministers, digestion and concoction. As soon as thou hast partaken of thy midday banquet, with the queen of beauty and the god of loquacious [MS mutilated] as thou hast dined with John and Dorothy. Thou wilt [MS mutilated] in my chamber, law-reading and chequer-playing, we [MS mutilated] mighty conqueror! Thou wishes to triumph over thy vanquished and prostrate foe, fill thy pocket with motley warriors, and I will furnish the field of battle, where thou mayest, till thou art satiated with victory, "sweep whole armies in the fight of Draughts—."

Fare thee well—

C. B. BROWNLOW

### EARLY LITERARY PROJECTS

In a letter from Wilkins to Brown dated April 29, 1792, we learn that both Brown and Wilkins were at work on literary projects and that the former had sent two odes to Wilkins, for his criticism. Wil-

kins begins by saying, "I have again perused your inestimable epistles," and continues with, "Your dissertation, as you are pleased to
style it, was ingenious and entertaining, and your assertions and
arguments receive my entire assent." The letter concludes with pertinent comments on the two odes:

Your two odes, which form a fine contrast to each other, I will preserve
as religiously as a papist would treasure the eye-tooth of St. Peter, the Prince
of Apostles, or the pincers of St. Dominic himself, the father of the holy
Inquisition. The novelty of composition in the *last* and the license of [MS
mutilated] sense into different lines which the absence of rhyme permits,
render it a little obscure unless read with attention or read several times.
I have read it frequently and think I discover new beauties every time. The
first surprised and pleased me more than you can imagine. I had not the
most distant idea that the same person and that person, my intimate friend,
inherited the poetical estates of Pindar, the Boeotian, and Peter Pindar, the
Briton. It is a union of such immense acquisition that I expect you will be
now worth a plum of poetry and hope you will liberally remember

Yrs. affectionately

W. W. W.

Brown was early afflicted with the writer's itch, and daily when
he left the law-office would hasten to his rooms, seize his pen, and pour
out his soul. Sometimes he would laboriously copy into his Journal
letters to and from his friends; or he would compose letters, such as
the Ellendale letters, to imaginary friends. These latter were no
doubt the ancestors of his early novels cast in epistolary form.

This severe tax upon his time was intended for improvement both
in thinking and in writing, and as a record of his progress. Always
eager to acquire a facile, correct, and graceful style, he early studied
with assiduity the writings of the best English authors; his later
writings attest his success.[28]

### A VARIETY OF INTERESTS

But it must not be presumed that Brown was ever devoted solely
to literature. All kinds of knowledge fascinated him; the whole
world, indeed, he took for his province. Henrietta knew of his predilection for geography and history, for in one of her letters she
remarked: "I could easily evince that your native disposition has
always been the same, and that in the midst of chronological tables
and geographical computations, of which I have been told you have
ever been singularly fond, it was easy to have discerned a mind susceptible of amorous impressions."

Another subject that held his lifelong attention was architecture.
Architectural drawings are found here and there in his Journal, and
his early writings show considerable interest in the subject. His

[28] Dunlap, I, 15.

unpublished journals confirm the fact that in the preparation of *The Carrils and the Ormes,* Brown sometimes sat for whole days planning mansions, castles, or cathedrals, or examining the proportions of some celebrated building of remote ages.[29] But his occupation with this favorite pastime was such that he could leave it at will and enter into a conversation on any topic with a fluency and copiousness that approached the truest eloquence.[30]

His Journal gives evidence of his varied interests. Mingled with letters, fragments of essays, elaborate architectural drawings, and floor plans are schemes for utopias, including part of an original alphabet, a new system of shorthand he is known to have invented, and tables and computations of many kinds. We also see that he was early occupied with literary schemes. In the Henrietta portion of the Journal he expressed his delight in composition, adding: "But it is useless as well as impossible to recount all my literary propensities, the duration of their influence, the order in which they succeeded each other, or the effects which they produced in the enlargement of my heart and the improvement of my understanding."[31]

Brown also essayed a curious form of writing, a cross between fiction and fictional history, published in the Allen-Dunlap biography as the *Sketches of the History of Carsol* and *Sketches of the History of the Carrils and the Ormes.* Although printed in Dunlap as if they were composed in Brown's youth, internal evidence suggests that they were completed much later, perhaps as late as 1806. These puzzling fragments pose the questions: What was the date of their composition? What is their significance? And what was Brown's purpose in all these performances? Was he merely getting practice in the historical writing which was eventually to become his main interest? Certainly he was making no effort to write actual history, for he deliberately mingled history and fiction, real persons and imaginary ones. Were these two sketches intended as part of a greater work? Were they utopian schemes to be considered as introductory to his favorite prospect of a perfect system of government?

Reading these works is an exciting because tantalizing experience. Brown gravely used historical facts, interlarded with the most preposterous inventions, presenting all alike in a convincing, scholarly manner, until the reader, dizzied by the incredible mass of detail, feels obliged to turn to a history text to discover what really happened. As in the *Faerie Queene,* the land is England (in *Carrils and Ormes*) or Sardina (in *Carsol*), and yet it is a ghoulish land, wherein a whole set of events unknown to history takes place. In the *Carrils and Ormes* fragment, we find real historical characters grafted on the

[29] *Ibid.,* p. 258.
[30] Dunlap, II, 89-90.
[31] "Love Among the Ruins," section 22.

family tree of the two extravagantly imagined families. For instance, Catherine Tudor, Henry VII's youngest daughter, who actually died in infancy, grows up and marries one of the Ormes heirs and leaves a permanent imprint on the family history. Hollywood itself could do no more!

Although *Carsol* is a pseudo-history of a kingdom in Sardinia and *Carrils and Ormes* is the story of an ancient family in England, there is considerable similarity of ideas in these two sketches. In both Brown devoted a good deal of time to the description of religious characters—particularly saints. A curious assumption underlay the formation of their religion: that God and Christ neither required nor expected worship or prayer, leaving to local saints direct intervention in worldly affairs. Naturally, then, all ritual was dedicated to the patron saint. Statues, nearly always miraculously created, formed the center of worship in every chapel. Next to religious matters, Brown was interested in economics and government. He described several schemes of government, but never developed any of them sufficiently for the reader to determine what his ideal plan would have been. He always sketched some economic details of the life in his community, but again there is hardly enough to give us a concrete idea of his beliefs.

### THE BELLES LETTRES CLUB

Another indication that young Brown was troubled by *cacoëthes scribendi* during the heyday of his law study was the fact that he and several friends of like mind founded a purely literary society under the name of the Belles Lettres Club. The suggestion for such a club came originally from John Davidson. Its exact membership cannot be definitely determined; but it included Brown, William Wood Wilkins, Timothy Paxson, Zachariah Poulson, Jr., Peter Thompson, Thomas P. Cope, Joseph Bringhurst, Davidson, and a Dr. Milnor, minister of a Presbyterian Church in Philadelphia. Apparently this club lasted from 1786 to 1793. At first Brown was reluctant to enter the club because he did not have a just idea of the improvement derived from such associations. But he soon became its leader. The object of the club was improvement in composition and eloquence.[32] The club no doubt fanned the flame of Brown's ambition to become an author. In the friendly rivalry among its members much ink was spilled and many a goose was minus a quill. Love lyrics, odes, essays poured from their pens.

Anyone familiar with Brown's Journal and the letters exchanged by members of this goodly company would come to the inescapable conclusion that Brown's one passion was to become an author in this new nation and be among the signers of the declaration of the literary independence of America.

[32] Dunlap, I, 15-16.

The formation of the Belles Lettres Club was probably the most powerful circumstance in the early life of Brown in deciding his future prospects and destiny.[33]  A youth of only sixteen, Brown demanded of Davidson "the relation, dependence, and connection of the several parts of knowledge," and his friend, instead of answering the questions, proposed a literary society.  Disappointment at this evasion only stimulated Brown's reflection on the various fields of knowledge, and he answered his own questions by recording in his Journal that he believed the general and true divisions of science to be the moral and the physical; that mind could never be considered except in conjunction with matter; that the science of mind in its essence is metaphysics; that our minds are continually employed in the exercise of apprehension, reason, and will; that the operations of the mind employed upon things foreign to itself are not metaphysics, but perhaps logic; that man must be considered in a variety of lights—in relation to other animals; that he is the subject of both moral science and natural history; that knowledge must not be departmentalized; that chemistry and anatomy have the same object and differ only in the nature of things on which they operate; that medicine is the art of curing diseases incident to both body and mind; and that man may be considered as one and alone, or as a member of a community.[34]

This is a remarkable analysis for a youth yet in his teens.  It shows an unusual familiarity with the main currents of eighteenth-century thought from Locke to Hume, from Descartes to Rousseau.  Such reflections undoubtedly impressed Brown's friends with his solid background in the literature, philosophy, and science of his century; in fact so high did he stand in their esteem that they chose him to deliver the keynote address of the first meeting of the club.  Only a few excerpts can be given:

In this essay I shall attempt to sketch the leading features of our constitution, and to unfold the most obvious relations between the laws and those whose conduct they are designed to regulate; the more minute and imperceptible lines in which its specific nature consists may be reserved for future and more accurate investigation.  To give a general idea of the spirit of laws[35] as they are peculiar to this institution is a task of no small labor and importance. . . .  Literary improvement is certainly the object which every one proposes to himself in becoming a member of this society. . . . He is already convinced that his mental powers only are the subjects of intended cultivation, but when he has once fixed the boundary in his mind, he is apt to think no further division is necessary; he gives his imagination full liberty to range without control through the whole circle of human knowledge, in the belief that whatever calls for the exertion of his mental

[33] *Ibid.*, p. 18.
[34] *Ibid.*, pp. 18-20.
[35] A phrase made famous by Montesquieu's *Esprit des lois*.

faculties is already within his reach and may reasonably be appropriated
to his own use. . . . The road to knowledge is open before him, the prize
of literary excellence is displayed in his sight, and personal assiduity and
attention only are required to remove every impediment between him and
the object of his ambition. . . . I will not even deny that this society will
fully answer his idea, but I am perfectly convinced of the possibility of
framing a system which shall gratify every propensity to enlarge the circle
of his faculties of which the human mind is capable—a system calculated to
employ at once the reason, memory, and imagination of man. . . . An idea
of perfection incompatible with the present state of things is generally the
object of contemplation with philosophers. . . . But though I am sensible
that dreams of absolute perfection can be realized only in another world;
that plans of government without defect, and men whose spirits have been
rendered perfect, can appear only in a future and unknown state of being;
yet, I cannot help thinking but that success in every pursuit will be commen-
surate to the ideas of perfection which we entertain concerning that pursuit.[36]
. . . But education can claim an unbounded dominion over the separate provinces of infancy and youth; whether she employs precept and authority as
the instruments of her purpose, or engages the passions of youth on her
side by means of example and emulation, she is able to instill into the uninformed minds of her pupils whatever sentiment or disposition she pleases.[37]
. . . The idea of a perfect commonwealth is not the same extravagant thing
in education as in politics. The settled depravity of mankind will never
yield to the gentle admonitions of the wise, and the stubborn and inveterate
prejudices of the vulgar will be always hostile to the kindly influence of
good government.[38] . . . It behooves us to make preparation for that awful
crisis in choosing our future parts. . . . Whatever his profession may be
(I speak of those of the liberal kind) he will soon feel the absolute necessity
of devoting some of his time to the study of polite literature.[39] If the native
beauty of the liberal arts be found unable to allure him his interests alone
will incite him to the pursuit. Thus he may owe the most valuable of intellectual treasure to motives the most sordid and interested. . . . Finally
overcome by the bewitching charms of this their favorite pursuit, they become regardless of the soothing pleasures of intoxicated fancy; the enthusiasm of poetry is no less strong and violent than that of religion; they flow
in separate channels, but are derived from the self-same fountain. . . . The
whole circle of human knowledge is indeed bound together by a strong and
indissoluble chain; they mutually receive and impart strength and lustre.

[36] This is a fundamental eighteenth-century concept in France, in England, and
in America.

[37] This is another dominant eighteenth-century philosophy, that education and
environment are all-important in shaping the destiny of man.

[38] This was Brown's earliest utterance on the question of political government—
a subject on which he later had much to say. This early condemnation of Utopian
dreams Brown never had occasion to regret. The Constitutional Convention, meeting at the same time and only a few blocks away from the club, furnished an
ample basis for Brown's apprehension. Was this boy of sixteen expressing fear
of democracy?

[39] Brown had apparently at this early date (1789) not decided to give up the
law, but he certainly did not intend to neglect "polite literature."

The several and distinct sciences which are derived from the reason, the memory, and the imagination are as intimately connected with each other as those powers are in the human mind. The traits of resemblance, for example between moral and physical science, are so many, so various, and so complex, that it is a task of no little labor and ingenuity properly to separate them. Philosophy owes its precision to history, and history is enlightened by the beams of rational philosophy. . . . The connection is not more exquisite between the spiritual and material worlds than between the several provinces of imagination and reason. . . .[40] To obviate the inconvenience of such an unnatural separation, to ornament the mind as well as to improve the understanding, is, I think the business of this society. . . . It even comprehends science and art within the same circle. . . . Different parts of the world, as well as different ages of it, may entertain different notions concerning the particular objects of study which should be ranked under this denomination. . . . Fashion may affix what stamp she pleases to the term of Belles Lettres, and this stamp must of consequence be in perpetual change. . . . Polite learning, sometimes under the name of humanity and sometimes of Belles Lettres, has long been the subject of academical education in the universities of Europe. . . .[41] Belles Lettres may be generally divided into three great departments—grammar, rhetoric, and poetry.[42]

After a lengthy exposition of language and its component parts, he briefly mentioned topics for further discussion in the club.

With the club now fully launched by this dignified and penetrating address, the various members took to their pens. Not content merely to write, they formed themselves in congenial coteries of three or four for reading the classics, discussing style, and holding high converse with the spirits of the mighty dead. Brown's particular knot of friends, Davidson, Bringhurst, and Wilkins, were boon companions. Brown and Wilkins, as we have seen, actually managed to persuade their parents to allow them to live together. To the Brown-Wilkins lodge Bringhurst and Davidson constantly bent their way. The society occasionally met at the home of Benjamin Franklin, who had just returned (1785) from his long and successful mission to France and who immediately upon his return, though old and ailing, threw himself into heated political and constitutional debate (1787-1790). Thinking to pay a pretty tribute to that illustrious American, Brown found occasion for his first ambitious effort as a member of the club: he indited a poem to Franklin. The untoward incident of its publication he recorded in his Journal. The blundering printer substituted the name of Washington, who therefore stands arrayed in awkward colors. "Every word of this clumsy panegyric was a direct slander upon Washington, and so it was regarded at the time."[43]

[40] Brown apparently was not familiar with the eighteenth-century speculation on this subject.

[41] Lectures on Rhetoric and Belles Lettres by Dr. Blair, of the University of Edinburgh (Brown's or Dunlap's note).

[42] Dunlap, I, 21-31.

[43] Ibid., pp. 17-18 (quoted from the Journal).

Apparently young Brown had sent his poem to his brother Joseph, then in the mercantile business in Edentown (Edenton), North Carolina, where on February 26, 1789, the poem was published in the *State Gazette of North Carolina.* Only recently have these facts been given to the public.[44] I print the poem here as a product of Brown's youthful poetic pen:

### An Inscription for General Washington's Tomb Stone

The Shade of great Newton shall mourn,
    And yield him Philosophy's throne,
The palm from her brow shall be torn,
    And given to Washington alone.

His brows ever shall be adorn'd,
    With laurels that never decay,
His laws mighty nations unborn
    And ages remote shall obey.

Him liberty crown'd with her wreath,
    Philosophy shew'd him her plan;
Whilst the Muses inscrib'd underneath
    The hero, the sage, and the man.

Let candor then write on his tomb,
    Here America's favorite lies;
Whose soul for the want of due room,
    Has left us to range in the skies.

His second performance was more fortunate in publication, and distinctly more ambitious. This was a series of original essays under the romantic title of *The Rhapsodist,* begun in the *Columbian Magazine* in August, 1789. As Alexander James Dallas, at the time editor of the magazine, had maintained a high standard and had been successful in enlisting the most distinguished literary talent for his publication, it was no small honor for a boy of eighteen to have his essays appear along with productions of older and abler men, for even in those days there was more competition than has been commonly supposed.

Brown evidently intended that *The Rhapsodist* should be complete in a series of five essays, one for each letter of his name, for the four which were published were signed *B., R., O.,* and *W.,* successively. Whether he wrote the fifth has not yet been determined, but it is a matter of no great moment, for the essays are little more than random and disjointed speculations on life in the manner of the late eighteenth century. Intrinsically they are of little value, but they are interesting as the earliest public appearance in prose of the first professional man

[44] For this bibliographical item I am indebted to H. R. Warfel. See *American Notes and Queries,* I, no. 7 (May, 1941), 19-20.

of letters in America. And to the student of Brown's life and works they reveal much of his character and style: his straining after the unattainable, his dissatisfaction with things as they are, and his glorification of life devoted to the happiness of others. In a world of fancied perfection he "peopled every object with ideal beings, and the barrier between himself and the world of spirits seemed burst by the force of meditation."[45]

In *The Rhapsodist* Brown tells us that his life was to be devoted to reason and dedicated to the task of making truth prevail:

I speak seriously [he said] when I affirm that no situation whatever will justify a man in uttering a falsehood. My opinions respecting this subject are somewhat singular. Truth is with me the test of every man's character. When I perceive the least inclination to deceive, I suspect a growing depravity of soul that will one day be productive of the most dangerous consequences. But I am not alone sagacious in discovering the faults of others. I am also careful to regulate my own conduct by the immutable standard. My scruples in this respect have been ridiculed by my friends.

Here can be seen the didactic spirit of the Brown of *Alcuin* and the novels.

Contrary to generally received opinions the essays have few marks of Dr. Johnson—called by Dunlap, Brown's first master of style—but many symptoms of the romantic tendency then at work in the world. The rhapsodist admits that he is no longer a complete rhapsodist; but he once was, and can thus define the type as "one who delivers the sentiments suggested by the moment in artless and unpremeditated language." He was wed to solitude:

The life of the rhapsodist is literally a dream. Love and friendship, and all the social passions are excluded from his bosom. Nature is the mistress of his affections, in the contemplation of whose charms he is never wearied. He pours forth the effusions of a sprightly fancy and describes the devious wanderings of a quick but thoughtful mind; but he is equally remote from the giddy raptures of enthusiasm and the sober didactic strain of dull philosophy.

In the days when he was a complete rhapsodist, he would not step on a cockroach or let a mouse remain in a trap—"if it were deed or bledde," but that was when he dwelt in the wilderness and could give himself as vehemently as he pleased to rhapsodizing, heedless of the astonished vulgar. He has just come from the "solitary banks of the Ohio, into the thronged streets of the metropolis." He arouses curiosity by hints at a wide range of adventure: "I have alternately spent my life in the wilds of Canadian woods, and in the seraglios of the East." But, as if he remembers his announced intention to say less of himself than of the perfect truth (a noteworthy alternative!),

[45] Dunlap, I, 40.

he interrupts his narrative in the third number with a letter from a censorious and argumentative reader, presumably himself, which is long enough to extend nearly to the end of the fourth number and to prove, it appears, fatal to the series.

The style of *The Rhapsodist* is neither pleasing nor impressive. Brown did not escape "the sober didactic strain of dull philosophy," nor did he achieve a sprightly fancy. But, for a boy of eighteen, there was in it promise both of the writer and of the thinker. The style is individual enough to be called original, though, like most of the prose essays of the latter part of the eighteenth century, it inclines toward heavy, often pedantic, sentences. There is a suggestion, however faint, of Dr. Johnson; but Brown's style cannot in any definite sense be said to resemble that of the *Rambler*. Brown is less formal than Johnson, but still less easy and natural than Goldsmith. Brown's knowledge of the Latin language did not lead him, however, to use a noticeably Latinized vocabulary. His diction in these essays is surprisingly simple, and his style is more concrete than "the wondrous buckram" of Dr. Johnson. In *The Rhapsodist,* as in his earliest speeches and essays, by actual count there are less than 20 per cent of Latin words, and only 25 per cent of the words contain more than one syllable. These figures would seem to refute the general impression that Brown's diction is Johnsonian. In sentence structure, on the other hand, there is a close resemblance to the balanced, antithetical form. But it has already been pointed out that in this trait Brown was a child of his age, and not the follower of any particular individual of that age.

His love of moralizing and philosophizing was in strict keeping with the high seriousness of the eighteenth century. In all the elements of his style, in manner as in matter, Brown, then, was unmistakably of the closing years of the eighteenth century. Critics have remarked his want of humor, yet have failed to point out that his was a serious age, which generally speaking was lacking in that saving grace. Men did not write so much of fops and fans as in the time of Addison and Steele, for there was little spirit of levity in those revolutionary days. What little humor there was became generally so overlaid with grim irony and satire that it really ceased to be humor; this is particularly true of the prose essay and the novel.

The date of composition of *The Rhapsodist* is unknown. There is, however, a suggestive but inconclusive editor's notice to contributors for the September (1787) number of the *Columbian Magazine*. In this the editor remarks that "The story, *The Rhapsody,* or whatever it may be called, cannot be inserted, till the writer furnishes us with a proper name for his composition, as we have, in vain, endeavored to frame one." There is a reference to titles in Brown's first essay that, in the light of the editor's remarks, may be significant.

"The title for these essays," he observes, "is a matter of equal moment; the reputation of the writer in a great measure depends upon it, among those who judge of the composition by the title, and not the title by the composition; I could hardly have believed that sort of prejudice existed in an enlightened mind." It may be thought that the editor refers to a story; if so, it was never printed in the magazine with the title of "Rhapsody"; and the word *story* may be used to refer to a kind of production that would include Brown's essays, for they are in a way a loose sketch of the life of a rhapsodist. If the above data are reliable, Brown was only sixteen when he wrote these essays.

### BROWN'S THEORY OF COMPOSITION

The members occasionally exchanged pieces for criticism, since self-improvement and mutual aid were motives for the establishment of the club. That such critical advice was sought and given may be inferred from a letter of Brown's to J. D——n (probably his friend and fellow club member, John Davidson). After considerable bantering about his beloved Henrietta, Brown concludes with a postscript, as follows:

I have read your dissertation with as much intuition as I could possibly bestow upon it, but considered merely as a series of arguments, in support of a controverted proposition, you must be convinced that I am far from being a suitable judge of its merits, that I am utterly incapable of analyzing its proof and weighing the propriety of every conclusion. The dialect of medicine is peculiarly unintelligible, but there is nothing in this performance which I do not fully understand, but as the basis of your reasoning are facts which have been discovered on experiment, or which are the results of actual inspection into the human economy, they only who enjoy opportunities of examining their validity by the same method can presume either to adopt or reject your opinions.

You are not ambitious of excellence with regard to composition, and aspire only to correctness and perspicuity, and in those qualities your essay is certainly not deficient. I know no one whose thoughts are more solid and judicious than those of my friend, or whose expressions are better suited to the subject and occasion which demand them. To write with classical elegance is the lot of few, but though this be doubtless a desirable acknowledgement it is far from being necessary. Skill in composition is the result of long and incessant labor and attention, but there is somewhat that disposes us to endeavor after its attainment and which renders our efforts successful—which can only be derived from nature. May it not be disputed whether the means are united to the end, whether more time and pains are not required than a reasonable being ought to bestow [on] it, whether those hours devoted to rhetorical exercises would not be far more usefully employed in storing the imagination with images and the understanding with ideas, in enriching our minds with just and valuable sentiments, in collecting and arranging the elements of knowledge? Those whose conceptions are ardent and vigorous cannot fail of expressing themselves with sufficient energy, and all the defects of composition may perhaps be outweighed by just arguments, useful relations, and humble perspicuity. May not your performances be highly celebrated, your own doctrines be incontestably established, and the position of your opponents be unanswerably confuted though you should be deficient in propriety of terms or harmony of periods or elegance of phraseology? And it can be known only by experiment whether nature has been propitious to us. Until the end be actually accomplished are we not uncertain whether it be in itself attainable? As it is doubtful whether the importance of the end will justify the labor of pursuit, it is also dubious whether our purpose, such as it is, be possible to be accomplished. Elegance of style is of no value when put into competition with solidity of thought. The power itself of thinking accurately and reasoning justly, and the means by which this power is acquired or improved, will necessarily induce such a degree of excellence in composition as will sufficiently secure us from contempt and not only exempt us from the inconvenience of writing or speaking unintelligibly in support of our opinion, but enable us to adorn our style with many valuable though simple qualities.

I confess that were I to consult only my own taste I should willingly assume a different opinion. I am seldom profited by instruction unless it be conveyed in elegant and pleasing language, but I know that the bulk of mankind are very differently affected, and that in performances which are designated to be generally useful, uncommon solicitude with regard to style would be not only useless but improper, that our language and ideas are to be reduced to the standard of common mind and familiar diction.[46]

I know that you will allege in opposition to those remarks that all literary performances are not destined for the amusement or instruction of the vulgar, that genuine elegance is so far from being incompatible with perspicuity that perspicuity is, in reality, one of its most indispensable ingredients, that its other qualities, though they tend to heighten the impression of our sentiments on polished and cultivated minds, are at least without any injurious effect in a coarse and vulgar comprehension, that while they entitle us to the praise of one of taste and genius, they will at least not diminish the approbation of common readers. You will probably observe also that to improve our style it is necessary to converse with men and books; that to limit our attention merely to science is impossible, or at least in this pursuit, by no means necessary; that [the] means which every one must use to make himself master of the style of Addison or Johnson will also unavoidably put him in possession of their sentiments; that the reputation of a writer will be more permanent and universal in proportion as he adds to the force of sentiment the embellishments of composition; that it is our duty not merely to offer but enforce the truth, and to make use of every method to arrest attention and facilitate conviction. You have often reasoned in this manner, and I know not whether it be possible to confute you. At least the present is not a suitable opportunity for attempting it.[47]

The young literati tried their hands at various forms of writing— including poems. We have already examined several early specimens

---

[46] The plea for familiar language was becoming rather general by the end of the eighteenth century. See Wordsworth and Coleridge.

[47] From the Journal.

of Brown's poetry. It was toward the end of the period of hesitation that he penned his most ambitious poem. He called it *Devotion: An Epistle*,[48] and aptly so, for it has the apperance of being the final and poetized letter to Henrietta. This poem was his best, and as late as 1801 he thought so highly of it that he laboriously copied it for his fiancée and future wife, Elizabeth Linn, in spite of its having been inspired by his former sweetheart, Henrietta. That the poem has genuine merit must be allowed. Perhaps F. L. Pattee summed up the consensus of critical opinion when he said:

Judging from his "Devotion: an Epistle" . . . there was genuine poetry in the youth. Even in England in 1794, four years before the *Lyrical Ballads*, few writers could equal certain passages in this poem. It is poetical autobiography: it throws light upon those unrecorded yet formative years after Brown had abandoned the law.[49]

Although the thought is sometimes hard to follow because of the long, wandering, and often incomplete sentences, it is evident that Brown was voicing those feelings of uncertainty and melancholy that dominated his mind during this period. Troubled by the religious skepticism characteristic of the Age of Reason, he struggled to find his way through doubt and insecurity, relying on Devotion, the subject of his poem, to be the "flame pointing to heaven." It mirrored the influences most potent during these troubled years: his friends, possibly Henrietta ("Virtue femininely clothed"), and his various intellectual interests. We obtain valuable glimpses of the restless, all-embracing mind that turned for solace to poetry, music, history, science, psychology (such as it was then), logic, and even "the thorny tracts that lead to nothing in the metaphysic wilderness." In the poem he visited, as later in *Alcuin* and other productions, ancient civilizations and examined great works of architecture. But after all these excursions into varied fields, he felt the need for

> The guidance which,
> with radiant finger, points
> To these divine abodes . . .
> the haven of eternal rest.

From a literary standpoint *Devotion* is, like much of his other work, uneven. Bearing marks of haste, incompletely developed thoughts, and lack of organization, it is nevertheless informed with sincerity and with noble feeling. The trite personifications and commonplace similes typical of eighteenth-century verse mingle with lines of strong descriptive power. As one would expect from Brown's broad literary background, the poem is vibrant with echoes of seven-

[48] "Devotion, an Epistle," *American Register*, III (1808), 567-578. See appendix A in this book.

[49] *Wieland*, ed. Fred Lewis Pattee (New York, 1926), Introduction, pp. xiv-xv.

teenth- and eighteenth-century sentiment. Though poetry did not naturally well up in Brown, still one is inclined to agree with Pattee that "there was poetry in the youth."

The days of Brown's law apprenticeship had now drawn to an inauspicious close. He had worked hard in the office, but without pleasure or hope of ultimate benefit to himself. His preparation had been made with a thoroughness that assured success, and his knowledge of history and philosophy, his command of language, and his keen logical faculty only added to the reasonable anticipation of a brilliant career. But Brown saw that legal success meant only money, a high-sounding name, and a careless disregard of moral values. In consequence he finally decided not to practice, and "neither the persuasions and arguments of his friends, nor his own sense of duty" could overcome his decision. Without money and the necessities of life, with the most unpromising prospects for other employment, Brown stood firm in his conviction that he was right. We have seen in the course of this study that it was not merely rebellion against the practice of law which led Brown to this momentous decision, but the persistent inner urge to become an author by profession.

# III

# LOVE AMONG THE RUINS

HENRIETTA G.

Now BEGINS a period of some years of hesitation and pain. The pitiful struggle through which Brown passed has never been fully told. Alienated from family and friends, and without a penny in his pocket, he was in a position almost hopeless; but with the indomitable Quaker spirit to support him he triumphed over the sorrow and the disappointments that everywhere lay in his path. Like Samuel Johnson fifty years before, Brown was set adrift in a friendless world to make a living by his own literary efforts. Letters in America, as in the England of Johnson's day, were by no means a gainful calling. Brown could scarcely have expected at once to win his bread with the productions of his pen, nor could he have hoped for much in any practical business, for both his education and his natural inclination had disqualified him for success in any trade.

His letters of this period read like pages from the *Journal* of Amiel, in the aversion to an active life, the love of self-analysis, and the faculty of morbid philosophizing. They are, as Matthew Arnold says of the *Journal Intime,* studies not in biography but in pathology. "I have not been deficient," Brown wrote to his friend Wilkins, "in the pursuit of that necessary branch of knowledge, the study of myself. . . . I sincerely lament that I ever gave you reason to imagine that I was not so happy as a gay indifference with regard to the present, stubborn forgetfulness with respect to the uneasy past, and excursions into lightsome futurity could make me."[1]

Amidst these sorrows and disappointments came one of the most momentous experiences of the young philosopher's life—his first serious love affair. He loved with an ardor that knew no bounds except the scruples of his sweetheart, as the pages of his intimate Journal fully reveal. This event in Brown's life Allen and Dunlap do not even mention, in all likelihood out of deference to the wishes of the family. The object of his violent passion was a young woman from Connecticut, apparently paying a protracted visit to her aunt in Philadelphia. All that we know of her is that she was "very beau-

[1] Quoted in Dunlap, I, 51.

tiful''; that she was three years older than her lover; that she was exceptionally well educated for a woman of her day; that her moral sensibility was much finer than Brown's; and that her name was *Henrietta G.* The letters which he wrote to her and hers in turn to him were copied into his Journal, here published for the first time. Those who persistently think of Brown as an inhuman prig should read the pages of this Journal and breathe the healthful atmosphere of a real boy, just out of his teens, in the throes of his first love, even though his love-making at times dangerously approaches the Godwinian formula.

Brown had apparently made the acquaintance of the beautiful Henrietta in the spring of 1792, for in that year her name is first mentioned in a letter to his friend Wilkins.[2] The acquaintance rapidly grew into intimacy, and intimacy to betrothal. The young philosopher urged immediate marriage, but the good sense of the woman prevailed, and no definite day for marriage was set. Apparently the one stumbling block to their anticipated marital happiness was religion. She, it seems, was not a Quaker—a sect that frowned upon any of its members' marrying outside the Society.

The Journal suddenly breaks off, and the reader is left to piece out the sequel. Apparently the beautiful Henrietta, alarmed at the prospect, took flight to the home of her kinsmen in Connecticut. Young Brown, estranged from his family, his friends, and his beloved, fell into a despondency that bordered on insanity. He even hinted at suicide in a letter to Wilkins: ''Had I never had friends and relations, I am convinced that before this time I had ceased either to exist, or to exist as an inhabitant of America.''[3] Hoping, apparently, to re-instate himself in the graces of his lady, he wandered off to Connecticut, ostensibly paying a visit to his friend Elihu Hubbard Smith. This in brief is the story of his first love; how the affair finally terminated is a sealed book.

These letters to and from Henrietta dwell on several dominant and revealing topics. Besides the considerable space naturally given to the absorbing subject of their love, we find valuable indications of Brown's tendency toward gloomy introspection, his early interest in literature both classical and modern, his uneasiness of mind, and the unsettled state of his personal affairs during this period (1790-1793). The interest of the lovers in all branches of literature is impressive, and Brown's literary criticism is remarkably astute for a young man of twenty. His condemnation of classical literature on the ground of morals, while rather ridiculous today, reflects the increasing eighteenth-century disapproval of the classics, growing out of middle-class Puritanical ideals. His opinion of the rights, the dignity, and the

[2] References to Henrietta G. occur in the Brown-Wilkins correspondence after May, 1792.

[3] Quoted in Dunlap, I, 52.

abilities of women reflects the most advanced thought of the time, as
do his discussions of such philosophical questions as the nature of
virtue, sincerity, the Neoplatonic union of souls, and the question of
immortality—in which he reflects the skepticism of David Hume and
other eighteenth-century English and French philosophers. In her
conduct Henrietta conforms (deliberately, as we shall see) to the ideal
of the typical eighteenth-century heroine of the sentimental novel.
In her independence and good sense (which show through the simper-
ing pose of the sentimental heroine) and in her desire for a more
extended education, Henrietta is the "new woman," who was to find
full development in *Alcuin,* and who evidently served later as the
model for the intellectual heroines in Brown's novels.

The question may be raised whether this series of letters may not
be a youthful attempt to write a novel in epistolary form. A careful
examination, it seems to me, will convince one that the work is autobiographical, representing an actual experience in Brown's life: it
was his custom according to Dunlap, who was intimately acquainted
with his writing habits, to copy into "his journal the epistles he received from his correspondents" (I, 15); the tone of the letters is
particularly intimate and personal, and quite unlike that in the epistolary novels of the author; several statements in the letters concern
identifiable events in Brown's life; and finally an irrefutable argument for their autobiographical nature is the fact that several of the
letters are signed C.B.B.—something Brown would scarcely have done
had the letters been part of a novel and his characters imaginary.

Since letters are by their nature discursive and digressive, ex-
planatory interpolations of key passages have been made to aid the
reader in spotting the subject matter in which he may have a particular interest. The letters are numbered as in the original. The punc-
tuation, spelling, grammar, and paragraphing have been modernized.

### THE JOURNAL LETTERS
### (c. 1790-93)

I [From Henrietta]                         Tuesday, morn, August 7.
   [*Occupations of a typical young lady of the eighteenth century: 1*]
I am never so happy as when employed in writing to my friend; and
I am willing to persuade myself that he receives no less pleasure from
answering than I from the composition of my letters. What a scribbler have I suddenly become! and how many of those hours do I now
devote to the pen which were formerly engrossed by the needle and
the book. It is true that your performances have made me more
attached to my music than I have formerly been. I pay more attention to it than is, perhaps, consistent with a prudent distribution of
my time, but that is of small importance when compared to the time
which I dedicate to our correspondence. I protest I think that if we

proceed for a considerable period in this manner I shall begin to imagine myself your rival in composition. I know you value yourself extremely, and with justice, on the ease and vigor and correctness of your style. Be assured, my friend, I shall never be able to contend with you in those qualifications, but in the facility of composition, a not inaccurate and ungrammatical facility, I really flatter myself that I shall at no great distance of time be equal to you. However, to whatever excellence I attain, it is to you only that I shall deem myself indebted for it.

[*Brown's personality: 2*] To me, however, the valuation of these questions is of small importance. My disposition is naturally serious. I too much resemble my beloved friend in this respect, and as love, no less than friendship, is founded on a conformity of disposition, to this cause among others I attribute my affection for him. How much more is my ear delighted in listening to thy amiable enthusiasm, to thy tender and pathetical effusions that bespeak the candor and sincerity of thy love than to all the volubilities and prettiness that compose a fashionable circle! Write to me as frequently as possible. I begin to be more and more uneasy in your absence. Supply your absence with your letters, but when it is possible to come to me in person I shall expect to see you, who in sleep or wakefulness are always present to the mind of [Harriet?].

P.S. Rachel will put this into your hand. A little gratuity would not be amiss. Gratitude will render her more faithful and exact in delivering my messages than any orders or injunctions from me. Such is her disposition, and it is surely laudable to profit by the knowledge of it. Farewell.

II [From Brown]                          Tuesday afternoon: Aug. 7.

What obligations do you continually heap upon me! How shall I discharge them? O loveliest of women! How inferior are the beauties of your person to those of your mind! Surely nature has enabled thee to [achieve?] excellence without the aid of education. With what emotion did I read your letter. How shall I express my gratitude, my admiration?

[*Brown's method of composing his letters: 3*] Surely you are jesting when you compliment me on my skill in composition. My dearest Harriet, what excellences do I display or what opportunities are offered you to judge my proficiency in the art of writing? You have seen only those performances which were dictated by my love, which were produced at the luminious and impassioned moment in which all my faculties were suspended in the contemplation of your charms, when my soul was elevated far above its usual pitch and endeavored to pour itself forth at your feet. Is it to be wondered at that at such a moment officious and unbidden eloquences awaited on my lips? My conceptions are often too big for words; they struggle in vain for utterance, and in the hurry and confusion which their multitude in thronging to my pen produces, I cannot hesitate in the choice of words. Whichsoever first offer themselves are instantly adopted. I have no leisure to reflect and weigh, to choose. I am unsolicitous of elegance or accuracy and am satisfied with the power of expressing myself intelligibly, regardless of that perspicuity which results from the use of words cautiously and deliberately selected and arranged, and of that elegance which is the effect of painful and laborious attention.

Why should I review and correct what I have written? And no otherwise than by incessant revision and correction can exactness be acquired. Preposterous! I might with the same propriety repeat what I say to you personally, in order to discover and correct improprieties of sentiment or inaccuracies in the expression. I am not that despicable thing that mopes away his hour in the dust of a library, that scrutinizes, with superfluous labor, the dress of borrowed or artificial sentiments. I deliver the suggestions of my heart. I speak in my native character. So rapid is generally the current of ideas, in writing to my angel, that I cannot mark their connection and dependence, and am sometimes fearful that the abruptness of my transitions has occasioned some degree of obscurity. But art thou not animated by a kindred spirit? Dost thou not honor me with thy regard and avow a passion for me, not less sincere, though perhaps less violent and ungovernable, than that which reigns in my heart? Thou needest not the aid of an interpreter; where to the vulgar or disinterested eye, all is darkness impenetrable, to thine, whom love has endowed with sagacity—"A crystaline transparency prevails." How was I affected by the conclusion of your letter! And am I, least of creatures, condescending angel! "always present to thy mind"? How does thy goodness overwhelm me! You will make me mad. Heaven be witness for me that your image is engraven in my soul, that death only can obliterate the impression. Death, did I say, alas! I should be miserable if I thought that, by death, we should be disunited forever, that the union of our minds would not continue to eternity.

[*Henrietta convinces him of immortality:* 4] You know I formerly doubted about the reality of a future state. That doubt was always sufficiently terrible. But how hideous would it now appear, when it would necessarily involve the possibility of separation from you. I have long since discounted this tormenting doubt in obedience to the command of my sovereign mistress. How can I believe that thou wast unable to have produced any arguments in defense of thy opinion? With what rapture would I have listened to my beauteous reasoner! Why should you refer me to the learned lucubrations of rugged philosophers—you who are so much better qualified to be my instructress?

But formal argument was indeed wholly unnecessary; I should have derived pleasure rather than instruction from it. For my conversion to your doctrines was effected by a single word. The simple declaration of your opinion was always equivalent to demonstration.

Shall I ever forget the time and place in which that declaration was made? Every circumstance is indelibly impressed upon my memory—the garden—the mild and tranquil evening—the cloudless sky—the moon walking in her brightness; the deep, the sacred silence that prevailed around—when all the noises of a great metropolis were hushed, when everything conspired to fix my attention and to sublime my spirit into rapture. I saw thee before me, thou blooming angel. I heard thy voice. What a revolution in my sentiments did a few words produce.

"My friend, my only friend, there exists a deity. He is wise; his benevolence is equal to his wisdom. Thou wast formed for happiness, but canst enjoy it only in eternity. Canst thou enjoy it only in eternity? Canst thou overcome thy abhorrence of non-existence? Canst thou derive pleasure but from the prospect of immortality? Dost thou need a stronger proof that thy being will never end? Unbelief is misery. Why then wilt thou not believe? If the soul be matter, if our being be finite, the period of our eternal separation will arrive. Do not you shudder at the thought? Let me take thee to my arms; for this embrace may be the last. I may never see thee more. When thou diest I shall never see thee more unless thy soul be immaterial and immortal."

[*Brown's idealization of Henrietta: 5*] Ah! thou heavenly teacher, was it possible for me to withstand such rhetoric as this? Belief instantaneously shot into my mind, luminous as a beam of revelation. That evening you appeared a thousand times more amiable than before. Sublimest of women! My love was mingled with a sacred awe; your purity was heightened into sanctity. The tenderness which I before held was now in some degree converted into veneration. I approached you with a kind of fear, such as may be supposed to be inspired by the presence of a superior being! I was alarmed at these emotions. A secret dread began to take possession of me. My eyes beheld a new object. I no longer saw the Harriet with whom I had been just conversing. I saw a different personage, whom my unworthiness rendered it sacrilege to touch, presumptuous to behold. "What," said I to myself "is reverence to take the place of love? How I love the mistress in the angel! Then I am miserable." But ah! As soon as you touched my hand and pressed me to your bosom, how quickly did my terrors vanish, and the tide of all my former reservations retreat. What miracles cannot the enchantments of your touch produce! My reverence was not diminished; you appeared equally sublime, exalted, and adorable. And yet I perceived that you were still a woman, that to think of you with melting fondness was not criminal. To love you appeared not only [not] criminal but laudable, to be a duty indispensably encumbent upon me.

[*Romantic sensibility: 6*] Never did I leave you with more invincible reluctance. As soon as you retired I sunk into despondency which I cannot describe. I lingered involuntarily; I could not force myself from your door. Gloomy and dispirited, I walked homeward; every step that carried me from you seemed to carry me to a greater distance from happiness. I left the highway and traversed the fields in order to avoid the sight of a human creature, though at that late hour it was not likely that I should meet a single passenger in a road so unfrequented. I strayed I knew not whither in the tall and thick grass; my knees were wet with the dews, which appeared to be extremely heavy; my hair was soaked with moisture. Autumnal dews are fatal to my constitution, but I was insensible of wet and cold. Never did the face of nature appear more desolate and gloomy; the moon seemed to struggle for a passage among the clouds which now flew by from the south and began to overspread the atmosphere. The landscape, as her glimpses made it occasionally visible, was absolutely hideous. Melancholy, in spite of all my efforts, came over me. I wept and sobbed, I scarcely knew why; I was agitated by conflicting passions. My imagination accompanied you to your chamber. She is alone (said I); her couch receives her; she sleeps. Why am I excluded? Would my presence profane the chamber? I yet feel the warmth of her embraces. They have made me miserable. To what a precipice have they conducted me? I dare not—dare not, even in imagination, contaminate her angelic purity. Encircled by those arms and leaning on that bosom—felicity unspeakable! And why is it forbidden! She indeed gives me much, but how much does she withhold! Ah! Wretch!—"a wretch, indeed a very wretch"—

I at length reached my chamber. I turned to the passage in *Comus* which you had, an hour before, recited with a grace and energy peculiar to yourself. I thought it would be effectual to delay the tempest of my mind, but it availed nothing, and, according to my usual custom, I had recourse to my pen, and wrote you that letter for which you so often and severely chided me. . . .

But surely pity was mingled with your anger. But death shall overtake me ere I again offend. But why have I recalled these circumstances to your memory? They are recent. And it is my interest that you should forget them. I know not why. I will not be answerable for the deviations and [wanderings?] of my pen. Thou enjoyest the peace of virtue. Thou art mistress of thy passions. Thy pen utters nothing but the dictates of truth. O! impart to me a portion of thy magnanimity; lead me to the shrine of devotion and let thy idea be mingled with that of my Creator and Preserver. Be my guide, my genius, and my *spouse*.

III [From Henrietta]                                    Wednesday Morn.

[*Henrietta rebukes her lover: 7*] I had not forgotten the affecting
circumstances which you mention. But the letter—ah! My capricious
and unaccountable friend! As thou valuest the continuance of my
regard, let me not again be affronted at the mention of it. How would
you be induced to write in that inexcusably licentious manner? I read
it with indignation and regret, but let this be the last time that you
recall to my remembrance that epistle or the circumstances which
produced it. I shall not forgive a second and equally flagrant violation of decorum. I blush for you.

I could not forbear weeping over some parts of your letter. Why
will you continue to write and cant in such a manner as gives me
perpetual occasion to upbraid myself? Why will you so often give
me reason to exclaim, "Lo! the ruins of the noblest youth that ever
[lived] in the tide of times." For surely he whose deportment is
regulated not by reason or prudence but by violent and domineering
passion; whose being is perverted from its original end, and whose
mind is made the slave of phantoms and chimeras may justly be considered as *in ruins.* Your attachment is to me a source of pure and
exalted pleasure, pleasure interrupted or diminished only by the consciousness that its effects upon yourself are very different. How far
are you from tasting that felicity which I enjoy, that stillness and
repose, that mental calm which only is worthy of the name of happiness? You pretend that my inclination is your law, that my will will
always be complied with as soon as it is known. I can easily conceive
a just idea of love. It appears to me to be simple, intelligible, and
consistent. But thy love I must confess to be wholly mysterious and
absolutely inexplicable. For notwithstanding the absoluteness of my
most reasonable commands, you obstinately refuse obedience to them.
It it not possible to subdue this contumaciousness? What think you,
my friend, of an expedient which has just occurred to me? Give me
in your next letter your opinion of it. I think its success will be in-
fallible. It is this: I will immediately leave this city and return to
Connecticut; I will send you a letter, to be delivered to you after my
departure, in which I will solemnly renounce all affection for you,
declare with all the virulence of female indignation that some parts
of your conduct have mortally and inexpiably offended me, and that
hereafter no correspondence or connection shall subsist between us.
What sayest thou? I hope thou wilt applaud the ingenuity of this
contrivance. It will doubtless be successful, but another more important question with regard to it remains to be considered, and that
is whether it be practicable.

Alas! I am apprehensive that its execution is impossible. I find,
O my beloved youth, that my soul is linked to thine by ties which will
not easily be broken. But nothing but necessity can part us. Some

other scheme must therefore be discovered which may more conveniently be carried into effect.

[*The sentimental heroine: 8*] But the disorder must be known before it can be cured. What is thy disease, my friend—the source of this perpetual inquietude? Thou talkest very obscurely. What! Dost thou regret the transformation, the fancied transformation, of thy mistress into an angel; but her chamber, her couch, her arms! Her bosom! Hah! I see—I see— how long has my sagacity slept! Was it possible to be so blind? A precipice indeed! Thou indeed art rushing to a precipice, from which thou wilt fall, but not alone. Thy Henrietta will fall with thee. Call thy courage to thee ere it be too late; assume thy manhood; shake off this drowsiness. Do not oblige me to look upon thee with terror instead of tenderness, to shun instead of saluting thy company, to regard thee as the foe of virtue, the bane of my peace, the destroyer of my honor. Ah, my friend, my much deluded and unhappy friend! The distress which this discovery has given me will not suffer me to proceed—

IV [From Brown]                                   Wednesday Noon.

[*Romantic despair and remorse: 9*] Distress! What have I written that has given you so much distress? And have I been the cause of your grief? Wretch that I am! I was born to be unhappy and to make those miserable whose felicity I must desire to promote. My life is ebbing, but a transitory moment and the scene will vanish. I cannot bear the weight of your resentment, but the consciousness of having afflicted as well as angered you drives me to despair.

How was I capable of harboring such atrocious guilt? Surely, my beloved creature, you have erred; you have misinterpreted my meaning. Am I capable of intending the disturbance of your tranquillity, the violation of your purity? Exalted and unblemished excellence! The mind of him who adores thee is not less pure and sinless than thy own. Thou, whose name is virtue, deem less unjustly of me, I beseech thee. Know me for the lover of thy soul. The graces of thy person, however unrivalled and transcendant, are abundantly eclipsed by the beauties of the animating mind. It is that to which I seek to be united, but am I not a man? And would you punish me for faults which are inseparable from my nature? Is it not enough that my errors are always followed by bitter and, I hope, effectual repentance? Permit me to remind you that—but I cannot write. I will throw myself at your feet as soon as possible, and entreat your favor and forgiveness there—Devout creature! May thy soul be ever a stranger to the tumults [by] which I am torn and harassed. But your presence is a cure for all my sorrows. When I hear your voice, when I press your hand, I shall be happy, supremely happy.

V [From Harriet]                                    Thursday Morn.

[*Henrietta's judgment of his sincerity coupled with gloom and passion—Wertherism: 10*] Come to me, my friend, as soon as possible; I have already told you that though your letters are pleasing, they are less delightful than your conversation. I have recovered from the disorder into which I was thrown by the perusal of your last letter, a disorder to the removal of which the one which I have just received has greatly contributed. It is impossible to doubt the rectitude of your heart, and though you may sometimes be hurried away by uncontrollable passions, I am confident that their dominion is transitory and the principles of honor and integrity will at length obtain the superiority, and teach you to conduct [yourself] aright.

I clearly perceive that there is a mode of speaking which is dictated by nature, and which it is impossible to [counterfeit]. Thou, my friend, speakest the language of sincerity, and amidst the utmost simplicity of sentiment and language art truly and sublimely eloquent: And why? For no other reason than because thou art sincere. Beware of me, my friend; be careful to deserve this exalted panegyric. Trust me—I am a woman of uncommon penetration. As soon as thy sincerity forsakes thee, I shall instantly discover it, and thou wilt no longer be accounted eloquent. This among other formidable consequences will result from thy apostasy.

You see how I labor to be gay and sportive. But I cannot instantly shake off the gloomy and foreboding melancholy with which some expressions in your letter have inspired me. "Life is ebbing." Horrid intimation! What do you mean by this? Thou dear Capricious! I shall at length obtain some knowledge of your character, and shall learn to lay less stress upon the most emphatical of your assertions without any impeachment of your veracity. Life is ebbing, sayest thou. Thou speakest falsely, that is, if thou really believest what thou sayest, but what thou sayest is by no means true. Will you venture expressions like these in my imperial presence? If thou wert dead, I would stretch forth my scepter to thee, and in touching it, thou wouldst revive. When have I heard from thy lips a phrase of such solemnity?

Ah! My friend, this second effort has availed me nothing. I am still the prey of a gloomy and unconquerable solicitude. "Life is ebbing!" In speaking thus I am certain that you spoke as you thought. What then must I conclude? Horrible conclusion! Vanish! Or felicity is fled forever.

Why should the passions of my friend be so impetuous and ungovernable? Is his youthfulness the cause? I am no more than three years older than himself, and the sincerity of my love is doubtless equal to that of his; and yet my serenity, unless when ruffled by the gust of his passions, is perpetual. I will exact an explanation from you of this mystery when I see you. Provide yourself with a plausible solution. I have already forgiven you. You will find me all mildness and placability. I will indeed be extraordinarily kind, and if you are very good, will perhaps permit you to seal this forgiveness on the lips of

HENRIETTA G.

VI [To Harriet]                                        Thursday Noon.

[*Romantic idealization of Henrietta: 11*] That indeed will be a blissful testimony of its truth. Imagination already bears me to your arms; my lips already feel the animating pressure. Sighs and transports are the only eloquence to which thou shalt then listen. But do you not dread the intoxication of the moment? That bosom which it is criminal to name, thinkest thou that I shall not be irresistibly tempted to touch, to gaze with too much greediness at its enchanting undulations? What, has your discretion forsaken you! Do not you perceive that I shall stand on the very brink of the frightful precipice, that reason will be powerless, that her throne will be usurped by passion? What then will become of you? Will angels shield thee from the contagion and breathe around thee uninfected airs?

Ah! No. My apprehensions are vain! Caution would be superfluous. For thou art all excellence and purity and I all reverence and adoration. Thou canst easily check the career of my impetuosity; I shall shrink from the rigors of a look; I shall not clasp thee without shuddering. Thou art too austerely, unvoluptuously beautiful!

Am I indeed eloquent? It is to love that the wand of Hermes is indebted for its magic power. But how far am I surpassed by you, whose silence produces all the effects of moving oratory? But if my eloquence shall always keep pace with my sincerity, I am confident that I shall always merit your encomiums; but the hour of our meeting hastens. I wait impatiently to salute you. I shall not forget the additional ceremony. No, by heaven, I shall not omit it. Why have you not always treated [me] with the same enchanting familiarity, and permitted me to touch as well as gaze? The constraint which you have imposed upon me was intolerable. It is now removed, removed forever. You will not hinder me from tasting the delicious fragrance of those lips; you will not sternly interdict my kisses; you will not banish me from that heaving bosom. What sweet, what nourishing repose shall I not taste in your arms?

VI [VII] [From Henrietta]                              Friday Morn.

[*She marvels at his knowledge: 12*] It is well, my friend! I was fearful that my indiscretion would produce its natural consequences. But be more cautious for the future, or I shall be obliged to be more reserved. Thou art a wonderful youth. Where didst thou get thy knowledge? Didst thou draw it from the fountain of inspiration?

Who was your preceptor in poetry? In sciences, in history? Are you a Grecian and Latinist? But I know you art. And how do you think I made the discovery? I will not tell you; you will laugh at my pretentions to knowledge and sagacity.

[*Educated women—Mrs. Elizabeth Carter, translator of Epictetus; note that a Mrs. Carter is soon to become the leading character in Brown's* ALCUIN: *13*] Will you teach me the Greek and Latin languages? Methinks I should be proud to be placed by the side of Mrs. Carter.[4] Was she not a linguist and philologist, the deepest of female scholars? Such, I have read, was the character of this illustrious lady, and amidst all her eruditions she was, if I am rightly informed, still a woman, and carried into the recesses of the library all the delicacies of her sex. What an extraordinary spectacle! The fingers of a lady soiled with the dust of the manuscripts of Epictetus.

Can you furnish me with her translation of that moralist? I should like to read it merely on account of the sex of the translator, and yet my friend is so frequently the subject of my thought that I have scarcely any leisure for indifferent avocations, and it is somewhat unreasonable to require your assistance to banish the idea by which I am thus incessantly haunted. Epictetus is also a man. Of what kind and species is that animal? I never heard him accurately described and am doubtful whether he be most the object of contempt or veneration. But Brutus was a Stoic. The amiable and exalted Brutus and the tender and heroic Portia, art not these sufficient to vindicate the name of Stoic from reproach and obloquy?

[*Avowal of her desire to pattern herself after Clarissa Harlowe: 14*] I, a poor unlearned, unphilosophical creature, shall never become a Stoic, never emulate the heroism or admire the exploits of Lucrece or Portia. I am a disciple of that religion and philosophy of which the effects are to be seen in the conduct of Clarissa. O best of men! Most eloquent of writers! It is from thy immortal production that I have imbibed the love of virtue; of moral harmony and beauty. From thee also have I gathered critical instruction and learned to speak and to write. How great then are my obligations to thee. But if thy spirit be a witness to the deeds of human kind, this confession will sufficiently reward thee!

[*Desirability of a literary correspondence; wishes Brown to be her tutor: 15*] Whither has my pen conducted me? I follow without scruple or examination its guidance. The incidents of the last evening have restored all my happiness and tranquillity. It is sufficient that I am writing *to* my friend, and find no difficulty in expatiating

[4] Elizabeth Carter (1717-1806), English poet and translator of Epictetus (1758); friend of Dr. Johnson, who praised her Greek scholarship. Compare this discussion of women's education in classical and modern languages with a historical sketch by Frank Pierce Jones, ''The Role of the Classics in the Emancipation of Women,'' *Classical Journal*, XXXIX (March, 1944), 326-342.

on indifferent topics. Why cannot I engage you in a literary correspondence? You suffer your imagination to dwell upon a single
subject so long that at length no efforts can elude or banish it and
you write with a sort of frenzy that saddens and alarms me. I beseech
you be more cool, collected, and dispassionate, and let [me] be gratified with the sight of one letter written in the capacity rather of a
tutor than a lover. And why should you not be my preceptor? It
will furnish you with a pretense to be more frequently my visitant.
Let us be mutually communicative of our literary stores. If you will
teach me the Greek and Latin I will initiate you into the French and
Italian.

[*Her desire to learn the classical languages; women and literary
pursuits: 16*] Why should women be outstripped by men in literary
pursuits? For is not female curiosity insatiable, and what other
passion is requisite to render learned labor successful? I am, in this
respect, a mere woman. Would you believe that I have sometimes
been ambitious of being versed in the jargon of the Mohocks and
Japanese, and of bearing away the palm of classic erudition from
learned people? What are your names? Yes, I remember them.
Flencher, Sealyer, and Vapius. I must conceive that a more ridiculous propensity never inhabited the female bosom, and should view
not with veneration but with laughter the Statue of Domina Dacier.
Domina? Is that right? Thou seest that I am already infected with
the contagion of Latinity. Tell me whether the Latin language be
to one in my circumstances worth the labor of acquiring, and what
period of time and what degree of application the acquisition would
necessarily demand. And Greek—methinks I have a strong desire
to read Euripides and Sophocles in their originals; to talk, in their
native dialect, with Xenophon and Plato.

[*Her treatment of him as a pupil: 17*] And what, my tutor, shall
I teach you in return? Thou wilt be a very docile and submissive
scholar, wilt thou not? I am excessively delighted with the prospect,
but what shall be my system of reward or punishment, what method
of reproof, when thou art negligent and inattentive, or of encouragement when thou learnest thy lesson with alacrity and readiness, shall
I adopt? I can smile upon him, it is true, and that perhaps, unless
he is very unreasonable, my pupil will esteem a sufficient recompense,
but to frown upon thee! Ah! that, dearest youth, is impossible. How
can I scowl, with eyes of unaffected indignation, on my beloved disciple, whose presence, ever pleasing and acceptable, constitutes my
felicity. But, when he is very culpable, shall I banish him for a certain time, prohibit his visit, refuse to see him or to read his letters,
whether expostulatory, exculpatory, or precatory? No, that would
be a greater punishment to myself than to him. But I hope he will
not need chastisement. This aptitude and inclination to learn, under

the auspices of his sovereign mistress, will render punishment unnecessary, and what shall I teach him?

I will teach thee—What canst thou teach him, vain, presumptuous girl? What knowest thou thyself? In what pursuit or accomplishment can thou justly be accounted a proficient? Yes. I am, at least in my own opinion, a woman of vast learning, I care not who knows. Wilt thou venture to contest my claim?

[*Their knowledge of the modern languages and music: 18*] I am conscious of my inferiority to you, but am I not best acquainted with those branches of literature of which you know the least? You are ignorant of French and Italian. I may reasonably claim some acquaintance with them. But I had forgotten. Of the French you are already master, and are not only well acquainted with its grammatical property, are able not only to read it with facility and precision but if I am rightly informed, to prattle in this dialect with the volubility and correctness of a Parisian, and the purity and propriety of an inhabitant of Blois. You can at any time, without my assistance, be personally acquainted with the author of *Eloisa* and the *Social Compact*,[5] and traverse every region of animated nature, in company with Buffon[6] or of organized and inanimate with Bonnet[7] and Saussure[8] and the De Luc's.[9]

But you are not as well acquainted with Italian. Indeed you tell me, but I believe you not, that you are totally a stranger to it; but have you ambition to become adept in this delightful language? I shall be able to be your instructress in it. I will tell you the reasons on which I found my pretentions. My uncle was my tutor. He resided several years in Italy and Switzerland.[10] He is violently enamored both of the country and its language and studied both in the bosom of Tuscany. He constantly frequented the literary and polished circles of Rome and Florence. He is a zealous *Cruscante;* has often been present at the meetings of the Accademia della Crusca,[11] and has, in his possession, an elegant copy of their *Vocabulario*, together with an excellent collection of French and Italian authors. He tells me that his library shall be mine at his decease. You will

[5] Rousseau's *Julie, ou la Nouvelle Héloïse*, was published in 1761; *Le Contrat Social* in 1762.

[6] Compte George Louis Leclerc de Buffon (1707-1788), French Naturalist and director of Jardin du Roi; coauthor of *Histoire Naturelle* (44 volumes, 1749-1804).

[7] Charles Bonnet (1720-1793), Swiss naturalist and philosopher.

[8] Horace de Saussure (1740-1799), Swiss professor of philosophy, did research in geology, physics, and meteorology.

[9] Jean André Deluc (1727-1817), Swiss geologist and meterologist. Brown clearly writes *the De Luc's*, but I have been able to identify only one De Luc.

[10] I have been unable to identify this American.

[11] The Accademia della Crusca, established in Italy in 1582, had as its object the "purification" of the Italian language, with the fourteenth century as its standard. Its great work was *Vocabulario della Crusca* (1612).

allow that this man must have been an accomplished preceptor, and was fitted to instruct me in all the elegancies of the Tuscan style and accent. What think you—am I not qualified to be your mistress? To be the mistress of your taste and understanding as well as of your heart? If you have no dictionary, I will stand in the place of one. The only books in this language which I brought with me are Metastasio[12] and Guarini,[13] but these are sufficient for all the purposes of instruction. You shall read to me. I will correct your pronunciation and explain to you the meaning of words and the propriety of beauty of construction, as far as I am able. You often oblige me to sing the odes of Metastasio. But how can you be pleased with unintelligible sound, if it be true that you art utterly a stranger to the language of the Imperial Laureate? At least, would not your pleasure be much higher and more rational if, to the music of the flute and harpsichord, were added the lustre of expression and the harmony of sentiment? You already listen with so rapturous an attention and perform your part in our little concerts with such spirit and sensibility as delights and astonishes me. How delightful will be our employment![14] How rapidly and easefully will fly the hours! O, why is it decreed that they should end!

HENRIETTA G.

VIII [From Brown]                                    Friday Noon

My fair declaimer! Yes. Thou shalt be my conductor in the tracts of knowledge. My mistress, my instructress, and my friend! Who, under such a guide, would fail of arriving at excellence? What impediment can hinder him or retard his progress, for whose sake love is willing to expound philosophy, when knowledge is encompassed by a million of attractions, and the fondness of the mistress is united with the austerity of the teacher?

[*Brown's opinion of Italian: 19*] Be not deceived. I know no more of the Italian than of the Spanish. It is the melody of your voice, the fascinations of your presence, and its own intrinsic softness, that give to the sounds of this language all the charms which it possesses and which I at present discover in it. Is not the pleasure which music affords distinct from that which results from the sentiment, and who, angelic creature, could listen to your midnight songs, however incomprehensible their meaning, without the rapture of unfettered and harmonious spirits? I am indeed incapable of conceiving a higher degree of pleasure, and the knowledge of the Tuscan could

[12] Metastasio (1698-1782), Italian poet and dramatist. His lyric dramas and operas (set to music by famous composers) were the rage of that day, but were superseded by the new school of such musicians as Gluck and Mozart.

[13] Giovanni Battista Guarini (1538-1612), Italian poet.

[14] In his letters and journals Brown makes many allusions to his passion for music.

not possibly increase the delight with which my ear is ravished in listening to your performances, whether vocal or instrumental.

But the Italian is undoubtedly superior to any other modern language in harmony and copiousness and, among those of antiquity, is exceeded only by the Greek, though it may perhaps be affirmed to be inferior in copiousness to the English. It is the dialect of poets and musicians and therefore he to whom music and poetry afford pleasure cannot but be eagerly desirous of being in some degree acquainted with it. In this class you will not question that I rank myself and therefore will not be surprised when I tell you that your proposal to become my teacher is in the highest degree acceptable. My beauteous and amiable Harriet! with what delight shall I hang upon your lips while you explain the rules of instruction and point out to me the particulars in which the dialect of Florence differs from the ruder speech of Rome or Venice or Naples.

[*Warning as to his probable conduct as a pupil: 20*] Are you not fearful that my attention will frequently be found in the graces of the fair instructress rather than on her lessons, and that my ardor will sometimes prompt me to enfold my teacher in my arms, banish all grammatical austerity from her tongue, and teach her lips another office? Shall I not be tempted to forget the demureness of my character, to lay aside the humble and timid deportment of the scholar, and act a part far more congenial to my disposition? I will not promise to exert any extraordinary degree of self-denial, and will not scruple to interrupt the most useful disquisition by a tale of love or by passionate caresses. Of these circumstances I have thought it proper to apprise you that you may not form vain expectations and place too much confidence in the docility of your pupil. But I shall nevertheless cultivate with uncommon assiduity the acquaintance of the illustrious Metastasio, and shall con the lessons which you shall prescribe, with indefatigable care and attention in your absence.

[*How he acquired—and forgot— his knowledge of French; association with French émigrés in Philadelphia: 21*] If the knowledge of French be desirable, that knowledge, notwithstanding the favorable verdict of rumor, is yet to be attained. How could you have been so egregiously deceived? I will tell you in what respects I deserved to be ranked with an inhabitant of Paris and of Blois. Eighteen months ago accident threw me into company with several Frenchmen[15] whose knowledge was equal to their politeness. I had, at a very early age, acquired some acquaintance with the rudiments of French, and this knowledge one of my foreign friends, with [whom I] suddenly and unaccountably became a favorite, undertook to improve, and by continual opportunities for hearing others speak, and [determined?] to be myself a talker, I gained a considerable degree of fluency in conversation, but never had the slightest pretentions to correctness and

[15] For further information on the French émigrés, see chap. ii, pp. 12-13.

propriety. They gave me permission to read all their books, and I in some degree profited by this privilege, and have traversed with my usual rapidity some thousands of pages of the immense compilations of Diderot and D'Alembert.[16]

You now see, my lovely friend, what credit is due to report. Half a year's disuse of this language, occasioned by the departure of my Parisian acquaintances for Europe, has nearly obliterated the impressions of their lessons. I find it easy to comprehend and difficult, or rather impossible, otherwise than by continual recollection or incessant practice to retain. I know not [to] what cause it is to be imputed, but certain it is that not only the sentiments but the language of those parts of the *Encyclopédie* with which I have formerly been most conversant would now be new to me, and I should scarcely be able to make my way through a single page without the powerful assistance of a dictionary.

[*Brown turns from reading to writing: 22*] I was formerly actuated by a boundless ardor for knowledge. My eyes were so constantly and intently fixed upon my book that when I chanced at any time to look at the objects around me, they wore an aspect of obscurity, and I felt the same sensations of which a man may be supposed to be susceptible on his rousing from a long and profound sleep, and whose opening eyes are saluted by a rural prospect and an evening sun. But the passion for study was quietly supplanted by the delight which I began to take in compositions and my hand was less frequently furnished with a book than with a pen. But it is useless as well as impossible to recount all my literary propensities, the duration of their influence, the order in which they succeeded each other, or the effects which they produced in the enlargement of my heart and the improvement of my understanding. It is sufficient to observe that they all vanished at the sight of a fair and amiable creature, and that love and poetry, beauteous and inseparable sisters, rushed at once upon my soul with a torrent that was not to be resisted and by which all other passions were excluded.

[*Brown's evaluation of classical literature; his severe judgment upon the Latin writers in particular; and his idea of poetry: 23*] Are you really desirous of wading through the crudities, obscurities, and discords of the grammatical chaos, of conning old Lillie's rule,[17] and talking with colloquial Cordier[18] and Erasmus?[19] It is obvious,

[16] Denis Diderot (1713-1784) and Jean Le Rond d'Alembert (1717?-1783) worked for twenty years on their famous *Encyclopédie*, with the aid of Rousseau.

[17] William Lily, or Lilye (1468?-1522), English grammarian and high master of St. Paul's school. He was coauthor of the Eton Latin grammar *Brevissima Institutio.*

[18] Mathurin Cordier (1479-1564) usually Latinized his name to Corderius. His Latin manual *Colloquiorum Scholasticorum* (1563), an imitation of Erasmus's *Colloquies,* was translated into English as the *Colloquies of Corderius.*

[19] Erasmus's *Colloquies,* begun as Latin exercises, were expanded into trenchant comments on the times and were extremely popular in the schools.

however, that the task would by no means be difficult to one that was already versed in the Italian, from which the Roman tongue differs so little that it is, as I have heard, on some occasions scarcely distinguishable from it. But what is there, ambitious fair One, in the Latin language that can reasonably excite your curiosity? The ancient poetry is bare and despicable. You will perhaps be astonished at this assertion, but it is nevertheless true. There is scarcely any that can be read with patience by a man whose morals are yet untainted. What exquisite and tender pictures of conjugal and filial affection has Virgil, who appears to me to be the most enlightened and exalted of the Romans, given us, and yet how few pages of his work are there which would not shock the eye of female delicacy, the eye of Harriet or Clarissa? The pastorals, so celebrated for their musical cadences and polished rusticity, are stuffed with the grossest impurities, and I am persuaded that after having read the Georgics once, you could never prevail upon yourself to read it again. What constitutes the excellence of poetry? Not beautiful expression, splendid imagery or artful and surprising machinery, but that powerful charm by which the heart is attracted and surprised. It consists in moral sublimity. How odious and disgusting are the licenses of Juvenal and of Horace, both in their lyric and satirical performances, and with regard to the applauded productions of Ovid, Tibullus, and Propertius, I shall only show that I think those amorous and elegiac bards in the last degree [are] poisonous and detestable, and that they prove, in the most forcible manner, the justice of that observation which I have somewhere read, that the Cupid of the ancients was a sensual deity and deserved therefore to be banished to the mountainous and woody haunts of savages. But is it not certain that they who have themselves felt the dominion of the passion find almost all descriptions of them insipid? They are occupied with their own emotions, and have not leisure to contemplate their effects or appearances in others. Hence with whatever purity or justness the passions should be described by a Greek or Roman poet, their picture would to us be either insipid or superfluous. O my beloved Creature, what pleasure can be derived from learned volumes equal to the rapture of mental converse, to the union of kindred souls, speechless lips, and throbbing bosoms? They are strangers to avarice and ambition. And what do almost all the poets of antiquity do but furnish fuel to the direful and ferocious passions? Can the harmony and energy of Homer shroud from our view the horrid forms of revenge and cruelty that stalk with rapid and gigantic steps through every page of the *Iliad*? Who does not turn with anguish and aversion from the spectacle of slaughter and destruction which is continually presented to him? You could not possibly receive pleasure from the brutalities of Anacreon and Aristophanes, the obscure flights of Pindar, whose progress is discernible only through the glosses with which you can be furnished only by scholiasts and antiquarians, the mysticism of Plato, or the subtleties of Aristotle. There is nothing, however valuable, for which too great a price may not be paid. Before you engage in any study it is to be considered whether the labor of pursuit and the pleasure of acquisition be proportionate to each other, and whether the time which is thus consumed might not be more profitably employed.[20]

[*Importance of studying English language and literature: 24*] It is of more importance to you to become an adept in your native language than in any other. It is sometimes said that this knowledge cannot be obtained without a previous acquaintance with the classic tongues, but of this objection I shall always consider the example of my Harriet as an unanswerable confutation. That the knowledge of Greek and Roman literature may be, in some degree, conducive to the attainment of skill in English, it is needless to deny, but this motive only is not sufficient to justify our application to those studies, since it is indisputable that the improvement would be still greater if the time which is thus spent were devoted to British authors.

I cannot admit that the knowledge of ancient languages is otherwise to be esteemed than as they humanize the heart and polish the understanding, and though I am sincerely of opinion that it does not merit even this encomium, which indeed I must confess to be extremely high. Yet I am willing to bestow it, but must ask whether the study of British, French, or Italian literature is not equally conducive to the same end?

[*Value of mastering the work of one poet; true use of books: 25*] But why should we uselessly and pompously enlarge the circle of our pleasure? A true poet, for example, can never be exhausted. The delight which his compositions afford will only increase by repetition. How barren and limited must be the capacity of that man who can

---

[20] ''If Brown was really acquainted with the Latin authors whom he cites, one can hardly interpret the statements which he makes here as representing a sincere judgment. Whatever one may think of the literary excellence of these writers, no informed person could with sincerity say that: (1) few pages of Virgil's work would not shock a delicate female, whereas actually there are few pages in Virgil which would shock even the most prudish person; (2) Horace indulges in odious and disgusting licenses, whereas there is very little in Horace that would need expurgation, especially in his lyrics—while there is 'objectionable' matter in Juvenal and Ovid, there is a great deal in them that is suitable for an 'eye of female delicacy'; and (3) 'revenge and cruelty stalk through every page of the *Iliad*,' when there are considerable stretches of this poem which are far removed from the more horrible aspects of war'' (interpretation of this passage by Dr. H. J. Leon, Professor of Classical Languages, University of Texas).

It is absurd to say that Latin differs so little from Italian that it is ''scarcely distinguishable from it.''

Some years later, when Brown came to write *Alcuin; or the Rights of Women*, he argued for coeducation, equal education in both language and science for boys and girls alike. Shelley a few years later maintained the same position.

be instructed or delighted only in contemplating and revolving the ideas of others. When you read, your books ought to be considered as a text to which your imagination must furnish a supplement and commentary. The ideas of others are to you of no importance and utility but as you render them by meditation your own and make them as the soil or stock, which, with proper culture, may become productive of numberless others, the products of your own labor, or the offspring of your own imagination. Is it possible for true taste ever to be weary of a single author who is really excellent? I know not anything more dreadful than to be hopelessly immured in bookless solitude, but though Germany abound with sublime and pathetic poets, yet I should be contented to linger for an age in the wild and sequestered recesses of the Alps, accompanied only by the works of Gessner.[21] In the solitudes of Wales or Cumberland I should find an exhaustless source of consolation in the affecting and romantic tales of Spenser, and Virgil and Tasso would furnish pleasure and employment to a life spent on a promontory or island of Calabria.

[*His knowledge of the classics: 26*] But whatever motive may excite you to the study of the ancient languages, how will you procure a suitable preceptor? I received some knowledge of the Greek and Latin at a Grammar School, but this knowledge will by no means qualify me to instruct others.[22] It scarcely enables me to read these ancient authors. And I am determined that, should my beauteous Harriet put herself under my tuition, all my instructions should be oral. I will not suffer those eyes to be fixed on any other object than myself while I am present, and yet without the assistance of a book nothing can be learned.

[*Romantic melancholy; gloomy forebodings: 27*] But shall I not be near you—oftener than heretofore? Shall I not more frequently gaze at the fluttering lawn, whose whiteness dazzles the beholder, and through which the whiter bosom which it covers is discernible! O heaven! What celestial charms lurk beneath its folds and wait to be drunk by the eye and discerned by the touch. Ah! when will the blissful moment arrive when thou, angelic Creature, shalt be wholly mine, and when, to whatsoever [lengths] my impetuosity shall carry me, I shall not transgress the limits of decorum, nor rouse your anger and resentment when your mind and person shall be equally my own. Pause, malignant and ill-boding spirit! I know already what thou intimatest. I know it is decreed that we shall never be united other-

[21] Salomon Gessner (1730-1788), Swiss artist and poet, was best known for *Der Tod Abels* (1758), written in rhythmical prose. Brown seems to have thought of the German-speaking district of Switzerland as part of Germany.

[22] Brown had what appears to have been a fair grounding in the classics at the Friends Grammar School, but he here questions the thoroughness of his schooling.

wise than mentally.[23] My hope is dead, eternally extinct. But as long as I am permitted to be near her, despair is at a distance. To see her, to converse with her, to bathe her hands with kisses, her bosom with my tears! This is happiness which, without illumining the darkness of futurity, diverts my attention from it. I feel my heart overwhelmed with joy. My intellects are momentarily disordered. All the powers of my understanding are suspended in the rapturous idea of the present, but as soon as this delusion vanishes with her presence, as soon as her absence shall sober my intoxicated senses, whither shall I fly, the refugee from the pangs by which my soul shall be rent asunder? Ah! then will the benevolence and justice of the deity be put to proof. Then will my soul hurry with dismay and trepidation from her untenable mansion, and rush unsummoned into the region allotted for the residence of spirits. My God, in rendering my burthen insupportable, will justify me in escaping from it, or at least, when called to his presence, to hear the sentence of retributive justice I shall plead in excuse for the deed, the immunities of frenzy.

[*Type of reading suited to his mood: 28*] But why, infatuated youth, dost thou paint with such malicious skill thy agonizing apprehensions? How unhappy dost thou render her, whom thou so fervently adorest, by those gloomy and disastrous portraitures of thy anticipating pencil? I know it. I endeavored to still it, to still my turbulent emotion, to engage my mind in pursuits that are indifferent, to fill my imagination with ludicrous or pleasing images. But my struggles are ineffectual. My hand involuntarily strays from volumes of mirth to those of melancholy. I open at *The Rape of the Lock,* but the pages are, by a sort of mechanical and spontaneous impulse, turned over till I reach the melodious complaints of cloistered Eloisa. I hurry with impatience and rapidity through the comic scenes of Molière. To view them is a task which I congratulate myself on having finished, and I hasten to indulge the mode of sorrow at the feet of Melpomene. The tragic spectacle has charms congenial to my soul, and I dwell with mingled sadness and delight on the scenes of Sophocles, Racine, and Rome. I listen to Electra and Andromaque, and pour my tributary tears at the self-told narrative of their distresses.

[*Neoplatonic conception of intellectual union: 29*] But to ponder on thy everpresent image and to write to thee are my chief employments. Books, whatever be the theme, I cannot read without an effort of painful recollection. To write to thee, my charming Harriet, to tell thee all my feelings—this is the occupation which in thy absence delights me most. And yet how impossible is it to describe my feelings! How unequal to the force of my conceptions is the energy of words! How often do I throw aside my pen, and say out in a vent

---

[23] This is the first intimation that some insurmountable barrier stood between their love and its fulfilment in marriage.

of frenzy, "Why should I thus fruitlessly labor? Are not my ideas fettered and degraded by the poverty of language? Is she not actually present? It is true she is not visible, but her image is within me. Her soul mingles with mine; our intercourse is intellectual. Are not the chords of harmonious sympathy continually vocal? Ye votaries of babbling eloquence! Where have you learned that passion is loquacious? Did ye, ever, in your noblest moments, reach the sublimity of silence? Trouble not, by senseless and unreasonable clamors, the stillness of my soul! While I think of her she is no longer absent. The tongue, weak interpreter, is motionless. Minds where union is so perfect want no outward instrument of communication, require not the impertinent assistance of corporeal organs. But ah! how frail, how inconsistent is humanity!" O my beloved, whither are now thy thoughts straying? What object engages thy attention? Thy image is indeed before me, but art thou also conscious of my presence? Is this consciousness irksome or delightful? Thou canst not answer me; thou hearest me not; thou art absent. I discern with astonishment and horror that thou art absent.

[*Midnight wanderings; Brown plays on his flute; a beautiful rustic scene: 30*] How charming are our interviews! How do I delight in recalling the circumstances of them to my memory! in communing with you, in spending the night as I spent the evening, in thinking over all the thoughts that were in my mind and in repeating all the words that flowed from my lips while in company with you. When I left you, on the last evening, I did not immediately return home. Midnight is a season that has grown familiar to me. I am never apprehensive of danger of annoyance in my nocturnal rovings. I am indeed careless of health and safety, in a degree that, to many persons, would be incredible. And I am as little concerned at the baying of a mastiff, as on approaching in desolate and gloomy solitude—at the hour when robbery and murder walk abroad—persons of a suspicious and ruffian-like appearance, as in listing to the clamors of the owl or bullfrog.

When I arrived at the end of [the] lane which leads to our habitation, I went in the opposite direction. The banks of Schuylkill are in some places considerably high and steep, and are surrounded by scenes which to one that, like me, has never [been] in a mountainous country, are highly beautiful and picturesque. I seated myself beneath the pines, by which the descent is overshadowed. The moon was declining in the west and her beams glittered with surprising lustre on the water. The murmur of the tide on the sandy shore, and of a gentle gale among the leaves of the trees that shadowed me, diffused a languor and tranquillity over my soul that was inexpressibly pleasing. Tranquil water and the midnight air are peculiarly favorable to pensive music, and, till the fall of the moon below the horizon, I played

my most melancholy and pathetic tunes upon the flute. How powerful is the influence of music on the most brutal and illiterate minds!
Two persons were whispering together among the trees, who, as I
approached, rose up apparently startled and alarmed, and were preparing to go, but as soon as I began to play they stopped, and resuming
their seats upon the grass listened all the time of my performance with
the profoundest silence and attention, and, when they found I had
finished, and saw me rising from my seat, they showed evidence of
regret, and, as I saw, were going to ask me to continue, but I hastened
away before they had time to make the request, because I could not
but have complied with it, and my compliance, at so late or rather at
so early an hour, for it was three o'clock, would have been very inconvenient. I went home and enjoyed the peaceful sleep of innocence,
and dreamt of my mistress and my friend. May prudence preserve
our union unimpaired, and may all my days resemble yesterday.

C. B. B.

IX [From Henrietta]                    Saturday Morn. 6 o'clock

[*Her belief that he has not really changed—the qualities of poet
and lover have always been latent within him: 31*] What a motley
and variegated performance is your last letter! My friend, you were
formerly the votary of science, but are now according to your own
belief the faithful disciple of Love. What a sudden and entire transformation hast thou undergone, and yet, were it excusable for a woman
to philosophize, I could easily evince that your native disposition has
always been the same, and that in the midst of chronological tables
and geographical computations, of which I have been told you have
ever been singularly fond,[24] it was easy to have discerned a mind susceptible of amorous impressions. I am inclined to imagine that love
is a generous and ennobling passion, and that [it] is a proof not of
the weakness or depravity, but of the purity, of the heart and of the
understanding of him who is influenced by it.

[*Her growing admiration for his talents: 32*] But this perhaps is
an interested conclusion, and the opinion of a lover with regard to
the dignity of this passion may be considered in the same light with
the decision of a man in his own cause. For how often have I told
you that I feel a reciprocal affection for my youthful friend, and that
I will not allow myself to be exceeded by him in the ardor and sincerity
of my attachment, and this attachment, instead of diminishing by
time, is, I find, growing stronger. Whether love be a consequence
regularly arising from opinions previously formed, I will not pretend
to determine, but whatever be the cause or original, it is certain that
it increases in proportion as we discover, by the aid of reason, greater
excellences in the object. That reason, if it cannot withstand or does

---

[24] Brown's Journal contains several architectural drawings and geographical
computations. See chap. ii, p. 17.

not produce, at least, by sanctioning with its approbation the dictates of the heart, consecrates the bonds of love, and therefore, it will not be wondered at that my friend becomes daily more passionately beloved, because his talents and his virtues become daily more conspicuous. In every letter I discover new motives to love and admiration, and shall begin to doubt whether it [is] possible, after the longest and most intimate connection, to be thoroughly acquainted with your character. Be as copious as possible, my dear friend, in your epistolary communications and let this assurance, that every letter will contribute more firmly to establish you in the possession of my heart, be an additional incitement to your industry. I am sure that a more powerful one cannot be proposed.

[*Her insistence on a literary correspondence: 33*] I know not whether to lament or rejoice at the pathetic manner in which you have concluded your letter. I wish to soothe the passions of my friend, to tranquilize the agitations of his bosom, and make his affection for me as much as possible subservient to his own advantage. For this reason I wish to render his attachment more calm and agreeable without making it less strong or less permanent, to banish those tormenting apprehensions and that frantic enthusiasm which incapacitate him for all useful pursuits, and which equally enfeeble his body and his mind, and for these purposes to engage him in the discussion of literary topics, to make our frequent conversations the vehicle of mutual instruction, and to pass the hours in which we are together, not in each other's arms, dissolved in tenderness and mingling tears of raptures and murmuring vows of constancy, but in more laudable and profitable avocations, in the improvement of each other's understanding and of the virtues of the heart.

These are the dictates of reason, but alas! How stern and rigid and impracticable do they appear at those softer moments when the object of my affection is before me, when he offers himself to my caresses and when every word and attitude is expressive of his joy. How is it possible to relinquish those topics which are naturally suggested by the occasion and which are adapted to the eloquence of love? How is it possible not to receive pleasure from these letters which are fraught with tender and pathetic sentiment and to prefer them to those in which the writer expatiates on cold and barren topics and which might without impropriety be addressed to any other person, and how, my friend, shall I apologize for my weakness in confessing that of the letter which I have just received the former part is less acceptable and pleasing than the latter, and yet there are passages in it which greatly disturb and shock me.

[*Their contrasting attitudes toward the future: 34*] How could you permit your fertile pencil to depict in so vivid color so direful a futurity? Cannot you gather satisfaction from the contemplation of the present, and it is not improvident to neglect the task of learning the duty of acquiescence in the dictates of necessity or of resignation to the will of Providence till the time arrives in which it will be requisite, not only to know but to practice it? At least is it not preposterous to torment ourselves with empty suppositions, to abandon the enjoyment of the happy and auspicious present, for the sake of suffering a future and contingent evil which from the predominance of a gloomy and foreboding fancy produces all the effects of absolute realities? Lay aside, my friend, those idle and unreasonable terrors. If you cannot be induced to be happy for your own sake, let thy consideration of my felicity prevail upon you, and be happy if [for] no other reason than because you will thereby contribute to the happiness of

Your faithful and devoted,<br>HENRIETTA.

P.S. [*The sentimental heroine again; virtue and prudence: 35*]

I intended to have set you an example in this letter of copiousness, but I am unreasonably interrupted by a visitant, and obliged to finish it more quickly than I intended. But I shall consider your letter as not having yet received an answer and shall take the earliest opportunity of resuming my pen. I shall probably talk to you at my second sitting in a strain of greater sprightliness and levity, at which I hope my grave and solemn friend will not dare to be offended. I indulged him, at our last interview, in giving me such evident demonstrations of his passion and in pressing so frequently and fervently those lips which had hitherto been sacred and inviolable that I shall expect from him in gratitude for this signal condescension, the most unlimited submission and invincible forbearance. Thou saucy and impetuous creature! Dost thou think thou has a property in my lips or that I will suffer such perplexing and incessant interruption from thy kisses? In good sooth I will act with more discretion for the future. I will banish thee, whenever thou offendest, to the distance of a yard beyond the reach of my arm, and my kisses shall be the pledges only of forgiveness and reconciliation. Thy lady will permit thee on solemn and particular occasions to kiss the hem of her imperial garment or to touch with thy lips the end of her little finger, but greater favor will be charily dispensed, and shall be granted only to secure thy allegiance and preserve thee from despair. But my visitant is waiting for me. She wonders, I suppose, how I am employed, and being told that I was employed in writing, will imagine that my correspondent is a personage of vast importance or that the emergency is very critical that can render me thus neglectful of politeness. And, in truth she will not much err in her conjecture, for who is of more importance in the eye of a woman than her lover, and what subject more peculiarly interesting than the barbarities of his pretended privileges and his future exclusion from the kisses and embraces of his mistress? But I must attend her: excuse my absence for an hour. Will you? I am sure you will. Why cannot I forsake my pen? I wish my visitant had gone to Peking before she conceived the design of honoring me with her company. I have just arisen, and I was determined not to leave my chamber till I had composed a long epistle to my friend. That moment your letter was presented to me, and I cannot tell you the pleasure which the pleasure [perusal] of it afforded me, and, O my friend, what an exquisite conclusion! This single sentence affected me in a more forcible and pleasing manner than all the other parts of your letter. When are you absent from my mind? You are never absent, and, would you believe it, are most intimately present when in sleep. The soul appears to be divested of her mental fetters, and to enjoy the interval of freedom in realizing the wishes of our waking hours. Beloved youth! Not a moment during the night after your visit was my spirit separate from thine, and methought the conversation of the evening had not suffered interruption, that our interview continued, but that the repetition of the *"additional ceremony,"* as you choose to phrase it, was absolutely prohibited and that our intercourse was that of friendship rather than of love. There is certainly, my friend, a powerful and inseparable sympathy between us, nor should I have enjoyed such happy slumbers had not the footsteps of my friend borne him to the bank of Schuylkill, and his lips given melodious utterance to his flute. And I must not forget to relate one remarkable incident. My dream ended and I awoke just at three o'clock, for on drawing my curtains I beheld the western sky faintly illumined by the rays of the orb that had just disappeared. O my friend, what felicity is ours and does not its continuance depend principally upon ourselves! Let us not complain of our destiny, nor murmur impiously at heaven which has showered all its bounties on us and has hitherto regarded us only with indulgent smiles. It is impossible for us to penetrate into the future designs of Providence or to discover whether the catastrophe of the drama shall be built on consolation or despair. And let us not exert a useless foresight or torment ourselves with vain conjectures, which can tend only to embitter our present joys without diminishing or abbreviating future evils. But how forgetful am I! I am absolutely uncivil. I must hasten to my gentle guest below, and entreat her pardon for my stay. She will doubtless readily forgive me, but if she first arbitrarily demand the reason of it, what answer shall I make? Shall I tell her that I was recounting to an amiable youth the dreams of the past night and listening to a similar relation from him? I will invent a more convenient answer as I go down. Stay thee, friend, in my closet till I return. As soon at I am disengaged I will devote another hour to this most pleasing occupation. Farewell.

X [From Henrietta]                                    Saturday Morn.

She is gone. I will open the closet and release you. Did I stay longer than I promised or than you expected? I could not avoid it. An innocent and blooming creature, her mind pure, ingenuous, and uncontaminated is susceptible of every tender impression, and might easily be led a captive in the chains of love, but her destiny has perhaps otherwise decreed. Her understanding may be perverted and her heart corrupted by a vicious education, by the levities of fashion and the glitter of wealth, and she may experience the fortune of the greater number of her sex, in being wedded to avarice or insensibility and in feeling no repugnance to the union, nor sorrow at her lot.

She has just parted from me, and if you will not be offended I will tell you that I parted from her with reluctance. Women are, in general, most happy in the company of each other. There is less necessity for reserve and caution and constraint in their conversation, but on the other hand a man is a being whom a woman cannot but regard with a certain degree of timidity and apprehension, and, if she be his lover there is still a greater necessity for vigilance and circumspection. My own experience has taught me this divination, at least such, till very lately, did I imagine to be true, but I must confess that my sentiments are now somewhat altered, and I believe that if a woman be conscious of innocent intentions, and has reason to confide implicitly in the honor of her lover, she will find her caution superfluous. What is there in the bottom of my heart which I would not willingly unfold to you? Am I conscious of any sentiments that either shame or prudence should induce me to conceal, and is there wanting any additional proof or assurance of the sincerity and rectitude of my friend? In his presence I am equally sure [as] in his absence. I feel no embarrassment or uneasiness at his caresses. They are the natural expressions of a passion, not less pure than ardent, and to discourage or forbid them would be useless and ungenerous. Or rather they would be promiscuous since they would occasion a belief that these liberties are criminal, whereas they are in themselves indisputably harmless and are later dreaded only as they pave the way for greater and more flagrant licenses. But what have I to fear? Precautions are useful only to those who have reason to suspect themselves, who find that to be guilty opportunities to commit it are only wanting. But this is far from being my condition, nor have I need to check the innocent expressions of a laudable attachment. I do not start as if terrified by the sight of an asp when my friend clasps me to his bosom and presses his lips with mine, because I place equal confidence on my own and on his uprightness. Suspicion and distrust! Avaunt ye, horrid spectres! Your aid is unnecessary, is pernicious. It is in reality impossible that I should have occasion for them, for their appearance would instantly annihilate my love, and against the blandishments of one that is indifferent or detested, what woman can require an auxiliary?

Will thou, my love, ever abuse this confidence? No, I shall as soon suspect a mountain of an inclination to move from his seat as thou to overstep the limits of decorum. And am I not supported in this implicit reliance on your honor by the unquestionable verdict of experience? Have you not been exposed to all the fascinations of opportunity? Have you not reposed for guiltless hours, for hours guiltless even in imagination, in the arms of unsuspecting and unguarded beauty, when all your nerves were alive and active, when sleep, the friend of innocence, was banished to a distance, when you heard nothing but the voice of tenderness and saw nothing but the glances of benignity and the smiles of condescension? And is not yet my purity and thy fidelity inviolate? What then have [I] to fear? Surely nothing. What motive can there be to reserve or constraint? None can I discover.

[*Passion and despondency: 36*] But have I not caught you in the snare which I laid for you? Have I not accomplished my wishes in engaging you in a critical disquisition? But what supineness! I do not endeavor to profit by the advantage which I have obtained, but I am afraid that you have already escaped through my egregious negligences from the toils in which I had, with such expense of time and pains, entangled you. I know that what I have just written will afford you an opportunity to exert your powers of pathetic eloquence, of which you will not fail to take advantage. You will again give the rein to passion and the sceptre to despondency; you will again plunge me into tears and oppress me with unsupportable affliction by your horrid pictures of futurity. But why will my friend thus causeless afflict himself and me? How often must I charge you to forbear, to speak the language of reason, content, and magnanimity? O that you were now a witness to the serene gayety, the sprightly composure of your Harriet, at this happy moment. See her sitting at the writing table, satisfaction depicted in her countenance, and betokened ever by the motions of her quill that meanders through the page with such celerity that it reaches the bottom almost as soon as it begins its progress at the top. Its career appears to be finished almost as soon as it is begun, and my fingers perform their part with ease, dexterity, and steadiness to which it is plain by visible and undeniable labors that yours are too often strangers. How must you be agitated, when even your fingers, so long habituated to the use of the pen, are almost disabled from performing their accustomed office. Let my example serve your emulations and endeavors to display the same evenness in your character and sentiments, and to amuse your Harriet by your wit as well as astonish and confound her by your eloquence.

[*Her suggestions that he change his type of reading, and be less solemn: 37*] Too frequently, my friend, have you appeared before me in the solemn pall of tragedy and spread infectious melancholy round you. It is time to throw aside the buskin and assume the sock, and dissipate, by chaste and pleasing levities, the dictates of Thales, the gloom which has hitherto overspread your letters, and which have testified the inspiration of Melpomene. Do not so hastily desert the volume of Molière or glance, with such contemptuous rapidity, over the pages of Belinda's part.[25] Withdraw your attention from the plaintive and voluptuous Eloisa, by whom no virtuous sentiment was ever inspired, and watch with all imaginable anxiety the momentous vicissitudes of a game at ombre. Meditate no longer on the sorrows of Electra and Orestes nor mingle tears with those of the wife of Hector and the mother of Astyanax, but let gayety mingled with tenderness flow from your pen, and when you call forth the tears be careful also to awaken the smiles of your Harriet. By these means may your letters be rendered still more acceptable to me, and your own inquietude be stifled or diminished, and therefore I entreat you to pay some regard to my injunction. If you will continually disobey me, shall I not begin at length to question your fidelity, and in consequence, renounce your allegiance. And this I suppose will be a terrible disaster, will convert the visionary into a maniac and crowd his fancy with horrid images of self-inflicted vengeance and destruction.

[*Her continued desire to learn the classics: 38*] And so you will not consent to become my preceptor in the learned languages: and you think that the time which would necessarily be spent in learning them would be uselessly employed? I doubtless must be of the same opinion since I have no opportunity to appeal from this tribunal to another, and I cannot form a judgment for myself, without a previous acquaintance with the literature, as an opinion, with regard to the beauty or deformity of an object, can be formed only by looking at it, but you will not furnish me with the means of obtaining this knowledge.

[*She teases him about his "Platonic" love: 39*] My friend, it seems, will not suffer my eyes to be fixed on any other object than himself while he is present; and no language can be orally communicated, but yet he has not forgotten that in quality of tutor, his visits will necessarily be more frequent than heretofore and that he shall enjoy more frequent opportunities of penetrating with audacious eyes the folds by which the bosom of his mistress is attempted to be hidden. How do thy letters abound in contradiction and absurdity. Thou, in whose adoration there is no impurity, where love is purely intellectual, who is affected only by the graces of the mind, is it in the bosom of thy mistress, in the folds of her handkerchief that thou reachest, with so much eagerness, for the object of thy passion? Is the soul to which only you seek to be united, susceptible of sight and touch? Be a little

[25] The reference is probably to the heroine in Pope's *The Rape of the Lock*.

more cautious for the future. Consider before you write, whether the language which you are about to use be reconcilable with the dialect of former letters, and congratulate yourself in knowing that I do not account inconsistency in a lover any proof of insincerity. But yet I suppose you will not deny that it is somewhat embarrassing to be detected in a manifest and glaring contradiction and that it may be useful to exhibit in your letters as exact a conformity of sentiment as possible, and though I shall expect that the divine enthusiast who clothes his mistress with the attributes of divinity and fixes his affections only on the animating mind will forbear to expatiate with so much ardor on external beauties and the symmetry and whiteness which furnish so ravishing a banquet to licentious eyes.

But art thou serious when thou prohibitest my eyes from wandering from thy person? I should be glad to know in what manner thou intendest to enforce thy prohibition, and whether it would be criminal to fix them for a moment on the starry firmament, or lift them in gratitude or devotion to the father of the Universe, though my impatient friend should happen to be present; and can you vow that the white veil of dimity will not elude your penetration, and that the white bosom, notwithstanding all your efforts, would not be invisible, but I am afraid that your curiosity cannot be eluded but by a thicker texture than ordinary. I therefore propose to procure a woollen habit, and wrap myself up in it like a nun, as soon as you appear; to show, according to the Turkish fashion, a veil on my face, and leave you to reach in the intellectual and interior habitation for that soul of which you are violently enamored. I suppose my plan will receive your concurrence and doubtless you will readily procure the stuff for me, and if I make the request, will you not yourself be the workman who will make it up in the manner which I shall direct? I will not, however, be exorbitant in my demands or require so severe a proof of your obedience, and will only tell you that you will please me more in proportion as you talk less of handkerchiefs and bosoms.

XI [From Brown]                                    Saturday aft'n. 3 o'clock

[*His idealization of her; his unbridled imagination: 40*] Ye powers! Whither has my careless imagination transported me? O shameful and pernicious letter! How suddenly did the sight of thee awaken the most furious passion! Incomparable woman! why art thou so fatally exalted? Are you not affected by the picture which your fancy draws? What a base and despicable wretch am I! What names of ignominy are unworthy of me? Why am I not fearful of approaching? Does not my presence stain the purity and cloud the radiance of your beauty? Banish me forever from your presence, if you wish to preserve your angelic innocence unsmirched by profane, by sacrilegious hands. Religion hides herself from me; virtue is a simple and

inefficacious name. I am driven by an irresistible impulse to the verge
of the precipice; I throw myself headlong without remorse or reluctance. I perish forever and thou, O best of women! art involved in
my destruction.

Into what fatal reveries did your letter plunge my imagination!
A momentary frenzy deadened my intellects and beguiled my senses.
Yes, you shut me in your closet. With what impatience did I listen
to hear your return! How was I tortured by your delay. But I hear
a step tripping lightly as an angel; I hear your voice humming some
melodious air—token of serenity, and then the chamber door is opened.
You enter. Your closet is unlocked and you suddenly burst upon my
sight in a blaze of charms, far more beautiful in the careless and
voluptuous elegances of a night dress than in the studied decencies,
the splendor of the noon or evening. How does the lawn flow in wanton promiscuousness about you! How dazzlingly white, how exqui-
sitely fine its texture! How suitably adapted to the purpose of love!
to shroud without obscuring your resplendent beauties, to shade without concealing that angelic [?] bosom. Could my eyes be otherwise
than intoxicated with the sight: the dusk which the light-excluding
shutters diffused throughout the chamber; the chairs in each of which
I thought I saw the forms of sedentary ease and amorous pleasure;
the couch from which you had just arisen, on which my Harriet had
slumbered, and of which the folds were still ruffled and unsmoothed;
on which the night had beheld your angelic form supinely displayed,
conscious that no human eye beheld, enjoying the security of secrecy
and loveliness, and careless of concealment or disguise. What effect,
my Harriet! must all these circumstances have unavoidably produced
on a rambling and unsanctified imagination like mine? Was it possible for my glance to have been less passionate and eager? You
turned from me in confusion. You endeavored to cover your flutter
[ing] and apprehensive bosom with your hand, and adjusting your
bewitching dress with becoming haste and trepidation as if you thought
it were too negligent, but amidst those unavailing precautions you
found yourself suddenly encircled by my arms and almost stifled by
my kisses. Your blushes but heightened the disorder of my senses,
and your struggle only augmented my impetuosity, and—O heavenly
creature! when so little was wanting to complete my frenzy, and
render me the most happy and most miserable of mankind, a word,
a look, from you extinguished my ardor in a moment and dissolved
me in tears of shame and regret. With eyes that pitied and upbraided
me at the same time, you cried out, in a fine and commanding tone,
"My friend! forbear." It was impossible not to obey you. I instantly
unloosed you from my arms, and falling on my knee, bathed your
hand with my tears of sorrow and remorse and supplicated your
forgiveness.

See, my fair, the triumph of virtue over the most imperious and despotic passions, and the consequences of your letter. Why will you write thus seductively? Alas! the slightest spark will set my combustible imagination in flames, and leave me no longer master of myself. Why cannot I emulate your purity, your perfection? My wishes are fruitless, my resolutions ineffectual. It is in vain that I endeavor to become worthy of my Harriet, and to tread in her shining footsteps. O, commiserate my weakness. Believe my intentions to be virtuous, and that I shall never forfeit the confidence which you repose in me. Those paroxysms of disbelief are transitory. They affect me only in your absence, and at moments when my vigilance and circumspection are by sudden and unforeseen accidents diverted from the proper object.

But O rash, indiscreet beauty! to show me your chamber and your closet was not sufficient, to reveal yourself to my sight, arrayed in all the alluring negligences of the morning. You have made me witness of a still more ravishing spectacle and absolutely robbed [me] of my fortitude. What inauspicious power presided over your pencil, and induced you to describe, with such pernicious exactness, the curtain drawn aside at midnight, the chamber yet illumined with the rays of the sinking moon, the beauteous sleeper awakening from a vision in which her active imagination was filled with the idea of her friend, and rising from her couch, the receptacle of beauty, the asylum of love, her delicate arms and luxuriant bosom defenseless and uncovered, her dishevelled locks flowing with voluptuous profusion over her snowy shoulders, and leaning over the side to view the gleaming moat and mark the progress of the peaceful hours? Where was I, her friend, her spouse, her faithful votary, her passionate adorer, at the happy moment? Where ought I to have been? Whither should the star of morning, the bridal planet of love have conducted me? But where am I now? Are not all the enchantments of the scene and hour present? Are not all the images of night and solitude, of yielding beauty, of melting love, of meeting bosoms and unutterable ecstasy, before me? Do I not see the sensuous pillow and participated [?] couch!—Benignant angel, forgive me. I do not recollect with less horror than yourself those lawless imaginations. I strive in vain to subdue them, to recall my wandering thoughts, and pin them on a less seducing image to view you in the decencies of dress. I make continued efforts to escape from this delirium, but the current of ideas is with difficulty checked and directed into another channel. I am still pursued by these fatal and delightful phantoms. I still riot unrestrained in this delicious banquet of the senses, and am plunging deeper into guilt, in proportion as I endeavor to disengage myself. But is it criminal to think of my charmer thus? Will an awful ceremony sanctify those thoughts and give me a religious claim to slumber on your bosom, and to taste unspeakable felicity in your arms, when it will cease to be criminal to avow and when it will be laudable to gratify my boundless and impetuous wishes? Will that desirable period never arrive? How distant is it from the passing hour? Is it not in her own choice to hasten its arrival, or defer it? Why then is the gratification of those eager and tormenting wishes postponed?

[*Impossibility of their being married: 41*] I am convinced, thoroughly convinced, by your reasoning; I know that our union is impossible, but that, if it were possible to take place, it would be an instance of the most inexcusable impudence and temerity that ages of repentance would be bought by moments of pleasure; and yet why, my angel, should you wonder if I sometimes murmur at the hard decree which makes me miserable, if I sometimes, in an agony of impatience, venture to doubt whether any serious disaster which might arise from our immediate union could equal the pangs which are produced by postponing it; and how is it possible for me to feel very forcibly that conviction which your persuasive eloquence has expressed when I reflect that this very evening your chamber might be mine, that supreme felicity is within my grasp, that it is placed beyond my reach only by cold motives of dubious discretion, for, on second thoughts, I cannot esteem our union impossible, for what is required but that a minister should recite a few words from his own ecclesiastical formulary in our presence and with our concurrence? Your apartment would serve instead of a more sacred place. Witnesses, if necessary, could be easily procured, and then—let me think upon the rapturous result. No. The illusion is vanished. The end of my being is to contribute to your happiness. I will never be that selfish and contracted wretch that gratifies his wishes at the expense of your felicity. Do with me what you please. It is sufficient that in acting thus or thus I conform to the desires of my Harriet. What! is it possible to disunite us? Is not my existence annihilated or rather absorbed in yours? Can I harbor sentiments different from yours? Your wish is mine; your happiness is mine. I enjoy nothing distinct from you, and I exist for you only.

[*Brown is cast into the slough of despond by the knowledge that they cannot be united in marriage: 42*] Alas! How am I agitated by opposite and irreconcilable emotions. My reason is a fluctuating sea, on which my shattered vessel is in continual danger of foundering. It is the sport of a thousand hostile and variable winds, and neither shore nor bottom is discoverable. At one moment the storm is hushed; the waves are calm, I begin to collect my thoughts, reflect upon my situation, and prepare to regulate my course at leisure, but on a sudden, my bark is overtaken by another tempest, the ocean is again in tumult, the motions of the helm are no longer obeyed and terror and dismay beset me.

[*Influence of her presence; pleads for her to marry him: 43*] It is only when listening to the melodious precepts of wisdom that flow from your lips; it is only in your presence that I am happy and serene. You have deprived me of my reason, but I feel a temporary restoration of it in your presence. Your eyes are far more powerful preceptors than your letters; the pressure of your hand produces a greater and more instantaneous effect than a thousand dissertations. Sweet excellence! Thou indeed hast reason to be fearless and cautious in the presence, in the arms, of thy lover: for it is only in your absence that my thoughts will not be controlled. Your presence—how can I describe its influence? It produces an entire revolution in my feelings. It is not the sight of you merely that can gratify the ardent wishes which I form in solitude, and yet as soon as I behold you, where have my desires flown? They cease any longer to torment me. I experience all the felicity which I had previously imagined could be derived only from the gratification of those wishes. And I am certain that were I to find you other than you now are, I should turn from you with horror and disgust. All your charms would fade as your purity and delicacy vanished. Am I not actuated by a double evil? By two principles, neither of which is more powerful than the other? I am miserable without possessing her whom I adore, and yet to possess her would be misery! How is this strife of passion to be appeased? Not by conferring superiority on one, but by reconciling them, by giving me the sacred name of husband, by superadding the nuptial ties to those of love.

O Virtue! Chastity! Ethereal power! Effluence of deity! incomprehensible Attribute! Sum and Source of excellence! of beauty! of Love! How shall I describe thy influence? With what rites will thou be worshipped? Where art thou visible? In the person of my beauteous Harriet. In adorning her bosom does she not decorate thy shrine? Is not the lustre of her eyes attempered by thee? And is not the empire of her charms the result of thy energy? Yes, angelic woman! My love is without limits and above control, but by what inevitable, inconceivable charm my passion was erected, it would be fruitless to inquire. But have I not found thee without a blemish? Is not thy purity immaculate? And with what rage and detestation should I view thee, were I conscious that thy purity were lost? How would thy charms be blasted by the spotted and malignant fever of licentiousness! What unbearable disorder would seize my intellect! What opiate but death could lull my despair?

XII [From Henrietta]                    Saturday night 10 o'clock

I have just left you and can now retire to my chamber, but finding myself not much inclined to repose, I shall spend all the hours in which I shall continue wakeful in writing to you. But I will a second time peruse your letter. Yet there can be no necessity for reading it again, and the impression which your eloquent incoherences have already made upon me do not require a repetition. I shall not easily forget your letter, but as it has for the most part been the subject of the conversation which I've just finished, I should perhaps, in attempting to answer it particularly, only repeat what has already been, with so much vehemence and copiousness, discussed. I shall therefore abstract my attention from and confine myself to other topics, and yet, my friend, how is that possible? By what efforts can I extricate myself from the maze in which your letter has bewildered me? By one passage I am thrown into a fit of indignation and resentment; by another my heart is overwhelmed by tenderness and pity, by love and admiration. One part of it I can scarcely forbear tearing into pieces, and I am ready to disclaim all connection with the author, while another softens all my soul into fondness and compassion and fills me with a vehement longing to furnish him with the most unquestionable proofs of the strength and sincerity of my attachment that can be given consistently with virtue. The conclusion justifies or rather excuses the introduction, and I confess to you that, notwithstanding some parts are so obnoxious, I cannot prevail upon myself to wish that those parts had been omitted, or that your letter had, in any respect, been otherwise than it is.

[*Her bewilderment at his complex personality: 44*] Inexplicable, unintelligible creature! When shall I know thee perfectly? When shall I become acquainted with all thy faults and all thy excellences? Each hour I discover somewhat that I had not before known and which I did not expect to find, and the discoveries of the last hours are equally unexpected and surprising with those of the first. My acquaintance with you has at least been productive of one advantage. It has taught me hereafter to place no confidence in external appearances, and to judge only in consequence of knowledge, and yet, at this early period of our intimacy and when I am conscious that I am far from knowing you thoroughly, I cannot help forming a very favorable opinion of you. This you will readily believe, for can you imagine that I should otherwise have consented to receive and answer your letters, or have so frequently permitted your personal visits? But have I hitherto acted indiscreet? It is true that I do not know you thoroughly, but do I not know enough of you to justify my confidence?

[*The circumstances of their first meeting; her analysis of his character and personality: 45*] How perfectly do I recollect all the circumstances of the origin of our friendship. Nine months ago how should I foresee that the youth whom I observed frequently passing my window and whose habit and demeanor gave no tokens of his real character, would at this time have acquired all my confidence, and bound me to him in the bonds of indissoluble affection? I saw you often, but I saw you only with indifference, until one morning as you passed the window, I observed you looking into it with a timid, but eager curiosity. When you saw nobody you appeared disappointed, and slackened your pace to examine more attentively. But you suddenly met my eyes. You were startled, were covered with blushes and confusion. You tremblingly hastened away and left me in a situation not very different from your own. Your behavior, considered superficially and unaccompanied with certain minute but uncommon circumstances, would only have excited indignation or scorn. I should have esteemed you contemptible, foolish, or unpardonably audacious, but the anxiety which was depicted in your countenance, a certain reluctance and fear of offending, mingled with invincible curiosity, sufficiently showed that you were not a transient nor accidental nor impudent nor silly gazer, and this favorable opinion could not but receive the strongest confirmation on observing the manner in which you acted when you saw that I was looking at you.

All that day your idea haunted me incessantly. I endeavored to amuse myself at the harpsichord, but it was impossible to pin my attention on it. In the midst of a tune my fingers sank into a kind of involuntary inaction. My eyes wandered from the notes. I mistook the keys, confounded the time, and blundered in the execution. I thought of nothing but the modest confusion, the ingenuous aspect, of the gazer. I turned over several pages of a book without knowing what it was that I held in my hand, and being visited by some young ladies in the evening was still as musing and thoughtful as ever, and all their sprightliness and vivacity were in vain exerted to recall me to myself, to rouse me from my reverie. I spent the greater part of the night unable to close my eyes; I continually saw you before me; your blushes, your embarrassment were still visible. I began to be alarmed at myself. Why (said I to myself) cannot I get rid of this object: Let me think on indifferent matters. This Thomson—she is an amiable girl and accomplished, polite. Why did he look in? Was he not searching for me? The poor youth is certainly in love. Alas! I am afraid that I also am infected by the same contagion. By love? for whom? An absolute stranger. Perhaps mean, unworthy, immoral, and illiterate. And yet why should I form so severe a judgment of him? There is nothing in his appearance inconsistent with genius and integrity. Has he not intelligent features? A penetrating eye? His modesty is unquestionable. How was he embarrased when he saw me! Perhaps he wanted to address me to excuse his presumption, to solicit my forgiveness. But I frowned upon him. My air of severity intimidated him. Why did I display this unreasonable haughtiness? He did not merit disdain; his deportment was all gentleness. But poor youth! methinks I pity him. I wish he had spoken to me and been his own introducer. But, if he be really in love, he will find a way to make it known. And who knows what excellences may be

concealed under that homely exterior? But why should I think of
him? He is—he can be nothing to me. Am I not becoming a victim
to love? What new emotions are these? Did I ever feel similar ones
before? This youth—I cannot exclude his image from my mind. I
fear it will make me unhappy.

In this manner did I muse and thus interrogate myself for a considerable time; sleep at length overtook me, but you still haunted my
imagination; I saw you under a thousand different shapes. At one
time methought you came to visit me in a magnificent equipage, with
a splendid retinue; at another time that you put on a mean disguise
and became a servant of the gardener, and that you threw down your
spade and discovered yourself to me as I happened one morning to
be walking alone in the garden. Afterwards I thought you overleapt
the garden wall by moonlight and suddenly appeared before me while
I was sitting in the Summer House reflecting on the circumstances of
your first appearance to me.

I will not recount all the fantastic incidents which happened during
the course of that night. I rightly conjectured that if love were your
disease you would speedily contrive a method of disclosing it. It was
happy for you that you found a condescending mistress, and fortunate
for me that I had not laid myself under any obligation to another
before I saw you, for whatever my previous obligations had been,
unless they had originated in love, I could not have resisted the emotions with which the sight of you inspired me, and should therefore
have been condemned to waste my days in an unhappy contest between
love and duty, and what effects would not my inexorable dislike or
invincible indifference have produced on the wild, impetuous, and
ungovernable passions of my friend? I tremble to think of what would
probably have been the consequence, but still notwithstanding all my
condescension and indulgence, you are still unsatisfied.

[*Her assurance that no barrier shall stand between them and
eventual marriage; they are already wedded in a Platonic sense: 46*]
Have I not told you that my resolutions are taken, that the grave shall
receive me before I give myself to the arms of another, and do you
think that this resolution can possibly be shaken? Let me assure you,
my friend, that my fortitude is equal to the severest trial which can
encounter it, and that there is no obstacle to our final union which
cannot be surmounted by female intrepidity and perseverance. Why
is not this assurance satisfactory? Will nothing content you but that
of which the acquisition is impossible? Awake, my friend: be no
longer the slave of shadows and chimeras. Why will you be still a
child? Enjoy the felicity which is allotted to you. Our union is
already begun—our minds are wedded to each other. We shall be
One to all eternity.

Forbear to make your letters the vehicle of such outrageous passions; moderate your transports, I beseech you, and endeavor to trans-

fuse into your letters somewhat of that purity and delicacy which distinguishes your conversation.

[*She wants his letters to be more literary and less sentimental: 47*] You undoubtedly entertain a meaner opinion of my capacity than my vanity can patiently bear, or why in the letters which you write to me are not the same topics discussed as in those which you communicate to your friend? I am far from supposing that I should be able to extend the knowledge or rectify the opinions of my friend, but I am certain that I should be greatly benefited by his instructions. Let this consideration induce you to give to your future letters a more literary or speculative cast than is visible in those which you have heretofore written. I have heard you say that you have had better opportunities of knowing mankind, been acquainted with a greater variety of characters and of scenes than any other person. This, my friend, is doubtless a very modest assertion, and nothing could with less propriety be mentioned as proof of vanity, but if this be true why will you not communicate a few particulars to me, and make me the same wonderful proficient as yourself in this most useful species of knowledge? Do you think I should not be highly interested in narratives which relate to yourself, and I am too well acquainted with the talents of my friend to imagine that he would be unable to give to the most common and familiar incidents the graces of novelty and the aspect of importance.

I will not prolong this letter, though I yet feel no inclination to sleep. It is not likely that I should ever [become] weary or slumberous in writing to my dearest friend and therefore it must be some other motive [than] sleepiness that can induce me to lay aside the pen, and the reason why I leave it now is because I think I have written sufficiently.

XIII [From Brown]                                   Sunday Morn. 7 o'clock

[*Brown in the country: 48*] I rose this morning before the day began to glimmer in the east. This is my customary hour of rising, and the incidents of that last evening were such as scarcely suffered me to sleep at all. My slumbers were short and were continually broken by vague and confused dreams, of which however, the general aspect was agreeable, and which have greatly contributed to the peace and serenity with which I begin this letter. Your piety will not suffer you thus to employ yourself on this day, and you have also thought it proper strictly to prohibit me from writing, but, my dearest Harriet, is it less criminal to think of you than to write to you on Sunday? And since it is impossible to exclude you from my thought, whatever be the sanctity of the time or place, I know not why I should be forbidden to converse with you. I endeavored indeed to fix my attention on the scenery before me as I wandered over the fields, and to watch the progress of day in the east, standing on a verdant eminence within some hundred paces from Schuylkill, but the charms of nature are less attractive than formerly. My attention is forcibly and irresistibly borne away to objects that are distant and to occurrences that have already happened. How different are the emotions with which I now view the rising sun from those with which I have formerly beheld it, and I long for the approach of day, and the re-animation of drooping nature for no other reason than because it shortens the intervals of absence from you, or enables me to exercise my pen and enjoy, in some sort, your company.

[*Description of rustic life; its crude aspects, etc.: 49*] The house at which I reside is distant about half a league from Schuylkill. We are conducted thither by a road, the skirts of which neither art nor nature has very lavishly embellished, but the sight of dewy verdure is ever pleasing, and the fields, though for the most part flat and level, are at this season rendered delightful to the view by being covered luxuriantly with rising corn. Is not some of the pleasure which a cultivated landscape affords properly to be attributed to the consideration which naturally suggests itself of the condition or happiness of those who cultivate it? How much is the beauty of the scene heightened by the appearance of beautiful, intelligent, or contented countenances? Nature seems to derive additional charms from the manners of the inhabitants, and the rudest dwelling on the bleakest and forlornest promontory could scarcely fail of pleasing the spectator when he should know that it was the residence of beauty and simplicity. And how quickly would the greenest copse or the most sequestered dell lose its charms, when it should be found to contain a nest of adders or a den of outlaws? If any pleasure can be gathered from the prospect of any part of this peninsula,[26] we must be indebted for it totally to Nature, for the manners of the people are to the last degree gross and brutal. The light neither of letters nor religion ever illumined this dusky spot, and the inhabitants appear to imagine that the end of their being is to carry radishes and potatoes, or what goes under the denomination of *truck* to market, and to hoard up the produce "for a rainy day." Avarice is their predominant passion on which every other principle of action is based, and they are universally sunk in ignorance and brutality. Though their speech be distinguished by few national peculiarities of pronunciation and their idioms be far more truly English than any of the provincial dialects of G. Britain, yet it is so perfectly the reverse of purity and elegance that my ears are shocked and disgusted at it. It also enormously abounds with blasphemies and impurities, and almost all their phrases are expressive of so strange a mixture of folly and wickedness that I am sometimes doubtful whether they excite more contempt or abhorrence.

[26] The Schuylkill flows into the Delaware near Philadelphia, forming the peninsula to which Brown referred.

[*Description of Nature in the environs of Philadelphia: 50*] I am afraid that the face of nature is little less disgusting. I live near the confluence of two small streams which fall, when united, into Delaware, a little above its conflux with Schuylkill. These streams are confined within artificial banks in order to secure the adjacent grounds from inundation, and roll through muddy channels, which at the falling of the tide afford a striking spectacle of desolation and deformity. The land which belongs to this farm is nearly encircled by these rivulets, and is one flat, uniform, unsightly level. It chiefly consists of marsh, from which the rays of the sun exhale the most noisome and unwholesome vapors. The garden, of which the cost has been great, is indeed the only place from which the eye can derive pleasure, and in a small building, erected in one corner of it, and which by placing a chair and desk in it and furnishing it with books and paper, I have converted into a sort of study, I am now sitting.

The hither bank of Schuylkill is steep and lofty, with a sandy shore, and is the only place within ten or fifteen miles of my residence, with which a solitary wanderer like myself can be much delighted, and here I am frequently to be found at morning and evening twilight, and am sometimes conducted hither by the genius of contemplation, at the dead of night. The descent is overhung by pines which diffuse over the scene a peculiar solemnity, which greatly heightens the pleasure which one of a pensive and melancholy disposition may derive from it.

[*His habit of solitary study and meditation: he studies Milton: 51*] This morning I repaired thither, before the east had exhibited any tokens of approaching light, with Milton's *Comus, Lycidas,* and *Il Penseroso* in my pocket, intending to devote the hours to those performances, and to investigate the principles of that divine philosophy which they teach, but alas! my thoughts continually wandered from the page before me, and the image of my beauteous Harriet incessantly interposed between the poet and the critic and entirely diverted my attention from the book. You know it is my constant practice to think aloud, and I could not but smile at the strange, incoherent, and unintelligible soliloquies of which I was guilty in consequence of thus dividing my attention between two objects and of forcing myself to repeat the poems and to weigh the propriety of each line and phrase, when it was impossible to be absent from you for a moment. I at length forbore my unavailing struggles and hastily returned, determined no longer to withstand my inclination, and, as you were personally inaccessible, to spend the day in writing to you.

Judge with what satisfaction I perused your letter, which I unexpectedly received on my return. How infinitely condescending is my lovely Henrietta in bereaving herself of repose for my sake and yet how cruel are you in recounting the circumstances in which you write, in telling me that, on retiring to your chamber, you felt no inclination to sleep, and therefore thought proper to employ the wakeful hours at your pen. How shall I banish from my imagination the fatal images that crowd into it—which the mention of your chamber, like the wafture of a magician's rod, have called into being? How can I innocently foster them? But, in compliance with your injunction I will exert the utmost magnanimity of which I am capable, and though I am unable to hinder the lawless excursions of my fancy, I will at least forbear to describe its rovings in this letter, and to speak in a manner in the least offensive to your delicacy. I will speak, if possible, on general topics and keep the peaceful tenor which you describe.

[*An apostrophe to his pen: 52*] How shall I amuse my lovely correspondent? How shall I agreeably and usefully employ my pen? For, O pen! I warn thee that thou art doomed to labor without intermission for ten or fifteen hours, or at least without any intervals of rest except those in which thy master shall employ himself in sharing the wholesome and temperate repast. Be therefore prepared to show thy skill and perseverance, and be sure to suffer nothing to escape thee which is likely to offend my mistress. I know thou art willing to perform all that is demanded of thee, but thou desirest to be told on what subjects thou canst expatiate in order to afford her pleasure. Listen to her. She herself informs thee that thou shouldst utter in her presence sentiments like those which thy lord dictates to thee when in company with his friend. But I know thy obstinacy. Thou refusest to comply with her requests. Thou thinkest it impossible to speak any otherwise than as the organ of love and tenderness and art skilful only in embellishing with thy eloquence the ardent or desponding conceptions of thy enthralled and infatuated master!

[*The minds of women are not inferior to those of men: 53*] It is not possible, my dearest creature, that you should imagine me impressed with a mean opinion of your understanding. I must indeed confess that before I knew you I deemed too contemptuously of the greater part of your sex, and supposed that the actual arguments of women are in general few and inconsiderable, and on a general position I see no reason for relinquishing it even at present; but I never conceived that the minds of women were naturally inferior to those of men.[27] I have always indeed strenuously maintained that you are originally foremost in the scale of being, and it is easy to produce examples which show that you are capable of outdoing us both in vice and virtue: and then, my fairest, who is there whose superiority I am less inclined to call in question; whose maxims I should more implicitly adopt, whatever subjects they regarded and whose guidance,

[27] During this early period in his life, Brown had arrived at this high opinion of women—an opinion which some six years later was to receive full and persuasive treatment in *Alcuin; or the Rights of Women* (1797-1798).

in whatever tract, I should less scrupulously follow? I am sensible
that if our intercourse were merely literary I should reap infinitely
greater advantage from it than yourself, and that even the sagacity
and erudition of my friend do not so justly entitle her to become what
he is at present, my guide and teacher, as the exquisite penetration
of refined taste and various knowledge of my Henrietta. Have I not
reposed in your hands the direction of my conduct and opinions?

[*Idealization of her: 54*] Am I not your vassal? I have given up
the privilege of acting and thinking for myself, and wait with all the
madness of impatience for that period when I shall add to those which
you already possess all the exterior symbols of sovereignty. When
you shall see in the person of your—(Ah! Name of rapture! when
shall I be worthy of thee?)—the same awe-struck votary, the same
prostrate adorer that now trembles before you, when the sacrifice of
masculine privileges,—hateful, arrogant, pernicious privilege—shall
claim the merit of being voluntary and constraintless.

[*His changed ambitions—the law no longer has any attractions for
him: 55*] But do not you see the impossibility of devoting his correspondence to indifferent topics? In writing to my Harriet shall the
phantoms of ambition be suffered to intrude? Shall I delineate those
splendid objects at which I was wont formerly to gaze, and assume,
amidst the brightest visions of accepted love, amidst the rays of benignant beauty, amidst the ravishments of tenderness and overflowing
ecstasy, the stern and rugged aspect of the critic and grammarian?
Exalt myself into a judge of rhetorical performances, and act as
arbiter of the claims of rival orators? No! My Harriet would justly
despise and resent such unreasonable pedantry. A lover has other
recreations than to write critical dissertations, and dispute about the
merits of Tully and Hortensius.[28]

But however acceptable my criticisms might be to my charming
Harriet and whatever delight she might take in the correspondence
of a second Atticus, I am not accustomed to counterfeit opinions and
mimic enthusiasm. My hours of political ambition are past.[29] I no
longer muse in a portico of Athens, in the grove of Academe. I no
longer listen to the dialogists of Tusculum,[30] nor frequent the schools
of Socrates, Quintilian, or Dionysius. What I formerly beheld with
rapture is now disgustful or indifferent. I have at length acquired
a relish for true felicity, and all that I now desire is to pass a life of
rural and noiseless obscurity in the arms of love and friendship.[31]

[28] Tully (i.e., Cicero) and Quintus Hortensius were famous Roman statesmen
and orators.

[29] To be a successful lawyer in Brown's day one had to be in politics.

[30] Tusculum, an ancient city of Latium, was the scene of Cicero's composition
of *Tusculan Disputations*.

[31] Brown had definitely given up the idea of following the profession of law.

My correspondence with my friend[32] is far from being such as you imagine and, though not less regular and copious than formerly, is dedicated to very different purposes. You will not be at a loss to discover them; for how should it be supposed that one in my situation can with any degree of coherence or propriety meditate or reason on a speculative topic? I have no leisure to examine whether this phrase be classical or that sentiment just, whether the orator has well or ill-arranged his arguments on a particular occasion, no inclination to imagine myself his opponent and compose an answer to his declaration. No, my dearest Henrietta, I formerly thought that ambition was the attribute of the noblest minds, that the science of rhetoric was the sublimest of studies, and regarded perfection in eloquence as the pinnacle of human glory and felicity, but my creed is now entirely changed. The sacred influence of two bright eyes has softened my heart and illumined my understanding and taught me to estimate the perishable praise of men at its real value and to court the shade of philosophical retirements, domestic peace, and nuptial transports, with as much ardor as I formerly aspired to the splendid reward of forensic, judicial, and deliberative oratory.

[*His high opinion of her talents and of the transforming influence of love: 56*] Of the utility of that eloquence which is exhibited in conversation, I have always been convinced, and I shall not scruple to expatiate, even in my letters to you, on that interesting and important subject, because as a woman, you may reasonably aspire to the knowledge and attainment of it; because it is not less momentous with regard to you than to myself and because the discussion of it is far from excluding your image from my mind, and diverting my attention to other objects will furnish additional motive for contemplating it. Since all my rules must be drawn from you and all my precepts be illustrated by your examples, for of that eloquence where shall I search for a more perfect model than yourself! O my little angel, to what unlimited gratitude are you entitled! How numberless are my obligations to you! By acquiring and displaying so many excellences, you have raised me above myself. In contemplating perfection do we not ourselves become more perfect? Do we not acquire some resemblance to the deity by constantly meditating on his attributes? To gaze at your image, by which I am constantly attended, is my sole employment, and from continually gazing at purity and excellence, I necessarily derive advantages. I become, in some degree, akin to yourself. I feel a gradual elevation of sentiments, and am actuated by a boundless desire of rising to the same extraordinary pitch of mental and moral excellence. How potent and how beneficial is the influence of true love! It chastens the wanton imagination; it con-

[32] Perhaps William Wood Wilkins, then a student of law in Trenton, New Jersey (see chap. ii).

verts arrogance into humility, and softens the rudest and most boisterous demeanor into affability and gentleness; it teaches us diffidence
of our own powers and deference to the opinion of others, and produces a general conformity in thought and actions, to the beloved
object.    These are the effects of this sublime and exalted passion, of
which I do not scruple to quote my own behavior as an example.
What changes has it produced in the appearance and deportment of
the awkward rustic, whose speech might have been quoted as a model
of uncouthness and inelegance, who could talk only on paper, whose
pen only was audible, and the stream of whose turbid and muddy
elocution only served to perplex or baffle curiosity and to hide from the
view of the understanding those ideas which it was employed to render
visible and obvious.    I now involuntarily and mechanically imitate, as
far as natural defects will suffer me, the captivating grace and musical
distinctness of your utterance and the splendid simplicity and unstudied elegances of your style.    Since my connection with you, I
begin to entertain a better opinion of my own abilities, and know not
but that in time my Harriet may discover in me some resemblance to
herself, and may deem me worthy of the panegyric which my vanity
has already pronounced.

[*The power of the imagination; a description of his ideal home-site:
57*]    When religious rites shall have completed our union, and fortune
shall have conducted us to some romantic and peaceful asylum decorated with the beauty and magnificence of nature, shall I not search
out some sacred and sequestered spot "embosomed high in tufted
trees?"    Shall I not call from her attic shrines the genius of architecture to erect and dedicate a temple to the *Deity of love?*    O thou
precious faculty!    Creative and propitious power of practical imagination!    At thy command an Eden opens in the wilderness.    How
ravishing and picturesque the landscape which is momentaneously
depicted by the pencil!    Ye rushing torrents and gigantic mountains!
Whose sides verdant with luxuriant shrubs, or gloomy with impenetrable forests, are contrasted with summits naked, bleak, and inaccessible,
columns of ice on rocky pyramids. Ye springs bursting from the mossy
stone, and hiding in the depth of echoing caverns their collected
streams, ye vales whose fertilizing streams and shadowy recesses, where
silence, with footsteps noiseless and inaudible, is wont to stray—are
nightly witnesses of heavenly conferences, and are thronged with spirits, vassals of the poet's invocation on the word of magic. Ye images of
rural magnificence and tranquillity, how rapidly do you glide before me
and tantalize with the prospect of felicity which I never shall enjoy.
Lo! the mansion of peace, the domicile of elegance and hospitality, the
residence of love and beauty, rising in the midst of the wild, decorat-
ing the bosom of a swelling dale, that terminates in the low and
flowery margin of a winding and transparent stream of which the

opposite bank ascends, in steep and rugged magnificence, into the clouds. That mansion, my Harriet, have my hopes selected for our future residence, and I will not cease to believe the accomplishment of those hopes at least within the verge of possibility.

The scenes by which I am encompassed are in general so little suited to afford me pleasure that the embellishments of fancy are absolutely necessary to make them be viewed with patience, and of these embellishments, I am therefore by no means sparing, and it would not be easy for an indifferent [person] to conceive in how many additional and adventitious charms the most gloomy and insipid prospects are arrayed when they present themselves to my eye.

But the sun has performed one third of his diurnal journey, and the morning meal awaits my participation. How then must I finish this epistle, but, as soon as my repast is taken, I will return and resume my pen.

XIV [From Brown]                               Sunday Morn. 9 o'clock.

[*Description of his lodge: 58*] Here am I again, my Henrietta; I dispatched my meal with the utmost expedition and retired with inconceivable satisfaction to this studious recess. A description of it would, I believe, amuse you. Surely never had philosopher so forlorn and comfortless a mansion. Time has worn the plaster from the walls; in most places, the bricks, unevenly and irregularly disposed, are visible. It is in this building as in all other productions of architecture, in that which the form of the structure requires to be concealed, less pains and skill are employed than those which are necessarily exposed to examination. The width or breadth of it does not exceed ten feet, and yet it has two doors and six windows. One of the entrances is shut up by boards which the plane never touched, and which are nailed across it without the least regard to neatness or regularity. The other, which may be supposed to stand in the front of the edifice, and leads into the garden in the northwestern corner of which the building is placed, is open and without a door, though, as I perceive, part of the hinges, almost devoured with rust, still remain. In the windows there is no appearance of glass or shutters, and in one only, before which I have placed a desk tottering on three legs, lockless and almost coverless, are there any remains of a sash. My door and window are adorned with a profusion of lilies and honeysuckles, and in the holes and crevices with which the wooden parts of the edifice abound ants and bumblebees without number have taken shelter, but seldom molest me by their near approach. The flooring is gone, except in that part which supports my chair.

During this season, this retirement is by no means disagreeable or uncommodious, and I have often remained here in defiance of the chilling blasts of September and the cheerless cloudinesses of March. It serves all the purposes to which I have dedicated it, and I have obstinately refused either to forsake this asylum, ruinous and naked as it is, or to suffer any reparation of it. Were my desk mahogany, my floor covered with a Persian carpet, and my walls impanelled with plates of polished silver and adorned with the treasure of famous Medici or Belvidere, I should receive infinitely less satisfaction from it than from the humility and rustic[ity] of its present appearance, and I am not less delighted or benefited in gazing at the loosened cement and straggling bricks than in contemplating the broken shafts and shattered entablatures of Tedmore [?] and Persepolis.[33]

[*Sound principles of literary criticism. The importance of observing and recording common objects and familiar occurrences: 59*] I am far from thinking myself entitled to the praises which you have so liberally conferred upon me. Indeed, I know no rarer or more valuable qualification than that of describing common objects and relating familiar occurrences in such a manner as to render them pleasing and instructing, but when this talent is acquired, materials on which it may usefully and properly be exercised can never be deficient. I cannot conceive that the character of any man is unworthy to be known, and believe that there is no person, the incidents of whose life, if skilfully related, would not furnish as much entertainment by their variety, and novelty as any fictitious narrative that ever was written.[34] Fiction, however polished and elaborate, could never yet surpass reality. The life of most men is a continual comedy, which nature has furnished with characters, events, and scenes which cannot be imagined by the strongest power of invention and which, if faithfully related or described, would render the aid of fancy superfluous.

[*Nature, man, and the artist—painter and writer: 60*] No man can reasonably boast of greater experience than another. He that has traveled over a greater extent of country, associated with a greater number of persons than another, is not to be necessarily deemed more thoroughly acquainted either with man or nature. There is no sphere, however limited, in which human nature may not successfully be studied, and in which sufficient opportunities are not afforded for the exercise of the deepest penetration, and as a philosopher is able [to] derive amusement [and] instruction from contemplating a post or a stone, so he whose descriptive powers are vigorous can always make the delineation of them a source of pleasure and improvement. The book of nature, like every other volume, is useful to the reader exactly in proportion to his sagacity and to the attention with which he peruses it, but what advantage can he derive from it, whose rapid and unsteady glances can produce none but general and indeterminate ideas,

[33] Persepolis, an ancient city of Persia, was captured and partly destroyed by Alexander the Great. The site is marked by the ruins of huge grey marble buildings. Tedmore I have not yet identified.

[34] Brown's statement anticipates Wordsworth's by many years.

who dwells not on a single object long enough to know its properties? Nothing is more common than this inattentive and unobserving disposition, and those circumstances which though continually passing in our sight we wanted either power, time, or inclination to remark will, when depicted in words and set before us in a light so [clear] and forcible that they cannot fail of arresting our attention, be viewed with singular satisfaction and advantage.

I have long been powerfully impressed with the justness of these opinions and have sometimes conceived the design of relating every domestic incident, and accounting every dialogue and describing every scene that shall occur within a certain and assignable period with the most excessive and elaborate minuteness, relations in which no circumstances, however frivolous and inconsiderable, should be omitted, and pictures in which should be comprised every appendage. It may be questioned whether the force and accuracy of words can be exceeded by the power of the pencil, though to the perfection of *verbal* portraitures, it is obvious that a greater versatility and copiousness of style or greater command of language is indispensably required than many persons have attained. For my part I shall not scruple to pronounce in favor of the writer, but the circumstances in which the representations of the poet and the painter differ have been so frequently explained and are in themselves so manifest to the most negligent observer that I shall not weary my lovely friend with a trite and tedious disquisition, or with attempting regularly to demonstrate my opinion.

My design, to which I have just alluded, I have carried into execution and find that my knowledge of the manners, characters, and mode of speaking of those with whom I live is far more accurate and extensive than before, or than could possibly have been derived from casual observation. I cannot deny that had I listened with equal attention, or examined with equal vigilance, though without any design of recording what I saw or heard, I should have experienced a new and astonishing increase of knowledge, and therefore am convinced that exact and useful observation is practicable without the intervention or assistance of the pen, but the resolution to describe induced a kind of necessity for procuring the materials of description and was a cogent and irresistible incitement to attention, and the permanence of written record furnishes opportunity for reviewing the scene and attending to the dialogue at leisure.[35]

Such, my Harriet, are the opportunities and advantages of silent, indefatigable observation, and though what I have asserted with regard to the number and variety of scenes and characters with which I have been conversant were not strictly true, yet might I not still claim the merit of experience and sagacity? To visit Europe is it

[35] This theory was to be carried out in Brown's novels.

necessary to cross the ocean? Cannot I traverse Connecticut or Carolina while sitting in my closet and admire the dignity and affability
of Frederick or Joseph[36] though I never dined or walked in company
with either, though I never traversed the ramparts of Berlin or
Vienna? And cannot I converse with Gellert,[37] Haller,[38] or Gessner,[39] though I never set my foot within the precincts of Zurich,
Göttingen, or Leipsic?

[*The importance of sincerity; his opportunities of learning from
experience and self-analysis: 61*] I hope I do not deserve the imputation of vanity, and yet if to praise oneself, whether praise be merited
or not, be a sufficient proof of vanity, I cannot hope to elude the charge.
Among the qualifications of my Harriet I very quickly perceived that
uncommon penetration was to be ranked, and I was conscious that she
would not fail to exert her utmost sagacity in scrutinizing the character of her friend. I have, therefore, always acted and spoken with
sincerity from the strongest and [most] invincible motives, from motives of immediate and apparent interest. Duplicity and affectation
will scarcely be employed by one who sees that, instead of producing
the end for which they should be used, they would only counteract
and obviate it. Faults are only [aggravated?] by hypocritical pre-
tences and ostentatious disguises, and sincerity can never be otherwise
than meritorious. I assure you that I am flattered by a consciousness
of my own integrity in this respect and cannot accuse myself of a
single act of craft or dissimulation, with disguising any of my sentiments, with asserting what I know to be false, with professing to believe without actual conviction, or with substituting on any occasion
appearances for realities, during my intercourse with you. I am
willing that my candor and disinterestedness should be imputed to a
noble motive, but it is certain that a conviction of the uselessness of
dissimulation is a cause of itself sufficient to induce me to avoid it;
the inefficacy of an expedient is certainly the strongest motive for
rejecting it.

If I have really admitted an elevated opinion of my own talents or
attainments, is not the concealment of it a proof of insincerity, and
therefore culpable? And by what artifices could I hope to hide the
self-applause from you? In confessing my vanity I only disclose what
is already known to you. But what is the consequence of this confession? It is surely not without some degree of merit. If it be in consequence of a determination not to deceive you nor to wear appear-

[36] Frederick the Great, King of Prussia (1712-1786); Joseph II, King of
Austria (1741-1790).

[37] Christian Fürchtegott Gellert (1715-1769) was a German poet, born in
Saxony. He wrote the romance *Das Leben der Schwedischen Gräfin von G.* (1746),
but was best known for his songs and fables.

[38] Albrecht von Haller (1708-1777), Swiss scientist and poet.

[39] See note 21 above.

ances which do not really belong to me, it may justly be regarded as a proof of candor, or if I forbear to dissemble only because I perceive that to dissemble would be useless, cannot I found on this confession some claim to sagacity, for by what other power was I enabled to discover the inutility of false pretenses?

See, my lovely friend, with what laborious ingenuity I contrive to derive applause even from the acknowledgement of a weakness. I am afraid that you will not much approve my skill and that you will be inclined to suspect that my openness and frankness is only a new refinement upon vanity. I own I do not thoroughly comprehend my own motives, and will repeat, without attempting to explain or palliate my behavior, that I believe myself to have enjoyed opportunities of observation and of acquiring a knowledge of the world which few others equally young have possessed. But I can discover no vanity in this acknowledgment. That I have been a witness of various scenes and experienced many vicissitudes of fortune is not proof of my superiority to others, but though to have enjoyed opportunities of knowledge is no subject of panegyric, yet not to have profited by those opportunities will furnish just occasion for censure. He whose grievance is inevitable is less to be despised than he in whom it is voluntary.

Excellence is either absolute or comparative. On comparing myself with those with whom it is my fortune to associate, I am seldom inclined to question my own superiority, but on examining what I ought to be, and measuring my own attainments by the standard of character, remote or ancient, the phantom of superiority quickly vanishes and leaves me to regret my measureless distance from absolute excellence.

[*A confession—Brown hints at his unhappiness with his family: 62*] But you require me to give you some account of past transactions and to communicate some part of that knowledge in which I so boastfully declared myself a proficient. Ah! my amiable friend, your requisition can never be complied with, nor can I ever be prevailed upon to reveal domestic incidents, not because in acting on such a manner, I should imprudently be guilty of any breach of confidence or any violation of propriety, but because the pain would overweigh the pleasure of attending to the narrative, and no instructions could be derived from the melancholy tale equal to the severity of those wounds which your sensibility would inevitably suffer. If I cannot preserve the reputation of experience but by such communications, I must, however reluctantly, relinquish it, and be contented to be stigmatized as ignorant and inexperienced like those above whom I am so far exalted by the powers of a vain imagination.

Do you know with whom, in moments of imaginary elevation, I am sometimes tempted to compare myself? Ah! my Henrietta, you know not half the weaknesses of your unworthy friend, and in the progress of those discoveries which you are daily making with regard to my character, I am afraid that at length you will find abundant reason to withhold your approbation and forbear your panegyric, but whatever may be your future opinion with regard to me, I shall never scruple to claim the merit of sincerity, and doubt not but that, on the most exact and diligent examination, your confidence in me will be in no degree abated. You will find me, amidst all my weaknesses, fully sensible of the charms of virtue and of the deformities of vice, always endeavoring to resist temptations, and never yielding to them without remorse and repentance.

I think it may safely be asserted that of all the virtues mankind is most universally deficient in sincerity, and the innumerable casuistical distinctions which the ingenuity of every man furnishes him extenuate the guilt of severity in the eye of him who commits it. He ventures not only to commit it without scruple but to acknowledge and vindicate the commission. How many motives are there for concealing our real sentiment, for counterfeiting approbation and conviction? And how many occasions are there, on which, if its immediate and temporary effects only be considered, sincerity is criminal, and when a strict adherence to it would be, not only an infraction of politeness but a deviation from rectitude? He who exhibits in his deportment appearances inconsistent with his real character is undoubtedly a hypocrite: but ofttimes though it appears to have rendered the disguise of our real sentiments, in many circumstances, indispensable, it cannot alter the nature of things; cannot convert vice into virtue or beauty into ugliness; cannot change sincerity into a crime or render hypocrisy laudable. If two persons be openly and equally applauded, and both are equally convinced of the penetration and veracity of him who applauds, he who freely intimates his conviction and scruples not to own himself conscious of his merit would perhaps be as vain and arrogant, while the other who studiously disclaims all pretentions to the good qualities which are ascribed to him will procure the reputation of modesty, though it be clearly seen that his diffidence extends no further than his words and that the sentiments of both are the same though their professions differ. Custom commands that in our intercourse with others we should wear all the exterior symbols of modesty and always voluntarily shrink from the praises conferred upon us, whatever be our real and internal sentiments, but I cannot conceive any occasion on which it is justifiable to dispense with the observance of sincerity, on which it is not our invariable duty to utter our genuine sentiments and act in a natural character.

Will you permit me to leave you for a moment and conclude my letter? Forgive the abruptness of this conclusion, and continue to esteem, in spite of his demerits,

C. B. B.

XV [From Brown]                                    Sunday Noon.

The air is perfectly still.  I have a double motive for retreating into this recess, and come hither not only to converse with my Harriet but to avoid the searching and oppressive heat.  Silence is as much the communicant of noon as the associate of midnight, and the stillness of the air as naturally invites to contemplation at one season as at the other.  With what pleasure do I stretch myself beneath the shade of a hazel or a lilac in this agreeable asylum, and deliver myself up to the power of excursive imagination, or sink, by degrees, into slumber? My slumbers, however, are remarkable havens of amusement or instruction and it's only in my waking hours that I see "such sights as youthful poets dream."  Fairy-land was always interdicted to my sleeping fancy, though formerly, watchfulness never failed to conduct my footsteps thither.

[*The changing nature of man: 63*]  The vicissitudes to which the human character and opinions are liable cannot be considered without astonishment.  No one more widely differs in his sentiments and dispositions from others than at different periods from himself, and those intellectual revolutions always correspond with external circumstances. We vary according to the variations of the scene and hour, and it is not less difficult to tell what our views and opinions will be twelve months hence than to foresee the particular circumstances in which we shall then be placed.  Man is a progressive being.  He is never stationary, but is always either returning from a certain point or leaving it behind him.  It is therefore incumbent on us that our motions be tending toward perfection rather than receding from it.

But what awkward and uncouth morality is this?  How dare those cold and rugged speculations intrude into a correspondence like this, sacred to more tender and more amiable purposes?  Are you not displeased with the asperity of those reflections and accustomed to a strain more congenial to my present temper?  Yet you will not suffer me to obey the impulse of my heart, to rave, to supplicate, to exult, to deplore, but have harshly limited me to the discussion of uninteresting topics.  I assure you I find it almost impracticable to submit to your injunctions, but my fortitude, I hope, will triumph over every obstacle. I am sensible that the only alternatives are cold philosophy or dreadful silence, and what would I not cheerfully undertake, rather [than] relinquish this employment, than forfeit the inestimable privilege of writing to you?  Yes, impose upon me, if you think proper, tasks the most difficult and disagreeable.  Command me to exert my faculties in the solution of a mathematical problem, or in the explication of some incomprehensible subtlety in metaphysics, and you shall admire with what alacrity I will engage in the arduous enterprise, with what intrepidity and perseverance I will encounter opposition and trample difficulties.  The conviction that I act in compliance with your wishes will be sufficient compensation for my toils and render pleasing what would otherwise have proved insupportably disgustful.

[*His opinion of women's talents: 64*] But are not the two sciences which I have mentioned the exclusive property of men? Instances may indeed be produced of women who possessed every masculine property. Examples are not wanting of female warriors, lawyers, and professors, but is it not generally true that women are by nature unfited for the pursuit of mathematical as well as military science? Is not the gayer region of morality and poetry their province? In calm sedentary and domestic avocations ye shine with peculiar and reverent lustre. Divine and amiable objects! The pen as well as the needle may safely be intrusted to your beauteous hands, and ye are equally qualified for excelling in the use of both. Your eyes and fingers may with not less propriety be employed on the poem or romance than on the decorated screen and variegated lawn and you are destined by your maker not only to rival but outstrip your masculine competitors in all the excellences of the heart and understanding.[40]

[*What he owes to her: 65*] My Henrietta! when shall I reach the elevation to which you have soared? When shall I become as wise, as amiable, as sagacious in discerning truth and rectitude; as eloquent in enforcing it; magnanimous in adhering to it? But though an equality with you in every admirable and attractive qualification should be unattainable, yet I am already infinitely exalted above my former polish, and though I should continue forever stationary at the point at which I have arrived, my obligations to you will be unspeakable, and the dues of gratitude I shall never be able to discharge. I indeed survey the past with the utmost astonishment. In comparing my former with my present situation, the revolution which has taken place in my sentiments and situation is almost incredible. I am sometimes almost in doubt whether he that was last year a visionary has not now become a lunatic, whether the objects around me be phantoms or realities, whether my reason be not overpowered by imagination, and these are moments in which I almost call in question the existence of my Henrietta. Had any one formerly predicted that I should at this time engage the affections and enjoy almost incessantly the conversation of a lovely and accomplished woman, the most exalted of her sex, with what invincible incredulity should I [have] listened to his intelligence; I should have deemed it absolutely impossible as well from the conviction of my own unworthiness as from the knowledge of my situation. Women were objects with whom I conversed only at a distance; I regarded them with the profoundest veneration. I felt myself capable of all the romantic enthusiasm of love, but imagined myself eternally excluded from their presence by the want of exterior accomplishments. I saw myself obscure and mean, enrolled by adversity in

[40] Compare the thought of this paragraph with Brown's position in *Alcuin*.

the lowest rank of mankind; distinguished from the rabble only by the love of literature, by propensities which without altering the duresses of fortune could only render me more sensible of its rigueurs and injustices. I had never practiced in the School of Justinian.[41] Though versed in the laws of politeness, I was wholly unacquainted with the rules of accuracy. In the presence of any of your sex whose rank, virtue, or capacity entitled them to respect, the power of utterance was lost in confusion and embarrassment. My faculties were bewildered, and my pain and distress when under the necessity of meeting their eyes amounted to agony. I approached them [with] terror and reluctance and fled from them with the utmost precipitation.

[*His early reading and literary interests: 66*] I loved to indulge in visionary transports, to paint the form of imaginary excellence and beauty and put speedily together the materials of many a surprising and pathetic tale. I for a time, withdrew my attention from all other subjects and endeavored to obtain from those writers who are most celebrated for their skill an accurate though speculative knowledge of human nature, in the present state of polished and refined manners. I ingenuously confess my attachment to fictitious history, and read, at the period to which I allude, all the romances, whether French or English, which I thought deserving of perusal, of which, however, the number is extremely small. I know little of any performances of this kind but those of Mademoiselle Scudéri,[42] Marivaux,[43] Richardson, and I have no ambition to know more of the human heart from books than may be derived from those performances. But the want of opportunities, of experience, and the consciousness of my obscurity and of the meanness of my situation confined me to the region of fiction, and the only source of entertainment from my powers consisted in my own reflection, but in a short time I discovered with rapture and astonishment that those emotions which I had hitherto delighted to feign had suddenly become real, that I was actually enamored of an object that visibly and indisputably existed. How lavishly did my imagination decorate your mind and person, and yet how far was her polite pencil from painting with the energy of truth. How many excellences were disclosed in a more intimate acquaintance of which I had not previously formed the least conception. I am conscious that the lover frequently discovers beauties in his mistress which, in reality, have no existence, and whether I am deceived with regard to the

[41] Justinian I (Flavius Petrus Sabbatius Justinianus, 483-565), ruler of the Eastern Roman Empire (527-565), codified Roman law in *Corpus Juris Civilis*, the foundation of modern continental European law.

[42] Magdeleine de Scudéri, or Scudéry (1607-1701), was a French writer of long romances, of which the best known is *Artamène ou le Grand Cyrus* (10 volumes, 1649-1653).

[43] Pierre Carlet de Chamblain de Marivaux (1688-1763), playwright and novelist. Brown was evidently referring to the psychological novels *La Vie de Marianne* and *Le Paysan Parvenue*.

character of Harriet G.[44] I shall venture not to determine, but I am at least certain that I am not conscious of deception and that my error, if it be one, is involuntary.

Have I not reason to exult in my destiny? How far beyond my hopes, beyond my merits, is the blessing which I have received? When I have so much reason to rejoice, would it not be impious to complain? And yet to forbear complaint is impossible. My felicity though truly great, is far from being perfect. To know you, to converse with you, to find my vows acceptable, to excite in your bosom the same emotions which actuated my own, I have regarded as the summit of my wishes, the completion of my happiness, but now what I possess is little when compared with that to which I audaciously aspire. Wedlock! sacred and blissful state! All the joys which formerly encircled me have now retired within thy hallowed limits. From me they are fled forever unless thy portals are unfolded to receive me. My Henrietta! To be allied to so much excellence!—but I must restrain myself. I would not for the Universe offend you. Forgive me for disregarding your commands. I shall very quickly solicit your forgiveness in person. Meanwhile honor, I beseech you, with your written notice these vague and hasty effusions of

C. B. B.

XVI [From Henrietta]                     Monday, Morning, 6 o'clock

My friend, you have indeed been unexpectedly liberal. I requested you to write copiously, and in this instance at least you have not scrupled to obey. Why will you not submit with equal readiness to commands far more reasonable? How happy would your obedience render you, for my commands are inspired for no other reason than because I value your happiness in preference to my own. It is your own interest only that I consult, and am ardently desirous of making your attachment to me the means of consolation to yourself.

[*Praise of his good qualities: 67*] If that event should hereafter take place which is equally desirable by both of us, do not you see what exhaustless mines of entertainment this correspondence will offer us? I shall preserve all the letters which I have received from you, with the utmost care. They are indeed highly valuable on various accounts —but I will not wound your modesty, and yet it is somewhat ungenerous wholly to forbear applauding you. You have lately been so lavish of encomium on me that it would be but equitable to discharge the obligation, and in return to give you a little praise. Should you implicitly credit all that I should say of you? If you would not, I must of necessity be ardent. However uncommon your attainments may be, I cannot praise you if I had any reason to imagine that my veracity would be questioned. I cannot bear to be suspected of a

[44] There is a Susan Godolphin mentioned in one of Brown's letters (Journal). Could Henrietta G. be a Goldolphin?

falsehood, and to be guilty of a falsehood with you, to you would be a proof of peculiar malignity. And yet he that wholly disclaims praise is not perhaps less willing to receive it than he who openly accepts it as a tribute unquestionably due to him, and the forms of politeness, though they render indispensable the appearance of modesty and professions of unworthiness, do not demand that our words and sentiments should correspond. But, notwithstanding those remarks, I will not insult you with my panegyric, and if you knew how difficult it is to suppress my admiration of your intellectual qualities, I think you would applaud my fortitude.

I will never part with those precious manuscripts. Many an instructive [hour] will I pass in reading them, and as Alexander is said to have always slept with the *Iliad* under his pillow, I will imitate his illustrious example, and nightly deposit your letters in the same place.[45]

----

The *Journal* breaks off after Letter XVII (see note 20) with indication that the latter portion has been lost. We do not know precisely how or why Brown's affair with Henrietta ended. Although she returned his affection, differences in their religion and their social status, together with the fact that the youthful, impractical lover could not support a wife, contributed to Henrietta's postponement of their marriage. Early in the summer of 1793 she went to her home in Connecticut; Brown followed her, ostensibly to visit his friend Elihu Hubbard Smith. How long he remained there we do not know, but he wrote his brother James from Hartford during the summer, and in September he accompanied Dr. Smith to New York City, where the young physician was shortly to hang out his shingle. Apparently the young lover and would-be poet was back in Philadelphia by late fall. The new year opened with his most ambitious poem, which was no doubt inspired by Henrietta.[46]

[45] Letter XVII, the last in the Journal, is addressed to ''J—— D——n'' (probably John Davidson). It appears in chap. ii of this volume.

[46] *Devotion: An Epistle.* See appendix A.

# IV

# A PERIOD OF SPECULATION

### THE SCHOOLMASTER AND *ALCUIN*

Upon his decision in 1793 to give up the profession of the law, Brown hastened off to friends in New England and New York. How long he remained with them has not been definitely determined; but it could not have been long, for he was back in Philadelphia at his father's home at the beginning of the new year. Brown's life during the next few years is most obscure, and his activity can be accounted for to only a limited extent. His various meanderings—known by hearsay and not by documentation—between Philadelphia and New York and wayside places are a maze, the unraveling of which would furnish ample materials for a typical Brown novel.

Of documentary evidence of his doings there is but little; of conjecture, too much. The directories of New York for 1793-1801 are silent, though the names of his friends Smith, Johnson, and Dunlap, with whom he lived, are recorded. It appears, then, that at no time did Brown become a legal resident of New York. The Philadelphia directories, however, for the same period throw some light upon the activity of Brown and his family. His father between 1785 and 1810 was at one time or other conveyancer, landbroker, and clerk in the United States treasury; his brothers James and Joseph were during most of that time merchants; and his brother Armitt was for a time a clerk in the Register's office of the Federal government, and finally a merchant.

But more important yet is the fact that a Charles Brown is listed in the directory for 1794 as one of the masters in the Friends Grammar School. Although his address is given as 117 North Second Street, it is probably a mistake for 117 South Second Street, the home of his parents. Then, too, Charles as a Christian name was very rare among the Browns of Philadelphia, the directories for the period 1790-1800 showing only two with that name: one a daily laborer, the other a master in the Grammar School.

To one familiar with the nature and circumstances of Brown's previous training and his natural bent toward the didactic, turning schoolmaster seems a very likely move for him to have made as the first step on the road to authorship. He had just returned from New York. Fired by the ambitions and deeds of his friends Smith, Dunlap, and Johnson, Charles Brockden rededicated himself to the writer's profession. But he was penniless and well aware that it would take some time to win his bread by writing; so it was but natural that he should turn to a congenial and remunerative employment such as teaching. He had often said that he wished to become a teacher of truth, and here was at least a small opening. He probably remained with the school but a short time. Brown may have found the work uncongenial; who can doubt that Alcuin was speaking straight from the heart and from the experience of his creator when he drew the vivid picture of the unhappy life of the teacher?

Of this obscure but quite important period in our author's life, Allen and Dunlap, who were in possession of all the facts, laconically remarked that Brown's brothers had invited him to become a partner with them in the mercantile business and "even go as supercargo to Spain and Germany," and that his brother Joseph had invited him to spend the winter with him on the solitary banks of the Roanoke, where there would be musty books to read and ample time to moralize. But so far as we know he did not go to Spain or Germany or to North Carolina, nor is there any definite evidence that he entered enthusiastically the countinghouse of his merchant brothers.

The Browns were small and apparently unambitious businessmen. At no time before 1800 was there opportunity for gaining wealth or fame in the mercantile business as it was conducted by Elijah Brown and his sons, and there certainly was little inducement for the young philosopher of the family to establish himself in that business. A careful search through newspapers and magazines and other contemporary records fails to show that the Browns were active in state, municipal, or religious affairs; apparently only Charles Brockden showed any special talent or even ambition to rise to more than ordinary heights.

Whatever Brockden Brown may have been ostensibly engaged in during the early and middle nineties, we know that his mind was teeming. During these years he read widely in history and acquired many sorts of useful knowledge. He speculated on various evils inherent in social institutions, and like so many ardent reformers of that time he was inclined to ascribe social evils and general unhappiness to ignorance and to positive institutions. The magazines of the day were filled with vigorous speculation on political and social questions. That young Brown found congenial reading in the more radical sheets cannot be doubted. Furthermore, it was during his first visit to New York, in 1793, that the most provocative chapters of Godwin's *Political Justice* were published in the *New York Magazine*. Over Godwin's pages Brown and the little band of New York friends doubtless spent many a wakeful hour.  In Godwin, Brown found strong confirmation of his early radicalism.  His reading and speculation during these restless years led him eventually to the utterance of revolutionary doctrines that proved embarrassing to him in a later period of life.

Apparently Brown had spent several months with his New York friends during the early summer of 1795, but he was back in Philadelphia by September.  Perhaps at this time, while in New York and under the spell of Godwin, Brown planned an ambitious, didactic work.  The exact date of *Alcuin* is not known, but it was composed late in 1796 or early in 1797.

### THE RIGHTS OF WOMEN

It is generally assumed that Mary Wollstonecraft and William Godwin were the earliest advocates of women's claims to equal political, social, and educational rights with men.  As a matter of fact neither Mary Wollstonecraft nor William Godwin was an original thinker on this subject, for there is nothing really new in them.  Mary Wollstonecraft in her *Rights of Women* (1792) and Godwin in his *Political Justice* (1793) and in his novels did, however, by clothing the arguments for the social emancipation of women in lasting form, establish their chief claim to a place in the literature of the movement. Charles Brockden Brown was familiar with the works of these writers, but he was also familiar with what had been done by others earlier than the time of the Godwins.  It can be shown that the revolutionary spirit stirred in Brown before the appearance of the *Rights of Women* and *Political Justice,* and that the influence of these two works upon Brown has been overemphasized.  Indeed he was familiar with the history of women's emancipation from Mary Astell's *Serious Proposal* (1694) to Mary Wollstonecraft's *Rights of Women* (1792).

Brown's political theories were shaped by Locke and his French and American disciples.  While Locke's plan of government did not specifically assign to women a place in the body politic, by implication, at least, they were acknowledged to have an important position in the social fabric.  Women were so hopelessly low in the social scale that only the bravest persons before 1790 ventured to suggest that women, like men, have political rights.  They had first, indeed, to be emancipated socially and intellectually before any thought could be given to their political and economic freedom.  Woman had for centuries been considered a shallow, helpless creature, to be petted, caressed, or corrected by her superior lord, or else a merely moral being whose virtue had to be constantly guarded.  The old Hebrew canon law was generally in force and was pointed to as authority for the enslavement of women.  The Scriptures were invoked to prove that woman was created solely for the comfort of man, and as such she had no liberty of active or independent judgment.  Her highest virtue was obedience to the will of her lord, and her chief occupation was childbearing. Indeed her whole life was regulated by these considerations. She had no part in the moral, intellectual, or economic direction of her home, and no authority over her children.[1]

Charles Brockden Brown was influenced by Thomas Holcroft (1745-1809), whose dramas[2] and novels[3] attacked pride of rank and wealth, and man's domination over woman; by Robert Bage[4] (1728-1801), who anticipated parts of Brown's second dialogue of Alcuin in maintaining that reason is the only reliable basis of action, that women should have a part in the choice of a husband, that marriage should be based on friendship and esteem, and not on love merely, and that it should be a contract between equals; Bage pleaded for humane divorce laws, for economic equality of women with men, to be achieved through better education for women; and notably by Mary Wollstonecraft (1759-1797), who put into lasting form the various pleas of the century for her sex. In 1787 she wrote *Thoughts on the Education of Daughters,* in which she denounced artificial manners and commended simplicity of conduct and practical knowledge. This pamphlet may be regarded as an introduction to her better known work, *The Vindication of the Rights of Women* (1792). The *Vindication,* though poorly planned and clumsily written, was a remarkable and daring plea by a woman for her sex; its boldness and its passionate argument assured it a wide hearing. Like her predecessors she argued for marriage based upon esteem and friendship, and for the same education for both sexes, so that sex distinctions might be minimized. But while she asserted woman's capacity for many trades, she insisted that her chief place was in the home, where she should have a voice in the education of her children. The sentimentalism of Richardson, Sterne, and Rousseau she vigorously assailed.

By the end of the century, however, a temporary reaction to the professional and economic aspirations of women had set in.[5] This shift in interest, under the spell of Rousseau's popularity, was shown in woman's proper education. By "proper education," one is to understand that peculiar variety sponsored by Rousseau, in which delicacy, softness, sensibility, obedience, and sexual attraction were considered the cardinal virtues. It was directly against the baleful

[1] For a full account of the struggle for the rights of women, see David Lee Clark, *Brockden Brown and the Rights of Women,* University of Texas *Bulletin,* no. 2212 (March 22, 1922).

[2] *The School of Arrogance* (1791); *He's Much to Blame* (1798); *Love's Frailties* (1794).

[3] *Alwin* (1780); *Ann St. Ives* (1792); *Hugh Trevor* (1794-1797).

[4] Chief works: *Mount Henneth* (1781); *Barham Dawns* (1784); *James Wallace* (1788); *Man As He Is* (1792); *Hermsprong; or Man As He Is Not* (1796).

[5] George Elliott Howard, *A History of Matrimonial Institutions Chiefly in England and the United States* (1904).

influence of the Rousseauistic books[6] embodying this ideal of woman's education that Mary Wollstonecraft centered her attack in her *Rights of Women* (1792) and Brockden Brown inveighed against in his *Alcuin*.

But with the coming of the French Revolution and the Industrial Revolution, women assumed a more important role in the economic and political life of the state.

### RIGHTS OF WOMEN IN AMERICA

During the last decade of the eighteenth century America became an asylum for the radicals and the political refugees of France and England, and as a rule these men threw themselves vigorously into the political disputes of the day. America was for a time a forum for the discussion of the rights of men and women. It is not surprising, then, that Brockden Brown, just growing to manhood, was stirred by the arguments heard on every hand. Especially from writers like Fénelon, Poulain, La Bruyère, and Rousseau, Brown learned of the feminist movement in France and of the fundamental philosophy behind the "natural rights" arguments for the emancipation of women. Space forbids a detailed statement of the considerable influence of French thought on the feminist movement in America in general and on Brockden Brown in particular. Without doubt, it was during these formative years that Brown's zeal for the freedom of mankind was first awakened. That he was also acquainted with the struggle of women in America for a more active political and economic life can be taken for granted.

In the formation of the American Constitution, as with the first French Constitution, the most radical thinkers became conservative to a marked degree, and the much-heralded theory of "natural rights" and "natural equality" of the Declaration of Independence was partially and in some instances entirely brushed aside. The question of suffrage was an all-important one, and, in the minds of the most liberal, the limitations put upon the exercise of the franchise were unjust and but one step removed from conditions in England. The several state constitutions had various qualifications, and between Federal and state limitations the actual voting population was but a small fraction of the male inhabitants. When all women, all slaves, all immigrants under a certain limit of residence, and all men who lacked the property qualification were denied the franchise, it was plain to many Americans that democracy in practice was far from the ideal government that the Declaration proclaimed.

Certain state constitutions, however, admitted women to a larger share in the life of the state than they could hope for under the

[6] Goldsmith's *The Citizen of the World* (letter XIX); *Female Worthies* (1769); Alexander's *History of Women* (1769); Lord Kames's *Loose Hints upon Education* (2d ed., 1782); Dr. Gregory's *Legacy to His Daughters* (1788); and Hannah More's *Essays for Young Ladies* (1789).

Federal government. This was notably the case in New Jersey, where from 1790 to 1807, women were allowed to vote, a privilege due largely, it seems, to the liberal-mindedness of the Quakers of that state. It should be noted, however, that they rarely exercised this right. But an occasion once arose in which the vote of women became the deciding factor and gave rise to a most lively discussion in the press. John Condit of Newark, a Republican, and William Crane of Elizabethtown, a Federalist, were in a close race for the legislature, and in an endeavor to defeat his opponent, Crane secured many women from Elizabethtown to vote for him. The newspaper war which followed, for and against woman suffrage, soon passed beyond the bounds of the state, and for some time centered attention on the rights of women.[7] This event, the exciting national election of 1796, and the criticism of the Jay Treaty, undoubtedly furnished ample incentive for Brockden Brown's *Alcuin; or the Rights of Women.*

To say that Brown was familiar with the great body of this literature of dissent would be, of course, an unwarranted assumption, but that he was acquainted with much of it is beyond dispute. Such zeal for knowledge and enthusiasm for the betterment of mankind as his was not at all singular in a boy reared amidst the bustle and shifting scenes of the nation's intellectual and political capital. Philadelphia, as we have seen, teemed with French political refugees. And during these stirring days Brown is reputed to have learned the French language in order to gain a firsthand knowledge of French literature. Such names as Fénelon, La Bruyère, La Rochefoucauld, Voltaire, Rousseau are scattered through the pages of his early essays and addresses. It must be remembered, too, that Brown frequented the society of liberal-minded Frenchmen; that he had access to the best libraries in the nation; and that he was a frequent visitor at the home of Benjamin Franklin. When all these facts are considered, one is not surprised that Brown showed himself familiar with all the current arguments for the social, political, and economic rights of women. It appears now that he had decided opinions on such matters before the appearance of the works of Mary Wollstonecraft and William Godwin, and that those opinions had been stimulated by his French reading. An analysis of *Alcuin* will show that Brown's sources were not specific, but general.

## ALCUIN; OR THE RIGHTS OF WOMEN

*Alcuin* is important as the first published volume of the first professional author in America, and it is interesting to the bibliographer as one of the rarest American books. Only eight copies are now known to exist: one each in the Library of Brown University, the New York Public Library, the Library of the Massachusetts Historical Society,

[7] E. R. Turner, "Women's Suffrage in New Jersey, 1790-1807," *Studies in History,* I, 165-187.

the New York Society Library, the Library of Congress, and the Library of Yale University, and two in private collections.

The curious student will search in vain for an accurate discussion of the contents of this rare production. According to Dunlap it was written in the ''fall and winter of the year 1797,''[8] and the same year has often been referred to as the year of publication. *Alcuin* was probably composed during 1796, and perhaps revised and continued in 1797.[9] It was issued in book form from the press of T. and J. Swords, New York, in March, 1798, and reprinted with revisions in the *Weekly Magazine* of Philadelphia (March 17–April 7, 1798) as *The Rights of Women*. Dunlap's statement that it was written in the fall and winter of 1797 has misled every subsequent critic of Brown's work. No one, it seems, has ever suspected the existence of a sequel to *Alcuin*, and yet by a curious circumstance it is the sequel or second dialogue, and not the original, to which Dunlap referred and upon which discussion of the book has been based.[10] The matter is easy

[8] Dunlap, I, 70.

[9] Professor Warfel states in his *Charles Brockden Brown* (1949) that *Alcuin* was written in the summer of 1797 for Dennie's *Farmer's Weekly Museum*, at the suggestion of E. H. Smith.

[10] (A) ''Brown's inquisitive and speculative mind partook of prevailing skepticism. Some of his compositions, and especially one on *The Rights of Women*, published in 1797, show to what extent a benevolent mind may be led'' (W. H. Prescott in Sparks's *Library of American Biography*, I, 129).

(B) ''Near the close of 1797 he published his first work, *Alcuin, A Dialogue on the Rights of Women*. It is not without ingenuity'' (Griswold, *The Prose Writers of America*, p. 107).

(C) ''He wrote in the fall and winter of 1797 a work which he refers to in his journal as 'the dialogue of Alcuin, in which the topic of marriage is discussed with some degree of subtlety at least.' It was published in the same year, but its crude and hazardous theories on the subject of divorce and other social topics attracted little attention'' (E. A. and G. L. Duyckinck in *Cyclopaedia of American Literature*, I, 397).

(D) ''His first work, 'The Dialogues of Alcuin,' published in 1797, to which he refers in his journal as discussing the topic of marriage, attracted little attention, and many of the theories advanced on the subject of divorce were subsequently abandoned by the author'' (*National Cyclopedia of American Biography*, II, 59).

(E) From Mary Wollstonecraft ''he derived the idea of his next work, *The Dialogue of Alcuin*, 1797, an enthusiastic but inexperienced essay on the question of woman's rights and liberties'' (*Encyclopaedia Britannica*, 11th ed.).

(F) ''It is not surprising, therefore, that his first publication, *Alcuin*, in 1797 dealt with the social position of women, and advocated a very advanced theory of divorce. This brief work, in the form of a rather stilted dialogue, made little impression'' (Trent and Erskine, *Great American Writers*, p. 15).

(G) ''In 1797 he published a work on marriage and divorce entitled *The Dialogue of Alcuin*'' (Wendell and Greenough, *A History of Literature in America*).

(H) ''The spirit of Godwin stirred eagerly in Brown during the early days of his freedom. Toward the end of 1797 he bore witness by writing *Alcuin*, a dialogue on the rights of women which took its first principles from Mary Wollstonecraft and Godwin'' (Carl Van Doren, chap. vi, *The Cambridge History of*

to explain. The original *Alcuin* as published by Swords, March, 1798, carried an "Advertisement" signed by E. H. Smith, which states that "the following dialogue was put into my hands, the last spring by a friend who resides at a distance, with liberty to make it public. I have since been informed that he has continued the discussion of the subject in another dialogue." Now the Smith *Alcuin* is, as I have stated, exceedingly rare—although a facsimile reprint was published in 1935—and it appears that no critic has ever compared it with the "copious extracts" in Dunlap's *Life of Brown*. It has simply been assumed that Dunlap quoted from the Smith *Alcuin*. A comparison, however, shows that only three and a half pages in Dunlap were taken from the Smith *Alcuin*—to serve, it seems, as an introduction to the second dialogue, published in Dunlap's *Life*. The Smith *Alcuin* is a small volume of seventy-seven pages or approximately eleven thousand words, and is divided into two parts to correspond to Alcuin's two visits to the home of Mrs. Carter, who conducts a Philadelphia salon. The dialogue as printed in the *Weekly Magazine* differs in many points from the Smith *Alcuin*. It is somewhat shorter; the title is changed to *The Rights of Women;* the hero is Edwin instead of Alcuin; significant references to certain famous characters and events are omitted; the slurs on the professions of soldier and barber are deleted; and the last thirteen lines of *Alcuin* are lacking in the magazine edition. Why Brown made these changes is not readily seen, and why he failed to have Smith make the same alterations in the volume published by Swords, since both volumes appeared in print during the same month, is even more mysterious.

The concluding paragraph of the Smith *Alcuin* clearly points to a sequel. "Here the conversation was interrupted by one of the company, who after listening to us for some time thought proper at last to approach and contribute his mite to our mutual edification. I soon after seized an opportunity of withdrawing, but not without requesting and obtaining permission to repeat my visit." The Smith "Advertisement" definitely states that the discussion was continued in another dialogue. That Dunlap's "copious extracts" are the continuation of the subject foreshadowed in *Alcuin* and clearly expressed in the "Advertisement" is beyond cavil. Then, too, the permission to repeat his visit which Alcuin sought is realized in the continuation

---

*American Literature*). But in an unpublished article put into my hands by Van Doren he took note of this confusion.

There is an entry in Dunlap's *Diary*, August 8, 1797, which lends support to the statement that *Alcuin* was published in 1797. He writes: "Now Smith showed me 2 dialogues called *Alcouin* sent on by him [Brown] to be forwarded to Danies paper." It is quite likely that Dunlap—none too careful with his spelling at any time—meant to write *Dennie's* instead of *Danies*. Joseph Dennie, a friend and correspondent of Smith, was at this time editor of *The Farmer's Museum* of Walpole, New Hampshire. It was not published by Dennie.

—which begins: "A week elapsed and I repeated my visit to Mrs. Carter." The continuation, referred to hereinafter as the second dialogue, was entitled *Alcuin* in the Philadelphia edition (1815) of Dunlap's *Life of Brown*, and the Paradise of Women[11] in the London edition of that work (1822).

It is safe to conclude, then, that it was to the second dialogue that Dunlap referred as being written in the fall and winter of 1797. Smith and Dunlap agree that the second dialogue was written after March, 1797. The time of the writing of the first is less certain, but more significant, as it was Brown's first publication. Reasoning from internal evidence alone, however, we can almost certainly establish the date as the fall of 1796. First: on page 11 of *Alcuin* the priggish schoolmaster speaks of the pleasure he derives during his leisure evenings from watching a declining moon and the varying firmament with the optics of "Dr. Young." Thomas Young (1773-1829), a noted British physicist, by his paper on the structure of the eye, read before the Royal Society when he was only twenty years old, had established for himself the name of founder of physiological optics. Young shortly thereafter went to Germany, and in July, 1796, received the degree of doctor of physics from the University of Göttingen. On his return to England he was hailed as a great genius. It is not likely that Brown would refer to him as "Dr. Young" before July, 1796. Second: significant, too, is Alcuin's remark, on page fourteen, that "the theme of the discourse was political. The edicts of Carnot, and the commentary of that profound jurist, Peter Porcupine, had furnished ample materials of discussion." Lazare Nicolas Marguerite Carnot (1753-1823) was a member of the French Convention, an important member of the Committee of Public Safety, and the guiding genius of the Executive Directory. He became a member of the Directory in 1795, and because of his opposition to the extreme measures of his colleague Barras, he was suspected of royalist sympathy and was sentenced to deportation in 1797. He spoke strongly against the violations of the Bill of Rights, and objected to the dictatorial and autocratic action of the Directory. But Brown's reference to the edicts of Carnot undoubtedly suggests the uncompromising measures which Carnot adopted during the troublous fall of 1796. In order to put down royalist and anarchistic plots, the Directory assumed abosolute power over the life and property of the citizen. It is quite certain, however, that Brown had in mind Carnot's instruction to Citizen Adet, the French minister to the United States, to address a note to the American Secretary of State reproaching the Washington Administration for the position of the President in his *Farewell Address* and for the Administration's attitude toward the Jay Treaty (1795). Citizen Adet declared that America had violated

[11] In Bage's novel, *Man As He Is* (1792), France is referred to as the "paradise of women" (II, 234).

her sacred treaty with the French Republic, and that as a solemn protest against that dereliction his government had instructed him to suspend his duties as minister. War with France or rather with the Directory seemed imminent.[12]

And last, Peter Porcupine, mentioned in the same sentence with Carnot and referred to as a profound jurist, was the pen name of William Cobbett (1762-1835). He was an English soldier, essayist, politician, editor, and farmer, who came to the United States in 1792 to seek a berth with the Washington Administration. Failing in this, he settled down in Philadelphia as a tutor in English to French political refugees. In 1794 Joseph Priestley also came to America and plunged immediately into the fight for republicanism. This action of Priestley drew Cobbett to the defense of the Federalists, and his vicious attack upon the friends of democracy stirred up the bitterest pamphlet war known in American history. Cobbett issued at Philadelphia a monthly pamphlet under the title of *The Censor* (January, 1796, to March, 1797) which he signed as Peter Porcupine. In this paper he was a vigorous and unreasonable advocate of everything British and a violent critic of everything republican. Cobbett even went so far as to place in the windows of his bookstore in Philadelphia pictures of nobles, princes, and kings—including the infamous George the Third. We first learn of him as Peter Porcupine in January, 1796, but if one may judge from newspaper allusions, he was not well known under this pseudonym until August of the same year. In September, 1796, he wrote, "What must I feel upon seeing the newspapers filled from top to bottom—with *A Blue Shop for Peter Porcupine, A Pill for Peter Porcupine, Peter Porcupine Detected,*"[13] etc. Cobbett reached the zenith of his ravings against American and French republicanism during the fall elections of 1796.

While these allusions to contemporary persons and events do not definitely fix the date of composition of the Smith *Alcuin,* they at least point to an earlier one than has usually been assigned.

### THE SMITH *ALCUIN*

The first dialogue of *Alcuin* is a thoroughly sincere and practical document, representing the most respectable democratic doctrine of the day. Indeed, it appears as, in part, Brown's contribution to the great debate between the Federalists and the Republicans during the stormy election days of the autumn of 1796, and registers his protests against the conservative American Constitution. Brown, with others, had been clearly disappointed in the failure of the framers of the Constitution to embody in that document the principles of the Declaration of Independence. The Smith *Alcuin* is, furthermore, the first

[12] Edward Stanwood, *A History of the Presidency,* I (1898).

[13] Selections from *Cobbett's Political Works,* being a complete abridgement of the 100 volumes which comprise the writings of Peter Porcupine, London, 1835.

extended serious argument for the rights of women that had yet appeared in America, and as such it merits the praise that is due the pioneer. It is the author's plea for the "natural right" of women to share in the political and economic life of the nation. In this claim for women Brown was, to be sure, not at all singular, for he only gave voice to a time-honored Quaker conviction of the essential equality of women and men. Furthermore, we have seen that this conception of women's rights and capabilities was of slow growth from Mary Astell to Brockden Brown, and that it was neither fathered nor fostered exclusively by any one person. But so much for the general character of the work.

As *Alcuin* is not readily accessible, a detailed account of it seems advisable. In each of the two parts the argument is conveyed in a conversation between the priggish schoolmaster Alcuin and the widowed Mrs. Carter, a Philadelphia bluestocking.[14] She is familiar with the current arguments for the rights of women, and generally takes a more radical stand than Alcuin. Her argument goes beyond that of Mary Wollstonecraft, whose plea was fundamentally for the emancipation of women from low social standards through an education similar to that for men. Mrs. Carter's contention is for political and economic equality with men. Indeed, her ideas on this and other subjects are so unusual that her home becomes a rendezvous for all liberal and respectable talent. Perhaps the strongest inducement to visit her home was not the attraction of the woman, but the brilliant society that foregathered there. Following the description of Mrs. Carter and her liberal coterie is a bit of philosophy on the comparative merits of reading and conversation as means of instruction. Like Swift, Alcuin sings the praises of conversation: books are too dull and insipid; he hates a lecturer, because his audience cannot canvass each step in the argument. Formal debate is also condemned. But conversation is free and unfettered and blends, more happily than any other method of instruction, utility and pleasure. Schoolmaster Alcuin spends the day in repeating the alphabet or engraving on infantile minds that twice three makes six, and the evening, until his acquaintance with Mrs. Carter, in amplifying the seductive suppositions, "If I were a king," or "If I were a lover." The schoolmaster longs for the liberalizing influence that only the conversation of the ingenious can give, and after a careful self-analysis he decides to become a frequent visitor at the home of Mrs. Carter. We are now, after fourteen pages of introduction, permitted to hear the dialogue between Mrs. Carter and Alcuin. The very dullness and narrow outlook of this prologue, the least attractive part of the book, stand in striking contrast to the charm of style and the liberal views that follow in the main work.

[14] Brown no doubt wished to remind his readers of the famous London bluestocking, Elizabeth Carter (1717-1806).

Alcuin, when the embarrassment of his introduction to the circle is over, respectfully withdraws to a corner of the room and there finds opportunity to engage the hostess in conversation. He somewhat awkwardly begins: ''Pray, madam, are you a Federalist?'' She evades the question, and replies indirectly that she has often been called upon to listen to political discussions, but never before has she been asked her own opinion. Mrs. Carter declares that women, shallow and inexperienced as they all are, have nothing to do with politics; that their time is consumed in learning the price of ribbon or tea, or in plying the needle. No wonder, then, she asserts, with Defoe, Swift,[15] and others, that women are narrow, and for the sake of variety they sometimes wander into the pleasant fields of scandal. Alcuin admits the force of this argument, but submits that the work of woman is not less useful and honorable than that of most men, notably that of barber and soldier. He dwells on the noble character of the practical, simple, everyday work of women.[16] He declares that they are the equals of men in all essential respects and morally their superiors, that the distinctions based upon sex differences are of no consequence, and, with the whole body of French and English advocates of the rights of women, maintains that whatever important distinctions there are between men and women are the direct results of differences in opportunities. Women are superficial and ignorant because they are generally cooks and seamstresses.

But, unlike those who believe in the infinite perfectibility of man, Alcuin takes a pessimistic view. He declares that it is doubtful whether the sex can be educated, and with Locke he rejects the notion of innate ideas, holding that man was born in ignorance, and habit has given permanence to error. Through ignorance or prejudice certain employments have been exclusively assigned to men, and the constitutional aversion of human nature to any change has confirmed this error. Mrs. Carter submits that of all forms of injustice that is most vicious which makes the circumstance of sex a reason for excluding half of mankind from the more useful and honorable professions. Alcuin falls back for a moment upon the respectable Whig doctrine of ''Whatever is, is right,'' and replies that the real evil lies in the fact that so much human capacity is perverted.[17] Then Alcuin follows the argument of Plato, More, and Godwin in desiring to have all tasks shared in common without distinction of sex, but unlike Godwin, Alcuin is not sure that such an arrangement would be practicable. He laments that, on account of a perverted civilization,

---

[15] Mary Astell, Defoe, Swift, Mary Wollstonecraft, and Godwin, whose ideas are paralleled in *Alcuin*, are not specifically mentioned; Plato, Lycurgus, Newton, and Locke are mentioned.

[16] Alcuin's reasoning here parallels in a remarkable way that of Fénelon in his *De l'éducation des filles* (1681).

[17] Cf. Poulain's *De l'égalité des deux sexes*.

large portions of mankind are doomed to toil, but he laments this not
because they are men or women, but because they are human beings.
[This turn of argument is in line with that of the humanitarian movement of the latter part of the eighteenth century, and is not exclusively
Godwinian.]   But Mrs. Carter insists that under any arrangement
women would bear the greater burden because of the duties of mother-
hood.   Alcuin replies that luxury and its attendant evils have greatly
increased that burden.   Mrs. Carter believes that woman's field of
usefulness is too much limited by a consideration of her function as
mother, particularly as regards the liberal professions.[18]   But Alcuin
insists that women are not really excluded from the higher professions,
that in Europe at least women are found in such professions.   He could
never wish woman to stoop to the practice of law, and as for the
ministry some sects [the Quakers and Methodists, of course] do not
debar women from the pulpit.   The Christian religion has done much
to break down distinctions of rank, wealth, and sex.   Mrs. Carter does
not try to refute Alcuin's argument, but points out that those professions which require most vigor of mind and the greatest contact
with enlightened society and books are filled by men only.   Alcuin
replies by attacking all the liberal professions, charging them with
sordid motives; with them usefulness as such is but a secondary consideration.   Benevolence, universal benevolence, should be the motive
force behind all the liberal callings.

At this point Mrs. Carter broaches the question of woman's education.   She takes the same line of argument as Defoe, Swift, and
others, that women have been educated for the profession of household
slaves and that women of quality are instructed in the art of the
coquette.   Men believe that women should be thus educated; consequently, they are excluded from schools and colleges.   Here again
Alcuin takes a wholly unexpected turn in his argument [more correctly his rationalization] by questioning the advisability of a college
education, even for men, for it seems unfavorable to moral and intellectual improvement.[19]   It would be indelicate to conduct mixed
classes in anatomy or other such subjects.   This idea of false modesty
gives Mrs. Carter an opportunity to inveigh against those who urge
the separation of the sexes on the score of delicacy.   With Mary Wollstonecraft and Condorcet she insists that nothing has been so injurious as the separation of the sexes.   They are associated in childhood,
but soon they are made to take different paths, learn different languages, different maxims, different pursuits, and different principles
of morals; their relations become fettered and embarrassed.   With the
one, all is reserve and artifice; with the other, adulation and affected

[18] *Ibid.*

[19] Fénelon in *De l'éducation des fiilles* takes this same position. See also John
Trumbull's *The Progress of Dulness* (1772-1773). The same strictures on college
education are found in the works of Hopkinson and Freneau.

humility. The man must affect ardor, the woman indifference—her tongue belies the sentiments of her heart and the dictates of her mind. While her early life is a preparation for marriage, her married life is a state of slavery. She loses all title to private opinion; she knows nothing but the will of her husband; and she may prevail only by tears and blandishments.

Alcuin maintains that this is an exaggeration, but Mrs. Carter asserts that the picture is exact, that her own life has suffered from a mistaken education. Man is physically stronger, she continues, and therefore in the primitive condition of society, woman was enslaved; but the tendency toward rational improvement has been to equalize conditions and to level all distinctions not based upon truth and reason. Women have benefited by this progress of reason, but they are not wholly exempt from servitude. Alcuin admits that the lot of woman is hard, but he points out that it is the preferable one, freest from the thorns of life—and then he trails off into a song in the praise of the needle and a panegyric on the hand that conjures a piano. Mrs. Carter replies that this is but a panegyric on indolence and luxury, in which neither distinguished virtue nor true happiness is found. Alcuin agrees that ease and luxury are pernicious and that the rich and the poor alike are denied real happiness and peace.[20] He concludes his argument by a statement that there is something wrong with society as it is now constituted, and appeals to Mrs. Carter to waive the claims of women and urge the much greater claims of enslaved human beings.

At the beginning of Part Two of the dialogue, Alcuin again inquires of Mrs. Carter whether she is a Federalist; again she protests that women have nothing to do with politics, that the American government takes no heed of them, that the Constitution-makers, without the slightest consciousness of inconsistency or injustice, excluded them from all political rights, and made no distinction between women and the lower animals. In the sense that she prefers union to dissension she is a Federalist; but if the term means the approval of the Constitution as a document embodying the principles of right and justice, she is not a Federalist.

It is when Mrs. Carter inveighs against the Constitution of the United States as harsh and unjust that she waxes most eloquent. She scoffs at the maxims of the Constitution which proclaim that all power is derived from the people, that liberty is every one's birthright and is the immediate gift of God to all mankind, and that those who are subject to the laws should enjoy a share in their enactment. These maxims are specious, and our glorious Constitution in practice is a system of tyranny. One person is denied a voice in the election of his governor because he is not twenty-one; another because he has not been a resi-

[20] This point is particularly emphasized in Poulain's *De l'égalité des deux sexes.*

dent for two years; a third because he cannot show a tax receipt; a fourth because his skin is black; a fifth *merely because she is a woman*. So what have we to boast in the name of divinest liberty when only a small fraction of our people have a voice in our government?

Here Alcuin takes refuge in the Quaker doctrine that the spirit is of vastly more importance than the form of government; that the value of any government is measured by the character of the men who administer its laws. But this subtle distinction between power and the exercise of power does not find favor with Mrs. Carter; for she wishes a voice in the choice of even the wise man. Echoing Plato, she is willing to admit that government by the wisest would be the best government, but how are the wisest to be distinguished from the mediocre, and how is one to know that the wise man cannot be corrupted? That government is best, all things considered, that consults the feelings and judgments of the governed. Alcuin insists, however, that some qualifications should be required of the voter. Mrs. Carter sidesteps by saying that she is not arguing the claims of mankind in general, but the rights of women in particular; for mere sex is so purely a physical matter that to make it a basis for excluding one half of mankind from the enjoyment of their natural rights is sheer folly.

Alcuin is most absurd in the eyes of Mrs. Carter when he suggests that women justly relinquish all claims to liberty and property when they marry; that they are contented with their present position; that they would not exercise the rights of citizens if the privilege were extended to them [this was a common argument in New Jersey, where at the time women had the privilege of voting but very seldom took part in the elections]. Alcuin admits that he is prejudiced, that he could never bring himself to sympathize with the claims of women to rights in business and politics; but he closes the argument by prudently acknowledging that since women are as thoughtful as men, and more beautiful, they are therefore the superior sex. Thus ends the first dialogue, or the Smith *Alcuin*.

## THE DUNLAP *ALCUIN*

Dunlap published the more Utopian second dialogue in the *Life of Brown* (1815). That Dunlap was acquainted with the first dialogue is evident from the fact that he recorded in his *Diary* (April 28, 1797): "Read today Smith's publication of Brown's *Alcuin*, 1 and 2 parts." Then, on the following day, he noted that he read Parts Three and Four, indicating that the second dialogue had been completed. That Dunlap thought highly of the first work may be gathered from an entry in his *Diary* (August 8, 1797): "there is much truth, philosophical accuracy, and handsome writing in the essay."

The second dialogue—a less distinguished essay—opens with Alcuin's declaration that he has just returned from a visit to the paradise of women. To allay Mrs. Carter's suspicion, Alcuin gives a lecture on the nature of the external world, following with almost verbal minuteness at times the argument which George Berkeley (1685-1753) advanced to show that the external world exists only in the mind that perceives it.[21] Alcuin states that the language of the people whom he visited is English, but that their buildings show traces of Greek and Roman models. In this island commonwealth both sexes are engaged in "awakening by their notes the neighboring echoes, or absorbed in musing silence, or engaged in sprightly debate." There are vast halls for musicians and dancers—halls where state affairs are the theme of sonorous rhetoric, or where the poet or annalist, or the chemist, or the mechanical inventor displays his gifts.

At this point Mrs. Carter checks Alcuin in his glowing description, demanding information unembarrassed by rhetoric or ignorant conjecture. In response he draws a picture of conditions as he observed them: there was no distinction in dress; the women shared equally with men in all recreational activities; in the matter of art, poetry, science, or debate the sexes mingled their inquiries, as all were votaries of reason. As Gulliver found it difficult to make himself understood among the Houyhnhnms because of the irrational meanings that he attached to words, just so Alcuin is rebuffed by drawing moral and political distinctions from a consideration of a difference in sex. His guide admits finally that he has heard of nations of men universally infected by error, and asks Alcuin to give an account of some of these errors. He mentions difference in dress, in education, in occupations, and in marriage. The guide replies that utility guided by reason should determine one's choice in dress; as to education it is preposterous to think that there should be any difference for the two sexes. With Locke, Alcuin holds that we are born ignorant, that ideas are received only through the senses, that our knowledge broadens with our experience. In this, nature has made no distinction in the sexes; education and environment are the deciding factors in one's career, and the proper educational ideal is a "curious" mind in a sound body. The young are admitted to the assemblies of their elders and are instructed by them, as in More's *Utopia*. Conversations, books, instruments, specimens of art and nature, haunts of meditation, public halls, and leisure are at the disposal of all without discrimination of age or sex—again suggesting the *Utopia*.

As all must be provided with food, clothing, and shelter, all must share in the production of these necessities. Agriculture is considered the most useful occupation, as in the *Utopia;* since all are obliged to till the soil, any drudgery that would otherwise be the lot of a few is

[21] *Dialogues*, 379 ff.; Commonplace Book, ed., Alexander C. Fraser, I, 92. It should be noted that Godwin in the second edition of *Political Justice* (1796) had a brief footnote on Berkeley's theory, but Brown does not seem to have followed him.

eliminated. One should share in the common labor, not because he shares in the fruits, but because he is being guided by reason and is susceptible of happiness. It therefore becomes one's privilege to promote the happiness of others. Alcuin suggests that women are usually thought to be too soft and delicate for rough and toilsome occupations, to which his guide replies that that is the argument of men.

At this juncture the conversation is changed to the specific subject of marriage. Mrs. Carter here interposes a caution against Alcuin's overstepping the bounds of modesty in discussing so delicate a question. She warns him that she is prepossessed in favor of the system of marriage, but she is willing to reason on the matter. With the preliminary sparring on questions of delicacy and sophistry over, Alcuin begins by declaring that in that paradise there is no marriage or giving in marriage. Mrs. Carter sees at once the course of his argument and accuses him of being in sympathy with that class of reasoners lately risen—meaning, most likely, Godwin and the whole French school—"who aim at the deepest foundation of civil society." She is thrown on the defensive and protests in solemn tones her belief in the institution of marriage, for without it all perception of moral rectitude would be destroyed. Mrs. Carter vigorously denounces Godwin's position on marriage and the sacred charities of family life [of course Godwin's name is not mentioned, but his pet phrases are repeated]. Alcuin reminds Mrs. Carter that she once submitted specific objections to the present system of marriage: it renders the woman a slave to the man and it leaves the woman destitute of property.

At this point Alcuin philosophizes at length on the nature of property and its relation to the family (following rather closely Locke's ideas). With the same authority he urges that since the family must have some head, the natural head is the man. Here, curiously, Mrs. Carter takes her main argument from Godwin in his condemnations of cohabitation as the destroyer of reverence, personality, opinion, liberty, and self-respect. But still Mrs. Carter insists that the institution of marriage is sacred, "but iniquitous laws, by making it a compact of slavery, by imposing impracticable conditions and extorting impious promises have, in most countries, converted it into something flagitious and hateful." Her remedy is spontaneous, unlimited divorce on the complaint of either party—such as obtained in France at that time. Then follows a gloomy picture of the ills of domestic life—such ills as often result from a marriage of convenience, but seldom from one based upon friendship guided by reason. She borrows Godwin's phrase "groundless and obstinate attachment"[22] to describe those affections that persist beyond reason.

Emboldened by Mrs. Carter's liberal views, Alcuin dares to advance a step further by suggestion that marriage is but a custom

[22] Godwin, *Political Justice*, II, 245.

after all, a suggestion, however, which Mrs. Carter rejects. She ends the dialogue by restating her position: marriage, she says, is a union founded on free and mutual consent; it cannot exist without friendship and personal fidelity; it will cease to be just when it ceases to be spontaneous. Thus ends Brown's most daring production.

As the author's first serious publication, *Alcuin* is outstanding. The style is simple, easy, and forceful, the descriptions vivid and accurate, and the argument persuasive. But as a whole the essay is crude and unorganized; it lacks effective disposition of the material and consistent grasp of character; and the conversation is not at all brilliant. Only the unusualness of the ideas could ever have made it interesting. But now that those ideas have been largely realized, one finds it increasingly difficult to read the book with sustained interest. Coeducation is general, the professions are open to both men and women, women now have a share in the enactment of the laws under which they live, and the marriage bond no longer makes a slave of the woman. Common as these things are now, they were in Brown's day most revolutionary, and for the advocacy of such ideas, many men and women were dogged by the law.

It does not appear, however, that *Alcuin* made the least stir in America; even among the author's friends this maiden attempt was received but coldly. The Smith *Alcuin* must have had only a small circulation, for it is now one of the rarest American books. The version in the Philadelphia *Weekly Magazine,* of course, reached a much larger public, but there is not the least evidence that it attracted any special attention. Smith in the "Advertisement" held out a promise of a second dialogue on the same subject if the first received a cordial welcome. It is to be observed that the second remained in hiding until 1815. Brown must have felt that his talent did not lie in the field of dialectics, for he immediately turned to the writing of romances to release the energy that stirred within him.

# V

# BROWN'S FIRST ATTEMPT AT JOURNALISM

## THE PLAGUE INTERLUDE

CHARLES BROCKDEN BROWN arrived in New York City on July 3, 1798, the proud author of one novel and with the incomplete manuscript of a second, *Wieland,* under his arm. He established himself in the bachelor quarters of his friends Elihu Hubbard Smith and William Johnson, at 45 Pine Street. He renewed his acquaintance with various members of the Friendly Club. During July and August, Brown was a busy man, feverishly applying himself to the completion of *Wieland* and to seeing it through the press. As if that were not enough, he began and prosecuted with vigor a third novel, *Carwin.* Brown also, according to Dunlap's unpublished Diary, attended meetings of the Club and was present at Mitchill's apartments on July 19, at the founding of the American Mineralogical Society, of which he became a member.

During July and August there were isolated cases of yellow fever in the city. Dr. Smith, who was in charge of some of them, reported that there was no need for alarm, because they were mild and under control. It was not until early September that the plague struck in full force, and in a particularly virulent form. Brown had written to his brother James on August 25 that "heavy rains, unclean sinks, and a continuance of unexampled heat" had given birth to the plague, but asked his family not to be alarmed, for he was far from the seat of the disease.[1] He insisted to them that his "mode of living, from which animal food and spirituous liquors" were wholly excluded, gave him the utmost security. On September 4 he wrote again to his brother, urging him not to credit newspaper rumors, and intimating that if the disease struck in his neighborhood, he would not flee.[2]

Brown's family in Philadelphia had, in the meantime, fled that city, and had written urging Charles to leave New York. Dr. Smith contracted the disease and, recovered in part, had just begun again to administer to the sick when he learned that an Italian doctor, Joseph B. Scandella, whom he had met in Philadelphia while in medi-

[1] Dunlap, II, 4.
[2] *Ibid.,* pp. 4-5.

cal school, had arrived in the city, and was down with the disease at
Tontine's Coffee House. Smith brought him to his apartments. On
September 17 Brown wrote to his brother James that Smith, after
attending Scandella, had had a severe relapse, and that Scandella had
died.[3]

Charles had by now the early symptoms of the disease; he was
under the care of Dr. Miller, to whose home he had been removed.
Johnson wrote to Dunlap on the twenty-first, saying:

Charles has gone to my brother's in Greenwich Street. Since Sunday he
has stayed with Dr. Miller. He is languid and pale, but having taken medicine by the advice of Dr. M. he wants only to be restored to strength. I wish
to get out of this hateful city. As soon as Charles is strong enough to bear
the fatigue of travelling, shall either visit you at [Perth Amboy?] or go to
Middletown.[4]

From Horace Johnson's Brown wrote on the nineteenth of September to his brother James:

My excellent friend Dr. Miller dissuades me from going to you. . . .
The number of physicians is rapidly declining, while that of the sick is
as rapidly increasing. Dr. Miller, whose practice, as his skill, exceeds that
of any other physician, is almost weary of a scene of such complicated
horrors.[5]

On the twenty-first Brown wrote to Dunlap:

Well, my beloved friend! It may afford you some satisfaction to recognize my hand once more, though vague and feeble in a degree that astonishes
myself. . . . I do not understand my own case, but see enough to discover
that the combination of bodily and mental causes have made deep inroads
on the vital energies of brain and stomach. I am afraid I cannot think of
departing before Monday at the least.[6]

In answer to a letter from his brother James, urging him to go to
Burlington, New Jersey, to recuperate, Brown said:

The weather has lately changed for the better, and hopes are generally
entertained that the pestilence, for so it may truly be called, will decline. As
to myself, I certainly improve, though slowly, and now entertain very slight
apprehensions of danger to myself. Still I am anxious to leave the city.
To go to Amboy and remain there for some time will be most eligible. This
calamity has endeared the survivors of the sacred fellowship, W. D., W. J.,
and myself to each other in a very high degree; and I confess my wounded
spirit and shattered frame will be most likely to be healed and benefited by
their society. Permit me, therefore, to decline going with you to Burlington—for a little while at least.[7]

[3] *Ibid.*, pp. 7-8.
[4] Dunlap's MS Diary, in Yale University Library.
[5] Dunlap, II, 10.
[6] Dunlap's MS Diary, in Yale University Library.
[7] Dunlap, II, 10.

By September 24 Brown had gained enough strength to journey with his friend William Johnson to Perth Amboy, in New Jersey, from where on September 25 he wrote to his brother James:

It is with great pleasure that I now inform you of my safe arrival at this place. . . . We left the city at two in the afternoon, and after a most auspicious passage arrived at Amboy at sunset. I already feel the sensations of a new being and am restored as it were by magic to a tolerable degree of health and cheerfulness.

Here I wish to stay, at least for some weeks, in the enjoyment of the purest air and wholesome exercise. The change from a pestilential, desolate, and sultry city to the odors and sprightly atmosphere of this village is inexpressibly grateful and beneficial; and I believe you may dismiss all uneasiness henceforth on account of my safety.[8]

Dunlap's *Diary* records, in part, Brown's activities during the next few weeks:

*September 24, 1798:* J. and B. arrive. Brown has quite recovered.

*September 25, 1798:* Walk with my friends. Read the beginning of Charles's last novel, called *Calvert* (proposed to be changed to Caillemour) or "The Lost Brothers."

*September 28, 1798:* Brown tells me the manner in which his mother breaks off his connection with Miss Potts. Brown's brother visits him from Princeton. J. has a letter from Tracey and others at Litchfield partly commissioned by Smith's parents to return thanks and make enquiries. Tracey in a postscript to Horace Johnson says, "Did Smith die a Deist? If you require, the answer will be kept secret." It appears that Mr. and Mrs. S. are anxious on this subject: Johnson is now happy that he can say nothing in answer, for our beloved friend was seized so violently that he was in a stupor until death. . . .

*November 15, 1798:* Brown arrives in N. Y. and stays at Miller's.

*November 24, 1798:* Johnson returns.

*December 6, 1798:* Call on W. Johnson and C. Brown; the latter read me proposals for a Magazine and gave me *Wieland*.

The fall and early winter, for the most part, Brown spent in recovering his physical strength, in listening to Dunlap's plans for a New York theater, and in passing criticism upon some of his friend's dramatic effusions. Brown must have busied himself, too, with "sketching" the novels which were shortly to appear.

### A MAGAZINE AND THE NEW YORK FRIENDLY CLUB

Toward the end of 1798, with health restored, Brown turned again to the projected magazine. In a letter to his brother Armitt, December, 1798, he went into details of plan and management for the magazine and his own financial prospects:

Eight of my friends here, men in the highest degree respectable for literature and influence, have urged me so vehemently to undertake the project of

[8] *Ibid.*, pp. 10-11.

a magazine and promised their contributions and assistance to its success that I have written and published proposals. Four hundred subscribers will repay the annual expense of sixteen hundred dollars. As soon as this number is obtained, the printers will begin and trust to the punctual payment of these for reimbursement. All above four hundred will be clear profit to me; one thousand subscribers will produce four thousand five hundred dollars, and deducting the annual expense will leave two thousand and seven hundred. If this sum be attainable, in a year or two you will allow that my prospect is consoling. The influence of my friends and their unexpected and uncommon zeal inspire me with a courage which I should be unable to derive from any other quarter.

The idea of a magazine as a mouthpiece for the New York Friendly Club had been in the minds of Dunlap, Johnson, and Smith some time before Brown took up his residence in the city. Dunlap recorded in his *Diary* on June 5, 1798: ''See Smith and talk of a weekly magazine for this place, to be printed by the Swords for their emolument, we having all power over it.'' Brown had arrived in New York July 3, 1798. On August 7 Dunlap wrote: ''Breakfast with S., J., and B. Talk over our project of the weekly magazine to be published by Swords under us.'' They were uncertain whether the magazine should be a weekly or a monthly. The original plan for a weekly magazine finally gave way to the idea of a monthly, and Brown was to be its editor.

It is fair to assume that the eight respectable and influential friends of whom Brown writes were members of the New York Friendly Club.[9] As these men were important in determining the direction of Brown's activities for the next few years, let us see who they were. Of several members of the Club there is little available information.[10]

Charles Adams, the second son of President John Adams, practiced law in New York. William W. Woolsey, Esquire, brother-in-law of William Dunlap, was a successful and influential merchant there. John Wells and Anthony Bleecker were both prominent New York lawyers, the latter being master of the Court of Chancery. Samuel Miller, a Doctor of Divinity, was the author of *The Retrospect of the Eighteenth Century* (1803). In this interesting account of the social, scientific, and literary life in England, France, and America,

[9] Concerning literary clubs in New York at this time, information is hazy and fragmentary. From the following sources the interested student may gather such material as is available, though much of it is incorrect or contradictory: William Dunlap, *History of the American Theatre*, I, 114, 220; John W. Francis, *Old New York;* Martha J. Lamb, *History of the City of New York*, I, 468; *Memorial of the Life and Character of John Wells*, pp. 45-46; Samuel Miller, *Life of Samuel Miller*, p. 320, and *Sketch of the Life of Dr. Edward Miller*, I, 8; *New York Mirror*, I, 265-266; James Grant Wilson, *Memorial History of the City of New York*, IV, 233.

[10] For a fuller discussion of the New York Friendly Club see David Lee Clark, ''Brockden Brown's First Attempt at Journalism,'' University of Texas *Studies in English*, no. 7 (1927), pp. 155-174.

the modern reader finds amusing his dire prediction that allowing men and women to work and study and play together "would convert society into hordes of seducers and prostitutes."[11]  Edward Miller, Samuel's older brother, was a physician of note, who began publication of the *Medical Repository* in 1797.  He was one of the early individuals in the medical profession to see the advantage of clinics and of pathological anatomy for medical students.[12]  Samuel Latham Mitchill, a civic-minded physician and United States Senator, helped to establish the New York Institute for the Deaf and Dumb. William Johnson, translator of Azuni's *Sistema universale dei principii del diritto maritimo dell' Europa* (2 vols., N. Y., 1806), served as reporter to the New York Supreme Court and also to the New York Court of Chancery.  James Kent, staunch Federalist and intimate friend of Alexander Hamilton, was a professor of law at Columbia and Chief Justice of the State Supreme Court.  William Dunlap, the chief influence in the introduction of German drama to America, was himself an artist and poet.  Elihu Hubbard Smith, poet and physician, published *American Poems: Selected and Original* (1793), the first noteworthy general collection of poems in the United States.  According to Mrs. Marcia Edgerton Bailey,[13] Smith took part in a "three-cornered poetical correspondence" in the *Gazette*.  The other contributors were "Bertha" (probably Joseph Bringhurst) and "Henry" (who may have been Theodore Dwight, Mason Cogswell, or even—less probably—Brown himself).  Smith as "Ella" contributed twenty-one of the thirty-five poems.

Such in brief was the character of the New York Friendly Club. The significance of the club lies in the fact that on its roster were the names of New York's young intellectuals and her leading professional men.  The versatility, the conservatism, and the sanity here represented worked a most salutary influence upon Brown's rather melancholy cast of thought.  When he left Philadelphia in 1793, a morose, unsocial young man, his mind was definitely made up for the profession of letters; but that mind was full of undigested knowledge and radical tendencies.  Brown needed sorely the stimulus and the corrective of just such a group as the Friendly Club.  Indeed, his intimacy with the members of the club—particularly with Smith, Johnson, and Dunlap—had a formative and an abiding influence on him. In company with them at various informal gatherings, the melancholy Jaques was made to cast his coat.  To the chastening influence of his association with such conservative men as James Kent and Samuel Mitchill, Brown's Journal bears unmistakable witness.  We read: "Last evening spent with the clubbists at K's.  Received from the candor of K. a severe castigation for the crimes of disputatiousness

[11] Dunlap, II, 287.
[12] Howard A. Kelley and Walter L. Burrage, *American Medical Biographies*.
[13] *A Lesser Hartford Wit: Dr. Elihu Hubbard Smith*, p. 44.

and dogmatism.  Hope to profit by the lesson that he taught me.''[14]
The fact that the strongest members of the Friendly Club were staunch
Federalists accounts, in part at least, for Brown's gradual conversion
to more conservative principles.  The influences which were changing
radical Europe into conservative Europe were also at work in America, and Brown reluctantly but candidly acknowledged the change.

The publication of the *Monthly Magazine and American Review*
was deferred, as has been indicated above, by the onslaught of the
yellow-fever epidemic which carried away Smith and endangered the
life of Brown himself.  In a letter to his brother Armitt, December 20,
1798, Brown stated that proposals for the magazine had been published and that if the magazine answered expectations it would commence in February or March, and would be very profitable to him.
A careful search through contemporary newspapers and magazines
from August 1 to December 20, 1798, has not brought the proposals
to light.

### THE PLAN OF THE *MONTHLY MAGAZINE*

The nature of the proposals and some idea of the editor's intentions
can be inferred from a communication, signed ''Candidus'' (perhaps
Brown himself), in the first number of the magazine:

You have undertaken to amuse the world with a monthly publication.  I
hope you will have well considered the difficulties that lie in your way, and
have not forgotten the old fable of the farmer and his ass.  In his eagerness
to please all, he displeased everybody, and most of all himself. . . .  I am far
from thinking that your publication will deserve the fate of the ass; but I
am afraid that such a fate will befall it. . . .

You seem to think that the tastes of all may be gratified.  You promise
to extract the quintessence of European wisdom; to review and estimate the
labors of all writers, domestic and foreign . . . and to speculate on manners
and morals in the style of Addison and Johnson.  You have promised all
this; but you will excuse me if I question your power to perform it. . . .

I cannot conceive what should induce you to promise so much.[15]

Further light is shed upon the original plan of the magazine in a
statement at the close of the first number (April, 1799).  Apparently
Brown's friends had urged him to exclude all political and controversial matter from the pages of the magazine:

Some deviations will appear to have been made from the plan originally
submitted to the public.  Those deviations were adopted after mature reflection, and it is hoped that they will be seen and acknowledged to be just
and proper.  These changes encroach but little on the original scheme, and
were prescribed by a due regard to the opinions of every class of citizens.
There already exists a sufficient number of vehicles of political discussion

---

[14] Dunlap, II, 94.
[15] ''On Periodical Publications,'' *Monthly Magazine*, I (April, 1799), 1-2.

and political information, and it is presumed that readers in general will be best pleased with a performance limited to scientific and literary topics.

Considering the political ferment of the times, with partisanship often verging on violence, one can understand the prudence of avoiding controversial topics.

Much can be learned about the plan and the success of the enterprise from a statement in the Preface to Volume III, January 1, 1800, on the occasion of Brown's quitting the magazine and returning to Philadephia:

*The Monthly Magazine and American Review* was undertaken with a foresight of the many difficulties which might embarrass and impede its progress for a time; but, feeling some confidence in the general excellence of their plan, and relying on the aid of friends and others well disposed to promote the literature of their country, the Editors were not intimidated by the gloomy prospect of the disastrous wreck of former adventures, or discouraged by the predictions of a similar fate, from renewing the experiment, and again trying the strength and durableness of public favor and patronage towards literary projects. Its appearance, too, at a time when no similar publication was known to exist in the United States, was justly deemed a circumstance peculiarly favorable to success.

With no very high expectations, and with no extraordinary efforts to obtain patronage, which has been chiefly voluntary and unsolicited, it cannot be supposed that any disappointment should be felt, if the success of the undertaking has not been hitherto equal to their wishes. The Editors have, indeed, experienced the most flattering species of encouragement, in the approbation bestowed by those whose judgment is a sufficient sanction in favor of any production relative to literature or science. Gratified in being instrumental in the establishment of a work which, from the nature and value of its materials and the respectability of the contributors, might add something to the literary reputation of their country, and tend, in some degree, to refute the censures of foreigners on the apathy and disregard apparently shown by Americans to literature and science, they indulged little expectation of any remuneration for their labors, but as a remote and dubious consequence of the prosperity of the enterprise. . . .

The thin population of the United States renders it impossible to procure sufficient support from any one city; and the dispersed situation of readers, the embarrassments attending the diffusion of copies over a wide extent of country, and the obstacles to a prompt collection of the small sums which so cheap a publication demanded, are, it is presumed, satisfactory reasons for altering and contracting the publication, so as to diminish, if not wholly avoid, those inconveniences. Their own experiences, as well as the observation of respectable friends, has led to a belief that a work chiefly or wholly devoted to literature and science would, in the present condition of the United States, appear more advantageously at less frequent intervals; and that, either as it may regard the Editors, or the Public, a quarter-yearly publication is preferable to one appearing at shorter periods. The completion of the *third* volume of the present work, and the commencement of another year, and a new century, render this a fit time for introducing such a change. . . .

The plan of the magazine, then, was for the most part conventional. There were the usual three sections, Original Communications, Selections, and Poetry.  To these Brown added a new department, The American Review, which became in time the most characteristic section of the magazine, as it was certainly the most important, for it was in the field of literary criticism that Brown was to excel as an editor.

### CONTRIBUTIONS AND CONTRIBUTORS

A fair impression of the nature and variety of the articles that appeared in the magazine may be obtained from an enumeration of the titles or themes of some of them.  There were essays on apparitions, cards, female charitable societies, longevity, punning, shaving, the style of Gibbon, biographical sketches of the leading men and women of the day, with a goodly number touching upon scientific discoveries and inventions.  Some of these articles were so spicy and vigorous that one does not to this day find them tiresome reading. Of course they are lacking in humor, as indeed the whole magazine was; the age was too serious for humor.  Critics often remark on the lack of humor in Brown's works as though it were a quality of style peculiarly wanting in him; they fail to observe that the closing decades of the eighteenth century, both at home and abroad, were strikingly deficient in that saving grace.

It will be observed that the quantity of original matter decreased perceptibly from the beginning.  While there were many and various articles sent to this department, they were of too ephemeral a nature to keep the magazine alive, and the editor more and more found it devolving upon himself to write the leading stories and essays.

While the most significant of the original literary articles were Brown's, the bulk of that department (Original Communications), though commonly attributed to him, was not positively his.  Algernon Tassin states in his very suggestive but not altogether reliable study of the American magazine that Brown was obliged to furnish almost the entire contents of the magazine from his own pen.  A careful study leads to a different conclusion.  It is true that the chief original material was Brown's; but of the fifty-two pieces or series making up the literary department, only four are positively known to be Brown's, although others, possibly a dozen, have been tentatively identified as his, reaching by actual count to slightly more than one-half of the total number of pages.  In three numbers[16] Brown's contribution to the original section is conjectural.  His known contributions during the entire course of the magazine were: "Edgar Huntly, A Fragment"; "Thessalonica—a Roman Story"; "Memoirs of Stephen Calvert";

[16] II, 2; III, 3; III, 6.

and a series of six original letters taken from what Paul Allen called Brown's first romance. Besides these pieces, it is almost certain that a "Lesson in Concealment, or Memoirs of Mary Selwyn," "The Trials of Arden," and two of the "Dialogues of the Living" were by Brown.

Of the actual contributions from the members of the Friendly Club to the magazine disappointingly little can be said. Smith had died before the appearance of the first number, though his poem on the occasion of the opening of the New York theater under Dunlap's management was published in the magazine for June, 1799, and his essays on the Hartford Wits were also printed. Professor Mitchill wrote four articles on the nature of alkalis and one on the anatomy of the shark. Samuel Miller, in a letter printed in the magazine, solicited the aid of all patriotic New Yorkers in his search for materials for a history of the state. Dunlap, from whom Brown must have expected considerable assistance, contributed an insignificant article on Chick Willow and two important ones on the comparative merits of the translations by Elizabeth Inchbald and by Anne Plumptree of Kotzebue's *Lovers' Vows*. No contributions from Johnson, Adams, Wells, Bleecker, or Kent have been identified, though many articles, generally criticisms of contemporary work in science, history, and literature, appear under such unidentified signatures as Francisco, Crito, M, L, N, A (the last Brown sometimes used as a pseudonym), Q, X, and T. Some of these may have been pseudonyms of members of the Friendly Club, but it is certain beyond doubt that no member of that society was a notable contributor to the magazine; and none but Smith and Dunlap became known for literary work.

Of the various contributors only a few were prominent. An article by L. M.—probably Lindley Murray, grammarian and noted literary critic who prepared many Quaker schoolbooks—on the character of Mary Wollstonecraft Godwin, mingling praise and disapprobation, called forth some comment. One of the most frequent contributors was John Davis (1774-1853), the English traveler and writer, who spent seventeen years in the United States.[17] Tutor, translator, bookseller, poet, novelist, and traveler—Davis was truly a jack-of-all-trades and good at none. As Miss Kellogg puts it: "Davis was himself . . . an odd combination of conventional morality and patriotism and conservative literary standards, with the wide tolerance and emotional freshness of his own day."[18] He was master of several languages, ancient and modern, but his favorite appears to have been French. Three of his *Monthly Magazine* articles, though descriptive of his travels in India and in South Carolina, and his voyage from Bristol to New York, were written in that language.

[17] For an excellent study of this writer, see Thelma Louise Kellog, *The Life and Works of John Davis*.
[18] *Ibid.*, p. 21.

It will be noticed that from the beginning the "American Review" section was vigorous and showed keen insight into the literary problems of the day. It was in this department that Brown evinced the greatest skill, and it was this section of the magazine that attracted most attention. Many of the reviews were unsigned, and while it would be unwarranted to assume that they were from Brown's pen, as editor and as frequent rewriter he would at any rate be to a degree responsible for them.

That Brown felt at home in the field of criticism is evidenced by the fact that the "American Review" bulked larger with each succeeding number. For the first few issues the "Review" averaged about ten pages per number, but it was gradually increased until in the last two volumes thirty of the eighty pages making up the magazine were devoted to that department. It became the most powerful as well as the most efficiently conducted section of the *Monthly Magazine*. Among the more important reviews were those of Benjamin Trumbull's *Complete History of Connecticut;* Benjamin Smith Barton's *New View of the Tribes and Nations of North America;* William Robertson's *History of America;* Count Rumford's *Essays: Political, Economical, and Philosophical* (a review of twenty-eight pages covering a most important scientific field and stimulating a renewed interest in farming and good government) ; Robert Proud's *History of Pennsylvania;* and Jeremy Belknap's *American Biography.* Undoubtedly the contribution that called forth the greatest stir was a letter to the editor from Noah Webster in defense of his *History of Pestilence,* which had been unfavorably reviewed by Brown. Review of contemporary English and American poetry was both extensive and discriminating. Brown's work as a reviewer will be dealt with in some detail in another chapter.

The poetry of the magazine was not particularly extensive, nor was it notable for quality. There were on the average two pages of poetry in each number, divided into "Original" and "Selected." But it is hard, often impossible, to determine what poems were original and what were not. The quality of the poetry that was unquestionably original was good as a rule, but there was nothing in it to lift it above the good brown earth. Of the eighty-odd poems in the magazine, thirty-three were by John Davis, seven by Richard Alsop—largely translations from the Latin and the Italian—five by Cowper, and the rest by numerous other writers. The meter and diction were of that transition variety between the purely neoclassic and the new romantic poetry. The heroic couplet was much in favor, and the moralizing tone was more prominent than in contemporary British verse of the same quality. Brown said of the poems of Davis that they had "merit seldom to be found in the fugitive compositions of contemporary poets. Simplicity and tenderness are their characteristics." The translations of Latin and Italian poems by Richard Alsop, the editor felt to be of superior quality. These included the "Oath of Hannibal" and the "Description of Hannibal," both from the Latin; and "A Song," from the Italian.

The section known as "Selected" took the whole world for its province. About fifteen pages of each number were allotted to this division, and the material was taken largely from English journals, with German and French also well represented. These selections are interesting, if for no other reason than that they give an idea of what generally pleased Brown and the public. In most cases the sources of the articles were indicated. There were memoirs of Cumberland, Hannah More, Cowper, Bürger, and other prominent personages. Much material of a scientific nature was extracted from European publications.

In Volume II an important department known as "Literary and Philosophical Intelligence"—both domestic and foreign—was added. This is valuable as a record of the literary and scientific happenings of the day; in fact these observations were often nothing less than short reviews in which the editor summarized the contents of the productions and sat in judgment. In writing of Dennie's essays, he reminded the public that, although the *Lay-Preacher* and *Farrago* were American, they had considerable intrinsic value and much individual merit. Another notice read: "Peter Pindar, with whose inimitable productions in *verse* the public have been delighted many years, is preparing a satirical work in *prose*, in the manner of a novel, of which Dennie speaks highly." On the appearance of the first number of Dennie's *Port Folio*, with its ambitious promise to devote its pages to Federal politics, to wit, to storytelling, to argument, to original essays, etc., Brown generously remarked:

Every lover of his country must smile upon efforts of this kind; and their repeated failure hitherto, while it is a subject of generous regret to the wise, should be a stimulus to patronage.[19]

In the February (1800) number a Theatrical Register of the New York (Park Street) Theatre was introduced. This feature did not recur until the November (1800) number, with report of the opening night of the theatrical season. A study of the offerings revealed the "double feature" program, usually consisting of a Shakespearean drama or a translation of a foreign play and a modern English or American production. William Dunlap figured prominently as a playwright and as a translator of foreign plays.

In speaking of the plays of Kotzebue, Brown deplored the hasty and inaccurate translations of that popular dramatist. He remarked that it was in "vain to look for Kotzebue's play either in the transla-

[19] "Port Folio," *Monthly Magazine,* III (Oct., 1800), 312.

tion or alteration.  To show the gross ignorance and stupidity of many of those translators from the German who have seized the pen and dictionary at the instigation of hunger and the call of fashion, we will mention a passage in the translation noticed above [Dunlap's] which we confess affords us no small amusement.''  The defects were then pointed out in detail, without, apparently, alienating the friendship of Dunlap.

The theater was open on Monday, Wednesday, and Friday nights; the audience, to judge from a contemporary article, obtained full value for their money (one dollar an evening) :

> The privilege of sitting, for four hours, in a crowd of all ages and degrees; in the midst of glaring lights, occasional clappings and hisses, with a motley and varying scene before you, cannot be enjoyed for nothing.[20]

### FOSTERING A NATIVE LITERATURE

Perhaps the most significant aspect of the magazine is the picture it affords of Brown's views on topics with which he was vitally concerned—particularly the question of a native literature.  We find a good deal, in both articles and reviews, about American literature, all branches of learning (especially science), American customs and attitudes, American history and politics.  Although he had expressly said that he would religiously exclude political discussions, he permitted a modicum of strictly partisan material.

As one of the first exponents of a native American literature, Brown made the issue a live one.  Native literature was in an unenviable condition at the turn of the century.  One article, signed *Candidus,* presents a vivid picture of the literature (or lack of it).  There were no professional authors in the United States, charged the writer.  Brown (if he wrote the essay) was evidently having fun at his own expense, for it was during this period that he was trying hard to be a professional himself.  Considering the lack of financial encouragement accorded to authors, the writer continued, it was understandable why men should not write for the sheer love of authorship.  In the sixteen years since independence, fewer than a hundred books on all subjects had been published.  There were hundreds of orations, sermons, and pamphlets on scientific and political subjects, but practically no poetry or other creative writing.  The most popular works seemed to be ''political invectives.''  The author's only regret was that there were so many of them.[21]

American magazines were also having a hard time, said Brown in the Preface to the February (1800) number.  They were admittedly inferior to those of Europe; they usually started small, and dwindled, but editors would soon learn and they should be encouraged in their

[20] ''The Men Worth Fifty Dollars,'' *ibid.*, p. 401.

[21] Candidus, ''On American Literature,'' *Monthly Magazine,* I (Aug., 1799), 340.

efforts.   To charge that "in America genius is a lowly, wild, and neglected shrub" was unfair, he insisted in another article.   Americans were too modest about their literary abilities:

> It has been frequent, of late years, with some writers to decry all the literary productions of their contemporaries, and to deny the votaries of literature in America every claim to genius, wit, or erudition.   If Americans possessed an inordinate vanity in this respect, it might be useful, perhaps, to repress or correct it, by asserting the folly of such vain pretensions; but the national vanity seems to be rather *political* than literary.[22]

The lack of books and magazines was certainly not due to the fact that Americans were not interested in reading.   They were a nation of readers, but principally of newspapers, avidly following news of national politics as well as of foreign affairs.

As to the question of remuneration for authorship, in a compact and vigorous essay Brown very justly reminded an irate writer that authorship seldom had been, in any age or in any country, a facile source of wealth and power:

> It would not be difficult to point out the causes why *authorship* is not a *profession,* and book-making a *trade* here, as well as in Great Britain, France, or Germany, and to prove that Americans are not endowed with less genius or less intellectual capacity and vigor than their fellow-beings on the other side of the Atlantic.   But such an inquiry would lead us out of our province; and we must be content, for the present, with some brief strictures on the passages which have been quoted.

> The complaints of *neglected merit* and genius *starving* with want are at this time almost stale; and, in general, few complaints are made with so little foundation in truth or reason.   They are too often the offspring of a disordered fancy, indolence, fastidiousness, or caprice.   In no country, are the paths of literature and science the direct avenues to wealth and power. The modest and retired votaries of learning and science must be content with the humble but dignified state they have chosen.   To repine at the want of opulence and power, while they disdain the only sure means by which they can be attained, discovers a childish folly which expects the laws of nature to be changed to gratify its impatient longings.

> If riches are the object of desire, they are within the reach of all who will grovel, with toilsome perseverance, in their pursuit.   If ambitious to lodge in a palace, or be drawn in a chariot, the closet must be exchanged for the countinghouse; Homer and Longinus, for the Lex Mercatoria and Daily Gazette.   He who aspires to a seat in the Senate must not support his claim to the suffrages of the people by proving his knowledge of the art of poetry, his skill in music, or his acquaintance with chemistry.   The man of action, not of contemplation, he who is ready to devote his days and nights with laborious diligence to the concerns of others is the person who will be selected for the management of their affairs and on whom they will bestow honor and

[22] Article LX (American Review), *Monthly Magazine,* III (Dec., 1800), 426-427.

profit, the rewards of his activity and meal.  He who will not thus devote his talents to the service of others in things which regard their immediate interest must be content to enjoy the admiration of the few and the pleasures which flow from the cultivation of his taste and understanding.[23]

Although there was a serious dearth of good poetry, Brown stoutly denied that America was incapable of producing it.  In fact it was his exuberant faith in what America held for the future rather than what she had actually accomplished in the literary field that characterized Brown's undying loyalty to his country and his lasting service to those of aspiring hope.  Read this astute but generous observation:

As Americans who feel a solicitude for the literary fame of our country-men, we wish ever to be among the first to announce and applaud the elegant productions of domestic genius.  We disclaim acquiescence in the opinion which some have had the freedom to declare that the atmosphere of America is ungenial to the spirit of poetry; and that, like Lord Chesterfield's fine gentleman, we must be content to listen to the music of strangers, without ever venturing to fiddle for ourselves.

We must, however, acknowledge that although our country can boast of several writers who have become entitled to the honors appropriated to the excelling bard, poetry is by no means as yet our staple commodity.[24]

America had, Brown maintained, ample and sufficient cause for inspiration within her own borders to call forth truly noteworthy poetry.  For instance, George Washington had become an inspiring symbol to Americans to awaken their "sleeping Muse," and his death the occasion for many poetic tributes.

An impartial observer cannot but highly approve of the unanimity with which the tribute of public veneration has been paid to this illustrious man. It is hoped that the honor of our country will be raised by the strains of eloquence and poetry which this occasion will call forth.  Pageantry and dirges, though suitable, are transitory and imperfect testimonies of our hom-age, and to genius must be committed the office of imparting to the world at large and to posterity faithful pictures of the sentiments which the memory of WASHINGTON excited in the hearts of his contemporaries and of those who have witnessed his achievements and partaken of his benefits.[25]

In noticing a particularly eloquent oration by Gouverneur Morris on Washington, Brown again published his faith:

From a tribute of mere eloquence, it might thus by versification be changed into homage of poetry, and might convince the sceptical world that, as Amer-ica produces heroes that engross all possible virtue and all conceivable wis-dom, she likewise nourishes poets that possess all the treasures of the muse.[26]

[23] Article LV (American Review), *Monthly Magazine*, I (Dec., 1800), 427-428.
[24] Article XXXIV (American Review), *Monthly Magazine*, III (Oct., 1800), 226.
[25] "Death of General Washington," *Monthly Magazine*, I (Dec., 1799), 447.
[26] Article (American Review), *Monthly Magazine*, II (Feb., 1800), 122.

The increasing number of "original sermons" afforded Brown the doubtful comfort that our literary independence was established in at least one field. But he by no means believed that native productions should be unqualifiedly and fulsomely praised simply because they were American. If they were bad, it was the critic's duty to say so, in the hope of stimulating more successful efforts. But this honest and forthright denunciation of mediocrity aroused not so much the sleeping muse of genuine poetry as it did the sleeping dogs of a cheap and blatant chauvinism. Why, one injured author was sarcastically represented as complaining (in the person of one *Americanus*), should American writings be judged by strict European standards? Did not the editor realize that America had her own language and her own standards? There was even "an American size of genius, corresponding to our youthful standing in the republic of letters. . . ." And finally, in a particularly pungent paragraph, Brown (if our ascription to him is correct) poured out his wrath on the sort of blind isolationism and boastfulness which have continued for more than a hundred and fifty years:

Sir, . . . we are a young country, and what is more, we are an *independent* country. . . . What though arguments be erroneous, unavailing, or ridiculous? What though the bathos and the bombastic perpetually alternate in our compositions? . . . Pray let us alone—we wish to be independent of all the world, in a literary as well as in a political sense. Such independence cannot be secured but by our adopting many peculiarities; and we hope nothing will be done by your critics in future to abridge our privileges . . . to prevent their being transmitted, inviolate, to our most distant posterity.

Brown welcomed the numerous books of sermons then pouring from the press as a sign that American ministers were vying with English divines in producing professional literature. He reviewed these works, criticizing them for content as well as form. He seldom took issue with their points of doctrine, but he did with broad-minded dignity protest against dogmas that he considered too narrow. Brown, sensing the interdependence of morals and religion in our national and international dealings, approved of those writings which stressed virtue and practical morality rather than those of a purely controversial nature; he ridiculed Noah Webster's theory that epidemics were a visitation of the wrath of an avenging God. In all that Brown wrote or said we detect the deeply religious and kindly tolerance of the Quaker that he was at heart.

Apparently the Rousseauistic idea of national standards versus the classical requirement of universality had gained some converts in America even at this early date, though Mme de Staël did not give it full critical expression until 1810, in *De l'Allemagne*.[27] Brown, how-

---

[27] Rousseau had first advanced the theory of historical relativism: that a writer is an inevitable product of his own age and country and is not to be judged by

ever, believed in universal, objective standards of taste; and, far from being too harsh with second-rate American writers, he protested that he was really doing both them and his country a genuine service by insisting on high standards of excellence. If strangers should read these productions, would they not, he queried, form a wrong idea of American ability and taste? Beware, Americans, of merely following European models or interlarding your work with classical quotations to show your erudition. Oh, countrymen, the time will come when you may justly prefer your native literature to a mixture of foreign.

### AMERICAN CUSTOMS AND MANNERS

Like all periodicals of the time, the *Monthly Magazine* displayed interest in contemporary customs and manners by admitting to its pages essays on shaving, hair powder, cards, styles, conversation, and so on. But aside from these conventional subjects, Brown was much concerned about more important customs. Of some, transplanted from Europe, he heartily disapproved, such as government lotteries. His Quaker upbringing rebelled against government authorization of lotteries, which to him were particularly pernicious gambling devices. But let us listen to Brown's thunderous Jeremiad:

As a mode of taxation it is unequal, oppressive, and unjust, falling principally upon the industrious poor. It is a legislative act for the encouragement of vice. It is a lure held out by the guardians of the people's morals (for such legislators are, or ought to be), to entice the mechanic and the husbandman to enter the lists as adventurers, speculators, and gamblers, turning their minds from the rational hopes of profit flowing from their usual wholesome and virtuous employment, to chimerical and ruinous visions, which change their habits, debase their souls, and often end in utter destruction. That this evil should flow from the lawgivers of the land is deplorable beyond all calculation; among the collateral mischiefs, a disrespect for the laws and the magistrate is not among the least. The loss of the first cost of a ticket is to the generality of those who purchase a serious evil; yet, happy is he who having once adventured escapes with simply that inconvenience. The farmer or tradesman, fully impressed with the idea that there is roguery in the management of all lotteries, leaves his profitable employment to attend the drawing; leaves his home, neglects his business, and, by the time his ticket comes up a blank, has increased its price many fold. In large cities, the encouragement which lotteries give to every kind of knavery is notorious; and their fatal effects upon adventurers have been the theme of many a heartrending tale. Lottery offices are opened in every street, and under the pretense of insuring numbers, &c. &c. ten thousand little lotteries or gaming schemes are made to depend upon the great one, and the wretch whose poverty would have

---

standards of the past. This was to become the chief rule of the romanticists, and Mme de Staël elaborated on it: " 'The rules . . . are only barriers to keep children from falling,' . . . genius is to be purely effusive and the critic, instead of serving as a check on genius, is only to enter sympathetically and comprehensively into its effusions" (Irving Babbitt, *Masters of Modern French Criticism*, p. 17).

excluded him from the participation of the evil on the great plan, is thus
sucked into the whirlpool and loaded with irretrievable misery.[28]

Another custom against which Brown poured out his wrath whenever and wherever the chance arose was dueling—a custom he laid
squarely at the door of our European ancestors:

Seduction and murder by duel are the remnants of the ancient manners of
Europe.  These have sometimes been more politely styled gallantry and the
point of honor; and such is the influence of names that gallantry and honor
are soft and inoffensive sounds, though their acceptation be precisely similar
to seduction and murder.

It is sufficiently manifest that these vices have accompanied the Europeans
across the ocean, and that the colony cannot boast of an exemption, in this
respect, from the faults of the mother country.  The degree in which these
crimes prevail in America, and the difference, in this respect, between the
integrity of the parent and the offspring, are questions difficult of solution.

Seduction is a secret guilt: there is no scale, therefore, by which its prevalence can be estimated either in Europe or America.  Duels, on the contrary,
though projected secretly are generally, when accomplished with or without
bloodshed, extremely notorious.  The parties, or their friends, commonly
think their honor concerned in telling the story to the world through the
medium of some newspaper.  In other cases popular curiosity is gratified by
the voluntary diligence of newsmen.

The number of duels is perhaps not of such moment, in a picture of manners, as the rank and condition of the duelist; but in neither case have Americans cause to boast.  Their most illustrious characters, those among the highest in reputation and in office, have either been actually engaged in duels,
or shown on different occasions a perfect promptitude to take up arms at
honor's bidding.  In Great Britain we find, in the catalogue of duelists, such
names as Grattan, Lansdowne, Fox, Pitt, and the Duke of York.

As to the number of encounters of this sort, Great Britain and Ireland
may safely be said not to furnish thirty instances in a year; but ten instances
in the United States constitute an extremely moderate computation.  The
British Isles are at least three times more populous than these States.  Hence
it appears that so far as the folly and depravity of national manners may be
estimated by the frequency of duels, and the prevalence of that principle
which leads to them, the United States, if it cannot bear away the palm of
infamy from all other nations, is at least upon a level with the corruptest of
them.[29]

Less fiery, though not less disapproving, was Brown's attitude
toward insincerity, a subject on which he wrote frequently and earnestly.[30]  In the *Speculatist*, II,[31] he complained that one seldom could

[28] "Dialogues of the Living," *Monthly Magazine*, I (April, 1799), 20-21.

[29] "The Point of Honor in America," *Monthly Magazine*, III (Dec., 1800), 408-409.

[30] "Journal," Letter to J—— D——n.

[31] Brown's authorship of the *Speculatist* is uncertain, but the views here expressed coincide so closely with those in the "Journal" that it is reasonably safe
to assign these essays to his pen.

hear a person's real views expressed. For example, he had the Speculatist cite a conversation he had heard regarding Mary Wollstonecraft's *Rights of Women*. One young lady who was incapable of reading anything requiring thought, nevertheless took her cue from one of the men and declared that she enjoyed the treatise. The other young woman, who really had read the book and admired it, did not dare to give her real opinion, for someone had remarked on the "indelicacies" of the author's frank speech. Of her Brown remarked:

Her greatest error is a punctilious nicety in regard to everything which sickly minds have sanctified with the name of delicacy. Her understanding is sufficiently awake to the merits of the authoress; she thinks that the volume contains a display of genius which adds lustre to the female character; her whole soul assents to the justness and force of Miss Wollstonecraft's eloquence; but on this occasion to express her admiration of a work that was styled indelicate, she felt to be impossible. She therefore chose to debase the purity of her mind with a falsehood rather than to incur the terrible opprobrium of indelicacy.

Interested though he was in American manners, Brown nevertheless considered it next to impossible for anyone, even a native, to give an all-inclusive description of them.[32] On this head he observed:

A picture of American manners! A view of our social, domestic, economical state! Such as foreign and future observers, as well as contemporary ones, shall point to and say, "This is the scene displayed by four millions of actors on the vast stage bounded by the ocean, Florida, Mississippi, and St. Lawrence, for the three lustrums ensuing the revolution, which made the Anglo-Belgico-Teutonico-North-Americans a nation." Are you aware of the many difficulties attending such a scheme?

Only reflect upon the motleyness, the endless variety of habits, ranks, and conditions in our country. The theatre itself is too wide for you to traverse: a thousand miles one way and fifteen hundred the other: various in climate from the ceaseless ardors of the tropics to the horrors of the arctic winter; divided into near a score of separate states, in each of which there are very great peculiarities of constitution and laws; each of which has climate, soil, productions, distributions of property and rank somewhat different from those of its neighbors.

One could not hope, continued Brown, as some European travelers did, to learn the customs and thoughts of Americans by merely traveling through the country, but one must live intimately with the inhabitants; Americans were not just merely transplanted Europeans: new conditions had made them a new people. In the same essay, with keen analytical insight Brown set up standards for judging personal and national characteristics, and by implication condemned the casual sojourner from Europe who spent a day here and a day there, then rushed back home and spawned a book on the national life.

[32] "On a Scheme for Describing American Manners," *Monthly Magazine*, III (July, 1800), 7-10.

It is true we derive little primarily from our own soil. We are all emigrants, or the progeny of emigrants from Europe and Africa. Thence came our language, dress, building, furniture, maxims of lucrative, sexual, and social intercourse, and modes of literature, avarice, and ambition; but these our new situation has considerably modified. Directly or derivatively we are English, French, German, and Dutch, it is true; but we or our fathers have entered into new relations of property and government by crossing the ocean, and these relations have had an influence on our character proportioned to their diversity from those which still betide the inhabitants of France, Holland, and Great Britain.

The merchant, the farmer, the mechanic, the man of liberal profession, and the servant, are in every country distinct from each other. Some personal circumstances, likewise, exist to make one of each class different from every other; but in a nation, divided like ours into numerous subordinate communities of such diverse modes and constitutions, the rank or profession itself is widely different in different places.

The influence of religion, likewise, is not to be forgotten. In America, every branch into which Christianity has shot out grows and flourishes with equal freedom from restraint. Manners and habits are greatly influenced by religious sentiments. How shall that influence be ascertained but by close, intimate, domestic observation?

Even if a man were to collect a great many facts, such as prices of all sorts of items, ways of sowing and planting and manufacturing, he still would be

far from knowing the social, moral, and intellectual condition of the people. He has acquired what, indeed, is necessary to perfect knowledge, but what constitutes the smallest part of what is necessary. These do not inform him what modifications of opinion, religious, moral, or political, prevail; what notions of duty, and honor, and decorum govern us; how men treat their neighbors, their parents, their wives, their offspring; with what eyes they survey external nature, and what the vice or virtue that adheres to, and what happiness or misery flows from, the settled tenor of their actions or reflections. If you ask how this knowledge is to be obtained, I answer, by coming, as it were, in contact with their actions and their principles; by hearing them talk, and seeing them act.

What echoes of these opinions have been heard since novelists of the "new regionalism" began complaining about the sometimes superficial methods of the nineteenth-century local color writers! But if descriptions must be written, Brown continued, they could best be done by a native:

He himself is a product of the soil, is a sample of the beings which a North American climate, government, and education, will produce. Those who are inquisitive as to their effects will closely and eagerly examine him, and he may contribute much to improve the science of human nature, and somewhat to a picture of his age and country, by minutely and faithfully portraying himself.

If Brown was dubious about the possibility of an adequate portrayal of American life, he was firmly opposed to the idea of an American language. He ridiculed Noah Webster's attempts to reform spelling and to make undue distinctions between the speech of Englishmen and of Americans. In his review of Webster's *Brief History of Epidemic and Pestilential Diseases*, he remarked:

Mr. W. will incur some censure . . . for while he is always and minutely careful to cut off a vowel from the end of some his words, (*famin, determin,* etc.) which ordinary writers retain, he is unreasonably negligent in more important matters. . . .[33]

He also gave temperate but definite expression to his opinions in the essay "On the Scheme of an American Language."

What is called the *amor patriae,* the national spirit, operates with wonderful force and in many ways. As to the rectitude and usefulness of this passion, it can only be approved, like other passions, when strictly disciplined and limited.

.    .    .    .    .    .    .    .    .    .    .    .

I have lately had occasion to observe the influence of this spirit in one of its most remarkable and faulty forms. Some of those among us who devote themselves to letters are extremely anxious that, as we are politically independent and distinct from other nations, we should likewise be so in literature and language. They are ambitious of obtaining not only a national individuality in policy and jurisdiction, not only a government that shall be American, but likewise an American *language.* For this end, they think grammars and dictionaries should be compiled by natives of the country, not the British or English, but of the *American* tongue.[34]

One trouble with the world, he said, was that there were too many languages and too much isolationism already. In the following paragraph he was prophetic:

Nothing more delights and exalts the imagination than the thought of all mankind talking and writing one language; and I, for my part, have reflected upon few things with more pleasure than what may with good reason be predicted, the diffusion of the English lineage and language through the whole extent of North America, and over hundreds of millions of the human race. Instead of any efforts to insulate ourselves from our ancestors and contemporaries in this respect, we should direct all our labors to the opposite purpose.[35]

Those misguided patriots, Brown insisted, who would pay heed to every trifling "dialecticism" would be hard put to it to determine what words should be considered American, for the speech of the New Englander is as different from that of the Georgian as the Virginian

[33] *Monthly Magazine,* II (April, 1800), 296.
[34] *Monthly Magazine,* III (July, 1800), 1-4.
[35] Article XIX (American Review), *Monthly Magazine,* I (Aug., 1799), 365.

dialect is from the Pennsylvanian. The very name "America" was a misnomer, he reminded the reader, for the United States really occupied, not America, but only "a small portion of its north-eastern coast." By all means he insisted, let us add our own distinctive words and new meanings of old ones to the language, but let us remember that it is still the *English* language.

### SCIENCE TO BE ENCOURAGED

Always interested in science, as were the leading men of the age, Brown carried this interest into his magazine. Every issue contained several articles of scientific interest, some of them running to five or six pages. In Volume I, for instance, of the fifty-four "Original Communications," eighteen were on scientific subjects; of the forty-three "Selected" articles, thirty were on scientific subjects. These articles showed an amazing catholicity of taste, dealing as they did with everything from alkalies to volcanoes, and treating with unusual thoroughness the nature of animals, from elephants to earthworms.

Brown also gave ample space to the activities of the American Philosophical Society, which afford an interesting commentary on the diversity of their projects. The Society as an institution, he maintained, was of great value to the new nation. Items in nearly every field of science found lodging in his magazine, from "Mr. Jefferson's mould-board plough" to the orbits of planets. The Society gave regular prizes for the best essays on the "promotion of knowledge and happiness."

Brown's lifelong interest in geography was reflected in the inclusion of numerous selected articles describing various foreign countries, as well as the essay, "On the Prevailing Ignorance of Geography." After citing amusing examples of people's lack of geographical information, Brown admitted that the study of geography, like that of any other science, was of no particular value unless related to the whole field of human knowledge.

He hailed joyously every new advancement in any field whatever. New books on astronomy, navigation, chemistry, biology alike aroused his interest and awakened a hope that our scientific horizon would be so enlarged and so broadened that America would soon take her place among the nations as a center of achievement of the human mind. Brown had no fear in pushing back the mental horizon: neither his religion nor his pocketbook—the two enemies of progress—would he allow to stand in the way of the onward march of the human spirit. Man must be free, and freedom can come only through knowledge. From this attitude of his the troglodytes of his day recoiled as if stung by an adder. Money-making must not be hampered by improvements, unless those improvements fetch in more money. Then, as now, the cavemen were busy keeping from the market, no matter what the cost in human welfare, those scientific improvements that would lead to the scrapping of the old with the consequent loss of capital. Brown had only scorn for the narrow-mindedness that led one orator to ridicule new inventions. With equal fervor he defended Thomas Jefferson's interest in science—in paleontology in particular—which led men like Gouverneur Morris to ridicule Jefferson. He condemned "that general, comprehensive, unqualified censure which distinguishes the uninformed, uncandid, and less cultivated portion of society."[36] Some investigations, he admitted, might seem impractical, but any thoughtful person would realize that theory must always precede actual accomplishment.

### AGRICULTURE AND THE GOOD LIFE

Agriculture, Brown claimed, was the basis of all wealth and of all human welfare. In a review of a book by J. B. Bordley[37] he pronounced his agricultural creed, which was essentially the agrarian philosophy of Thomas Jefferson. Like Jefferson, Brown called for a progressive, scientific approach to the problems of agriculture; like Jefferson he maintained that

A prosperity built on the basis of agriculture is that which is most desirable to us, because to the efforts of labor it adds the efforts of a greater proportion of the soil.

Agriculture is our wisest pursuit because it will in the end contribute most to real wealth, good morals, and happiness.

We have now lands enough to employ an infinite number of people in their cultivation. Cultivators of the earth are the most valuable citizens. They are the most vigorous, the most independent, the most virtuous, and they are tied to their country, and welded to its liberty and interests, by the most lasting bonds.[38]

I am conscious that an equal division of property is impracticable. But the consequences of this enormous inequality producing so much misery to the bulk of mankind, legislators cannot invent too many devices for subdividing property. . . . The earth is given as a common stock for man to labor and live on. . . . It is not too soon to provide by every possible means that as few as possible shall be without a little portion of land. The small land holders are the most precious part of a state.[39]

Brown's words, indeed, have a prophetically modern ring to them —listen to this Henry Wallace of the eighteenth century:

The present age has been emphatically called the age of improvement. In nothing has the spirit of amelioration been more strikingly manifested, or more usefully exerted, than in the increase and extension of agricultural knowledge. By the unwearied industry and laborious researches of . . . eminent agriculturists in Great Britain, a prodigious collection of useful facts

[36] Article XXI, *ibid.*, 370.
[37] "Essays and Notes on Husbandry and Rural Affairs," *ibid.*, pp. 439-42.
[38] Edward Boykin, *The Wisdom of Thomas Jefferson*, p. 109.
[39] *Ibid.*, p. 112.

and important local information has been made; and agriculture, which before the present age was debased by prejudice and enchained by ignorance, is now elevated into a rank among the sciences, and receives the liberal aid of her sisters in philosophy.

The United States, as well from their colonial origin and progress as their maritime situation, seem unavoidably destined to be a great commercial nation. But the state of their interior and the immense extent of rich and cultivable soil which it comprehends at the same time indicate that the great majority of the people must be powerfully impelled to become cultivators of the earth. We might here indulge in much pleasing speculation on the future condition of America, but we must restrain our imagination and forbear the expression of our wishes or anticipations and attend to the subject immediately before us.

The rude state of American agriculture has been often remarked by ingenious European travellers in our country. That our farmers persevere in many agricultural practices which have been exploded, and neglect to adopt better and more profitable modes which have received the test of experience in France, Italy, and Great Britain, cannot be denied. Yet the husbandry of the United States, though faulty when compared with that of Europe, may be easily accounted for and in many instances justified from peculiar local circumstances. And whoever impartially and candidly considers the situation of this extensive region, over which the inhabitants are so sparsely scattered, will not think the American husbandmen deserving of all the censure which has been bestowed upon them by some of their European visitants. There is a great difference between a *new* and an *old* country: and allowance must be made for diversities of climate, soil, situation, population, and numerous other local circumstances. But, although we are disposed to vindicate our farmers from the precipitate judgments of superficial and hasty observers, yet we are far from supposing that they are in no need of improvement.

They have *much* yet to learn; and the progressive settlement and population of the country demands a correspondent change and amelioration of their systems of husbandry. For this purpose they ought to be acquainted not only with what has been done in Europe but with the experiments which have been made by intelligent men in their own country.

The number of these experiments should be multiplied, and the different series of operations should be recorded, collected, and made public. The basis of the science of agriculture must be *facts,* and the more extensive the collection the more solid will be the super-structure.

### FOSTERING AMERICAN HISTORICAL WRITING

Historical writing also found a place in the *Monthly Magazine.* There were a few essays both in the "Original Communications" and the "Selected" departments, but Brown's enthusiasm showed itself chiefly in his reviews of histories. Regarding Benjamin Trumbull's *A Complete History of Connecticut,* he said:

The progress of the American States from small and obscure colonies to their present respectable station as independent and confederated Republics is an object of very just curiosity to all who take delight in contemplating the history of human society. . . .  The author of this work, therefore, has made a present to his countrymen, which, from its very *subject,* will secure, we doubt not, a large share of their attention and patronage.

There are few parts of our country which furnish matter for more instructive history or more lucid examples and proofs of the importance of virtue and religion to the preservation of public tranquillity and the promotion of public happiness.  In this point of view, a good history of Connecticut has for some time been a desideratum in the literature of America.[40]

Condemning the employment of "vague tradition" so common in historical writing, Brown applauded the author's careful use of factual source material—a practice, he added sagely, "which we trust will be followed by the future historians of America."

He was sure that American readers would gladly welcome another, more ambitious, historical work on America: *The History of America,*[41] by the distinguished contemporary Scottish historian, William Robertson:

The history of our native country will always deserve to be of chief moment in our eyes; and the discussion of this subject by the most eloquent historian of modern times cannot fail to afford us uncommon gratification.

Brown remarked on the "petty causes" leading to the discovery and settlement of America.  And yet the establishment of the colonies turned out to be "the greatest event in the history of mankind."  He revealed his own intellectual interests when he recommended the work, in the review of the above history, "to the study of all those who desire the knowledge of their native country, who are curious observers of mankind, or who delight in contemplating the productions of genius and taste."

The self-consciousness of Americans at this period of "the Great Experiment" is echoed in Brown's review of Hannah Adams's *A Summary History of New-England.*:[42]

The history of our native country justly merits the highest place in our regard; if not on account of the magnitude and singularity of its revolutions, yet for the unbounded influence of these revolutions on the happiness of us and our posterity.  It constitutes an instructive and inestimable spectacle, because we are fully qualified to understand it; because its lessons are of indispensable use in teaching us our duty as citizens of a free state, as guardians of our own liberty and happiness, and of those of that part of mankind who are placed within the sphere of our activity and are best entitled to our affection and beneficence.

However, he was worried over the fact that, though many histories of various colonies and of the revolution had been written, original source materials might be lost forever:

[40] Article I (American Review), *Monthly Magazine,* I (April, 1799), 45.

[41] Article IV, *ibid.* (May, 1799), 130-132.

[42] Article XXVIII, *ibid.* (Sept.-Dec., 1799), 445-449.

National occurrences since that period remain, for the most part, still dispersed in public offices, fugitive pamphlets, diurnal gazettes, and in private manuscript collections; and an historian of the United States, in the fullest sense of that term, is still wanting.

He approved of the action of certain patriotic Bostonians who had established the Massachusetts Historical Society in order to preserve "rich materials for the natural and civil history of the United States" that might otherwise have been destroyed. He urged that other states either form similar societies or consider the Boston society a national institution "and make it the grand repository of our historical treasures. . . ."[43]

### PARTY POLITICS TO BE ESCHEWED

On the question of politics Brown was cautious. In a period of intense political feeling, when ferocious journalistic attacks on opponents were accepted as a matter of course, Brown declined to take part in the conflict and closed the pages of his magazine to partisan communications—to invective and name-calling in particular. His magazine, he insisted, was to remain nonpartisan—a difficult status to maintain, he was soon to learn. For, as the acid-tongued but shrewd Candidus (who, as has been suggested, may have been Brown himself) said in the opening Communication:

If you aim to shun the evil by studying a medium between opposite opinions, or, as mediums are hard to hit, content yourself with stating mere facts, and suppress all reflections, you will gain the repute of a time-serving, equivocal, or lukewarm wretch. If you drop politics altogether, matters will be worse still; you will not be criticised indeed, but then you will not be read.[44]

Again, in Number 2 of his "Dialogues of the Living," Brown expressed the dilemma of the editor:

With respect to *politics,* I should be glad, myself, to see a part of the work devoted to this subject. But here, also, there is a difficulty still more formidable. What can the Editor do? If he should open his mouth to utter a political sentiment, however moderately and discreetly it might be delivered, he would not fail to offend one half his readers. Nay, some of them have been already offended at his taking notice of different political characters and writers with respect in a literary view. I know several who were angry at his inserting *Clery's* account of the imprisonment and death of the King of France among his selections, which they considered as a proof that he regretted the fate of that unfortunate monarch, and was therefore a royalist in his heart. Others, and a still greater number, were vexed at the account

[43] Article I (American Review), *Monthly Magazine,* III (July, 1800), 47. It is interesting to note here that in 1809 Brown, along with Joseph Dennie and Timothy Dwight, became an honorary member of the New-York Historical Society (*Ormond,* ed. Ernest Marchand, p. xlv).

[44] "On Periodical Publications," *Monthly Magazine,* I (April, 1799), 2.

of a singular clawed animal introduced into the last number, because it came from the pen of Mr. Jefferson, who, they said, had better be employed in writing letters to *Mazzei*. "The Editor," added they, "must certainly be an admirer of his, or he would not have done him the honor to reprint his little snivelling production." These things being considered, I cannot help thinking that the Magazine had better be entirely free from theological and political polemics. I am willing to give up my share of them from this prudential consideration.[45]

Besides, he protested in another article,

The mind of a candid reader, on either side of the great political question which now agitates the public, can feel little pleasure in the extravagant effusions of *pure party spirit*.[46]

Brown's personal attitude toward journalistic invective and his sense of editorial responsibility are persuasively and cogently expressed in the following passage:

Truth requires no weapons but those which are furnished by reason, and it is ever injured by causeless crimination and illiberal abuse. But while pride or prejudice prevents the granting of any indulgence to an adversary, a proper sense of his own dignity, as well as of the subject in which he is engaged, should lead a writer to reject the language of contumely and scorn.[47]

As to Brown's own political beliefs, they are difficult to discover from the magazine alone. We know that in his early days he was strongly pro-French and radical. But most of the members of the Friendly Club were, as we have seen, Federalists and conservative; and Brown, under their influence, became more moderate in his own beliefs. Hints here and there define some of his attitudes. For instance, in a review of a political pamphlet,[48] he gave a temperate but revealing essay on prevailing political terminology. This careful discrimination has for the modern historian considerable value in shedding light on the contemporary use of such terms as "tory," "whig," "federalist," etc. Compare the essay below with Jefferson's endeavor to define these terms, and note their close similarity.

The names of *roundhead* and *cavalier, whig* and *tory,* so famous in English history, and the latter in our own, have nothing in their intrinsic meaning which would lead one ignorant of the history of the political events of the times to a knowledge of their signification. The term *federalist* appears far more significant and descriptive than that of *whig*: yet no one mistakes the meaning of the latter, or thinks it necessary when he uses it to give a formal definition.

The appellation *federalist* was intended to designate a person attached to the *union* of the American States under one general compact, and was adopted

[45] *Monthly Magazine*, II (Feb., 1800), 98-99.
[46] Article L (American Review), *Monthly Magazine*, III (Nov., 1800), 378.
[47] Article LX, *ibid.* (Dec., 1800), 452.
[48] Article LVI, *ibid.*, 433-441.

at a time when, from the weakness and impotency of the old *confederated* form of this *union,* there was danger of a dissolution of the compact and the establishment of separate and absolutely independent sovereignties.

Those who were more attached to the independency of the State governments than to the union and to that new constitution deemed essential to its preservation were denominated *anti-federalists.*

No terms could be found better adapted to express the leading trait in the political characters of the two parties; and the history of governments will not furnish any so significant.

Changes take place in the political circumstances of the nation and the general opinion of the people, by which the meaning attached to a name becomes enlarged, or restrained, or modified to suit the new ideas which have been introduced, while the original name continues the same, or experiences some slight modification.

Thus the political discussions of the latter years, produced by the French revolution, have introduced among us the terms *aristocrat* and *democrat, monarchist* and *republican.* These have been bestowed or assumed by the respective parties according as they supposed their political principles favored the one or the other of those characters.

The anti-federalists, or *soi-disant* republicans of the present day, though composed of mixed characters, are yet well known by their original appellation.

Though it is presumed the *republican* would not have the folly or audacity to assert that the federalist had discarded *republican* principles; yet the new-adopted name was too strikingly distinctive in its popular sense not to be abused to catch the ignorant and unwary. The federalists have, therefore, assumed the addition of republican, and *federal republican* appears to us as significant an appellation for that party which this writer chooses to call constitutionalists, as any that can be found. It has the advantage also of retaining its original characteristic, *federalism,* or an attachment to the *union,* rather than to the State governments.

It would be unjust to say that there are not many in the anti-federal, or republican party, attached to the constitution, in its present form, and might therefore be truly denominated *constitutionalists,* which renders this new appellation quite as objectionable as the old. That party, as well as the other, is composed of men of various characters; many of these are new accessions, derived from the turbulent fluctuations of the European governments.

Thus the friends of government, of order, and peace, whether monarchical, aristocratical, or republican, arrange themselves on the side of the supporters of the present government and its administration, though they may essentially differ in the most fundamental principles of government. On the other hand, the true *democrat,* the Jacobin, the discontented opposer of all law and government, as well as the sound republican, are found united with those who are in the opposition to the ruling power. Yet there is no man at all acquainted with the history of our constitution and government, as well as with the character of our citizens, that can be deceived by the present names that distinguish the two parties.

Brown did not formally align himself with either the republicans or the federal republicans, much less the democrats or Jacobins, but he declared his loyalty to the government and the Constitution. He was a warm admirer of Jefferson both before and after his election to the presidency, but he never let his preference appear in the *Monthly*.

### AMERICA SHOULD HAVE A WISE FOREIGN POLICY

Like most other Americans, Brown turned from his early admiration of the French to indignation toward them for their treatment of the United States. He praised Jedidiah Morse for his exposure of "French villainy," but urged moderation and avoidance of hysteria. During the heated discussions of the issues raised by our relation to France and the French Revolution, America, as we have pointed out in the Introduction to this volume, divided sharply into warring factions. Any editor who "took sides" greatly endangered his usefulness to the public at large. Though Brown tried to follow the middle path, he leaned more and more toward the Federalist point of view. In answer to an oration warning Americans against "the Gallic faction" in this country, Brown even went so far as to suggest that Americans were ready to fight the French—or the puppets of France —if necessary.[49] As for other countries, Brown hoped that friendly relations could be maintained.[50]

He urged moderation between internal factions, and diplomacy in our dealings with other nations. In a review of a jingoistic political article[51] he ridiculed the idea that America was in danger of immediate destruction. He strongly disapproved of conquest of the colonies of other nations in North America, saying that any one who advocated it had a "shallow and imperfect knowledge of our national policy." In this respect Brown stood almost alone, for in the beginning of the new century the tide of westward expansion and aggrandizement was running strong. But we shall see that, by 1803, Brown came to modify this view by countenancing the doctrine of "manifest destiny." In his dream of rapid and vast expansion of American industrial, commercial, and agrarian life, Brown would admit no one element of growth at the expense of others. His utterances place him squarely on the side of Adam Smith and the angels of "free enterprise." The following vigorous paragraph as surely embodies his vision of a great people rising to wealth and power by honorable means as it prophetically sets forth the actual course which the nation was to follow for years to come:

That the United States are, and will be, a great commercial nation, is too obvious to be denied; and government ought not, nor can, by regulation or restriction, prevent the growth of this spirit of trade. But whoever is ac-

---

[49] Article XXIII (American Review), *Monthly Magazine*, I (Aug., 1799), 374-375.
[50] "Thoughts on the Origin of the Claims of Europeans to North America," *Monthly Magazine*, III (July, 1800), 16-18.
[51] "Review of a Political Survey," *ibid.* (Aug., 1800), 131-137.

quainted with the character of the people will perceive that if suffered to take their own way, they will go on with sufficient strides towards commercial grandeur and opulence; and that this progress will be equal to, if not greater than, that of agriculture, which constitutes the basis of the strength and riches of this country. Instead of wasting a scanty population and revenue in 'extending our empire and renown' by foreign conquests, the possession of which must ever be precarious and dependent on the will or caprice of other nations, we should seek in our own uncultivated regions a field of conquest worthy a hardy and virtuous people; in subjecting which to the hand of culture and art, we shall acquire the rich rewards of honorable toil and a fame not tarnished with crime or stained with blood.[52]

In our dealings with foreign nations he recommended, as we have seen, a wise neutral policy, and approved of Washington's and Jefferson's warnings to keep out of entangling foreign alliances. He warned that Great Britain would naturally seek her own interests and would not hesitate to sacrifice ours to further her cause. He maintained that nations, like individuals, are ruthless when their commercial interests are at stake, and that they act on the sole principle that might makes right.

Furthermore, in the light of this temperate and rather conservative political and social philosophy in his mature years, we are not surprised to find Brown, the fiery young author of *Alcuin,* now speaking cautiously about universal suffrage. Brown apparently found himself in agreement with the views expressed by this contributor:

Whether our *fair sisters* will acquiesce in the justice of their exclusion from the exercise of political rights we presume not to conjecture. They may in some degree be reconciled to their condition by the very courteous and plausible description of Mr. K., who artfully appeals to them for their decision in his favor.[53]

As we look back on Brown's first venture into the treacherous sea of American journalism, we must pronounce the voyage a success. Measured by the length of life of his first magazine, by the high quality of original literary contributions, by the sound critical reviews, by the editor's ability to hold an even keel in the turbulent political waters, the astute critic will allow that Charles Brockden Brown reached a high place in early American journalism. In his battle against American isolationism, he made a plea for understanding among the various political factions of the day, and he encouraged native writers to build their literary structures on solid principles and not to bank too much upon the fact that they were Americans. These accomplishments should give to Brown's journalistic work a secure place in the esteem of his countrymen.

[52] Article XII (American Review), *ibid.,* 134.
[53] Article VI (American Review), *Monthly Magazine,* II (Jan., 1800), 57.

# VI

# BROWN AS A NOVELIST

## THE NOVEL BEFORE BROWN

AMERICA WAS NOT READY for a native fiction until nearly two hundred years after the landing at Jamestown. As we pointed out in the Introduction to this volume, two factors apparently caused this delay: namely, Colonial conditions that confined all activity to the conquering, settling, and building up of a new country; and the Puritan spirit that held novel-reading to be an insidious device of the devil for perverting unsuspecting youth. Then, too, the colonists never lost sight of the fact that they were Englishmen and therefore inheritors of whatever England produced. Before the appearance of Charles Brockden Brown there were current in America only some four or five native novels, mainly tales of seduction, clumsily handled because of the authors' attempt to placate the Puritan spirit. From them Brown drew no inspiration, in either matter or manner. They had, however, established the validity of works of fiction in the minds of the American public, and they had prepared the soil for sturdier growth. Brockden Brown saw this opportunity for creating a purely American fiction, and he seized it. The result was not great, but it was considerable.

## BROWN'S EARLY AMBITION TO WRITE NOVELS

We have seen that Brown's only attempts at creative work before 1793 were *The Rhapsodist,* some philosophical essays, and a few didactic odes. His Journal and letters covering the period of his law apprenticeship bear unmistakable signs of his determination to devote himself to the profession of letters. Apparently, however, he had no notion before 1793 of undertaking a work of fiction. That he entertained such a notion in the summer of 1793 while in Hartford and New York may be seen in an unpublished letter to his brother James, dated October 25, 1796, from New York. Since this letter is apparently unknown to the public and since it throws considerable light upon Brown's early ambitions as a writer of fiction and upon the problems with which his mind was then busied, it is herewith extensively quoted:

I have been away for this good many days past, and have allowed the weariness of some hours dayly occupation at my pen to unfit me for this employment. I received your last letter in good time, and thank you for your punctuality, a virtue in which it seems my destiny to fall short of most people.

I believe the yellow fever has taken its final leave of us, at least for the present season. Not even the name of it has been mentioned in my hearing, nor the idea of it, scarcely occurred to my mind, since I last wrote you. When you talk of the necessity of circumspection to escape its ravages, I can not but admire the exaggerations of rumor, and the multiplying and enlarging efficacy of distance. Physical objects are diminished by distance, and even vanish altogether as we go farther from them. Not so the yellow fever and the like imaginary spectacles which cling closer, grow into gigantic dimensions, in proportion to their actual distance from us.

Plague operates by invisible agents, and we know not in what quarter it is about to attack us. No shield, therefore, can be lifted up against it. We fear it as we are terrified by dark in which tho much of our panic be, doubtless, owing to the influence of education, and may be removed by habitual exposure to it, yet our defenseless condition and the invisible approaches of danger may contribute to our alarms. I am not even wholly uninfected by this disease, because strong is the influence of early association; when in the dark, if an unlucky incident calls my attention to the imperfect gleam which may be darted from a neighboring lamp along the ceiling, or to that more imperfect glimpse which will be produced by the faintest starlight when reflected from irregular polished surfaces, I find myself seized by unwelcome shrinkings and hasten to the asylum which sleep, or light, or company, or abstract meditations may offer me. I have never had recourse, in this phantastic distress, to the best expedient, but when all others fail me, that is, the endeavor to *reason down* my perturbations, and dispeople by mere energy of argument the aerial work of 'calling shapes and beckoning shadows dire!'

These impressions are, in general, very early, perhaps when arrived at a certain age, and covered with a certain degree of experience, they cannot be produced. They are, therefore, a striking example of the importance of stamping on the infant mind right impressions. . . . But how came my pen to make this wide excursion into the mysterious regions of conjuration and necromancy? I remember; I was talking of the yellow fever, or rather of the plague. . . . When I mentioned to you my treatment [of it] at Hartford in ninety-three, I was half disposed to instruct myself, and possibly amuse you, by recalling and putting [it] on the paper before me, during a residence of two or three days there. Such a design was prompted and recommended by many considerations; and I was deterred from the execution of it only by the consciousness that more time would be requisite for such a task than could just then be reasonably bestowed upon it. Many reflections, as well as many incidents, occurred at the time and many new reflections would now occur the recording of which, in the epistolary way would be useful to myself and productive of some sort of entertainment to my brother. Every man's transactions are of moment in his own eyes; they are valuable as portions of the history of human nature; and may be read or heard by some individuals with an interest flowing from their relations to the hero of the tale. . . . The affection which you bear me would render you an attentive auditor of Tales which should possess little intrinsic importance. If, therefore in the future, my pen should [MS here unreadable] stray into cheerful or melancholy, general or minute [word missing—perhaps *representation*] of my own story, its course will not be checked by the [word missing] persuasion that I am talking to one whom my narrative will disgust or fatigue and whom civility alone will induce to pay me any attention. I shall pursue the task without any scruple of this kind.

The important fact which this letter affirms is that as early as 1793 Brown's mind was busied with plans for works of fiction, and that the subject then uppermost in his mind was the yellow fever, out of which two of his most powerful novels subsequently grew. There is every reason to conclude, however, that his pen, which he represented as so busily employed, did not as early as 1793 yield a work of fiction based upon the plague. If he did write such a work, we hear no more about it for several years.

Brown again visited his friends in New York in the summer of 1795, but was back in Philadelphia in September. From there he wrote that he was busily engaged on his "Philadelphia novel." This work has not been definitely identified. Could it have been that early work, spoken of in 1793, which later was to mature into *The Man at Home?* But whatever its name or nature, the following excerpts from his Journal tell us that Brown was engaged on yet another—probably a lost—novel:

Soon after my return, I began the design of which we talked so much. I had planned so that I could finish a work equal in extent to *Caleb Williams* in less than six weeks; and wrote a quantity equivalent to ten of his [Godwin's] pages daily till the hot weather and inconvenient circumstances obliged me to relax my diligence. Great expedition does not seem desirable. Tenets so momentous require a leisurely and deep examination; and much meditation, reading, and writing, I presume, are necessary to render my system of morality perfect in all its parts, and to acquire a full and luminous conviction; but I have not stopped—I go on, though less precipitately than at first, and hope finally to produce something valuable for its utility./

Four months later, in January, 1796, he again wrote to Dunlap:

After wandering through fifty pages, the experiment was sufficiently made, and the thorough consciousness that I was unfitted for the instructor's chair, that my style was feeble and diffuse, my method prolix and inaccurate, my reasoning crude and superficial, and my knowledge narrow and undigested, suddenly benumbed my fingers: I dropped the pen, and I sunk into silent and solitary meditation on the means of remedying these defects.[2]

### *SKYWALK:* BROWN'S FIRST NOVEL

As *Skywalk* is Brown's first definitely identifiable work of fiction, its date, its subject matter, and its fate call for brief notice. The first

[1] *National Portrait Gallery,* IV.
[2] *Ibid.*

known published mention of *Skywalk* appeared in the *Weekly Magazine* (Philadelphia) for March 17, 1798, under the signature of *Speratus;* a week later, a brief (1700 words) excerpt from the novel was given in the same magazine. The extract shows the influence of *Caleb Williams* (1794), a work which Brown probably would not have been acquainted with before its appearance in America early in 1795. On March 29, 1798, Dunlap recorded in his *Diary:* "Yesterday Smith showed me a letter from C. B. Brown, in which he describes himself as assiduously writing *novels* and in love." Novels here must surely refer to *Skywalk* and *Wieland*, for on April 12, Dunlap, while in Philadelphia, wrote in his *Diary:* "Dine with C. Brown: he reads to me the beginning of a novel undertaken since 'Skywalk'—he calls it 'Wieland,' or the Transformation. This must make a very fine book."

On April 11, 1798, Dunlap recorded in his *Diary:* "Call on Brown who goes with me to the booksellers, . . . and gives me some account of his 'Skywalk.' He says that it is founded on Somnambulism." As Brown and Dunlap had been on intimate terms for upwards of five years, it seems unlikely that the theme of *Skywalk* could have been news to Dunlap in 1798.

Recording the completion of *Alcuin* in 1797, Brown wrote in his Journal:

When this was finished, I commenced something in the form of a Romance. I had at first no definite conceptions of my design. As my pen proceeded forward, my invention was tasked, and the materials that it afforded were arranged and digested. Fortunately, I continued to view this scheme in the same light in which it had at first presented itself. Time, therefore, did not diminish its attractions. The facility I experienced in composition and the perception of daily progress encouraged me, and my task was finished on the last day of December.

I hardly know how to regard this exploit. Is it a respectable proof of perseverance or not? Considering my character in its former appearances, this steadiness in application might not have been expected. What is the nature or merit of my performance? This question is not for me to answer. My decision is favorable or otherwise, according to the views I take of the subject. When a mental comparison is made between this and the mass of novels, I am inclined to be pleased with my own production. But when the objects of comparison are changed, and I revolve the transcendant merits of Caleb Williams, my pleasure is diminished and is preserved from a total extinction only by the reflection that this performance is the first. That every new attempt will be better than the last and that, considered in the light of a prelude or first link, it may merit that praise to which it may possess no claim, considered as a last best creation.

It was at first written in an hasty and inaccurate way. Before I can submit it to a printer, or even satisfactorily rehearse it to a friend, it must be wholly transcribed. I am at present engaged in this employment. I am afraid as much time will be required by it as was necessary to the original composition. I do not fear but that I shall finish my labor, barring all extraordinary accidents.

Brown clearly states here that the first draft of the work "was finished on the last day of December," and that he was now engaged in revision; he calls the romance his first; Dunlap says that "the first novel he wrote was entitled 'Skywalk,' " the "extract" from *Skywalk* suggests that the novel was written under the influence of Godwin; and as soon as Brown has finished his unnamed romance he compares it with *Caleb Williams.* If the revision was as difficult as Brown feared it would be, consuming "as much . . . as was necessary to the original composition," one may readily believe that the work was not fully revised before the middle of February (1798).

That *Skywalk* had been completely revised and the manuscript in the hands of his friends by April 21 is certified to by Dunlap's *Diary*, April 21. They were reading it on April 21, 22, 23, and 24:

[April 21]: Smith reads in 'Skywalk, which interests us all very much. [April 22]: Call on Smith and Johnson and bring home with [me] 'Skywalk'; begin to read it to my wife. [April 23]: Read 'Skywalk' to my wife. This is a very superior performance. [April 24]: Afternoon read 'Skywalk.' Smith came and stayed after the others, reading 'Skywalk' to the end. I give high credit to Charles for this work, yet I am not satisfied. Is not Lorimer too much exalted—too fascinating? Why are we not satisfied as to the pistol of Avonedge? And how are we to account for the dagger, so opportunely ready in the chamber of Mrs. Courting?—perhaps these are trifles—the work is masterly.

When the work was finished, Brown viewed it with mixed feelings, offering a weak apology for its evident shortcomings:

You will be good enough to inform your readers that, in a short time, their patronage will be solicited to a work in which it is endeavored to amuse the imagination and improve the heart. A tale that may rival the performances of this kind which have lately issued from the English press will be unexampled in America. . . .

It is indeed a poor plea by which to shield ourselves from the indignation of criticism, that our work, like ourselves is juvenile [he was twenty-seven years old at the time] and that, aided and fostered by encouragement and levity, the seed that is at present so inconsiderable may in time expand into the loveliness of the rose and the deliciousness of the banana. . . . This writer does not rest his hopes upon the indulgence due to the unripeness of his age and limitedness of his experience. All that he can do to make his book a good one of the kind, he has done. . . .

Brown's first novel, like his first published poem, suffered an untoward fate. In the words of Dunlap:

It was never published, owing to the death of the printer, who had undertaken to publish it at his own risk. Mr. Brown being then altogether unknown to the public, and the work, nearly printed, being left with executors, who did not choose to finish it and would not or could not sell the sheets for such price as Mr. Brown's friends thought proper to offer for them. After

Charles had made New York his place of residence, he incorporated parts of 'Skywalk' into other works of imagination, as his memory retained them. In *Edgar Huntly,* for example, the wild district of Norwalk had its prototype in *Skywalk.*[3]

### BROWN'S FORMULA FOR A NATIVE FICTION

The "Advertisement" to *Skywalk* gives us an insight into Brown's idea for a native fiction:

To the story-telling moralist, the United States is a new and untrodden field. He who shall examine objects with his own eyes, who shall employ the European models merely for the improvement of his taste, and adapt his fiction to all that is genuine and peculiar in the scene before him, will be entitled at least to the praise of originality.

. . . Our ecclesiastical and political system, our domestic and social maxims, are in many respects entirely our own. He therefore who paints not from books, but from nature, who introduces those lines and hues in which we differ rather than those in which we resemble our kindred nations beyond the ocean may lay some claim to the patronage of his countrymen.

The value of such works lies without doubt in their moral tendency. The popular tales have merit, but there is one thing in which they are deficient. They are generally adapted to one class of readers only. By a string of well-connected incidents, they amuse the idle and thoughtless; but are spurned at by those who are satisfied with nothing but strains of lofty eloquence, the exhibition of powerful motives, and a sort of audaciousness of character. The world is governed not by the simpleton, but by the man of soaring passions and intellectual energy. By the display of such only can we hope to enchain the attention and ravish the souls of those who study and reflect. To gain their homage it is not needful to forego the approbation of those whose circumstances have hindered them from making the same progress. A contexture of facts capable of suspending the faculties of every soul in curiosity may be joined with depth of views into human nature and all the subtleties of reasoning. . . .

. . . Some part of his tale is a picture of truth. Facts have supplied the foundation of the whole. Its title is 'Skywalk' or 'The Man Unknown to Himself' . . . An American Tale.

Though saddened, but not daunted, by the fate of *Skywalk,* Brown at once began another novel. It was to be a work portraying American life and native scenes, and it would, by exhibiting "the man of soaring passions and intellectual energy . . . enchain the attention and ravish the souls of those who study and reflect." The new novel would be based upon his own experiences in the plague-ridden city of Philadelphia, and he would call it *The Man at Home.*

### THE MAN AT HOME

Epidemics of yellow fever were not unknown in America before 1793, but they had generally been of a mild form. The frequent visits

[3] Dunlap, I, 259.

of the plague were largely due to insanitary conditions and especially to the increased activity of our merchant marine following the Revolutionary War. Ships plied between this country and almost every known port in the world, often returning with one or more of their crew ill of some disease, usually of Asiatic origin. The port of Philadelphia had been for some time the center of American trade, and, as the national capital, it attracted foreign "visitors" and refugees from the French wars in the West Indies. The yellow fever, endemic to the West Indies, often made unpleasant visits to our shores. The terrible plague of 1793 was brought directly from the West Indies by French refugees from Cap Français in July, 1793. Philadelphia was not particularly unclean, but the drainage was poor, and the streets narrow and dirty. These general unhygienic conditions invited disease and made difficult its control when in epidemic form. During August, September, October, and November of the year 1793 the city was a scene of desolation.

There are many contemporary accounts of the pestilence, the most faithful-to-fact portrayal being Mathew Carey's *A Short Account of the Malignant Fever* (1794). Carey made no attempt to gloss over unpleasant facts or to give to history the glow of passion; that was left for Charles Brockden Brown. But Brown did not write wholly to entertain. He had himself witnessed the early scenes of the plague of 1793; had been in the city during the plague of 1797, which was almost as severe as that of 1793; and he was a victim of the fever in New York in 1798. These awful scenes and experiences lingered in his mind, and in part explain his somber outlook on life. He came to question the goodness and the power of God and to look upon man as insignificant in the scheme of the universe. So the ravages of the plague, he thought, would form a fitting background for depicting the ills of society.

We have already noted that Brown as early as 1793 saw the value of the plague as a literary asset. Though it now appears that he wrote nothing on it at that time, it was certainly his intention to make use of his own experiences with the plague as the basis for fiction. Apparently, nothing was written before 1798. On February 3, 1798, *The Man at Home* began its appearance in the *Weekly Magazine* (Philadelphia). If we except the ill-fated poem to Franklin, this is Brown's second appearance in print. *The Man at Home* was continued regularly through the next twelve issues of the magazine, and reached the length of approximately 28,000 words.

The story is fragmentary and awkwardly handled—there are no fewer than five digressions from the main theme. Briefly, *The Man at Home* is a tale of "lofty crime," of great energy spent in strengthening the arms of virtue and in dissipating the follies of the vicious, thrown against a background of a city in the clutches of the yellow

fever. Dissertations on the dignity of honest labor and the pernicious-
ness of wealth, on debtors' prisons, criminals, Rousseau, Howard,
Hawkesworth, on untoward events that flow from ungovernable curiosity, on the consequences of opening "mysterious iron chests," and
on "the duties of men and the principles of social institutions," with
amusing digressions on the vocabulary of a sailor and the immunity
of Indians and Creole Frenchmen to the plague, make up the larger
part of *The Man at Home*. It must be admitted, however, that despite
inexcusable awkwardness and confusion in the development of the
story, the author shows a masterful hand in picturing the horrors of
the plague. Here was material congenial to his nature, and by an
almost ghoulish force he has succeeded in achieving a Defoe-like verisimilitude. Brown's genius was analytical, and minute descriptions
delighted his soul. The plague furnished the opportunity to exercise
his powers. Brown rightly judged that his genius lay in the direction
of minute analysis of feelings and motives awakened in moments of
great passions; he felt that he had really achieved success in his plague
scenes.

This first public appearance in the field of fiction exhibits Brown's
chief faults, faults that clung closely to him to the end: his apparent
inability to tell a story simply; his weak and inconclusive endings;
a tendency to work up to powerful climaxes that never come off; an
almost fiendish delight in lecturing his readers; and a heavy, involved,
verbose style.

### WIELAND; OR THE TRANSFORMATION

*Wieland* was the first of Brown's novels to be published in book
form. It was begun in February or March, 1798, and finished late in
August. Arriving in New York on July 3, Brown took up his abode
with Dunlap. That day Dunlap recorded in his *Diary* that Brown
had "brought on his second novel, but not completed"; and on July 4:
"Walk with Brown; read in *Wieland*." On the following day Dunlap
set down: "After supper, Brown reads his novel to self and wife as
far as he has gone"; on July 22: "Read Brown's continuation of
*'Wieland'* to my wife"; on July 25: "Drink tea with Smith, Johnson,
and Brown and read part of the remainder of 'Wieland,' the first
proof of which was under correction of the trio," and finally on July
26, "Finish reading *Wieland* at S and J's. We had some conversation
in respect to proposed alterations suggested to Brown." Brown evidently made the corrections, for on August 6, Dunlap recorded: "See
Smith, Johnson, and Brown and read the addition of the latter to his
*Wieland*." Apparently, then, *Wieland* was complete, except for the
last ten pages, by August 6, 1798. The last proof was read in early
September, and the novel issued from the press of T. and J. Swords,
New York publishers, on September 5, 1798, a neat volume of 298
pages. America's first important novelist was now introduced to the
world.

That Brown thought highly of *Wieland* may be seen from his letter to Thomas Jefferson, soliciting his opinion of the work and hoping that he would use his good offices in gaining it a wider audience.

December 15, 1798.

SIR:

After some hesitation a stranger to the person, though not to the character of Thomas Jefferson, ventures to entreat his acceptance of the volume by which this is accompanied. He is unacquainted with the degree in which your time and attention is engrossed by your public office; he knows not in what way your studious hours are distributed and whether mere works of imagination and invention are not excluded from your notice. He is even doubtful whether this letter will be opened or read, or, if read, whether its contents will not be instantly dismissed from your memory; so much a stranger is he, though a citizen of the United States, to the private occupations and modes of judging of the most illustrious of his fellow citizens.

To request your perusal of a work which at the same time is confessed to be unworthy of perusal will be an uncommon proof of absurdity. In thus transmitting my book to you I tacitly acknowledge my belief that it is capable of affording you pleasure and of entitling the writer to some portion of your good opinion. If I had not this belief, I should unavoidably be silent.

I am conscious, however, that this form of composition may be regarded by you with indifference or contempt, that social and intellectual theories, that the history of facts in the processes of nature and the operations of government may appear to you the only laudable pursuits; that fictitious narratives in their own nature or in the manner in which they have been hitherto conducted may be thought not to deserve notice, and that, consequently, whatever may be the merit of my book as a fiction, yet it is to be condemned because it is a fiction.

I need not say that my own opinions are different. I am therefore obliged to hope that an artful display of incidents, the powerful delineation of characters and the train of eloquent and judicious reasoning which may be combined in a fictitious work, will be regarded by Thomas Jefferson with as much respect as they are regarded by me.

No man holds a performance which he has deliberately offered to the world in contempt; but, if he be a man of candor and discernment, his favorable judgment of his own work will always be attended by diffidence and fluctuation. I confess I foster the hope that Mr. Jefferson will be induced to open the book that is here offered him; that when he has begun it he will find himself prompted to continue, and that he will not think the time employed upon it tediously or uselessly consumed.

With more than this I dare not flatter myself. That he will be pleased to any uncommon degree, and that, by his recommendation, he will contribute to diffuse the knowledge of its author, and facilitate a favorable reception to future performances, is a benefit far beyond the expectations, though certainly the object of the fondest wishes of

CHARLES B. BROWN

On January 15, 1799, Jefferson replied:

SIR:

I received on my arrival here some days ago the copy of the book you were so kind as to send me together with your letter, for which be pleased to accept my thanks. As soon as I am in a situation to admit it (which is hardly the case here), I shall read it, and I doubt not with great pleasure. Some of the most agreeable moments of my life have been spent in reading works of imagination, which have this advantage over history, that the incidents of the former may be dressed in the most interesting form, while those of the latter must be confined to fact. They cannot therefore possess virtue in the best and vice in the worst forms possible, as the former may. I have the honor to be with great consideration, Sir.

Your most obed. servt.<br>TH. JEFFERSON

It is not known whether Jefferson read the novel or made any public or private commendation of it.

The novel carried a Preface setting forth the nature, purpose, and justification of the work, and further developing the author's formula for an American fiction. Brown wrote:

The following work is delivered to the world as the first of a series of performances which the favorable reception of this will induce the writer to publish. His purpose is neither selfish nor temporary, but aims at the illustration of some important branches of the moral constitution of man. Whether this tale will be classed with the ordinary or frivolous sources of amusement, or be ranked with the few productions whose usefulness secures them a lasting reputation, the reader must be permitted to decide.

The incidents related are extraordinary and rare. Some of them, perhaps, approach as nearly to the nature of miracles as can be done by that which is not truly miraculous. It is hoped that intelligent readers will not disapprove of the manner in which appearances are solved, but that the solution will be found to correspond with the known principles of human nature. The power which the principal person is said to possess can scarcely be denied as real. It must be acknowledged to be extremely rare; but no fact, equally uncommon, is supported by the same strength of historical evidence.

Some readers may think the conduct of the younger Wieland impossible. In support of its possibility, the writer must appeal to physicians and to men conversant with the latent springs and occasional perversions of the human mind. It will not be objected that the instances of similar delusions are rare, because it is the business of moral painters to exhibit their subject in its most instructive and memorable forms. If history furnishes one parallel fact, it is a sufficient vindication of the writer; but most readers will probably recollect an authentic case, remarkably similar to that of Wieland.

Here Brown clearly goes beyond his formula as stated in the preface to *Skywalk;* in these paragraphs he denounces the puerile Gothic novels, and the sentimental stories of love and seduction fathered by Richardson, and adopts the principles of the Novel of Purpose, made prominent by Holcroft, Bage, and Godwin. Henceforth he will lay bare the hidden motives of men of soaring passions and raging wills; he will choose for his characters men and women who are under some horrid mental or moral delusions, some obsession or perversion of mind.

The plot of *Wieland* is remarkably simple. With the exception of *Jane Talbot*, there are fewer digressions than in any other of Brown's major works of fiction.

The story is autobiographical in form, and is carried forward by letters from Clara Wieland to her friends. To prepare the reader for the unparalleled events of the main plot, she gives a detailed account of the life of the older Wieland. He was reared in the big friendless city of London amid the laborious duties of the counting house. His education had been entirely neglected—the world of the printed page being almost unknown to him. He was in a state of mind to become completely enthralled by new ideas, when he discovered in a dusty garret a book containing an account of the sect of Camissard, one of the Albigenses or French Protestants. He now secured a Bible and the Camissard Commentaries, the reading of which wrought a profound change in his mind. "Hence arose a thousand scruples to which he had hitherto been a stranger. He was alternately agitated by fear and by ecstasy. He imagined himself beset by the snares of a spiritual foe, and that his security lay in watchfulness and prayer." His moral nature was likewise changed: "all levities of speech and negligences of behavior were proscribed. . . . He labored to keep alive a sentiment of fear and a belief of the awe-creating presence of the Deity." He felt himself called upon to disseminate the truths of the gospel to the ungodly nations, and as the American Indians seemed to be in the most hopeless condition, he embarked for Philadelphia. But stories of the savage nature of the Indians arousing fears in him for his own safety, he decided to postpone his work among them and buy a farm on the banks of the beautiful Schuylkill. Here he lived for fourteen years a married life of useful labor. But the old desire to "save" the Indians seizing him, he spent many years of toil and privation among the savages of the Ohio valley.

Wieland's religion was a religion of nature: he followed no man-made creed, and he did not believe in public worship; prayers to be efficacious must be offered up in private. Therefore he built for his own personal use a temple high upon a hill overlooking the river; to this temple he repaired for prayers at noon and at midnight. Eventually he grew melancholy and complained much of pains in the head. After a day of unusual restlessness, he retired to the temple for his midnight orisons; a great explosion was heard and a flame as of fire was seen. His family rushed to the temple; they could hear the groans of Wieland, but the flame had disappeared on their approach. A careful examination of the body revealed some astonishing facts. It was scorched and bruised. "His right arm exhibited marks as of having been struck by some heavy body." His clothes had been reduced to ashes, but his slippers and hair were untouched. Wieland lived for two hours after the disaster, and gave an imperfect account of what had happened. He related that while he was engaged in prayer, "with thoughts full of confusion and anxiety, a faint gleam suddenly shot athwart the apartment. His fancy immediately pictured to itself a person bearing a lamp. It seemed to come from behind. He was in the act of turning to examine the visitant, when his right arm received a blow from a heavy club. At the same instant, a very bright spark was seen to light upon his clothes. In a moment, the whole was reduced to ashes."

The reader is now prepared for the main action of the story. Clara and Theodore Wieland, children of the older Wieland, left to the care of a maiden aunt, grow up with Catherine and Henry Pleyel as companions. Their education is Rousseauistic; their religion a worship of nature. Young Wieland determines upon agriculture as his occupation. But like his father he grows melancholy and austere; he delves into religious doctrines and weighs them. He becomes a religious "enthusiast": "Moral necessity and Calvinistic inspiration," says Clara, "were the props on which my brother thought proper to repose." Pleyel, a disciple of Godwin, is the champion of intellectual liberty, and rejects all guidance but that of his reason. The author by means of such contrasts and by keen analysis of the springs of human action gives a vivid picture of these four young people caught in the crosscurrents of eighteenth-century thought. After many years of strenuous living, the little band is destroyed by the machinations of an escaped convict from Ireland—Brown's villains are usually Irish—one Carwin the biloquist, whose life in Europe in the service of Ludloe has been a life of blackest crimes. Carwin chooses from this happy group young Wieland, upon whom to employ his diabolical tricks of ventriloquism. He feels that Wieland should be taught a lesson against religious credulity. According to Carwin's later confessions, he meant no real harm to anyone, but he insists that he had set in motion a machine over which he did not have full control, that the doctrine of Calvinistic necessity had tainted his mind. He had made Wieland believe that Heaven commanded the destruction of his wife and children and his sister. From the time Wieland makes up his mind that the voice is the voice of God, he never for a moment hesitates. The story rushes to a powerful climax in the murder scene with a rapidity unusual in Brown's novels. A lull—the inevitable suspense—then follows in Wieland's trial, confession, imprisonment, and escape. Wieland yet feels called upon to murder his sister, and another climax ensues, one even more terrible in its awful suspense. His sister is finally saved by the intervention of Carwin, but Wieland, before leaving his sister's room, puts an end to his own unhappy life.

Such in brief is the story. The story of the elder Wieland and his death by spontaneous-combustion is valuable as explaining the mind of the younger Wieland. It prepares the reader for the main plot by showing him the importance of hereditary and environmental influences in molding the character of younger Wieland. His father's death by the mysterious means of spontaneous-combustion produced a lasting impression upon him; he felt that this was the work of a supernatural agency, and his brooding over its mystery led to melancholy and superstition. It is the author's purpose to show the evil effects of credulity and superstition thus early lodged in the mind of young Wieland. Brown had deemed it necessary to dwell at length on the psychological effect that the mysterious death of his father would have on the mind of Wieland; it was a new thing for the novelist to venture into the field of abnormal psychology, and Brown never lost an opportunity of making his reader feel that he was dealing with facts, mental and physical. During the last two decades of the eighteenth century, if one may judge from the numerous references in contemporary literature, particularly in magazines, considerable progress was made in the study of what is now familiarly known as abnormal psychology. It was to the field of the unusual, the abnormal, that Brown looked for materials for his novels. No one doubts the perfect congeniality to his mind of such explorations into the world of unusual phenomena.

In the Preface to *Wieland,* we have seen that Brown felt called upon to disarm criticism at once by an appeal to the intelligent reader. He searched the journals of his day for cases of spontaneous combustion. In a footnote at the end of the second chapter of the novel, he noted that ''A case, in its symptoms exactly parallel to this, is published in one of the Journals of Florence.'' The case of Dan G. Maria Bertholi, a priest, is particularly interesting as furnishing several parallels with that of the elder Wieland—parallels too exact to be accidental. In each case groans were heard; each victim was stretched on the floor; the skin on the greater part of both bodies was scorched; in both, the right arm appeared to have been ''struck with a club''; certain articles of clothing were untouched; mortification had set in in the right arm of each and soon spread to other parts of the body; not a single hair of the head had been touched; a faint flame was observed; a bright spark of fire was seen to light on the clothes, and in a moment reduced them to ashes; in each case the night was clear and calm. The only important addition which Brown made, one calculated to heighten the mystery, was the dying Wieland's hint that he was purposely withholding part of the awful truth that there had been Divine interference.

The story of the younger Wieland had a remarkable American parallel. Brown had said: ''If history furnishes one parallel fact, it is sufficient vindication of the writer; but most readers will probably recollect an authentic case, remarkably similar to that of Wieland." The first suggestion of an actual parallel is found in a footnote to a review of *Wieland* in the *American Review and Literary Journal*.[4] The reviewer cited a story in the *New York Weekly Magazine*[5] for July 20 and 27, 1796. It is important to note that the story here related is not a contemporary event, but happened in December, 1781. Miss Marble's statement that the theme was suggested to Brown by an "occurrence just before the tale was written"[6] is obviously misleading. The title of the article is "an account of a Murder Committed by Mr. J—— Y——, upon his Family, in December, A.D. 1781."

The parallels between the "account" of the unfortunate Mr. Y—— and *Wieland* are many. Both Wieland and Y—— made confessions of guilt, both protested their innocence of a conscious desire to commit such awful crimes, and both acted according to what they thought was the Divine Will. The sister in each case was attacked, but each escaped to tell the horrible story; both Y—— and Wieland had four children; both were put in dungeons and each escaped twice, only to be recaptured.

If these are the sources of *Wieland,* one can perceive readily enough the superiority of Brown's story. He has taken the bald facts and vitalized them. In the account the murder of his wife and children by Y—— is described in detail; in *Wieland* it is left to the reader's imagination, only the fact being made known. The crude machinery of the two spirits and the burnt Bible does not appear in Brown's story. Instead, the author of *Wieland* found a natural explanation in the art of the ventriloquist, then a newly realized and mysterious power.

Man—frail, ignorant, selfish, superstitious man—was for Brown a perennial subject for meditation. He deplored the fact that man has always been wont to ascribe to supernatural agency any phenomenon which transcends his power of explanation. Like Voltaire, for instance, he was mortified that the apparently intelligent accepted the view that the Lisbon earthquake was the expression of the wrath of a benevolent God because the city contained a few wicked people. The religion which called for the adoration of such a God was in Brown's mind a dangerous religion. His native state had harbored many curious and fanatical sects, some of them dangerous to both mind and body. It cannot be doubted that *Wieland* was a direct protest against the consequences of such religions. It was a sermon against credulity

---

[4] I (July, Aug. and Sept., 1801), 335.

[5] Brown gave the reference as II, 20-28, which should read II, 20 and 28. For a discussion of this error in citation see Carl Van Doren, *Nation*, XCIX (Nov. 12, 1914), 577-578.

[6] Annie Russell Marble, *Heralds of American Literature*, p. 296.

and religious fanaticism. In fact, the greatest merit of the novel lies in the masterful picture of the progress of Wieland's religious "enthusiasm" until it terminates in a wild frenzy. As the title suggests, Wieland had been transformed from a man into a very beast by the power of "creed" religion. It is this religious theme of the story that is most gripping, and about which the reader's memory clings longest. Indeed, the whole novel is directed toward that end.

It was precisely this element of fanaticism which so deeply impressed John Greenleaf Whittier that, when he wrote his essay on fanaticism, he used a passage from *Wieland* to drive home his point.[7]

Brown had had ample opportunity of observing in his own native city and its environs the evil effects of religious fanaticism. Pennsylvania had become the refuge of more religious eccentrics than any other American state. While the evil genius of Carwin is devilishly fascinating, the author has endeavored to center the mind of the reader on the final destruction of the mind of Wieland by religious fanaticism.

As a work of art *Wieland* has considerable claim on our attention. Although the narrative is slow and awkward, the action too often delayed by long, philosophical speculations, the Stuart-Conway-Maxwell episode irrelevant to the main theme, Carwin's actions too obvious, and the catastrophe strained and premature, *Wieland* has its positive qualities. Wieland, helplessly driven to crimes of the blackest nature, even against the humanity that rises up in him, and Carwin the biloquist, impelled to wickedness, not because of innate maliciousness, but because of the fascination of evil itself, are powerful and impressive studies in speculative pathology. They are characters that linger in the mind long after the events with which they are associated have been forgotten. Carwin is undoubtedly one of the most horribly fascinating characters in fiction. We follow him, yet we hate him. The author also achieved a marked degree of unity by making almost every event bear directly upon the character of Wieland. The catastrophe, awkward and unnatural as it is, has been carefully and rationally prepared for from the beginning. A feverish atmosphere pervades the novel and gives to it an incomparable driving power.

### CARWIN, THE BILOQUIST

*Wieland* made a stir in its day, and—what was to be expected—Carwin was the drawing card. The fascination of this character and his mysterious past at which the author had hinted induced Brown immediately to begin another novel with Carwin as hero. For September 14, 1798, Dunlap's *Diary* reads: "Read C. B. Brown's beginning for the life of Carwin; as far as he has gone, he has done well; he has taken up the schemes of the Illuminati." But the work was

---

[7] "Fanaticism," in *Writings*, Riverside ed., VII, 391-395.

interrupted a few days later by the plague which then raged in New York, and we hear no more of *Carwin* until November, 1803, when Brown needed it as "copy" for the *Literary Magazine*. The work was published posthumously in book form in 1822, in London.

The story is simple. Carwin, a youth of great natural ability and endowed with the power of ventriloquism, is observed by an enlightened and mysterious European by the name of Ludloe, who induces Carwin to accompany him to Ireland. All the luxuries and attractions of Ludloe's home are shared by Carwin. He is allowed to browse at will among the master's books, so that he may gradually become imbued with the same views concerning the ills of society. After a period of proper tutelage Carwin finally accepts Ludloe's primary principle that the end justifies the means, and, like his master, is willing to go to any length to effect a worthy end. Carwin, thus advanced in knowledge and dissimulation, is sent to Spain to get a firsthand view of the Inquisition. While there he plays many foul tricks on the monks and nuns by means of ventriloquism. This power, however, he has kept secret from Ludloe, despite his promise to disclose every detail of his life.

When Carwin has returned to Ireland, he is let into the secret of his master's profession. Ludloe tells him of a great Institution whose purpose he will not yet make known to his disciple. Much about the designs of this association, however, Carwin—a typical Godwinian spy—learns from a map of an unknown island which he discovers in Ludloe's closet. His curiosity thoroughly aroused, Carwin expresses a desire to become a member of the society. Ludloe assents, but warns him of the perils to be encountered, of the pledge of absolute secrecy, and of the necessity for a full confession of his life. Carwin then confesses everything but his biloquial powers; but Ludloe, whose insight into Carwin's past is remarkable, is not satisfied with the confession, and promises to give him another chance the next day. The story is left in a fragmentary state.

*Carwin* is not a sequel to *Wieland,* for it is the story of the life of that remarkable character before *Wieland* opens. It should be read first, for it throws much light on Carwin's subsequent machinations in *Wieland.* But even with this knowledge the reader is unsatisfied with his actions, for there appears to be no motive for the calamity which he brings upon the Wieland family. We may be induced to accept the principle that under certain conditions a worthy end may justify the use of ignoble means, but what is the result in this case? What was the worthy end? Was it to warn against religious fanaticism? As *Carwin* was never completed, the reader should not expect to find a well-motivated story. Such unanswered questions as we have asked in connection with this fragment would doubtless have been satisfactorily answered in the completed work.

*ORMOND; OR THE SECRET WITNESS*

In another connection we have seen that in September of 1798, after a severe outbreak of the plague in New York, Brown with his friend William Johnson fled to Perth Amboy, New Jersey, the home of William Dunlap. Here Brown remained for six weeks and regained his health. The three friends—Dunlap the dramatist and theater manager, Johnson the lawyer and court recorder, and Brown the aspiring author—took long rambles over the countryside and discussed plans for a memoir of Smith. Brown was also busied with plans for a magazine and with seeing his next novel, *Ormond,* through the press. It was published January 21, 1799.

The circumstance of the composition and publication of *Ormond* is described in a letter by Brown to his brother Armitt, December 20, 1798:

> What excuse to make for my long silence I know not, unless the simple truth be sufficient for the purpose. Some time since I bargained with the publisher of *Wieland* for a new performance, part of which only was written, and the publication commencing immediately, I was obliged to apply with the utmost diligence to the pen, in order to keep pace with the press. Absorbed in this employment, I was scarcely conscious of the lapse of time, and when the day's task was finished, felt myself thoroughly weary and unfit for a continuance of the same employment in any new shape.
>
> I call my book *Ormond, or The Secret Witness.* I hope to finish the writing and the publication together before New Year's day, when I shall have a breathing spell.

Despite this hasty and haphazard method of composition *Ormond* marks an advance over *Wieland* and *Carwin* in motivation of plot and in delineation of character. It is also a better illustration of Brown's professed thesis that the world is governed by men of "soaring passions and intellectual energy," and it exhibits more fully than its predecessors the author's avowed purpose in writing novels: "to enchain the attention and ravish the souls of those who study and reflect." Here are soaring passions and intellectual energy in great sufficiency.

The theme of the novel is virtue in distress, and its method of development is Godwinian.[8] Stephen Dudley, an honest, benevolent apothecary of considerable means, is suddenly reduced to indigence by the intrigue of his apprentice Craig. In order to win a living, Dudley is driven to daily labor. He finds employment as clerk in a law office, where "he was perpetually encumbered with the rubbish of law, and waded with laborious steps through its endless tautologies, its impertinent circuities, its lying assertions and hateful artifices." This grind, this hollowness, breeds in the hero an unconquerable

[8] Cf. Professor Warfel's divergent and in my opinion erroneous interpretation in *Charles Brockden Brown* (1949), 130-131.

melancholy. Other troubles follow. His wife dies of melancholia, and he himself is blinded by cataract. Thus the support of the family devolves upon his sixteen-year-old daughter Constantia. She does not falter. Her mind is powerful and cultivated, for her education has been "regulated by the peculiar views of her father, who sought to make her, not alluring and voluptuous, but eloquent and wise. He therefore limited her studies to Latin and English." Instead of the amorous effusions of Petrarch and Racine, the works of Tacitus, Milton, Newton, and Hartley become her daily food.

When calamity comes, the Dudleys move from their mansion in New York to a tenement in Philadelphia. Constantia gets employment as a seamstress. The small pittance she receives is barely enough to satisfy their wants. To add to her burdens and alarms, yellow fever breaks out. But Constantia is brave and resourceful, and by wise management keeps the family supplied with food and shelter. She then loses her job, and her savings are nearly gone when the heartless landlord forces the family to vacate. They find smaller and cheaper quarters, and reduce their food to "hasty pudding" and water. By this means they can live four months on three dollars. But fuel is expensive and, as they have no means of getting any, the poorhouse seems the only alternative to death.

At this critical moment Ormond makes his appearance. He seems the soul of benevolence, and immediately supplies the family with necessities. We are at once prepossessed in favor of Ormond, who continues to grow in our esteem until we learn of his relations with Helena Cleves and his associations with Thomas Craig. The suspicion that Ormond has been the cause of the calamity which befell the Dudleys now comes to our minds. The suspicion increases when he declares his love for Constantia and renounces Helena, whom he has seduced and brought from New York. Ormond puts the Dudleys under every obligation that his fertile brain can devise; and when this fails to win Constantia, he resolves to use every means in his power. Her virtue is assailed, but without success; all his arguments against the sanctity of love and marriage cannot move her. He now forces Craig to murder Constantia's father and thus prepare the way for the blackest crime. Constantia lays plans to escape him, but Ormond forestalls her and loses no time in trying to execute his design.

It is dark and Constantia is alone in her apartment. When Ormond enters, finding Craig lurking in the building, he kills him and proceeds to Constantia's room, driven on by a power which he cannot resist. The scene which follows is one of the most powerful in fiction. Constantia endeavors to escape from the building, but all exits have been secured; she threatens suicide if the villain tries to lay hands on her. However, instead of killing herself, she plunges the knife into the heart of Ormond.

Here is Brown at his best; here are all the "soaring passions and intellectual energy" that one can reasonably crave. Although the readers is not fully aware of it, every movement from the very beginning points directly and inevitably to this catastrophe. There is no lack of motivation as in *Wieland,* no premature and awkward solution, and when the end comes, horrible though it is, the reader is satisfied. For once Brown has achieved a unity of impression rare with him.

Constantia Dudley is Brown's conception of the ideal woman— noble, generous, self-reliant. She is most sympathetically portrayed, and the reader follows her with more personal regard than he follows any other of Brown's characters. The author never really succeeded in making a character live, but Constantia is unquestionably his nearest approach to such achievement. Shelley was fond of her; and if we can believe Peacock, she "held one of the highest places, if not the very highest place, in Shelley's idealities of female character."[9] There is no evidence to sustain the contention of a recent critic that Constantia was a victim of homosexuality or that she failed because she lacked the bulwark of religion.[10]

*Ormond* is a tragedy—a tragedy not of an already weak and impotent mind as in *Wieland,* but of a powerful and enlightened mind, wrecked by a master passion over which the victim has no control. Ormond is moved, not by the fascination of evil as Carwin was, but by an overwhelming desire to conquer and possess whatever the heart craves. His is a mind that brooks no defeat. There is nothing too sacred or too powerful to stand between him and the object of his desire. Ormond is one of those "high-minded" villains, political and social enthusiasts, endowed with noble and generous impulses, who begin life in benevolent service, but who, on being caught in the web of social errors, turn fiends and like Macbeth cut their way out regardless of the cost. Ormond had early embraced the doctrine that a worthy end always justifies the means. He can stand before Constantia and tell her in the typical Godwinian dialect that he murdered her father out of a spirit of benevolence, since "his death was a due and disinterested offering at the altar of your felicity and mine. . . . At his age, death, whose coming at some period is inevitable, could not be distant. To make it unforeseen and brief and void of pain . . . was the dictate of benevolence." As Dudley's life is of no value to the world and no pleasure to himself, but a direct obstacle to the happiness of others, therefore, argued the fiend, he has no "moral" right to life.

Ormond is Brown's most accomplished villain; he is not only an adept in the major sphere of villainy but also a transgressor of all the

[9] Thomas Love Peacock, *The Memoirs of Shelley,* ed. Humbert Wolfe (1933), II, 328.

[10] Warfel, *op. cit.,* pp. 130-131.

ordinary conventions and safeguards of society. He holds religion and the institution of marriage in contempt. In these and many other respects, he resembles Falkland in *Caleb Williams*.

There cannot be the least doubt of Brown's indebtedness to the author of the latter novel. But this debt has been much exaggerated, because critics have not taken the time or had the inclination to give the proper orientation to Brown's novels. In addition to the works of Godwin, the novels of Holcroft and Bage, the works of Rousseau and the philosophers of the Enlightenment, the generous impulses and benevolent feelings generated by social and political revolutions at home and abroad, the rapid advance of social and moral science, ideal schemes for social uplift—all these and more form the proper background for Brown's novels. Brockden Brown was decidedly a child of his age, a proponent of all advanced social and political opinions fathered by the French Revolution.

We have said that Brown's villains remind us strongly of Godwin's, but there is a difference—a significant difference. This difference lies in the motives behind the villainy. Brown's criminals are systematic and ''large-minded'' villains, clothed with mysterious powers, governed by an invisible Empire whose object is the salvation of the world. But Falkland, the typical Godwinian villain, on the other hand, becomes a criminal in a sudden burst of passion and then degenerates into a hardened sinner. Falkland has been schooled in the gentleman's code of honor, a blind irrational system which holds its devotees as in a vise and destroys their reason. Godwin was bent upon the destruction of an outmoded system; Brown, upon portraying the nefarious consequences of blindly following principles based upon cold logic. In reality this is a refutation of Godwinism. Ormond, Carwin, Ludloe, and Welbeck are villains by premeditation and for noble ends; not so with Falkland. This difference is not merely accidental; it is fundamental, and represents, I believe, Brown's indebtedness to the Society of the Illuminati.[11] Although Brown never mentions in his novels the Society by name, there can be no doubt about the matter. His frequent discussions of the ideals of the Illuminati in the *Monthly Magazine and American Review* show that the Society had had considerable fascination for him. The probable influence of the principles of the Illuminati upon Brown's fictional characters will be examined in some detail in another section of this chapter.

Apparently Brown, by now having exhausted this vein of fiction, turned once again to his native heath for materials for his next novel —*Edgar Huntly*.

## EDGAR HUNTLY

In July, 1799, Brown had ready for the press another novel, *Edgar Huntly; or Memoirs of a Sleep-Walker*. This production, as already

[11] See discussion of the Society, pp. 188-190.

pointed out, was in part a recasting of the materials of the ill-fated *Skywalk,* a recasting the exact nature and extent of which cannot be determined, but judging from Dunlap's description and the fragment printed in the *Weekly Magazine* it was was considerable.

The nearest approximation to the fulfilment of Brown's threefold purpose in writing fiction is seen in *Edgar Huntly.* It ''enchains the attention'' more completely than any other of his novels; it ''instructs the mind'' by pointing a moral; and it portrays distinctively American scenes. The work unites Old World intrigues with the hazards of a New World civilization. The story of Huntly and the Indian massacres is in striking contrast with the moral decadence of Europe as seen in the Clithero narrative.

The story in brief follows: Edgar Huntly's friend Waldegrave has been mysteriously murdered; a strange, half-naked man is discovered at night furiously digging under the elm where Waldegrave's body had been found; he is a sleepwalker and proves to be Clithero, a laborer lately arrived from Ireland. Suspicion connects him with the murder; Edgar Huntly in pursuit, Clithero flees into the wilds of Norwalk. After some thrilling adventures, and hard pressed by Huntly, he confesses, but not to the murder of Waldegrave. His story is a web of family feuds, murders, and incest, through which Clithero has played the high-minded villain. Out of self-defense he has murdered the vicious brother of his beloved patroness; and from a motive of ''pure benevolence'' he decided to kill her; he was, he insisted, crushingly impelled to the most heinous crimes by a Demon against whom no human power could contend. To escape, Clithero, like Carwin, put on beggar's clothes and fled to America.

But these two elements are so interwoven as to give to the novel a unity rarely achieved by Brown. Even the Weymouth episode has a closer relation to the main threads of the story than is commonly suspected. But Brown certainly intended the main interest of the novel to be the analysis of unusual mental states, a study of somnambulism and insanity. A careful reading reveals that Clithero had inherited a weak mind, that more than once he had been temporarily insane. And Huntly, brooding over the mysterious death of his friend Waldegrave and deeply moved by the plight of Clithero, turns somnambulist and sojourns in the dim borderland between the sane and the insane. That keen insight into the springs of human actions, that subtle analysis of morbid conditions of mind, that almost ghoulish force in calling forth terror from the common facts of life are nowhere in Brown so well displayed as in the novel before us.

Brown evidently intended the Huntly adventure to form the main element of his novel. He did, at least, bring the whole action to a climax in the Indian ravages. Edgar's encounter with a panther; his spooky adventures in a cave; his fight with the Indians, and the rescue of a white girl are told with a passion and a sweep that lift the novel above the idealizations of a Fenimore Cooper. Old Deb, or Queen Mab, the embodiment of various traits of Indian character, is skilfully and sympathetically portrayed. In fact, she is the most highly individual character in the novel.

Brockden Brown's ideas of the Indian character show little or no affinity with contemporary European writers bred on the ideas of Lord Shaftesbury and Rousseau. Shaftesbury's idealization of the virtues of primitive man or "the noble savage," supplemented by Rousseau's ideas of a purely imaginary State of Nature, had had a far-reaching effect on the thought of the eighteenth century. The praise of out-of-doors life and the noble instincts of men in a natural state found an honored place in a vast body of literary productions; philosophers and divines vied with each other in glorifying "the noble savage." They contrasted the corrupt and decadent civilization of Europe with man in a state of nature, and, to substantiate their claims, they cited "the noble natives" of some peaceful island in the Pacific Ocean; or later, when the American Revolution brought this country into prominence, the American Indian became the type of noble savage dear to the doctrinaire. Indians were induced or forced to accompany European travelers back to their native land and to suffer the indignities of being caged and displayed to the astonished vulgar as the natural man. Indeed, European enthusiasts looked upon Americans generally as the sturdy product of nature.

This idealization of the Indian character and of primitive life found little place in the works of native American writers. They knew the Indian, not from enchanting distance, but from actual and often bloody contact. Nevertheless, early American novelists saw a wealth of material in our Indian heritage; cunning, crafty, hardy, nimble, bloodthirsty, the Indian appealed to them as the basis for a genuine native fiction, and to Brockden Brown goes the honor of first demonstrating the worth of that material. Mrs. Ann Eliza Bleecker, in her *History of Maria Kettle* (1793), had, to be sure, preceded him by four or five years, but her treatment was purely incidental. Brown, on the other hand, made a conscious effort to put the Indian in fiction. He was prompted partly by the novelty of the material and partly by the desire to foster a purely native literature. The Preface to *Edgar Huntly* shows Brown's disgust with the ordinary Gothic means of exciting terror. One merit

the writer may at least claim: that of calling forth the passions and engaging the sympathies of the reader by means hitherto unemployed by preceding authors. Puerile superstitions and exploded manners, Gothic castles and chimeras, are the materials usually employed for this end. The incidents of Indian hostility and the perils of the western wilderness are far more suitable; and for a native of America to overlook these would admit of no apology. These, therefore, are, in part, the ingredients of this tale, and these he has been ambitious of depicting in vivid and faithful colors.

The climax in *Edgar Huntly* as in *Wieland* is artistically weak, for the expected does not happen. Clithero turns out to be a maniac; his patroness has only swooned, not died; Waldegrave has been killed by an Indian; and Huntly is left a bewildered man, musing over the train of events which his ungovernable curiosity has set in motion. Clithero and Huntly have been living under "horrid delusions." Indeed, the novel is a fascinating, if not a powerful, study in abnormal psychology.

### ARTHUR MERVYN

From this curious mixture of native with Godwinian and Rousseauistic materials, our author now turns for his next novel to that subject matter which he knew most intimately—yellow fever. The conviction, based upon his success in *The Man at Home,* that his forte lay in realistic treatment of the impact of the plague upon life in crowded cities, perhaps induced Brown to continue this vein in another novel, *Arthur Mervyn; or Memoirs of the Plague Year 1793.* This work, undertaken apparently in the spring of 1798, began its appearance in the *Weekly Magazine* (Philadelphia) on June 16, and continued with a brief interruption until August 25, when the magazine was suspended owing to the death of the editor, James Walters. Brown had left for New York on July 1, engaging to supply Walters with weekly instalments of the novel. This engagement Brown apparently did not always keep, for no instalment appeared on July 21. The editor's note gave the probable reason: "The distance at which some of our correspondents reside, or their indisposition, necessarily subjects us to the hazard of a pause in continuous original productions. This is the only excuse we have to offer for a temporary suspension of *Arthur Mervyn.*" The work was resumed on August 4 and continued regularly till August 25. The editor did not know that the severe pestilence which had broken out in New York in the summer of 1798 had put a stop for a time to Brown's literary activity.

We hear no more of the novel until December 20, when, in a letter to his brother Armitt, Brown wrote: "Together with your letter, I received one from M. proposing the publication of *Mervyn* on the terms and in the manner mentioned by you. I wrote him an immediate answer, assenting, perhaps too hastily, to the publication, and promising, when my present engagements [he was then completing *Ormond*] were fulfilled to finish the adventures of A. Mervyn."[12] When *Ormond* was published on January 21, Brown immediately resumed work on *Arthur Mervyn.* Part I, a complete novel, was in the printer's hands sometime before February 15.

[12] Dunlap, II, 93.

The story may be briefly told. Arthur Mervyn, a country lad, leaves home because of his father's hasty and suspicious marriage with a milkmaid, and seeks his fortunes in the city. He reaches the metropolis (Philadelphia) penniless and falls victim to yellow fever. Mervyn is picked up on the street by a benevolent Dr. Stevens, who acts much as did Brown's friend E. H. Smith later in rescuing the Italian Scandella. Mervyn is nursed back to health only to be apprehended by a Mr. Worthley on the ground that he is connected with a swindler named Welbeck. Mervyn, to justify himself before his benevolent friend and rescuer, is forced to reveal his history. He has been induced, it seems, by philanthropic Welbeck—the counterpart of Falkland as Mervyn is of Williams—to become his secretary. Welbeck's activity is kept secret from the lad. He lives in a mansion with his sister and has a mysterious air about him. Mervyn's curiosity being aroused, he tries to manufacture a romantic past for his patron. Welbeck's enjoining absolute secrecy as one of the conditions of Mervyn's employment only increases an already active curiosity; and Mervyn, like Caleb Williams, constantly hounds his master for the story of his past. Welbeck finally confesses. He has, it appears, committed a forgery, murdered a man for fear of exposure, and squandered the wealth and ruined the morals of the woman represented as his sister.

This confession is followed by an unsuccessful attempt of Welbeck to commit suicide by jumping into the river at night. He is rescued and in four days returns to find Arthur in possession of the twenty thousand dollars in bills which the latter suspected had been stolen from Signora Lodi. Welbeck's master passion is the love of wealth, and his endeavor to regain the bills brings about the climax in the main story.

Since *Arthur Mervyn* in both idea and plot has a closer affinity with *Caleb Williams* than any other of Brown's novels, a brief summary of Godwin's novel will help clarify our discussion of Brown's work:

Caleb, a lad of unusual ability, the son of a small farmer, has become the secretary of Falkland, his landlord. In his anxiety to discover the cause of fits of melancholy and insane wandering which at times affect the benevolent and accomplished Falkland, Williams is led to believe that his patron is really guilty of a murder for which he has once been tried and acquitted. Henceforth, his passionate curiosity, to whose satisfaction, he says, he would have sacrificed liberty and life, leads him to attempt every means to discover the truth. Falkland comes upon Williams in the act of lifting the cover of a mysterious chest, and in a passion of impatience tells all the story of his guilt, and his determination to hide it at any cost. Williams still loves and admires his master, whom he considers criminal only through the force of circumstances acting on his really noble qualities. But Falkland distrusts his devotion, maddens him by a petty tyranny of suspicion, and drives him to an attempted flight. Caleb is captured and imprisoned on a charge of theft arranged by Falkland.

Williams escapes from prison, but is prevented by Falkland's emissaries from leaving the country. In London he lives the life of a hunted creature, constantly recognized by Falkland's spies and driven to new disguises, until he is seized and taken before a magistrate. Maddened by the long-drawn terror of his hiding, he denounces Falkland, only to be reproached with adding lying to theft. Falkland appears and tells Williams that the apparent persecution was only a test of the lad's fidelity to his oath, a test in which he has failed. Henceforth, wherever he goes, he will always be in his patron's power, and always be pursued by his revenge. To Falkland reputation is the dearest thing on earth; therefore his revenge will be to take reputation from Williams.

Thereafter Williams is followed from place to place by emissaries of Falkland, who, by spreading the story of his theft and ingratitude, made him an outcast from each community that has sheltered him. Deprived of his livelihood, his friends, his betrothed, he forgets the reverence for Falkland which has persisted through all his sufferings, returns to his native place, and brings a solemn accusation against his former master. Confronted with the feeble, almost dying Falkland, Williams is overcome with grief for what he has done. Falkland, convinced too late of Caleb's sincerity, praises his heroic patience, acknowledges the crime, and dies. Godwin leaves his hero a prey to eternal remorse, dramatically inquiring, "of what use are talents and sentiments in the corrupt wilderness of human society?"

The reader will perceive at once remarkable parallels between *Arthur Mervyn* and *Caleb Williams*. In each a country lad, brimming over with curiosity, is employed as secretary to a villain; Welbeck and Falkland differ in the circumstances leading to their villainy— the former being moved by a boundless passion for wealth, the latter by a desire for reputation. Each of the villains is pursued by the ceaseless curiosity of his secretary until his crimes are confessed. Falkland's motives are not so sordid and mean as Welbeck's; but, on the other hand, Mervyn is more admirable than Williams.

There are some forceful scenes in *Arthur Mervyn*—notably Arthur's arrival in the plague-stricken city, his adventures in a bedroom, his quarrel with Welbeck, the murder scene, and Welbeck's attempted suicide. These are worthy of any writer's pen, but most readers will feel that the author failed to realize the full value of these situations. Brown could create stirring scenes and powerful plots, but he could not resolve them. Whatever may be the shortcomings of the novel, it must be admitted that the author has in the plague scenes achieved a powerful realism.

We have already, in a previous chapter, noted Brown's interest as a writer in portraying minute details and in laying bare the innermost secrets of the human heart. In this power he challenges a place among the great realists of English fiction, and in this particular field he wins a berth beside Defoe of *The Plague Year*. A quotation will show Brown's power:

The city, we were told, was involved in confusion and panic, for a pestilential disease had begun its destructive progress. Magistrates and citizens were flying to the country. The numbers of the sick multiplied beyond all example—even in the pest-affected cities of the Levant. The malady was malignant and unsparing.

The usual occupations and amusements of life were at an end. Terror had exterminated all the sentiments of nature. Wives were deserted by husbands, and children by parents. Some had shut themselves in their houses, and debarred themselves from all communication with the rest of mankind. The consternation of others had destroyed their understanding, and their misguided steps hurried them into the midst of the danger which they had previously labored to shun. Men were seized by this disease in the streets; passengers fled from them; entrance into their own dwellings was denied to them; they perished in the public ways.

The chambers of disease were deserted, and the sick left to die of negligence. None could be found to remove the lifeless bodies. Their remains, suffered to decay by piecemeal, filled the air with deadly exhalations, and added tenfold to the devastation. . . .

. . . These tokens were new, and awakened all my panics. Death seemed to hover over this scene, and I dreaded that the floating pestilence had already lighted on my frame. I had scarcely overcome these tremors, when I approached a house, the door of which was opened, and before which stood a vehicle, which I presently recognised to be a *hearse*.

The driver was seated on it. I stood still to mark his visage and to observe the course which he proposed to take. Presently a coffin, borne by two men, issued from the house. The driver was a negro, but his companions were white. Their features were marked by ferocious indifference to danger or pity. One of them as he assisted in thrusting the coffin into the cavity provided for it, said, "I'll be damned if I think the poor dog was quite dead. It wasn't the *fever* that ailed him, but the sight of the girl and her mother on the floor. I wonder how they all got into that room. What carried them there?"

The other surlily muttered, "Their legs to be sure."

"But what should they hug together in one room for?"

"To save us trouble, to be sure."

"And I thank them with all my heart; damn it, it wasn't right to put him in his coffin before the breath was fairly gone. I thought the last look he gave me told me to stay a few minutes."

"Pshaw! he could not live. The sooner dead the better for him; as well as for us. Did you mark how he eyed us, when we carried away his wife and daughter? I never cried in my life, since I was knee-high, but curse me if I ever felt in better tune for the business than just then. Hey!" continued he, looking up, and observing me standing a few paces distant, and listening to their discourse, "What's wanted? Anybody dead?"

Such scenes were not exaggerations of a romancer's idle brain: they were living pictures of the facts as they were. Brown was a realist, and this was the spirit of realism then finding its way into fiction. Of this novel Mathew Carey, who had himself witnessed the plague, wrote: "*Arthur Mervyn* gives a vivid and terrifying picture, probably not too highly colored, of the horrors of that period."

The numerous subplots of *Arthur Mervyn* defy summary, for they have neither beginning nor end. The author excites our interest in an episode like that touching the fortunes of Mrs. Wentworth or the Hadwin family only to leave it suspended in midair. This was Brown's clumsy way of preparing his reader for a sequel. And a sequel there was. Part II of the novel, according to a letter to his brother James, was ready for publication by April, 1800. It proved to be greatly inferior to the earlier work. The threads of the plot are loosely held together, and the unity of the story is lost in the confusion of detail piled on detail. Brown was indeed successful in achieving the "horrible" in the first part; but the second suffered the usual fate of sequels.

### CLARA HOWARD

In a letter to his brother James, dated April, 1800, Brown wrote:

Your remarks upon the gloominess and out-of-nature incidents of *Huntly*, if they be not just in their full extent, are doubtless such as most readers will make, which alone, is a sufficient reason for dropping the doleful tones and assuming a cheerful one, or, at least substituting moral causes and daily incidents in place of the prodigious or the singular. I shall not fall hereafter into that strain.

Here, then, is Brown's revised formula for novel-writing: no longer will he present the high-minded villain of soaring passions and intellectual energy; no longer will he portray the horrors of the plague. And he might have added that henceforth the radicalism with which his pages had bristled will be superseded by a philosophy less extreme in its implications.

On the failure of the French Revolution to achieve its avowed ends, the radicals of Europe as of America deserted to the ranks of the conservatives. The once challenging and inspiriting doctrines of perfectibility, equality, and natural rights had been considerably modified or entirely discredited by the failure of the Revolution. This turn of events acted powerfully in changing Brown's philosophy of life, a change which we see in his letters and in his magazine articles. This change in philosophical outlook, however insignificant, was to modify the thought and the materials of his subsequent novels. It represents a renunciation of the more radical of Godwin's tenets. It must not be thought, however, that Brockden Brown's way of thinking had undergone a complete revolution. With him the change is much less noticeable than that which marked two of his distinguished English contemporaries—Wordsworth and Coleridge. Brown still remained a radical, but not of the old stamp.

Begun soon after the publication of Part II of *Arthur Mervyn*, *Clara Howard* exhibits much of Brown's new way of handling his material. Its theme is the sanctity and nobility of simple love and life. No villains or bloodletting or soaring passion adorns these pages; everything is so quiet and monotonous that the reader sighs for just a little villainy. Brown's method in this novel is the method of analysis; consequently, nothing happens. One or two sentences will suffice for the story; only a reading of the novel itself can give an adequate idea of the character analyses and philosophical meanderings which fill its pages. Philip Stanley, a gifted rustic turned watch-tinker, loves and is loved by Clara Howard, a sort of humanized Constantia Dudley. Philip has, however, been long betrothed to Mary Wilmot, for whom he has no love. Clara, discovering this fact, very properly insists that he must go in search of his Mary, who has fled the city, and Philip as properly obeys. When at last Miss Wilmot is found, she is engaged to another man (the only approach to villainy). This action frees Philip, and he hastens to his Clara, who in a "melting scene" of some magnitude swears eternal love to her charming Philip.

This is the first of Brown's novels with a woman in the title role. Clara Howard is resolute, self-contained, educated; older and more sophisticated than her lover, she is also his superior in strength of will. Philip's love for her reminds us of Arthur Mervyn's infatuation with Mrs. Fielding, whose "superior age, sedateness, and prudence" gave to his "deportment a filial freedom and affection," and in whose hands he was but "wax," as he naïvely remarked. Though the disparity in age between Clara Howard and Philip Stanley is not great, there is the disconcerting picture of the strong woman leading the weak, vacillating youth. She goads him to action and sets about a course of instruction for the lad. "I am in hope," she says, "that time and reflection will instill into you better principles." And in her last letter, she could write: "My maturer and more cautious judgment shall be counsellors and guides to thy inexperienced youth. While I love and cherish thee, as a wife, I shall assume some of the prerogatives of an elder sister and put my circumspection and forethought in the balance against thy headlong confidence."

This is Brown's ideal woman; she is perhaps a reminiscence of his beloved Henrietta, who acted in real life much as Clara does in the novel. We saw the beginning in Constantia Dudley; here is the perfection: a happy mixture of brains and sensibility. This is the New Woman whom Brown dreamed of in his *Alcuin*: self-reliant, resourceful, tolerant—none of your pink-ribboned, melting, swooning Emmelines among Brown's heroines.

## JANE TALBOT

*Clara Howard,* published in 1801, was Brown's last novel written in New York, After a tour of two weeks, in July, 1801, through New York and several of the New England states, Brown settled down in Philadelphia and became a partner with his brothers in the mercantile business. But he found time during the year to write and publish *Jane Talbot,* his last novel. It is an "affecting story," and in some respects suggests that Brown had forgotten his new formula and returned to his earlier pattern, for it is a novel of soaring passions. Jane Talbot has been forced by her father to marry her cousin, a Mr. Talbot, a man whom she cannot love or esteem. The expected happens: Henry Colden, a disciple of Godwin, a man of striking appearance and powerful intellect, has just returned from France. He crosses Jane's path, and she at once realizes that here is the man of her choice. He visits her home and pours into her credulous ears his philosophy of religion, love, and marriage. He hints at a dark and mysterious past, but appears to be the very soul of benevolence and human sympathy. In the meantime, the gossipy, evil-minded, but thoroughly conventional, and thus respectable, Miss Jessup has seized upon the indiscretions of Jane to poison Talbot's love for his wife and at the same time win him for herself. This she succeeds in doing by the forging of letters. Jane and her husband are finally separated; Talbot marries Miss Jessup, and Jane's heart is then free for the man she really loves.

Mrs. Fielder, Jane's adopted mother, protests and, by playing on the filial sympathies of her daughter, finally induces Jane to renounce her lover. Colden, feeling that the situation is hopeless, decides to leave his native land and seek consolation in foreign travel. He is gone four years. In the meantime all obstacles to their happiness having been removed, Colden and Jane hasten to the altar.

*Jane Talbot* is not a great novel—it is inferior in many respects to the novels of Brown's heyday. There is too little action, too few of the gripping scenes characteristic of the author's best work. But when all is said, it must be allowed that the author keeps alive our interest in the lovers to the very end. If inability to lay the novel aside before the last page is reached is a test of its power, then *Jane Talbot* will rank with novels otherwise admittedly superior.

Its drawing power, however, does not lie in the skill of the narrative or in the good disposition of the materials of the plot, but rather in the philosophy of social emancipation working itself out in the lives of Jane Talbot and Henry Colden. The heroine, although still possessed of many of the characteristics of the "sensibility" school, is undoubtedly a woman of the new type. She is affectionate and impulsive, but she differs from the ordinary run of contemporary heroines in her insistence upon an exercise of independent judgment in matters that vitally concern her. Jane is of an analytical turn of mind, self-scanned and self-schooled. A number of books then considered dangerous for women to read had fallen into her hands; from them she learned self-confidence, and through them she was brought to the notion that a human being, man or woman, must be allowed to speak, act, and love for himself. It is this new confidence, this new assertion of self, that lends to Jane Talbot an unmistakable air of modernity. She might pass any day for a twentieth-century heroine, were it not that she still wears the cloak of "sensibility"—a fact that brings much sorrow to her and her lover. Jane could not be shaken by the brutal threats of her brother or the cruel insinuations of Mrs. Fielder, but the moment that either appealed to her affectionate sensibility, her heart would melt and become agreeable to any course of action. Weak though she is, the distance between her and the helpless, sighing, drooping creatures of eighteenth-century fiction is immeasurable. Though she marries the man she hates, is browbeaten by her brother, and is lectured by her adopted mother, Jane Talbot remains an individual of essentially independent mind.

Jane is undoubtedly a stronger character than Clara Howard, and the novel is distinctly superior in the unified effect and in the driving power of the story. Though Colden's personality permeates the novel, and his ideas of social and intellectual uplift form the meaty portions of the book, the character of Jane Talbot dominates it. Many of the stock phrases of the new freedom are repeatedly heard from her. "The world, in estimating my merits," said Jane, "never forgot that my father was rich." The amassing of great fortunes through speculation she regarded, in consonance with the Godwinian precept, as criminal. When driven to marry the man she does not love, Jane soliloquizes: "What a fatal act is that of plighting hands when the heart is estranged! Never, never let the placable and compassionate spirit be seduced into a union to which the affections are averse." Yet Godwinian philosophy received a merciless denunciation from Mrs. Fielder. "Colden had imbibed that pernicious philosophy," she said, "which is now so much in vogue . . . these letters show him as the advocate of suicide; a scoffer at promises; the despiser of reverence, of Providence, and a future state; an opponent of marriage, and as one who denied [shocking!] that anything but mere habit and positive law stood in the way of marriage, nay, of intercourse without marriage. . . ." But Colden was not always thus. A most fascinating book (Godwin's *Political Justice*) had fallen at length into his hands, and changed in a moment the whole course of his ideas. What he had before regarded with reluctance and terror, this book taught him to admire and love. "The writer," insisted Mrs. Fielder, "has the art of the grand deceiver; the fatal art of carrying the worst poison under the name and appearance of wholesome food; of disguising all that is impious, or blasphemous, or licentious, under the guise and sanction of virtue.''

Such is the character of Colden as seen through Mrs. Fielder's eyes, but not through Jane's. Colden confesses to her that he had once been criminal, and now has only one merit and that lately acquired, the devotion to truth. He looks backwards with humiliation and remorse, and forward with confidence. In fact, Colden is a high-minded, benevolent seeker for truth, but he is enchained by error. He even hints at being in the clutches of the Illuminati.

But Jane has profound confidence in Colden, and feels that she can reform him. ''If your opinions be adverse to religion,'' she writes to him, ''your affections are not wholly estranged from it. Your understanding dissents, but your heart is not yet persuaded to refuse.'' She hopes that she can awake him to rational activity. ''In you I found not one that disbelieved, but one that doubted. . . . I find it possible for me to disbelieve and retain their claims to our reverence, our affections, and especially our good offices.'' That Jane was successful in reforming Colden is to be inferred from his last letter: ''I have awakened from my dreams of doubt and misery, not to the cold and vague belief, but to the living and delightful consciousness of every tie that can bind a man to his Divine Parent and Judge.''

Another new and promising vein for fiction is struck in this novel: the fascination of the sea. Here for the first time in American fiction do we find emphasis on the significance of the sea in shaping man's life and character. Brown's lifelong interest in geography finds expression in descriptions of voyages to distant lands and of strange people in faraway islands and empires. The detailed picture of Japan and the curious life of its people has considerable interest just now. Voyages to various Pacific islands are mentioned or are given in scenic detail. Indeed, Brown's mind appears to have been moving toward a new type of fiction based upon the sea; for what may have been his last novel, ''Don Manuel,'' is in part a sea-story, containing a vivid and diabolically fascinating description of a storm in the Mediterranean. It is a novel which could be called a worthy forerunner of Melville.

### BROWN'S MINOR FICTION AND FRAGMENTS

In the course of Brown's career as a writer of fiction he turned out several minor pieces, really short stories, such as ''Thessalonica,'' ''The Trials of Arden,'' and ''Mary Selwyn.''[13] In these pieces, it may be plausibly maintained, Brown was the creator of that native American genre—the short story. Brown also left a number of fragments, as ''Adini,'' ''Jessica,'' ''Stephen Calvert,'' and ''Don Manuel.''

[13] These stories Brown published in his *Monthly Magazine*, May, 1799, and July and March, 1800, respectively.

The "Adini" fragment, twenty-nine pages in Allen-Dunlap, gives us only a slight clue as to its probable theme.[14] Signior Adini, a mysterious Italian, comes to America and settles down with his ten-year-old daughter. Mr. Ellen, the guardian of the young narrator of the story, gradually wins Adini's confidence and induces him to spend some time in his home at Ellendale. Adini holds advanced views on education and reform, and always gives the impression of being a stranger looking at the folly of Europeans. He makes mysterious allusions to "Socratic-land," and to islands in the South Seas. The Ellens erroneously conclude that he is insane, but Adini is only a member of the Society of the Illuminati, bent upon establishing Utopias in South America. The Ellendale letters in Brown's unpublished Journal have strong affinity with the "Adini" fragment.

The "Jessica" fragment is longer and more ambitious than the "Adini." It occupies more than sixty compact pages in Dunlap (1: 108-169), and is there untitled. Dunlap said that Brown planned to complete it but never did. The fragment was revised, however, and used, in part, in the author's last novel, *Jane Talbot*.

"Jessica" can be briefly summarized: Jessy (or Jessica) tells Sophia about Courtland, who has offered his "vows." She refuses his advances because she feels unworthy of him and because she does not love him. Courtland subsequently turns his attention to Sophia and writes her father asking for permission to court her. The father answers that she is already engaged to her cousin Watkins, then in Europe. Sophia, who has not known of this transaction, is furious, declaring that she cares nothing for Watkins and will never marry him.

The matter is dropped for one of more immediate interest—the arrival of a boarder, Colden, at Jessy's home. Jessica is much upset at the idea of a strange man about the house, but soon allows him to engross all her thoughts, though he seldom speaks to her. Determined to learn in order to talk intelligently to Colden, Jessy begins to read industriously Mosheim's *History*, which he had been skimming. She is much puzzled by the accounts of religious persecution, and determines to ask Colden the meaning of what she has read. That afternoon she asks Colden why people should be burnt for becoming Protestants. He gives her one dreadful look and dashes from the house. Heartbroken, she wanders out into the fields until dark, where Colden comes upon her. He apologizes for his rudeness, and she is transported by his kindness.

Just as the reader becomes interested in this evidence of a rapidly developing romance, the fragment ends. But brief as it is, it foreshadows the characteristics that Brown was to display in his completed

[14] I have in my possession an unpublished journal in which the *Adini* seems to be continued. Transcription is in progress.

novel, *Jane Talbot*.  The heroine, though modeled on the Pamela type, is a real person.  Colden, too, begins to acquire reality in the brief scope of the story.  Far from being the rake of the Lovelace type, he appears to be a noble and intelligent man, with some dreadful mystery clouding his life.  Knowing Brown's method from his other novels, one is justified in concluding that Colden was to be the "high-minded villain" of the Ormond type—a secret member of the Illuminati, who would stop at nothing to achieve his purpose.

Hurriedly written as this piece evidently was, it yet bears evidence of Brown's ability to create suspense.  His adroit suggestion of mystery surrounding Colden, his gradual unfolding of the emotions growing in Jessy's simple heart, rouse the reader's interest.

Perhaps of most interest in the fragment, however, is the moral and philosophical strain apparent in dialogues and incidents echoing the subjects which had evidently early occupied Brown's mind.  There are, of course, the conventional eighteenth-century dissertations on friendship and immortality, and discussions of women's education and of religious tolerance.

Even this brief fragment, then, reveals to us the fact that Brown was interested in the intellectual as well as the emotional content in fiction.

There are a number of significant parallels between "Jessica" and the later novel, *Jane Talbot*.  The most striking similarity is the patron-protégé relationship of Jane Talbot and Mrs. Fielder.  Colden is common to both novels and in both is described as physically of "middle size" and "scanty frame," not handsome, but with exceptionally expressive eyes.  As was to be expected, Colden in the earlier piece, "Jessica," was a revolutionary and probably would have developed into the typical Godwinian "high-minded villain," driven by an all-consuming purpose, the promulgation of the Illuminati creed.  The Colden of *Jane Talbot*, though addicted to questionings and discussions of economic, social, and religious topics, had no very sinister mystery in his past.

"Stephen Calvert," although filling 199 compact pages in Dunlap, was said by its author to be only the first act of "a five act drama."  This novel was begun immediately after Brown had completed *Wieland*.  This we learn from Dunlap's *Diary* which reads: September 25, 1798: "Walk with my friends.  Read the beginning of Charles's last novel, called *Calvert* [proposed to be changed to Caillemour] *or the Lost Brothers.*"  The fragment is a story of religious persecutions.  Calvert's ancestors renounced Catholicism and played a conspicuous part in the Wars of Religion.  With the revocation of the Edict of Nantes persecutions were renewed, and the two surviving members of the Calvert family were exiled to Holland.  From there one went to England, where he married into the nobility and became involved in the intrigues to reinstate the Stuarts on the English throne. The other brother came to America, married into a humble family, and lived a simple but honorable life. The narrator—a descendant of the brother who had come to America—disgusted with corrupt society, is now living as a disillusioned recluse on the banks of Lake Michigan. The novel no doubt would have been an extensive contrast between the Rousseauistic philosophy of man in a state of nature and Godwin's man in a decadent society. Some of the most gripping scenes Brown ever wrote are in the *Stephen Calvert* fragment.

The fragment, "Don Manuel," which is designated in the unpublished, extant manuscript[15] as "Volume Two, part One," opens with an exciting rescue at sea, during a raging storm, of the heroine Victoria, sister of the distinguished Italian Count Ariosto, by the faithful Hippolyto, referred to later as a Negro—perhaps a Moor from Spain. The lady has apparently been kidnapped by Don Manuel, the head of one of two rival, feuding Spanish families, and the hero of our story. Chapter I ends with the rescuing party's being washed up on the coast of Provençe, near the French-Italian border. Chapter II tells of their reception at a monastery in the vicinity, and makes known the identity of the leading characters of the rescue party. Victoria, the reader learns, is none other than the distinguished Italian Countess Victoria di Modena. The remaining two chapters of the fragment are concerned chiefly with the unraveling of the very complicated threads of the story, with incisive analyses of motives and intrigues of various characters and the faked marriage of Victoria to Hippolyto.

The fragment is a thrilling story by Brown at his best, though the style is heavy and verbose. Although the date of the fragment cannot be determined with certainty, it has many earmarks of being late Brown.

### BROWN AND THE ILLUMINATI

In the course of this study frequent mention of the Society of the Illuminati has been made. Since the principles of that Society had considerable influence on the character of Brown's heroes, they will here be briefly explained.

The Society was founded by Professor Adam Weishaupt at the University of Ingolstadt, in May, 1776, "to reform mankind." Weishaupt was an ex-Jesuit and a foe of man-made religious and social institutions. He conceived the idea of a society made up of enlightened men only. Such a society, he hoped, would dissipate the forces of superstition and error. At first only youths of great natural ability were to be admitted; but later the privilege was extended to include men whose minds were free from fears and prejudices. Each new member was under the tutelage of an Illuminatus whose duty it

[15] Now being transcribed by me.

was to impress upon the young mind the value of truth, to point out the errors of social and political institutions, and to fill the mind with the noble ideals of the Society. The Society was based upon the belief that the majority of mankind are ignorant, but are capable of vast improvement through proper education, and that it is the bounden duty of the wise or Illuminated to expose all the fallacies and prejudices inherent in social, political, and religious institutions. In order to bring about this end, no means must be spared; not even the most cherished conventions of society must stand in the way.

The connection of Brown's villains with such an Order is evident. Ludloe's guardianship over Carwin and the latter's subsequent actions can be explained in no other way. Ormond, Welbeck, Adini, and Colden hint at the existence of such a society, an invisible Empire to which they belong and whose commands and behests they must not challenge. Let us examine Carwin's convictions.

Carwin, a farmer's son—strong, capable, athletic, but uneducated— is, as we have seen, possessed of great curiosity and love of learning. He encounters Ludloe one morning—an Irishman of rank and apparently rich, who talks learnedly on many subjects. Believing that Carwin can use his voice to convert the ignorant to his desires and thereby accomplish many noble ends, Ludloe invites him to become a novice in the Society. The sum of human duty, Ludloe teaches him, is to be just and to square one's ideas and conduct. Ludloe dwells on the "duty of unfettering our minds from the prejudices which govern the world." He loves to expatiate on the evils of cohabitation, and maintains that all artificial ties of society must be broken before real liberty can come. Carwin, tiring of loafing, asks Ludloe to suggest something for him to do to help mankind. Ludloe replies that Carwin lacks knowledge and that it will take at least three years of study to make him a "man." Books alone will not suffice—one must study men. Thus it is determined that Carwin will travel in Spain and study men and manners. Carwin is taught to dissemble for good ends; he professes belief in Catholicism in order to study the priesthood. Ludloe teaches him that the evils that infest society are to be ascribed to the errors of opinion; that the absurd and unequal distribution of power and property gives birth to poverty and riches; and that these and not the defects in the moral constitution of men are the sources of luxury and crimes. Ludloe labors to prove "that man is the creature of circumstance, that he is capable of endless improvement; that his progress has been stopped by the artificial impediment of government; that by the removal of this, the fondest dreams of imagination will be realized." Carwin has by now seen the light; he dreams of an empire where reason will supplant force; where justice will be universally understood and practiced; where the interests of the whole and of the individual are the same; where the public good is the end of all activity; where the tasks of all will be the same and the means of subsistence equally distributed.

After Carwin has told Ludloe of his dreams of an ideal state, Ludloe for the first time intimates that he is connected with a society. After condemning the schemes of the Jesuits, Ludloe hints that an association resting on fidelity and zeal has been established in the heart of Europe. Its influence is boundless, and it stands as a great moral structure of wisdom and justice. Ludloe impresses upon Carwin the necessity of going through serious tests before he can be admitted to the society. "Until you are thoroughly tried out you will be unqualified for that post." It means death to reveal secrets, death to him that tells and to him that hears, for "our spies will find you out."

Since Brown left the story in a fragmentary state, the reader never learns whether Carwin became a member of the Society of the Illuminati.

An analysis would disclose that other leading characters had as close connection with the principles of the Society as Carwin; it would show that in its general aspects the philosophy of the Society differed but little from that associated with the Enlightenment in general and Godwin in particular.

Apparently, this connection of Brown's heroes with the Illuminati attracted little attention in his day. Only Dunlap, so far as is known, took note of this fact, for he recorded in his *Diary:* September 14, 1798: "Read C. B. Brown's beginning for the life of Carwin; as far as he has gone he has done well; he has taken up the schemes of the Illuminati."

That the Illuminati movement profoundly impressed Brown may be inferred from the numerous references to it in his magazines and other publications besides his novels, but that he never became a convert to its insidious doctrines is certain, even though its principles may have modified his social outlook. Brown's mature social philosophy might well be expressed in his own words:

Men are liable to error, and though they may intend good, may commit enormous mistakes in the choice of means. While they imagine themselves laboring for the happiness of mankind, loosening the bonds of superstition, breaking the fetters of commerce, out-rooting the prejudice of birth, by which father transmits to son absolute power over property, liberty, and lives of millions, they may, in reality, be merely pulling down the props which uphold human society, and annihilate not merely the chains of false religion but the foundations of morality—not merely the fetters of commerce and feudal usurpations upon property but commerce and property themselves. The apology which may be made for such is that though their activity be pernicious their purposes are pure.

Students of Brown usually classify his novels with the Gothic romances. To do so is to use the term loosely. Horace Walpole in 1764 had a nightmare and wrote an extravaganza of bloody scenes, hooting owls, swooning maidens, pictures dripping gore, ghosts in armor, mysterious figures in dark subterranean passages, secret trap doors, rolling balls of fire, cold clammy hands of murderers grasping the velvety neck of innocent damsels, robbers, and premature burials—and called it *The Castle of Otranto;* and the School of Terror was established. It is not necessary here to trace the influence of this abortion of fancy on the novels of Clara Reeve, William Beckford, Anne Radcliffe, Matthew Gregory Lewis, the Shelleys, and Charles R. Maturin; suffice it to say that the fashion of "suspending the soul" was on, and these writers, seeing that it was good, tried to realize its full value. This type of novel began as a joke and with an apology, and never associated with it any serious or high-minded aim. To shock, to thrill, to stimulate swoons—this was its sole purpose, and in that it succeeded admirably.

With this school Brockden Brown had little or no kinship. In the Preface to *Edgar Huntly* we have seen that he denounced its "puerile superstition and exploded manners, Gothic castles, and chimeras." Brown was a realist, and he sought his material in fact, though often on the dim borderland between fact and fancy; he rummaged the latest medical journals for stories of the abnormal; he studied the man in the street or the passengers in a carriage that he might mark any aberration from the normal; and he had a keen eye for the unusual. His method and manner of observation are aptly put in a passage from *Arthur Mervyn.* Mervyn is making a journey, and has as companions a Creole Frenchman, two Negroes, and a monkey:

> I sometimes gazed at the faces of my *four* companions and endeavoured to discern the differences and the samenesses between them. I took an exact account of the features, proportions, looks and gestures of the monkey, the Congolese, and the Creole Gaul. I compared them together and examined them apart. I looked at them in a thousand different points of view, and pursued, untired and unsatiated, those trains of reflections which began at each change of tone, feature, and attitude.

Brown was interested in the human side of life and the daily routine of the world, the natural and the marvelous rather than the supernatural. Disorders of mind and diseases of body were to him far more powerful agents of terror than haunted castles; Indian massacres were calculated to excite more fear than Alpine robbers; the fangs of a panther were more horrible than ghosts in armor. Brown's method of achieving terror, then, was an appeal to the realities of life: insanity, fanaticism, master passions, ventriloquism, somnambulism, yellow fever, savages. These were the forces behind his heroes and heroines. This difference between Brown's novels and the Gothic romances is not accidental: it is significant and fundamental; in fact, it is this difference that separates him from the School of Terror and puts him in the ranks of the Revolutionaries, with Holcroft, Bage, and Godwin. It is more accurate to describe his novels as novels of purpose, their purpose being the dissemination of the radicalism then stirring the peoples of two continents. Whatever opinion one may entertain of the worthiness of the cause or the methods employed, novels of purpose were infinitely superior to Gothic romances.

It is from this group of writers, then, that Brockden Brown derived. Their purpose was the same; their method similar in the main; and their ideas remarkably alike. Thomas Holcroft was the first and the most original of the group. His *Alwyn* (1780), *Anna St. Ives* (1792), and *Hugh Trevor* (1794-1797) were a vigorous arraignment of the social, religious, and philosophical humbuggery of the times. He was not unknown in this country; Dunlap's *Diary* records the fact that the little band of New York savants, of which Brockden Brown was a leading member, read him. Robert Bage's *Man as He Is* (1792) and *Hermsprong, or Man as He Is Not* (1796) were even more revolutionary than Holcroft's. They embody almost every phase of radicalism then known.

It was from his friends, Holcroft and Bage, that Godwin received the impulse to translate the theories of *Political Justice* into a successful novel, *Caleb Williams* (1794). This novel became immediately popular on both sides of the Atlantic, and its influence on Brockden Brown was great, though hardly so great as is usually claimed. It was largely as a model of style that the influence was felt, for Brown's philosophy was already shaped, and his materials were, as we have seen, essentially native and his own. But as has been already pointed out, many of his situations and several of his characters were modeled directly on *Caleb Williams*.

### BROWN'S PLACE IN AMERICAN FICTION

Charles Brockden Brown's place in American fiction is a minor one, but it is secure. He was father of the American novel, and by the volume and power of his work he offered a challenge to the future. But he had no following; he created no school. His influence, however, made itself felt in the works of Fenimore Cooper, Edgar Allan Poe, and Nathaniel Hawthorne. To the first, he demonstrated the wealth of our Indian heritage; to Poe, his minute analysis of motives and feelings of souls under great stress was a source of inspiration as well as a model of form and method. Who can read Brown's description of Edgar Huntly's experiences in the cave and Poe's *The Pit and the Pendulum* and not feel the kinship? Hawthorne's fascination with the mysteries that lie just beyond human ken and his "solutions" of those mysteries are strong reminders of Brockden Brown.[16]

Charles Brockden Brown was not a great artist; he had no carefully formulated principles of the art of the novelist; but he did know human nature, both from study and from experience. His wide reading in the literature of England, and, indeed, that of other modern countries, had instilled in him almost unconsciously a sense of the rightness of phrase and the correctness of form in the many genres of literary work. In his keen analysis of human motives and his incomparable powers of observation, Brown possessed the elemental foundations for a great novelist. His gift of discerning the hidden springs of human action was a gift that could not be gained from books or experience—it could come only from nature. No doubt Brown early realized that he possessed such talent, which he felt impelled to increase. Although essentially a recluse, he did move among men, and his spongelike senses absorbed all they touched. It was this ability to take in all at one glance that was at the bottom of his power to lay bare the heart of his characters under storm and stress, to create with a Defoe-like realism scenes as powerful as are to be found in any writer, and to picture vividly appropriate physical background against which to portray the high-minded villains, his men of soaring passions and fascinating intellects.

But with this strength there was weakness: Brown's inability to make his characters live. They are shadowy figures moving about in a strange, unnatural world, driven by the weird forces of heaven and earth. Their creator pushes them around at will; almost never are their actions the result of the inevitable workings of their own impulses. The scenes in which they move live vividly in the reader's mind long after the names of the characters are forgotten. Then, too, while Brown had the power to build up incomparable scenes and striking episodes, he was never able to resolve those scenes and give them artistic meaning in the whole scheme of the work. They stand out too frequently as mere episodes independent of the main plot. The reader in the end comes to think of Brown as the creator of great scenes, and not the writer of great novels.

[16] Brown's influence on Poe was considerable. See "Sources of Poe's 'The Pit and the Pendulum,'" *Modern Language Notes*, XLIV (June, 1929), 349-356, by David Lee Clark.

# VII

# BUSINESS, LOVE, MARRIAGE, AND FAMILY

### DISAPPOINTMENT IN LOVE AND LITERARY REWARDS

THE YEAR 1800 found Charles Brockden Brown in a state of gloom. It had been increasingly evident to him and to his intimate friends that the *Monthly Magazine* had not been a success, financially at least; then, too, it had devolved upon the editor to supply the bulk of the magazine from his own pen, his friends of the Club having failed him. Even more important, the springs of his creative writing had also apparently dried up, and the novels he had published had not been financially rewarding. We may be certain that his brothers, seeing his plight, were ever pleading with him to join them in the mercantile business.

One day in the summer of 1800 Joseph invited his brother to visit him in North Carolina, but Charles refused with the comment, "I know not why, scarcely. Seldom less happy than at present. Seldom has my prospect been a gloomier one." That his refusal to visit his brother and that his gloomy state of mind were due, in part, to his literary responsibilities we may infer from a letter from New York to his brother James, in April, 1800:

DEAR BROTHER,

I received your letter and the volumes, by Mr. D., but not till several days after he received them from you, in consequence of a stop which he made at Woodbridge and Perth Amboy. It is a source of some regret that M. is so reluctant and dilatory in the fulfilment of his promises, but allowances must be made for his indigence on one hand and his sanguine and promiseful disposition on the other.

Yesterday the due number of copies of number three of the Magazine was put on board the stage for your city, where I hope they have seasonably arrived. This once the printers have been tolerably punctual, and, hereafter, I have reason to think that they will be regular and exact in their publication. I know how much depends upon punctuality and regularity, and nothing shall be wanting on my part.

I gave you, I thought, a good reason for the temporary suspension of *Calvert*. It will, in the ensuing number, be resumed, and I hope not again checked in its course till its course be finished.

Your remarks upon the gloominess and out-of-nature incidents of *Huntly,* if they be not just in their full extent, are doubtless such as most readers will make, which alone is a sufficient reason for dropping the doleful tone and assuming a cheerful one, or at least substituting moral causes and daily incidents in place of the prodigious or the singular. I shall not fall hereafter into that strain. Book-making, as you observe, is the dullest of all trades, and the utmost that any American can look for in his native country is to be reimbursed his unavoidable expenses.

I know not whether the advantageous publication of *Mervyn* (the sequel of it) can be brought about in this city, but shall have it done in the way you mention. The saleability of my works will much depend upon their popularity in England, whither Caritat has carried a considerable number of *Wieland, Ormond,* and *Mervyn.*

Adieu,<br>C. B. B.

But his low spirits were also in part due to emotional entanglements. As we have previously noted, Brown was always in and out of love. His infatuation with Henrietta was a characteristic attack of the disease. Shortly after his taking up permanent abode in New York, in 1797, he had fallen in love with Miss Susan A. Potts, about whom we know nothing beyond two enigmatical entries in Dunlap's *Diary.* The first, dated May 1, 1798, reads: "Call with Smith and my wife to see Miss Potts, C. B. B's wished for." The second notation, even more tantalizing, makes us wish that Dunlap had been more of a Pepys or a Boswell. On September 28, 1798, he wrote: "Brown tells me the manner in which his mother breaks off his connection with Miss Potts." Parental objection, probably because she was not a Quaker, again had prevented the happy termination of his love affair. (For other reasons see Letters 4 and 6 to Elizabeth Linn, pp. 200-202.)

Brown was now unhappy and restless, finding only a brief solace in a visit to Philadelphia, perhaps once again to make his peace with his parents, and perhaps to talk over final arrangements for him to become an equal partner in the firm of James Brown and Company. While there he wrote, on September 1, to his old grammar-school teacher, Robert Proud, a letter enigmatic in the extreme. Some burden lay heavy on his heart; what it was the reader does not know; he can only surmise that it was the unhappy end of the affair with Miss Potts. Yet he referred darkly to an important "plan" or "deal" of the previous November as having gone awry, as having cast a cloud over him. Was this perhaps some new literary scheme which he had had up his sleeve, and which had failed to materialize? To Robert Proud, after two inconsequental paragraphs on the weather and his health, he wrote:

What then were the recommendations of a change? I had no engagements that detained me in New York, and so I came hither not to see different scenes, to breathe different airs, but merely to see a different set of faces. I stayed in Jersey, at Newark, Brunswick, and Princeton half a week, and now have I come back to my ancient neighborhood.

All the inanimate objects in this city are uniform, monotonous, and dull. I have been surprised at the little power they have over my imagination, at the sameness that everywhere reigns. A nine-months absence has cast upon surrounding objects not a gleam of novelty. All the old impressions seem to exist with their pristine freshness in my memory. Under this sun I discover nothing new, but this sameness pleases not. More irksome, more deadening to my fancy is this city, on its own account, than ever. I am puzzled to guess how it happens, but it is of little moment to inquire, since walls and pavements were never anything to me, or at least were next to nothing, social and intellectual pleasures being everything. . . .

The last time I saw thee I was far from giving that satisfaction which a friend might claim. I was unreasonably reserved and while it appeared that something lay heavy on my heart, my lips were inviolably closed. I saw a letter to my sister in which thou accountest for my silence in a way not very flattering to me, but a way which I do not know how to prove erroneous. Erroneous it surely was, but how to convince thee of thy error otherwise than by candid explanations is the difficulty.

And why not practice candor? What lay heavy then, time has made light. What troubled me then molests me now but little. Such is the variable fleeting nature of this thing called thought. One idea, in spite of every effort to retain it, will gradually loose its hold and though it still occasionally come in sight and flit about us, it stings and vexes us no longer. Thus it is, with that idea which I brought with me from New Jersey, last November, and which spread a cloud over me. It is gone, yet not totally. It revisits me now and then, but holds no formidable place in my thoughts. When I see thee, I will tell thee what it was; I think I will. 'Tis a fantastic apprehension that withholds me. If I do not see thee, it will do to be written. . . .

C. B. B.

Brown returned to New York by the middle of September and remained there until he had edited the last issue of the *Monthly Magazine* (December, 1800). What he did with himself during the next six months has not been determined.

### JOURNEY THROUGH NEW YORK AND NEW ENGLAND

In the summer of 1801 Brown made a trip ''with an amiable and intelligent companion,'' William Coleman, through New York, Massachusetts, and Connecticut, recording his impressions as usual in his Journal.[1] The Journal gives unmistakable evidence that, with the burden of the magazine gone from his shoulders, even though his prospects for the future were problematic, Brown was again carefree and happy.

As he notes in his Journal, they made their course up the river past the villages of Peekskill, New Windsor, and Newburgh. He read

[1] Dunlap had access to journals of Brown which are not now known to be extant. These journals are extensively quoted from in Dunlap's *Life*.

the Captain's copy of Goldsmith's *Citizen of the World*, which he found to contain sentiments and observations "far from judicious or profound." The boat carried him from civilized country into the more remote or frontier territory.

They left Lebanon on Tuesday afternoon, traversing beautiful country to Pittsfield. By Thursday night they had arrived in Hartford, and on Saturday, July 18, in New Haven, where they became the guests of Timothy Dwight, President of Yale. Within a few days they were back in New York.

## BROWN BECOMES A BUSINESSMAN

At last his family persuaded Brown to settle in Philadelphia and associate himself with his brothers James and Armitt in the commission mercantile business, under the firm name of James Brown and Company. The three brothers were to share equally in the management and profits of the business. Charles now applied himself as assiduously to mercantile law and political economy as he had formerly done to editing and writing. But at no time did he lose interest either in literary pursuits or in his New York friends, as indicated by a letter to Anthony Bleecker, one of his Friendly Club cronies. His opening lines are largely a commendation of his friend who is able to reconcile poetry and the "austere guides and crabbed implements of the law," of the man "who retains the pure taste of a literary devotee, without disrelish and aversion for naked science and mere business."

## LOVE AND MARRIAGE

Once over his infatuation for Miss Potts, Brown again fell in love —again with a non-Quaker, Elizabeth Linn, the daughter of a New York Presbyterian minister, William Linn. Brown had met her in November, 1800, in Philadelphia, while she was visiting her brother John Blair Linn, then a minister in that city. As the unpublished letters below indicate, Brown paid court to her assiduously, and sometimes despairingly, for nearly four years. His uncertain financial affairs, combined with Miss Linn's reluctance (possibly on religious grounds), delayed their union until 1804.

The reader, even while gazing through the eyes of the adoring lover, gains a rather unflattering impression of Elizabeth. She constantly indulged in morbid self-deprecation. She may, of course, simply have thirsted for the never-ceasing flow of adulation and reassurance that Brown poured out upon her. Ostensibly because of her lack of training in both penmanship and composition, she rarely wrote letters to her lover—perhaps not more than a dozen in the four years—and when she did, to his great despair, she demanded that they be promptly returned or destroyed. And what wounded her lover even more deeply was her consistent returning of his letters after a first reading. At this distance we are at a loss to explain this coldness or indifference on her part. One wonders whether she had ever seen the Henrietta correspondence and, knowing Brown's incorrigible journalizing habit, had feared a like fate for her own letters. At any rate, hardly a scrap of her writing has survived. She appears to have been jealous (which is not surprising, considering his past record), and, either because of a genuine conviction of his inconstancy, or as a part of a woman's campaign, several times accused him of insincerity. Letter 5 indicates that early in their courtship she was ready to hand him back to a former sweetheart, perhaps Miss Potts.

All of these characteristics may, of course, have been exaggerated by Brown's melancholy, romantic nature. He was still probably pretty much the same youth who had, during the Henrietta episode, wandered over desolate fields and played the flute in the light of a declining moon. Perhaps unconsciously, in these letters he placed himself in the role of the chivalric lover, helplessly adoring, endowing his lady with impossible attributes of perfection, and suffering agonies of suspense and sorrow. One suspects that Elizabeth was hardly so cruel, cold, and variable as his letters imply, for their marriage was apparently a very happy and an unusually placid one. In fact, the whole tone of the series reminds us of a prose *Amoretti* with the despairing lover and the cold, supremely beautiful lady.

### EXCERPTS FROM BROWN'S UNPUBLISHED LETTERS TO ELIZABETH LINN

[There are thirty-nine letters, not counting the numerous journal-like entries, as separate letters. The chronological order of these letters is uncertain, but from the few that are dated and from internal evidences, the order here given, indicated by the date and number in brackets at the head of each letter, is reasonably accurate. Only those letters revelatory of Brown's state of mind or emotions are here included. The reader will perceive that most of these letters passed between the lovers while Elizabeth was staying at her brother's home in Philadelphia. The paragraphing here varies slightly from that of the originals.]

[1]                                                    Thursd. Morn. [December, 1800?]

So, says my domestic physician, you must not encounter this sharp breeze. Sore throats are dangerous and the state of yours requires caution. *I* will do the out o' door business, myself. . . .

Since I cannot talk to my friend, I must, I believe, write, and give it her when we meet. Yet why write? I can hardly tell. This is a sort of conversation. A substitute for something better. My impatience has been restrained thus long, and now, the direct gratification being not possible, my thoughts must overflow in some way. . . .

And now what shall I say to my ———? By what name shall I call her? No name is too tender and too sacred for my feelings; but let me carefully

CHARLES BROCKDEN BROWN

at the age of thirty-five. Engraved by L. B. Forrest from a
miniature by William Dunlap.

confine myself to the limits she prescribes, and call her—my beloved sister and best friend.

Let me thank her for the pure delight which her conversation on our last two interviews afforded me. The first is delightful in remembrance, because it proved that she has a generous interest in my welfare, that there is a noble and generous heart to whom my weal or woe, my life or death, is of some weight in the scale of her happiness. The second interview was no less precious by adding new hues and lineaments to the portrait which, beyond all others, I desire closely to scrutinize and perfectly to know; and because these lines and colors were all graceful and attractive. Yet there was a jarring string, a cloudy spot. It was when you shut up close all your sentiments upon "the Cave of Fancy" not for want of sentiments, but because no one like your Susan [Elizabeth's sister] was present to receive them.

Deep was my humiliation and keen my disappointment when I compared this confession with one made not long before. How soon were lost the rights of one who had admitted to share your affection even with that darling Sue.

You have not then, and far am I from wondering that you have not, that unlimited reliance on the candor and affection of your new, as you have upon those of your old friend. My hope and consolation is that one day you will admit me into full copartnership with Sue. You will admit me, will you not? When I am worthy of the favor; and shall I not in time prove myself worthy? I will: so believes, so vows,

C. B. B.

[2]                                                         Sat. Aft. [1801]

Little thought I that Saturday would come without the opportunity of a single half-hour's visit.

So it is, however, and I almost fear that the wish to see you must not be gratified till Monday. So says my unseasonable indisposition, of which no consequence has been more regretted by me than of losing your society thus long. I cannot talk; cannot read: and can only write—thus much—

[3]                                                  Tuesd. Aft. Feb. 17 [1801]

When with you, it is your province to talk, to delight me with the effusions of that noble and ingenuous mind; and so seldom does the occasion offer on which my fastidiousness will permit me to *say* what I find no difficulty in *writing*.

Would to Heaven you would lay aside scruples unworthy of yourself and unjust to me! You can't imagine how much you distress me whenever you talk of *fearing* to write to me. It mortifies excessively, besides cutting me off from the prospect of the only good that can reconcile me to future separation from you.

When you leave us, do you think I can have patience with your silence? No, I shall insist upon your writing, as the only proof admissible that you have not forgotten me. When will you have absolute reliance on my candor and attribute to me that illusion which converts even your foibles into merits, which changes even personal defects into lovelinesses, and makes everything belonging to you, merely because it belongs to *you,* inestimable?

I often smile wonderingly when you express dissatisfaction with your personal appearance, and profess your belief that all others must despise and dislike! That you should be so much a stranger to that trick of fancy which makes beautiful and precious every external attribute belonging to the mind we love. There is one eye, my friend, that sees you often, in which everything about you is lovely and engaging, and that knows no privilege more dear than that of listening to your tones or meditating your features.

What a length I have run to! I must positively come to an end.

Adieu.

[4]					Frid. Mo: Feb. 20, [1801]

What a melancholy, mortified, perplexed hour has my unkind, unaccountable friend given me. I have scarcely strength enough to lift the pen.

"I love; I am still loved; I still cherish the hope," you say. How much power is yours! The pleasure you have often given me attests that power. The pain you have now given me no less cogently bears witness to it. . . .

She for whom my attachment was founded chiefly in generosity proved fickle and capricious; who, even while all circumstances smiled, was capable of indifference, and almost of antipathy, who offered, who solicited me to absolve her from her ties, who eagerly caught at a plea that never would have weighed a feather with one who loved, and harshly and without hearing or appeal abjured me forever! [Brown is here referring to his affair with Miss Potts.]

An interval of grief succeeded, but I was not so poor a wretch as to bear forever a servitude so ignominious. No. The yoke was speedily shaken off, and every new reflection for the last two years has added new strength to my conviction that, at the price of temporary sorrow, I have bought exemption from the eternal misery to flow from the union of minds unakin, unpaired. All this I have told you before: yet you talk to me thus of *cherishing the hope* of future union, of that constituting my *security* from your influence.

You don't do well, my dear Eliza; indeed, you don't. I will not say you sport with my feelings: but you wound them sorely. If what you impute to me were true, I have already forfeited that honor which you conjure me to regard, for what have I not already said to you? Have I not made you mistress of my destiny, made it optional with you to place me *highest* in your regard? What temerity, what wickedness in me thus to act, if my feelings left me in any doubt of my ability to (I will not say) to requite, but to challenge, to outrun your tenderness.

I have *no* security, I tell you, against *you*. Thank Heaven I have not. The bar to supreme happiness exists not with me. If I am still lonely and forlorn, if no heart beats in unison with mine; if that good which I deem the greatest under Heaven, the regards of an Angel who will condescend to assume the guardian office, even *before* death, be still denied me, it is not *my* fault, Eliza. 'Tis nobody's, my sweet friend. Least of all is it yours, whose merits it is that I love, and whose preference is valuable to me, because you are so excellent. Why, I wonder, does this imputation discompose me so much? I feel that it would be of little moment from any lips but yours. But you, who possess facts that show the true state of my heart; you, to whom my deportment and professions are, at least inconsistent with preference of another: I can not bear this imputation from you.

Regulate your feelings with regard to me by as cold a standard as you will. Construe as coldly as you please *my* professions of esteem for *you;* but, if you value my peace, cease to believe, and cease to ascribe to me, a *greater* love, a *more* tender preference for any *other* human being. Your power over my destiny is boundless. Use that power as you please, but do not wound me by denying you possess it, or by ascribing to another a power greater than yours, for that, you know, is to question my veracity, my honor.

But let me turn away to a new page. What is it that alarms my dear girl? What is it that shocks her delicacy? But let me hasten to appease her tumults. Who and what has told me that you prefer me to all humankind? Alas! Would to Heaven it were in my power to tell you who and what; that such a declaration had ever passed your lips. No, no, no, Eliza, you have been sufficiently careful to maintain the *sisterly* relation, to make me know my place as third or *fourth brother;* I have not forgotten with how much solicitude I was classed even with the married man Romeyne [or Remeyne] and the mercantile and phlegmatic Phœnixes.

The charge you assign me shall be faithfully performed. I will point out whenever my friend violates the law of delicacy. She shall always know when I see reason to blush for her. *Now,* there is no such reason, and I may safely pronounce, you never will o'erstep the bounds of true delicacy. But what a whimsical kind of transgression is this? There would be guilt in avowing what you did not feel; in avowing what you *do* feel there is truth and delicacy.

My Eliza is dearer to me than all my brothers and sisters. It ought to be so: for what is brotherhood, the mere physical [MS mutilated] compared with the attachment founded on moral sympathies? Heaven knows I am not indifferent to my family, but my supreme affection must necessarily be garnered up in no brother's or sister's bosom.

Recurring to the passage in my note, you will find the wish that startled you, a general wish merely. 'Tis true, Eliza is *preferred* by me, but thou, only beloved friend, can tell me how wide the field that must be crossed before Eliza equally prefers

C. B. B.

[5]                                              Sat. Febr. 28, [1801]

So, it seems, my note placed things on their right footing. 'Twas just as it ought to be. To die and be honored with thy tears is just the suitable and becoming destiny which my good angel would assign me. Upon my word! I am much obliged to thy benevolence! I have really no small vengeance rankling just now in my heart, but, alas, I am powerless. I have no such hold on thy feelings as to enable me to wreak my vengeance on thee. Thou art such a sovereign and independent creature, who may make others suffer at thy pleasure, but cannot be made to suffer in thy turn!

O! what a beauteous sun; what a bland air is this! Yet I cannot call my beloved to the fields. Her company must be given to another, be denied to me. Such is her decree. . . .

[6]　　　　　　　　　　　　　　　　　　Frid. Morn. Mar. 6, [1801]

Let me overlook—let me erase, not only from the paper but from memory, all in this letter that is mortifying and distressful. For all the pain that parts of it have given me let me find compensation in the precious concession that my devotion to you is *not* infatuation; that the sacrifice it may hereafter demand from you will *not* be a painful sacrifice; that my life and my peace of mind is of some value in your eyes. I cannot comment on the conclusion of this penciling. My heart is too sore from such reiterated strokes. I cannot be distinct enough to be understood. O! May you never be cruel and unjust to me, in the thought of being kind and just to another. May your compassion be enlightened, and may never the fate be yours of merely making *one* miserable, while your only aim was to make *another* happy.

O! may you never forget that to reject my love is not to restore it to another; that to disbelieve *my* representations in a case where *I* only can judge, cannot alter my opinion; that your belief of parity of minds and capacity of material happiness between me and one of whom you know nothing cannot sway *my* beliefs, cannot destroy the evidence to the contrary that *I* possess. O! may [you] never forget that the way to secure her peace is not to take away *mine,* that *my evil* is not *her good;* that—but I said that I would not comment.

My good Angel! Make all future comments on this theme needless. Save my half-distracted soul from any new source of terror or perplexity. Be not thus cruel in your kindness. Let my life and my peace be of the utmost value in your eyes, or, by scorning and abhorring me utterly—kill me quite. . . .

[7]　　　　　　　　　　　　　　　　　　Tuesd. Morn. Mar. 10. [1801]

I hope, my best friend, thou wilt be abroad this fine day. If I cannot disengage myself for the same purpose, or am not so fortunate as to meet thee in thy rambles, I will console myself with thinking on thy gratifications.

We are odd creatures. The misery of those we love is sometimes grateful. To know that the pleasure of your walk was marred by your not meeting me would make my heart glow. Now this seems cruel. How shall we reconcile these emotions to humanity? We surely value the happiness of those we love, but then we wish them to owe that happiness to us. We rejoice that they seek their good in our store, and eagerly lavish on them all our treasures; but we are sorry to find them neglectful and independent of us. That they can do without us is our woe.

How is it with me in relation to a certain dear girl? Surely I desired her happiness. Can I ever lament, can I ever cease to rejoice that she is happy? O! no, never. But then I am unspeakably more delighted with that happiness she owes to *me* than that which another confers. Methinks I see you, arm-in-arm, on a summer's evening with your charming Sue, on the terrace of the battery. Your thrilling voices are equally attuned to gayety. They mingle, in mirthful key, on my fancy's ear. Would not such music cheer my heart? O yes! Did it reach me in the grave, it would—"Soothe the dull, cold ear of death. . . ."

How different are we, in some respects, my friend. When I write, *this* is the strain: I am grateful for leave to write to you. That you deign to accept, and to keep gives me joy.

You scarcely ever put epistolary pen to paper.  When you do, you never say—Now will I please my friend.  Any token of affection, any proof of confidence, delights him, and delight him, poor fellow, I will.  No, you only take out the pen when you have some wish of his to thwart, some request to refuse, some mortification to inflict.  What your cautious pen indites, you insist upon having immediately returned.  You are full of doubts, mistrusts, misgivings as to the possible use that may be made of your *pennings*.

I, on the contrary, am all confidence and trust.  To act as if I doubted your discretion, to be partial, hesitating, conditional in my confidings, either by tongue or pen, would seem to me to belie that love and reverence which I profess.

My scripts you are always prompt to return.  When I would fondly flatter myself that they are of sufficient value in your eyes to produce a wish in you to keep them, you press them upon me.  When you are tired of possessing these billets, when they become trash and incumbrance in your cabinet, spare me the mortification of returning them to me.  You need only *burn* them.  That is what I should do with such remembrancers of a contemned or slighted affection.

But how now!  I meant not to sink into complaint.  I meant merely to answer an indirect inquiry of yours.  When I last saw you, you talked of your expectation and your promptitude to return these papers.  Keep them till the possession becomes irksome or indifferent: then burn them, but do not tell me that you have burnt them.  I would fain be saved from that mortification.

I mean not to publish "Jane Talbot."  My reasons for a change of plan, I will tell you, when I have all your ear.

[8]                                     Thurs'd. Aft. [1801]
What words can sufficiently convey my gratitude for this precious billet!  Dost thou wish me to be with thee; to punish thee, my Angel?  For that wish am I thy everlasting debtor.

Robed in purity, arrayed in smiles of candor, sweetness, and affection was my dear creature this morning.  O! how my heart exulted in the thought that such a being was mine own Eliza, exulted on perceiving her features pregnant with happy meaning and bespeaking a soul at peace with itself and with me.

Forgive thee, Love!  What effect has such a demand upon me.  It calls up the spirit of self-accusation.  I have been to blame.  This morning's note was acrimonious.  It flowed from a culpable spirit.  Deeply I regret my giving it to you.  I shall not have peace till you have pardoned me, and *sealed* that pardon. . . .

[9]                                     Tuesd. Eve. M. 17, [1801]
What would I not give that every evening for years to come were spent like the last, with some improvements, I mean. . . .

Some still, retired place will better fit where seated on a sofa, unmolested by impertinents the lips might freely utter and eyes communicate whatever hearts, touched by divine sympathy, might dictate.

What courage has last night's conversation inspired!  'Tis well, my love, I have a stouter heart than thou. . . .

I have often considered the terms of our intercourse. I implicitly subscribe to them. Let us be brother and sister in the world's eye. When that eye is distant or closed, let tenderness and love shake off their irksome fetters.

For an heart truly impassioned, thine is the most fluctuating, fearful, self-doubting in the world. How much pain have thy misgivings, thy discouragements given me. Yet it is consolation to reflect that prize of so much value may well compensate the sufferings endured in the pursuit.

How much pains hast thou taken to convince me that a few months' separation will probably occasion me to be forgotten and another preferred. But I hope, now that we fully understand each other, all such drawbacks on my peace and my confidence in you may disappear.

Many things in last night's interview are remembered with ineffable delight. How greedy am I of praise from such lips. Cannot Eliza be prevailed upon in time to feel and to express all that I feel and say? . . .

[10]                                        Wednesd. Aft. Mar. 18. [1801]

How bleak, cold, lowering is the air. Yet all within me is serenely bright. My mind is cheerful and my health perfect. How, I wonder, is my gentle friend. But such a day as this, if I mistake not, she prefers to all others. It is favorable to agreeable contemplation, and secures her solitude at least. The time must come when your solitude shall have no duty but to lay up stores for conversation, and I shall thus obtain a share of all your social and all your lonely minutes.

People differ from each other chiefly in their notions of happiness. An agreement, in this respect, is the great source of harmony between minds. Methinks, my friend, thou and I are very much alike in this particular. On that account I love thee. Our minds in this most essential point touch each other. What a scene could I now draw, in which the delights of love, benevolence, and reason are united. I am always dreaming of it, but a single dream is a volume full. My pen can not be just to its beauty and variety. My tongue, I hope, can at these precious moments when I have none but my Eliza by my side. . . .

Thy heart, my love, seems differently moulded. How do you shrink from censure or ridicule. Your soul is agonized by scorn. That it is unjust or unmerited appears to supply you with no courage.

I am not very sorry for this immoderate sensibility. I know that the issue will be ultimately prosperous and that on me will devolve the great privilege of making you happy. I know that I shall be fully equal to the trust.

Some six years ago I wrote a poem. [This no doubt refers to the poem entitled "Devotion: An Epistle."] Perhaps for the writer's sake, of whose mind, at the time of composition, it is a faithful picture, my dear girl will deign to read and to keep it. I will have it with me when I see you next.

[11]                                        Monday Morn. Mar. 23, [1801]

So, you wish me to [be] your task setter. Charming pupil, whom my whole life shall be devoted to instruct in that wisdom that makes happy. Of what value is any other wisdom? The art of extracting from every event causes of gratitude and joy, of lifting ourselves above the prejudices and passions of others; of preserving our contentment unimpaired by their misconduct, while their virtue and prosperity increase our happiness, is the only valuable art. In this do I desire to be, by turns, thy teacher and thy pupil.

But how shall I proceed with my love? . . . Lately she has been despondent. Her eyes have overflowed for an hour together. And for what? Because she is ignorant in her own eyes, destitute of worth, comparatively so. She flatters me by allowing me to think the source of her humiliation to be comparison with me, who love her. . . .

How, at this distance, and through this cold medium, shall I contend with your despondency; inspire you with self-respect, and convince you that, among all the women that I know, your purity, your good sense, your taste, your sensibility, your liberal curiosity, your knowledge, your dignity, and gracefulness of carriage are pre-eminent.

How easy would it be to particularize, to supply examples. They hourly occur in my intercourse with you. Never had I cause to blush for you. A thousand times have I exulted in the gracefulness of your deportment, in the justness of your taste, in the unaffected delicacy of your feelings. . . .

You lay stress on fortune; on beauty. You deem yourself wanting in these requisites—you can't imagine my feelings when you talk thus. . . .

It never entered *my* head that *my* person would ever prove a bar to my acceptance with you. Character, I thought, was everything with a rational female, and I know that an impassioned heart dotes even upon imperfections, merely personal, or rather converts them into genuine beauties.

When you have praised my features I have delightingly accepted the praise. Why? Not because I considered your opinion in this respect as a test of the general opinion, but as flowing from the influence of that power which changes the rudest wild into an Eden and touches the basest pebble into gold.

What is my ambition? Only this: to be thought beautiful, to be prized above all the human race by one inestimable creature, by one who has already become to me the most beautiful, the most precious of her sex.

To praise the object of my love for complexion, for symmetry would surely insult her, since her reason would hence infer that I loved her merely on account of such external, dubious, transitory qualities. Did you possess them, I should endeavor to forget them in the contemplation of the softness of your temper, the delicacy of your taste, the vivacity of your feelings, the native, unbought, unstudied rectitude of your sentiments, for these are the true sources of that divine enthusiasm which I call love, and these are the qualities in my Eliza which bewitch me.

Yet how greatly do you err, when you think yourself eminently deficient in mere physicals. Among mere physicals the chief requisites, in the common estimate of handsomeness, are shape and stature. These are not (the last of them *is*) absolutely perfect in you. In whom are they so? But to judge of them comparatively, where in the females of my acquaintance can I hope to find more symmetry, more elegance in these particulars, than you possess?

I remember, shortly after our acquaintance began, Miss T—— after meeting you at Colden's observed to me—"Betsy Linn looked *very pretty,* tonight. Her face, as I saw it, was very pretty."

I commented on her words, by saying that your *shape* was lovely and attractive at all times, but that the most bewitching circumstance about "the Linns" was their voice. On a subsequent occasion she praised Susan very much, and added, "Take care of your heart, Mr. B——"

"You might better warn me against the elder than the younger. Voice, the most love-inspiring of all qualities, merely sensible, they both have, but the elder has the shape and the grace which the other wants."

And this, my dear creature, is my first lesson:—Respect yourself. My second is—Love me. What is my third? Perhaps it ought to have gone first, but let it come now—Rely, in all things, on the wisdom and goodness of that Providence, to whom you ascribe universal presence and unlimited power. Trust to him, for giving, sooner or later, here or elsewhere, repose to all your earthly cares, fruition to all your just hopes. And what lesson do I give for present use? 'Tis this—

When I next see you, be gentle, affable, kind, as you so well know how to be. If my longing for a tête-a-tête be gratified, be more than kind: be tender; and let every sorrow flee away at the assurance that you do indeed *love*. The little meriting, but ever fond and ever grateful C——.

I have been endeavoring to find out the anniversary of my first interview with you. It was some day, I think, in this month; was it not? I mean to keep it as a festival.

[12]                                          Tuesd. Morn. Mar. 31 [1801]

I parted from you last night with some uneasiness. I had done something wrong in the sequel of our conversation. While talking about Miss B—— your words, your looks disapproved. They censured me, it seemed, for being too credulous; too prone to admire and confide. . . .

For my Love to talk of refusing to write because she does not write *well* is very strange. The beauty of your phrases I might praise with sincerity; their correctness and their elegance; but how unfeeling and absurd would I be to have an eye for these qualities in a paper that contains the effusions of your heart.

Suppose a zealous lover to reject the precious confession of requiting love, because it was written—in a bad hand, because it was not *penned* well. No folly was ever more preposterous than that. Yet there is a folly quite equal to it. That of suffering incorrectness or inelegance of *style* to poison our delight is equally inexplicable and insane. . . .

I have labored to recollect what words of mine they were that suggested your first inquiry. I have no secret sorrow, my friend, no peculiarity of situation which deserves a moment's regret. Blessed with your love, I ought to deem myself the most fortunate of men. The blissful day that shall make us inseparable and shall realize my dreams of domestic felicity will be put *very* far off by *nothing* which I can now foresee. Would it not then be impious and ungrateful for me to repine? . . .

Your second question I hardly know how to answer. Why did I once *greatly prefer* your Susan? You cannot mean—Why did I once *love* her. You can only mean, why, when mere acquaintanceship subsisted between us three, I talked to her rather than to you. Can any other cause be assigned than the casual prepossessions imbibed from others, and swaying me before

I had the means of judging for myself, than the transient, momentary biases which govern us previous to knowledge?

But I am accounting for a fact of which I myself know nothing. I do not recollect the time when your graces of conversation and deportment were not far superior to hers—in my eyes. It seems to be impossible but that this superiority should be equally evident to you.

Have I answered your inquiries satisfactorily? . . .

[13]                                                   April 1. Aft. [1801]

What impertinents are headaches! I am more out of humor with *this,* because it may possibly hinder or mar the walk that we propose to-night.

I should be unworthy of my happiness if I did not offer thee the warmest tribute of my gratitude. What a dreary interval of six or eight years has been my life, and to whom but to my good angel, in Eliza's form, am I indebted for the joyous and serene element that now surrounds me.

Where was I, a year ago? In New York, not at home. I seldom or never spent a fine evening at home. 'Twas moonlight and mild, and at that time my lonely rambles on the battery were more frequent than before they had been. Probably I was there. I sighed for a companion. Had my thoughts inquisitively pierced into futurity, and the question occurred—What will be my situation at this hour of night on the last of March next year? What answer would some propitious and attendant spirit have returned? This:

"Traversing a shady walk, in company with one lovely friend, pressing her hand to your lips, offering and receiving the tenderest expressions of affection. . . ."

"Do I know her?"

"No. Never saw her in your life. She resides in this city, has heard much of you; has read your compositions; knows your person; yet you never saw her."

"Shall our intercourse take place here?"

"Your acquaintance shall commence here, but you shall separate, nearly as much strangers as at present. You shall meet again eight months hence, at a distance, and there you shall gradually learn to love each other. That event, however, is further, if possible, from her imagination than from yours."

Into what endless reveries would such a prediction have immersed my soul! How manifold, yet how vague would have been my conjectures!

Hope ought always to live and bloom in considerate breasts. Time is perpetually teeming with events which foresight would pronounce to be impossible.

Perhaps, on that very evening, you likewise, were strolling on the battery. Suddenly, your Ariel plucked you by the elbow, told you to cast your eye back, and pointed out the figure of a man, leaning on the rails. He was too far for you to recognize his form.

"That will be the man with whom in less than a year you will exchange hearts, and that man is C. B. B."

What would you have thought, my friend? . . .

[14]                                                   Sat. Aft. [April 11]

. . . I would fain now be very wise, be very monitory, very lessonful. I would play the tutor with you: the elder brother with his head a mere store-house for the harvest of experience; retailing his wisdom with the authorita-tive air of eldership—But, well-a-day, I am more fit to be your pupil than preceptor. The great art of being happy, of regulating my affections, of subjecting my conduct and my motives to the government of a rational piety, I am more deficient in than thou, and in that science—worth all the rest in the circle—I must learn of thee. There is something inexpressibly charming in that part of your character. Your nightly orisons, your rational, unosten-tatious, unobtrusive devotion adds sanctity to your character.

Have I any influence over you? Yes, I have. What a glowing zeal does that belief awaken in me. What a sacred duty to employ that influence in cherishing in you the seeds of excellence.

Confide in the never-ending watchfulness and fervor of my zeal to do you good. It is not vanity that says I deserve your confidence.

This air is mild and temperate. I hope to find you enjoying it abroad. Business may interfere with my present purpose of meeting you. If it does, I must endeavor not to murmur. Tomorrow aft. I hope to see you. . . .

O! I have not thanked you for your comments on my poem. How de-lightful were they, my friend. They answered my fondest, vainest hopes. Indeed, they far surpassed my hopes. I bless myself for recollecting this poem, and getting it transcribed for you. Shall I do the same by some others that are in my possession? I want, methinks, to put all my former, as well as present self into my Eliza's hands.

I called yesterday on Mrs. Higginson. Miss Templeton, the Millars, had their portraits slightly touched by her hand. Some short allusions to the history and present situation of G. H. Smith and his Margarette, *The Powers of Genius,* and *The Farmer's Boy:* all supplied us with transient topics.

I was disengaged at nine, and found no small difficulty in turning my steps away from you. I despaired of seeing you alone, and was not a little mortified at this disappointment of hopes that I had cherished through the day. I thought I'd take the opportunity and call on Mrs. H. I stayed with her an hour.

You must make haste and dismiss your indisposition. I hope it will shortly disappear. Moonlight has commenced its reign once more, and sum-mons from their fire-side Lorenzo and his Jessica. But you must be more careful than you have been. The inconveniences to which our love of each other's company has subjected us are no topics of serious complaint. Curious subterfuges and expedients are lovers obliged to resort to. They are subjects of amusement on recollection, and will form the sweet discourse of many a winter evening to thee and me hereafter, when our fates are one. . . .

I asked you about your opinion respecting the *Rape of the Lock,* and *Essay on Man,* merely because I want to multiply the memorials you possess of me. I met with very elegant editions of these poems, and the thought occurred of procuring one for you. I am jealous of the influence of time and absence on your heart. I seem to have, as yet, precarious hold of your affections, and my cause would be served by multiplying round you objects which might remind you of him who adores you. Goldsmith, you say, is most your favorite. Shall I get [it] for you? Before I give it you, I can read it myself and mark the passages that please me most. I judge, fondly perhaps, of you by myself. Such notes by your hand would render a volume inestimable to me.

[15]                                              Jan. 15. Sat. Aft. 1802.

I wished to greet my dearest friend this lovely morning, but was disappointed. You got the start of me and were already abroad. I wanted to know the cause of last evening's sadness and, if possible, to dissipate it. I wanted to talk *with* you and *to* you.

I have *just* returned from your house, after a walk with your brother. It was a communicative walk. I hope his displeasure, which your pencil hinted at, and which I saw before I left him in the afternoon, is now removed.

I wish I could call on you this afternoon but I am afraid I shall be engaged. This evening, however, I shall see you and I hope in good health and good spirits.

How sensible of defect, how anxious to excel is my friend! Inestimable qualities are these, if so managed as not to make you unhappy. O! that you could be just to yourself; that you could build your happiness on foundations firmer than the praise of others; that you would estimate merit not by the fair outside!

Study to be happy, for to be happy is to be wise, and the more numerous your pleasures, the fewer will be my cares.

[16]                                              Tuesd. Dec. 7, 1802.

How did your paper delight and pain me! Delight me by the proofs of your affection it contained, and pain me by the humiliations and despondencies which it breathes. Why will not my dearest creature be just to her own merit? Why will she not pay such deference to my understanding as to think of herself as *I* think of her?

Painful delight! Bewitching melancholy was the fruit of thy communication. I opened it in expectation of a few short lines—of what tenor they should be I could not guess. I hoped and was afraid: but how agreeably surprised by thy week's history! To comply with my importunity; to give me pleasure it was written and nothing damps that pleasure but the slights upon thy dear self of which thy pen has been guilty, and the persuasion that, upon the whole, the task was irksome and unpleasant to thee.

You hint at the propriety of my unbosoming myself upon my own affairs. What hitherto has deterred me? Nothing but the sense that the *detail* of my affairs would be unintelligible. The general truths, that I have an equal share in the gains of my profession, with my brothers, that those gains were, one and two years ago, such as to secure thee and me in the possession of affluence, I have often told you.

Misfortunes (I have not concealed from thee) have since come. I have endeavored to find consolation in endeavoring to—(Excuse my blundering. Two children are hanging upon me and striving to get my notice) in reflecting that the event has not realized all my fears; that others have fallen much lower from a much greater height; and now what remains but to build up again the half-fallen edifice; not to suffer the disappointment of the highest hopes to extinguish Hope altogether.

How much this disappointment has cost me I have concealed from you. Your sympathy in that distress should have alleviated that distress. But no. I cannot derive the lessening of my own pain by giving pain to you. Have you not enough already on your own account? [In these paragraphs Brown is referring to the losses which his company had suffered from storm at sea and from the Napoleonic Wars.]

Yet great as the disappointment is, on my own selfish account, (for need I again assure thee, that all hopes of earthly happiness are concentered in thee?) not small has it been on thine. Dost thou not justify the dear belief that union with me would for its own sake give thee some pleasure, and I am sure to be the mistress of thy time, thy house, thy company would be no small happiness.

Alas! Would to Heaven I could give thee and myself all this happiness tomorrow! When it may be hoped for it is impossible to tell. Sooner or later it must and will come. Meanwhile, let us, my Love, make each other as happy as we can by love, confidence, and communications the tenderest, the sincerest, and the most unlimited. Let us, likewise, my dearest friend, make some efforts to obtain the happiness which virtue (if virtue be more than name) and piety (if piety have any grounds in truth) secure to its possessors. After all, life is transitory. The highest and most stable bliss is necessarily precarious. While we anticipate future good and repine at present evils, let us not unthankfully and impiously forget the blessings in possession.

Excuse this preachment. I recommend to you the path in which I daily strive to tread. My perpetual source of consolation, amidst all troubles, is your life, your health, and your love. This good is mine and is a present one. All my future hopes are built upon the reality and the continuance of this one. . . .

I will shortly supply you with a book suitable for all your reveries and extracts.

[17]                                        Thursd: Aft. Mar. 27 [1803]

What a peevish, discontented wretch was I in my last to thee, my friend. The demon of impatience had got hold of me. Not to be amply, doubly compensated for any disquiets, by what bewitching confession! Will my beloved creature pardon me? I cannot be at ease till you forgive me.

How oughtest thou to congratulate thyself on such a friend and sister as is thy Susan! How ought I to rejoice for thy sake! Whenever anxiety hovers over you, one thought that such a friend and sister is yours should put the pesterer to flight. That her arms are ready to receive you when you return home, shall somewhat console me for your absence.

You will not forget me, will you? You will appropriate some few minutes of each passing day to telling me how you fare. You will lay aside coldness and punctilio. May I not demand this of you? Have we not exchanged hearts?

Me you shall hear from, oftener, I fear, than you wish. All my feelings and adventures shall be put down, daily, for you. From your epistles, I *will* anticipate nothing but incitements to fortitude, and ever flowing consolation. Mine shall only supply you with new proofs, that, if tenderness and constancy can create for me any merit in your eyes, I am not unworthy of you.

Did I tell you that Eliza was all that the fondest heart could wish? I believe I did; but 'twas not true. No: you are very different from the image which my dreams delight to portray. But how does Fancy's picture differ from truth's? . . .

[18]                                                                    Mar. 30. Aft. [1803]

I write in odd situations. With some always present, generally several and these talking, to me or to each other. How sacred, how desirable is privacy, especially on occasions like these, when the mere presence of another inspires us with some embarrassment.

Love is watchful, is timorous. I might amuse you by an account of my break-offs. A score or two take place in the course, frequently, of one billet. Some question or topic is started, to which my attention is demanded. Some one enters whom civility requires me to greet and to talk to as just now happened. I laid down my pen at the word timorous, and talked and heard another talk, an half hour, about sharks, whales, king-crabs, and flying fish.

How opposite to each other, how incongruous are the tenor of these billets with that of the conversation which is going on at the same time. Attention will fritter and divide itself after a strange manner. Most whimsical are the accompaniments of my pen. At this moment—such topics, so remotely foreign from those images which form thy train. And all are heard.

But what pesters me most is the peering, overlooking eyes, which seem to ask, and sometimes actually do ask, "What are you writing?" O! How desirable is privacy. To write to my Love, or talk to her, seems equally to demand seclusion, but neither of these seems it possible to gain but for short moments and few. I regret the want of it most in talking to you. Though I write to you in company, and with all the sounds, tools, and symbols of the gain-pursuing merchant about me, you only see what I write—but the absence of all others seems requisite when tongues and eyes commune.

Dr. Gregory was an egregious fool, Eliza. Never consign thy conversation and behaviors to his government. If I remember rightly, his errors are properly exposed, in the "Rights of Women." How remote, indeed, from simplicity and rectitude, are the systems of theorists on the laws of sex. How far those are practically adhered to, I am not qualified to judge. Yet in my narrow and indirect experience, I have met with scarcely anything among women, but exceptions to the systems of punctilio.

What shall I say of my friend? Her character is new to me. Love has not displayed itself in her deportment as I would have painted it in an imaginary picture. She has differed from my imaginations, but then she has surpassed them. Reason and passion reign in different spheres. My passion has often appealed to Oracle Reason, and always received the testimony of "Well done." Indeed, Eliza, I love thee more than heartily. My reason, as well as my heart, is thy worshipper. Heaven grant the future may be propitious.

Do you ask of what I think most busily and constantly? Of you, of course. You enter, the moment I awake, in the morning and I try to keep myself awake at night to think of you. The last conversation generally supplies my musings with materials. So it was, with Saturday's—if you knew the effect of your tenderness on my feelings, you would burn your "Gregory" that moment, and, so far from thwarting the kindly impulse, you would summon fondness to your looks and words and actions. All your kindnesses on Saturday eve I call up incessantly, repeat, and revolve. How bewitching are you, my love, at those moments, when unpunctilious. I could convince you now how good a memory I have, but I won't repeat the words that charmed me in the saying, and continue to bewitch me in remembrance.

Pish! There's another interrupter, from whom I cannot hope to 'scape to my dear pen, this evening. So, adieu, my love. I mean to call tonight, and tomorrow night too if your brother's society do not keep me away, by meeting at your house.

[19]                                                                Mar. 25, 1804.
I intended this to be a busy day, but can do nothing. My heart is oppressed with sorrow. I can think of nothing but melancholy themes. The first impulse, this morning, was to fly to thee but, alas, I shall not find thee alone, and thou wilt be restrained by the stranger's presence from giving me the consolations of thy tenderness. The next expedient is to say on paper what I shall not have an opportunity of saying to thy ear. I will call this afternoon, however: perhaps my Love may be alone.

What sad news has this day brought! Some three months ago we sent a vessel to St. Domingo with a valuable cargo; a young man, our particular friend and kinsman, the hope and joy of a numerous and worthy family, went as supercargo. This day tells us that he and the captain are dead, and by their death the vessel and cargo, worth $15,000, are probably lost and certainly exposed to great delay and imminent risk.

The young man was one of the most excellent and amiable and a large family placed their chief hope of being kept above poverty on his exertions. The total loss, or even the delay, in the return of the property (the last of which is certain) will be heavy evil to us. Both evils together have reduced my little courage for the present to nothing. How much does my heart at this moment stand in need of your tenderness!

Your brother does not preach, it seems, tomorrow. Let thou and I go together to Chr. Church, in the morning. I will call on you in due season.

Despite her apparent coolness toward her lover and her lack of enthusiasm for their approaching marriage, and under a threat of excommunication from his family and friends, on November 19, 1804, Charles Brockden Brown and Elizabeth Linn were married. The expected happened: he was promptly read out of the Society of Friends. Thus he at last defied and suffered the consequences of the dictum that perhaps had been instrumental in breaking off his engagement to Henrietta, and to Miss Potts. The unpublished certificate of dismissal, read at a Monthly meeting of the Society of Friends, of Philadelphia on February 20, 1805, states:

Charles Brockden Brown of this city who had by birth a right of membership in our religious society—having accomplished his marriage by the assistance of an hireling minister—to a person not in profession with us, it became our concern tenderly to treat with him on that account, but not appearing duly sensible of the impropriety of his conduct, we testify that we cannot consider him a member among us, yet desire that thro' submission to the operation of Truth he may be qualified to condemn his transgression to the satisfaction of this meeting and become united in religious fellowship with us.

This was indeed an inauspicious beginning of marriage. In spite of this excommunication and in spite of the usual financial uncertainties which had dogged him all his life and which were soon augmented by the growth of his family, Brown looked upon his marital state as full of promise of happiness. In fact he understood as no one else could just how much he stood in need of that steadying influence which only a sensible, lovable woman can give. That his expectation was realized can be inferred from a letter, November 6, 1805, which he wrote to William Dunlap:

PHILADELPHIA, November 6th, 1805.

MY DEAR FRIEND,

I wish, notwithstanding my neglect of your last, you had favored me with another telling me how you had fared, where you have been, and whither you are going. I have been looking for you hourly this fortnight past, agreeable to your plans and prospects, when we parted, but have neither seen you nor heard from you. I must therefore, though tardily, take up my pen to find you out and provoke some information from you. What excuse shall I make for not keeping up the correspondence as I projected? I have none, I fear, that you will deem sufficient. When I received your last, my apprehensions and hopes seemed to be monopolized by one domestic image. Some one says that the happiest man is still miserable, inasmuch as every human good is precarious and pent with danger, and the more he values the goods in his possession, the more fearful is he of the accident by which he is liable to be bereaved of them. My domestic felicities were so great that I shuddered at the approach of an event by which they were endangered. The event, however, came, and instead of depriving me of an adored wife, has added two lovely children to my store. They are sons, counterparts to each other, with all their members and faculties complete, and, enjoying as far as we can judge, after two months trial of life and its perils, the admirable constitution of their mother. Do not you congratulate me on this event? I was always terribly impressed with the hardships and anxieties attending the care of infants and was at the moment appalled by the prospect of a double portion of care; but when I had seen the little strangers with my own eyes and beheld the mother in perfect health and safety after all her perils, my terrors were exchanged for confidence, and now after two months experience I find, and their mother finds, that the two healthy and lovely babes are a double joy instead of being a double care. And now that I have told you my chief concern, pray tell me yours. Let me know what you have been doing, what new prospects a few months have opened to you, whether you persist in your scheme of publication and what success has hitherto attended you. When, particularly, may we hope to see you amongst us once more?

C. B. B.

During the four years' courtship of Brown and Elizabeth Linn, Charles became intimate with the whole Linn family—the distinguished father, a Presbyterian minister in New York, the almost equally famous poet-preacher brother, John Blair Linn, and Elizabeth's three sisters, Susan, Mary, and Rebecca, to whom, indeed, he became a big brother. Letters to members of the Linn family indicate that Brown adopted Elizabeth's sisters as his own, and that he remained always intensely interested in their welfare. Letters, in the Allen-Dunlap biography to "Miss R——," evidently Rebecca, and to W. Keese, her husband, show how completely and lovingly Brown had been received into the family.

With John Blair Linn, assistant pastor in the First Presbyterian Church in Philadelphia, Brown became a bosom friend. Linn's life affords several parallels to Brown's. According to a biography written by Brown[2] soon after his brother-in-law's death, and originally published as Introduction to Linn's poem *Valerian* (1805), John Blair Linn was born in 1771. He entered Columbia College in New York when he was thirteen. Early attracted to literature, he published a book of poems at seventeen. Like Brown, he was persuaded against his will to study law, under the direction of no less a personage than Alexander Hamilton. Linn, less fitted for that profession than Brown was, in a year quit in disgust for reasons very similar to those which had dissuaded Brown. According to Brown, Linn's "attachment to poetry acquired new force, by the contrast which the splendid visions of Shakespeare and Tasso bore to the naked abstractions and tormenting subtleties of Blackstone and Coke."

On the occasion of his giving up the law, Linn wrote to his father: "My aversion to the bar had something else in it than the mere loathing of taste. I could not bear its tricks and artifices; the enlisting of all one's wit and wisdom in the service of anyone that could pay for them."

In 1799 Linn was called to Philadelphia as co-pastor of the First Presbyterian Church. He was an eloquent and popular minister, who continued his interest in literature. He published several books of poems and was an active contributor to Brown's *Literary Magazine*, under the initials "I. O." That Brown had not completely severed his connections with the New York Friendly Club's magazine and that he was in New York in July, 1802, on a mission from Linn and also in behalf of the *Review*, is seen from excerpts of the unpublished letter which follows:

[2] This biography was reprinted in the *Port Folio* (1807). The editor thus introduced it: "This elegant specimen of affectionate biography is the production of Charles B. Brown, a relative of the deceased, and a man of letters by profession, who is distinguished by many publications both of beauty and utility."

N. Y., July 8, 1802.

MY DEAR FRIEND,

The review is exceedingly behind hand, and my friends have imposed on me the task of reading and reviewing half a dozen books, which, without their injunctions, I should never have looked into. This had been an irksome undertaking, and which nothing but a kind of necessity could reconcile me to. To criticize without reading would be absurd, and to read not for instruction or amusement would be galley slavery. The next number is very long in making its appearance, and I suppose will scarcely issue from the press in less than a fortnight. When it reaches you, I am afraid you will be but little pleased with the alterations they have made in your pieces. I have prepared them to expect some displeasure from you, and they have earnestly besought me to apologize for them. I have told them, however, that they have little to expect from an advocate who thinks them in the wrong, and that I shall make but a poor defence against a displeasure, which I think has been merited. . . .

Present my affectionate respects to Mrs. Linn and to Rebecca. Tell Rebecca that I hope to bring her a copious letter from her sister by way of atonement for past omissions. Mary has been disabled for some weeks, in her better hand, by a fellon which had like to have robbed her of her forefinger. She is getting the better of her enemy.

I shall be glad to kiss the little stranger and to call him by his name, if he has one. I hope he grows, at least, an inch a day.

How fares your poem? I hope it has made some advances towards the light in my absence. If it has not, I shall begin to lose all faith in printers yet, to say the truth, my confidence in that tribe has never been great. . . .

Though I expect to see you so soon, it would give me great pleasure to have a line from you ere I return, assuring me of your welfare. Any thing directed to the care of W. J. Esq., Pine St., will reach,

Your affectionate

C. B. B.

Your sisters are in health. The prospect of removal to Albany has not added much to their felicity.

Linn's melancholy was aggravated by ill health. After a sunstroke in 1802, he suffered from vertigo and intense depression, and finally developed tuberculosis. Brown's remarks on Linn's illness must have come from a mind already burdened with anticipations of how his own life was to end. Linn died in August, 1804, ending a friendship that had meant the fuller development of both young men and a richer life for Brown in particular. Indeed, Brown's marrying into the Linn family had been most fortunate for all concerned.

### FAMILY AND FRIENDS

During his last years Brown worked arduously, and in many capacities; he was editor and chief contributor to two magazines, running currently for a short period, and he was an active partner in a mercantile firm with two of his brothers from 1801 until 1806. After the dissolution of the firm in the latter year, Brown continued until his death to conduct a small retail business alone, selling pots and pans by day and editorializing by night.

Despite these manifold duties he found time to carry on a voluminous correspondence with various members of his own and his wife's families and with numerous friends. Brown was also an unusually devoted family man; he loved to read to his wife, and he spent much time in romping with his growing children, particularly the twins.

To Charles Brockden Brown and Elizabeth Linn were born four children: Charles Brockden and William Linn, twins; and Eugene Linn and Mary Caroline. The latter two died young—Eugene on April 1, (?), 1824, and Mary on March 11, 1830. Charles Brockden, Jr., died without issue. It was from William Linn, who became a distinguished lawyer, that the numerous Brown progeny derives. Charles Brockden Brown's descendants were substantial business and professional men. William Linn, Jr., was for thirty-six years treasurer of the Pennsylvania Company.

In 1806 Brown wrote most affectionately to young Susan Linn, expressing a sincere desire for a visit from her and looking forward to the pleasure of seeing "under the same roof, and that roof our own, the three persons dearest to me upon the earth"; he wrote about the studious nature of his own Mary and told Susan about his composition of a "great book" and the hours of work entailed. He concluded the letter with a comment on the "charming health and spirits" of the twins, who, he said, were making little progress in speaking.

There can be little doubt that the "great book" referred to in the preceding paragraph was the *Complete System of Geography*, a work Brown was known to be writing at the time of his death. Brown's lifelong interest in geography had at last resulted in the beginning of "a great book," of which unfortunately only the Prospectus is known to exist. But the original contract—apparently in the handwriting of Paul Allen—for the completion of the work by Paul Allen and its publication by C. & A. Conrad of Philadelphia was found among the manuscripts placed at my disposal by the novelist's grandson, the late William Linn Brown. Following is a transcript of the contract:

It is agreed between Elizabeth L. Brown and Paul Allen, that he engages to compleat an unfinished, "Compleat System of Geography" now in his hands and prepare the first volume for the Press in six months, and the whole, within eighteen months from this date, or as much sooner as practicable. Upon the Plan, and agreeably to the contract the said E. L. Brown and C. & A. Conrad & Co. are to pay her—one half out of the first payments and the other half out of the second payments, receivable from them.

Philadelphia 13th June 1811

P. ALLEN
E. L. BROWN

In October, 1807, he wrote at length to his brother-in-law, Rebecca's husband, in answer to a letter announcing the arrival of a son:

That the new comer is not a girl, is, you tell us, a great disappointment to you, and you have been obliged to play the philosopher on the occasion; but, my good friend, one smile of the little stranger, a few months hence, will perform more for your consolation than all the reasonings in the world. You will then bless yourself that the bantling is exactly what he is. I have often checked myself in forming wishes as to the sex of my children, from the utter uncertainty of their future destiny, be they of what sex they may. Their happiness must depend upon their temper; and mine, so far as it relates to them, upon the opportunity I may have of witnessing their fate after they have reached maturity; and, when I reflect on the innumerable chances against my living to the critical time, I give all wishes to the air. The chances for happiness, in either sex, seem to me nearly equal, yet, as a man, I must necessarily regard a daughter with more tenderness than a son, provided they are equal in all other respects: an equality, however, which is quite impossible.

Since the newcomer was named for him, it was in this letter that Charles Brockden Brown expressed a wish that the name Brown had a little more music and dignity in it and his mortification "in looking over the catalogue of heroes, sages and saints, to find not a single Brown among them." He added the hope that the newcomer might become "a vindicator of the name."

On June 17, 1806, from Albany, New York, where he had gone in search of health and copy and to visit his wife's family and his distinguished friend Chancellor Kent, Brown wrote to his wife of the journey. He gave a vividly descriptive account of the eclipse he witnessed as he walked the last twelve miles. The tedious, unpleasant trip by water was somewhat relieved by the conversation of "Little Paine," the only person on board who was tolerable. Other intimate letters of Brown's include that of August 25, 1806, to John Howard Payne, his new-found friend. The letter expressed a desire that "something like friendship might be grafted on mere acquaintance"; Mrs. Brown, who had accepted all of Payne's good qualities on her husband's word, was eager to see him and already "loves you by proxy." As might be expected, Brown was especially interested in Payne's academic progress, his studies, his books, and exercises. On February 22, 1809, Brown wrote again to Payne, urging a full account of his two years' work. The Allen-Dunlap biography gives numerous letters to his family and friends, written during this period of Brown's life.

# VIII

# BROWN AGAIN TURNS TO JOURNALISM

## THE LITERARY MAGAZINE AND AMERICAN REGISTER

In October, 1803, Brown, at the solicitation of C. and A. Conrad of Philadelphia, began the editorship of a purely literary periodical, under the name of the *Literary Magazine and American Register*.

In plan and purpose the work resembled the best British journals of the day, and it was by far the most imposing magazine that America had yet seen. In the three years which intervened between the *Literary Magazine* and the earlier *Monthly Magazine and American Review* Brown had learned much about magazine-making. Among other things he had now succeeded in gathering around him a score or more of talented men as contributors to his new magazine. Despite the mortifying fact that he had to squeeze most of the original matter from his own brain—at least during the hot summer months when the energies of his colleagues ran low—Brown had reason to be encouraged by the assistance which his friends in New York and Philadelphia rendered.

### THE VICISSITUDES OF EARLY AMERICAN MAGAZINES

The magazine opened with an address to the public, detailing the purpose of the work. Aware of the pitfalls in the path of every new magazine, Brown wrote:

Many are the works of this kind which have risen and fallen in America, and many of them have enjoyed but a brief existence. This circumstance has always at first sight given me some uneasiness; but when I come more soberly to meditate upon it, my courage revives, and I discover no reason for my doubts. Many works have actually been reared and sustained by the curiosity and favor of the public. They have ultimately declined or fallen, it is true; but why? From no abatement of the public curiosity, but from causes which publishers or editors only are accountable. Those who managed the publication have commonly either changed their principles, remitted their zeal, or voluntarily relinquished their trade, or, last of all, and like other men, have died. Such works have flourished for a time, and they ceased to flourish by the fault or misfortune of the proprietors. The public is always eager to encourage one who devotes himself to their rational amusement, and when he ceases to demand or to deserve their favor, they feel more regret than anger in withdrawing it.[1]

It is surprising that though acquainted with the vicissitudes of American magazines, Brown uttered in this prospectus never a word about them. He knew that the *Columbian,* for instance, although successful and popular, was forced to discontinue because of oppressive postal laws and uncertain delivery:

The law which charges for monthly publications the postage rate on private letters or packages is a prohibition as injurious in its consequences as the principles on which it is founded are partial and oppressive. . . . The operation of this unequal and oppressive law having rendered it impossible to convey this miscellany to their numerous subscribers in the interior parts of this country but at the expense of losing a great proportion of them through a bad conveyance, they have determined to relinquish the undertaking and employ their time and capital in a way which may be more conducive to their private interest.[2]

So wrote the *Columbian* editor.

Mathew Carey, editor of the vigorous *American Museum,* had expressed one of the main reasons for failure of early American magazines: the slowness and laxness of subscribers in paying their subscription:

After a careful examination of the various shoals on which periodical publications have been wrecked in this and other countries, I am in dread of only one—which I am almost ashamed to intimate. This shoal is a want of due punctuality in paying the subscriptions. These being small, each individual is but too apt to suppose it a matter of great indifference whether he pays his quota at the time appointed or in six or twelve months afterwards. This is a great mistake. It is further to be observed that the expense of sending twice or thrice or, as is often the case, four times for the amount of a subscription bears no small proportion to the sum received.[3]

Professor Algernon Tassin gives a succinct account of the rise and fall of the early national magazines based largely on preface announcements of the *New York Magazine.* This magazine's difficulty lay in the insufficient number of paid subscriptions which resulted from the unfavorable reception of literature in the United States. Lack of financial security made it impossible for these gallant editors to devote much time to their magazines or to develop them into objects worthy of attention.[4]

[1] "The Editors' Address to the Public," *Literary Magazine and American Register,* I (Oct., 1803), 3-4.
[2] Algernon Tassin, *The Magazine in America,* pp. 14-15. Quoted from *Columbian Magazine,* Dec., 1792.
[3] *Ibid.,* p. 21. Quoted from the *American Museum.*
[4] *Ibid.,* pp. 24-26.

That Brown was aware of these difficulties cannot be doubted, for he was on intimate terms with several of the editors and knew of their struggles to keep their heads above water. He, too, had had some mortifying experiences as editor of the *Monthly Magazine,* which, it will be recalled, he set forth in the preface to the last volume of that journal.

In the face of these untoward conditions and with the knowledge of others' failures, Brockden Brown had the temerity to publish the following ambitious yet carefully guarded address to the public describing his new magazine:

Useful information and rational amusement being his objects, he will not scruple to collect materials from all quarters. He will ransack the newest foreign publications, and extract from them whatever can serve his purpose. He will not forget that a work which solicits the attention of many readers must build its claim on the variety as well as copiousness of its contents.

As to domestic publications, besides extracting from them anything serviceable to the public, he will give a critical account of them, and in this respect, make his work an American Review, in which the history of our native literature shall be carefully detailed.

He will pay particular attention to the history of passing events. He will carefully compile the news, foreign and domestic, of the current month, and give in a concise and systematic order that intelligence which the common newspapers communicate in a vague and indiscriminate way. His work shall likewise be a repository of all whose signal incidents in private life which mark the character of the age, and excite the liveliest curiosity. . . .

In an age like this, when the foundations of religion and morality have been so boldly attacked, it seems necessary in announcing a work of this nature to be particularly explicit as to the path which the editor means to pursue. He, therefore, avows himself to be, without equivocation or reserve, the ardent friend and the willing champion of the Christian religion. . . .

As, in the conduct of this work, a supreme regard will be paid to the interests of religion and morality, he will scrupulously guard against all that dishonors or impairs that principle. Everything that savors of indelicacy or licentiousness will be rigorously proscribed. His poetical pieces may be dull, but they shall, at least, be free from voluptuousness or sensuality, and his prose, whether seconded or not by genius and knowledge, shall scrupulously aim at the promotion of public and private virtue.

As a political annalist, he will speculate freely on foreign transactions; but, in his detail of domestic events, he will confine himself, as strictly as possible, to the limits of a mere historian. There is nothing for which he has a deeper abhorrence than the intemperance of party, and his fundamental rule shall be to exclude from his pages all personal altercation and abuse.[5]

The editor concluded his remarks by reminding the public that there was at least one circumstance in his favor:

[5] "The Editor's Address to the Public," *op. cit.,* p. 5.

There is not at present any other monthly publication in America; and that a plan of this kind, if well conducted, cannot fail of being highly conducive to amusement and instruction.[6]

### THE PLAN OF THE MAGAZINE

The plan of the magazine was, like that of the *Monthly Magazine*, conventional.  The sections varied in name and content from number to number but the usual titles were "Communications" (original contributions); "Criticisms" (sometimes original, sometimes copied from British journals); "Poetry" original and selected; "Selections"; "Summary of Politics"; and "Remarkable Occurrences."  Later a section called "Literary and Philosophical Intelligence" was added, which when finally expanded to "Literary, Philosophical, and Agricultural Intelligence" became a catchall for bits of heterogeneous information.  The original matter, at first much less in bulk than the selections, was gradually increased, except for one or two issues in which the editor, hard pressed for material, used selections almost entirely.  With the beginning of Volume IV, Brown, discarding his plan of careful divisions, simply stated the titles of the articles, mingling original and borrowed items indiscriminately.  In Volume VII he even reprinted three articles from his old *Monthly Magazine*.[7]

### SUBJECT MATTER AND CANONS OF JUDGMENT

The articles were on all conceivable subjects, but there were fewer book reviews than in the *Monthly Magazine*.  Apparently no effort was made to review all the latest American publications.

Brown succeeded in eliciting for his second journal more contributions from his friends and from others than he had obtained for the *Monthly Magazine*.  Besides single independent articles, there were several outstanding essays in serial form, on divers subjects.

A brief analysis of several of the series will give the reader an idea of the critical judgment and the literary taste fostered by Brown's journal.  One of the most important of the series was "Critical Notices," consisting of nine articles—five unsigned and four by I. O.—now known to have been Brown's intimate friend and future brother-in-law John Blair Linn, the distinguished young Philadelphia minister. One might reasonably suppose Linn to have written the entire series, were it not for Brown's own implied avowal of the authorship of Number VIII.  In a letter to Linn (July 4, 1804) he wrote:

The number for June you will probably meet with in New York before your return.  I am afraid it will not greatly please you.  You will find but

---

[6] *Ibid.*, p. 6.

[7] "American Newspapers" is taken from *Monthly Magazine*, III; "Prevailing Ignorance of Geography," from *Monthly Magazine*, III; "On the Use of Almanacs," from *Monthly Magazine*, I.

a single communication in it (Valverdi), all the rest of original prose, I have been obliged to supply myself. . . .[8]

Since "Critical Notices," Number VIII, appeared in this same June (1804) issue, it may, on the authority of this letter, definitely be ascribed to Brown. Further evidence that the whole series was not by Linn is the striking disparity of view between Number I (Linn's), a thoughtful, deeply appreciative criticism of Milton, and Number VIII, which though well done contains what the author himself admitted as "carping" attacks on certain of Milton's images.

Interest in classical writers was represented by two essays on Virgil. On the eighteenth-century English poets, Goldsmith and Gray were eulogized; but Linn, in Number IV, censured Wordsworth severely. As a whole "Critical Notices," couched for the most part in moderate terms, reflected the critical judgment of late eighteenth-century America.

The longest of the series, "Adversaria," running to nineteen numbers, was written by John E. Hall, a lawyer and aspiring author—a thwarted literary man forced to turn to a more lucrative profession. "Adversaria" holds a special interest as the subject of an unpublished letter from Brown. The letter tells us of the struggle of the editor to keep one jump ahead of the printer; of his journey up the Hudson in search of health and of copy; of his meeting with John Howard Payne, the glamour boy of "Home, Sweet Home," and of Brown's relation with him; of Brown's amiable nature as friend and as family man; and finally of his wide acquaintance with classical lore. Excerpts from the letter follow:

PHILADELPHIA, July 26, 1806.

JOHN E. HALL, ESQRE.
BALTIMORE.
MY DEAR SIR,

I congratulate you most cordially on the success you have met with in your profession. You used to lament the disappointment of your literary projects, but I hope you now rejoice in their failure as much as I used to predict that you would. If that time has not yet arrived, I am persuaded it soon will. Your good genius has been at work for you, and by forcibly turning your steps from the paths of authorship and editorship has been promoting your lasting and solid welfare.

I saw your version of the ode in New York and intended laying felonious hands upon it. However, I wanted first to consult you about some particulars in the introduction. One would naturally infer from your words that Moschus and Bion were inhabitants of modern Persia rather than of ancient Greece. Your terms Oriental and Asiatic are never applied to Greek poets whether they happen to be born on the Eastern or Western side of the Icarian Sea. Manners, language, and taste were the same among the Greeks of Peloponnesos, Italy, or Asia Minor. Homer and almost all the lyric poets were,

[8] Quoted in Dunlap, II, 111.

geographically speaking, Asiatics, but this appellation when applied to manners or taste denotes not only a residence much further east, but is confined to such bards as Solomon or Hafiz. The Greek philosophers and rhetoricians of Antioch and Alexandria have never been called Orientals or Egyptians, though they were born, some of them, like Lucian and Dionysius Longinus, in the East and others in Egypt. But excuse me for thus criticizing what, very probably, you are able to defend. In that persuasion I have republished the verses with their introduction.

Dunlap, you tell me, brought me a number of the *Adversaria*. I set so high a value on that—what's its name?—that, I am sure, if I had actually received it, I should not have mislaid or neglected it, yet I am loath to charge our friend Dunlap with negligence or forgetfulness. Are you certain that you sent it? If, on searching, you chance to find it among your papers, pray send it to me. It will do, you know, for the ensuing number.

I have attended to your request about sending you the odd sheet containing the present number of your *Adversaria*. By the way, it is very short. Does the law or the ladies occupy so much of your time and thoughts that you cannot be as liberal of your lucubrations as you used to be?

I have not been long returned from a very pleasant journey to Albany, Ballston, and so forth. I went in pursuit of health and did not quite miss my aim. Pleasure and instruction, though I counted little on finding them by the way, were not wanting. One of the most agreeable incidents I met with was a meeting with one who is commonly called *Little Paine*. Perhaps you have heard of the author of the *Thespian Mirror,* whom Coleman took so much pains to make notorious last winter. This is the same. If you are here in the autumn, I shall probably have an opportunity of introducing him to you, as he purposes a visit to Philadelphia when his college vacation occurs; for, you must know, he has consented to turn hay again and go to school. . . .

Once more, adieu.

C. B. Brown

The "Adversaria" consisted of brief items on a variety of subjects, with literary matters predominating. As a rule the articles were of little interest, although some of the longer ones were very pleasantly and briskly written. The author most admired Dr. Johnson, Pope, Dryden (a special favorite), Sir John Denham, and Voltaire. Popular subjects were women, dress, dueling, and novel-reading. An article condemning French manners and morals and praising British uprightness in both public and private virtues may be an indication of the editor's swing away from earlier admiration of French revolutionary principles.

An essay, in three parts, *On Education,*[9] signed "W. W."—probably Bishop William White of Philadelphia—was written in an unusually liberal and forward-looking tone. In sentences clear, terse, and colorful the author advocated ideas advanced for their day. The writer pointed out the importance of early training of the child and

---

[9] *Literary Magazine,* VIII (Aug., Sept., and Oct., 1807).

advocated the use of undeviating firmness, restrained only by the milk of human kindness. The author was thoroughly schooled in the philosophy of his day—which maintained that the mind, though endowed by nature with certain powers, for all practical purposes was a product of its environment and of its training—in other words, the author held to the current doctrine of perfectibility through knowledge. The parent was urged to select the child's profession, even as early as birth, and direct every effort toward rousing his interest in that profession and training him for it. Poor hapless child who, destined for statesmanship, was required to read from infancy only those books dealing with political morality and devious ways of legislators, and whose rewards "should consist in philosophical, moral, and political books"! Except for this extreme view, however, the good bishop's remarks deserve to be given a place on pedagogical shelves.

The author of the "Visitor" series, eight in number, who signed his name *F*, has not been identified. The series, though general in nature, laid emphasis on literature. Probably the most interesting is the lament for the decay of belles-lettres.[10] The author recognized the decadence of the classical school, but he was at the same time unwilling to admit the excellence of the new romantic school. He would, to paraphrase Byron, rather err with Gifford than shine with Wordsworth and Coleridge:

That the efforts of modern writers are greatly defective in these points the examination of their works will fully prove. When I look back upon the works of many of the writers of the last century, and see the ease and elegance of their style, the sublimity of their ideas, and the novelty which distinguishes their thoughts, I regret that so few are to be found who can rival them with success. . . .

There is now no description of writers to whom want of novelty may more correctly be ascribed than the poets whose works are frequently as destitute of merit as they are numerous. The ease and elegance of Pope, the fervor and sublimity of Gray, the tenderness of Collins are seldom to be found. Never more in number than now, never did fewer attain to extraordinary excellence; paltry imitations, dull, insipid, drawling sonnets, rhymes jingling without sense or meaning, now aping the ridiculous style of Wordsworth, and now the luxuriance of Darwin. Nor is this the worst. We behold some prostituting their pens on that kind of poetry which should only accompany the volume of Rochester. The most delicate allusions on subjects on which the pen should forever be silent are dressed up in the garb of the muses and sent forth to the destruction of good morals and the annihilation of modesty. With all the captivations of elegant poetry, the ideas they constantly excite are such that, while they corrupt, they (to use the words of Blair) lay the foundation for lasting bitterness of heart.

Still, however, "in these degenerate times," poets are to be found who deserve that name, who satirize the follies and vices which are seen around them with justice and who please and instruct. Many have heard of and

10 "Visitor," no. IV, *Literary Magazine*, III (June, 1805), 468-470.

read the productions of Wolcott (Peter Pindar), and have laughed at his merry tales and witty remarks.  Though his strokes are often laid on too hard, and sometimes unjustly, he is surely as excusable as those who, in every age biased by party, have substituted prejudice for candor.  Gifford, his rival and opponent, possesses all the qualifications of a true poet and has greatly contributed to correct false taste and erroneous judgments concerning literature.

But this critic was not wholly infected with the virus of a decadent classicism, for listen to his indiscriminate praise of classicists and romanticists in the same breath:

The child of nature, Bloomfield, arrests attention as a votary of the muses, and as such bids fair to live long after his mortal tenement is mouldered into dust.  The attractions of Campbell, of Rogers, and Southey, and some others, will preserve them from oblivion.  Bayley [probably Peter Bayley (1778?-1823)], a poet of later date, has claims to merit when compared with many of his contemporaries; and from Hunt much is expected, as he has already done much.  His poems written at sixteen far exceed those of many others written at maturity, and his later years, it is hoped, will far exceed his days of youth and inexperience.  To this list, in conclusion, we may justly add the name of Fessenden, lately sprung up to do honor to his country, and increase the common stock of literature.

Then our critic turned to lament the fate of two of our own hapless bards who had given promise of somewhat redeeming the time, but suffered the fate of many young poets:

Thus in youth fell Clifton, as sweet a poet as America ever could boast of; whose strains are charming, and therefore please; few, and therefore rendered more estimable, particularly when we consider their author was an American, born and cultured beneath our native sky.  Thus, too, fell Linn, and much about the same age, who did honor to his country as a man of letters, a poet, and a divine.  Among modern poets, he had already attained a conspicuous station and would have arisen to greater excellence had not death asserted his claim and stopped his "tuneful breath" forever.  *Genius,* whose *powers* he has so ably described and illustrated, was his, in the strictest sense, nor could sickness or debility destroy its force, or deaden its energy.

The "Melange," in seven issues, was what its name signified—a medley of items, long and short, on every subject from pin money to Homeric mythology.  Betraying the mark of several styles, the series was probably composed of odd items by various contributors.  One was signed "Cento"—the pen name of John E. Hall, the author of "Adversaria."  The difference in style of the "Adversaria" series and the "Melange" essay may possibly be accounted for by the types of subject matter, the "Adversaria" being principally literary and the "Melange" a study of manners and morals.  At any rate, the same barbed pen that wrote the Cento number apparently wrote parts of others, for the amusing though severe remarks on human frailty, boiling up from intense moral indignation, bear evidences of the same origin. Listen to his encomium on the man of honor:

And shall we then say that no man who withholds from another what law, or justice, perhaps, calls his own, or who greatly and boldly deprives him of such property, is a man of honor? Heaven forbid I should say so! Is honor truth? No. It is not in the lie's going from us, but in its coming to us, our honor is injured. Doth it then consist in what the vulgar call cardinal virtues? It would be foolish to suppose so, since we see every day so many men of honor without any. In what then doth the word *honor* consist? Why, in itself alone. A man of honor is he that is called a man of honor; and while he is so called, he so remains, and no longer.[11]

Turning from the man of honor our critic—perhaps Brown himself—writes a pungent, stinging paragraph to the housewife. From this passage the social historian can gain considerable insight into the life of the time. His satiric picture of women who sacrifice everything for show might conceivably have been based on the critic's personal experience; in any case it gives voice to Brown's personal opinion, for he detested show:

As, after all her exertions, her situation in life does not allow of her being genteel in everything, parsimonious economy and heedless expense take their turn. To be as smart, not as her equals, but as her superiors, it becomes necessary in that prudent forethought which enables a good wife to proportion the family expenditure by the regular order of necessities, comforts, conveniences, and superfluities: this gradation must be reversed, and superfluities take the lead. Expensive wines may be introduced on great occasions, by a daily retrenchment of small beer; and wax lights may be had for routs, by limiting the number of kitchen candles. If her husband and children dine on hashed mutton, she can provide ices in the evening; and, by leaving their bedchambers comfortless and inconvenient, she can afford more drapery for the drawing-room. Even white morning dresses will not be so very expensive, provided you are expert in haggling with the washerwoman, and do not dislike being dirty when you are invisible; and if you know cheap shops, and the art of driving bargains, you may even save money by making useless purchases. New-modeling your household and personal ornaments is, I grant, an indispensable duty; for no one can appear three times in the same gown, nor have six parties without one additional vandyke or festoon to the window-curtains. These employments will therefore occupy your mornings till the hour of visiting arrives; then you must take care to dismiss the bed-gown and work-bag, and, having crammed every thing ungenteel out of sight, assume the airs of that happy creature who has nothing in the world to do, and nothing to think of but killing time.[12]

The "Olio," unsigned, ran for seven dreary numbers. A series of generalized essays on such topics as virtue, death, religion, politeness,

[11] *Literary Magazine*, VII (April, 1807), 216.
[12] *Literary Magazine*, VIII (Aug., 1807), 33.

it was a prime example of what Mark Twain would have called "sentimentalism gone to seed." Its subject matter was trite, and its typical sentimental euphemisms and elegant circumlocutions were strained, as these tidbits will attest:

Large crystalline drops of heavenly commiseration coursed each other from their azure orbs, and gave her youthful cheek the beauteous appearance of a newly expanded rose, bathed in the dew of the morning. . . . The moth, when hovering round the alluring flame, is too striking a resemblance of those incautious females who, in the simplicity of their hearts, tipple on the precipice of destruction, which too often awaits them.[13]

Brown must indeed have been hard pressed for copy to print such obvious nonsense. With the exception of one or two, the "Olio" essays as a whole fell far below the usual standard of the magazine.

There were other brief sets of essays, never carried beyond two or three issues. The "Gleaner" (unsigned—could the author have been Judith Sargent Murray [1750-1820], whose effusions had been published in 1798, under the title *The Gleaner?*) consisted of excerpts, for the most part, from little-known writers of earlier times, on such diverse topics as education, physiognomy, and marriage. The essays on agriculture, by one Rubricola, contained digests of two books on the subject and reflected the contemporary interest in botany as well as the economic concept of agrarianism.

Two essays, one on wealth and one on poverty, formed companion-pieces. Good-natured and philosophical, sometimes verging on the sentimental, the writer furnished the usual remarks in the best Addisonian style. "Thoughts on Wealth," in two instalments, presented the well-worn thesis that all men foolishly desire wealth above wisdom or virtue. The following paragraph must have made Brown nod in agreement:

Yet let not those who have disdained to tread the intricate paths which lead from poverty to wealth, from obscurity to splendor, from neglect to distinction, blame fortune; she sets a price on her favors, and whoever chooses may purchase; if they were unwilling to pay it, it is evident they thought the price too high; they are indigent from choice and not from necessity, and as they have preserved that which they esteemed the most valuable, ought to be contented with the situation in which they have been placed by their own inclinations.[14]

Regarding poverty no one, sagely declared the author, really prefers it. Those who praise poverty are either the rich who know nothing about it, or the poor who try to rationalize their condition. Some voluntarily embrace poverty, but only under the compulsion of duty or superstitious fear of wealth. The sufferings of the poor are some-

[13] "Olio," I, *Literary Magazine,* VII (March, 1807), 91; IV, *ibid.,* VIII (July, 1807), 1.

[14] *Literary Magazine,* II (June, 1804), 187.

what mitigated by their tendency to live each day without consideration of the next.

## BROWN'S ATTITUDES AND OPINIONS

The most important single author was, of course, Brown himself,
although he did not write so much for this journal as he did for the
*Monthly Magazine*. The only pieces of fiction were the two-part
Oriental romance of "Omar and Fatima," and "Carwin the Biloquist." He also wrote a few travel sketches, such as "A Jaunt to
Rockaway." His thoughtful and significant "Student's Diary" and
his shorter articles and reviews furnish material for an analysis of
his ideas.

As in the *Monthly Magazine*, the editor's attitudes and opinions
are of special concern to the biographer. Brown continued his deep
interest in all types of informational topics. Despite a pronounced
note of conservatism in almost all his views, Brown's tendency to
fairly objective presentation of facts rather than of personal opinions
characterized the *Literary Magazine*. Dispassionate essays on the customs and manners of the day continued to flow from his pen. His
remarks on women's dress occasion amusement today (as indeed they
probably did in his own time) : French fashions, he opined, would
disgrace women if they did not actually lead to their premature death,
for low-cut gowns and thin materials were too airy for the cold Philadelphia climate. But apparently the world gave the sage no ear, for
in a later article he wrote:

On the whole, I can never on a cold day behold a young lady in her Cham-
berry or muslins, her transparent drapery and her nudities, without a sympathetic shudder; and when I seriously reflect on the manifold dangers to which
she is exposed, I lament that so fair a thing should be so perishable.[15]

Was this the Brown whose youthful ardor made his Henrietta threaten
to wrap herself in a woolen habit?

The editor's gentle Quaker blood still boiled at the mere mention
of dueling. It is the "tyranny of custom," he contended, for so long
as men feel that their honor is at stake, just so long will they be "proof
against argument and jest, against religion and law." Alexander
Hamilton's tragic death afforded him a dramatic example of the dreadful folly of dueling:

The abhorred and sanguinary prejudice, vulgarly called *honor*, offers to
the understanding, in the influence it is found to have over strong and enlightened minds, a paradox the most bewildering and humiliating that ever
existed. . . . While reason and common sense exclaim against the *folly* of
duelling; while religion with its loudest voice condemns its iniquity; while
the civil laws of the state load it with the heaviest penalties and rank it with
the foulest and deadliest crimes of which human nature is capable; while so

[15] "Female Clothing," *Literary Magazine*, VI (July, 1806), 23.

strong is the current of popular opinion against it that no one is hardy enough to be its public defender or apologist, we daily see men that fill the first rank in a great state making this appeal to violence, fearless of legal prevention and legal penalties.

The wise and good, while they lament *this* death for its own sake, will regard it with peculiar regret, when they reflect that the example of a Hamilton has thus been given to the inhuman and pernicious practice of duelling.[16]

Less bloody, but hardly less reprehensible, he thought, was legalized lottery.  Various states were lending the odor of sanctity to this damnable custom by conducting lotteries as a means of raising money. As a result many people who would otherwise have disapproved took part in the gamble:

That they are authorized by laws and encouraged by the legislators of the nation is an additional reason for your discountenancing the practice; for who shall bear testimony against immorality, if those who know it as such and see its destructive consequences join in the commission, because it is sanctioned by the ignorance or tolerated by the vice of the individuals who ought to watch over the happiness of the republic? If you commit a robbery, you do an act of injustice highly reprehensible; but there is little to be apprehended from the consequences of such an action flowing from the force of your example upon your fellow-citizens, for the wise would pity your error and the ignorant would be deterred from imitation by the penalty of the law; but in purchasing a lottery ticket you encourage many to join in this most pernicious species of gambling, by the sanction which your action gives and by the impression which must be received that the practice is approved by your deliberate judgment; you encourage legislators to persist in this most pernicious mode of taxing the people.[17]

In spite of such "imported vices," as Brown called them, the country was rapidly growing in both wealth and population.  Various types of manufacturing were coming to the fore.  Like Jefferson, whose views had changed since the days when he advocated that America remain entirely agrarian, Brown, though not an isolationist, saw the advantage of our becoming economically independent of Europe as soon as possible.  In scanning the following glowing paragraph a reader could easily almost forget author and period, for it is strongly reminiscent of the puffing that issues from our modern Chambers of Commerce:

We have had occasion lately to announce the introduction of several important branches of manufactures in our country, in addition to the great number which have been gradually and almost imperceptibly progressing since the revolution, but we know of none which, as a collateral branch, affords us more real satisfaction than the recent successful effort of Mr. John Harrison, of this city, in the manufacture of oil of vitriol; after many unsuccessful

[16] "Death of Hamilton," *Literary Magazine*, II (Aug., 1804), 337.
[17] "Dialogues of the Living," *Monthly Magazine*, I (April, 1799), 20.

attempts in other parts of the union, and, indeed, knowing as we do that many parts of the continent of Europe are still tributary to Great Britain for this important aid to their general manufactures, we think it no common cause of congratulation.  The progress of science and the arts is eminently promoted by it. . . .  We therefore repeat, we think it no common cause of congratulation that a native American, by a series of laborious exertions, has succeeded in rendering us independent of Britain in one of the most useful aids to our infant manufactures. . . .  Upon the whole, we know of no undertaking which embraces so many useful objects, or deserves the applause and support of the American people more than this.[18]

A new type of native wool received Brown's editorial approval:

The exertions which Mr. Custis is making to improve the quality of American wool are highly meritorious, and rank him, with Colonel Humphreys, among the true patriots of our country.[19]

He also noted the far-sightedness of Dr. Thomas Ewell, who offered prizes of land as incentives for the discovery and development of native medicines:

To any person who will write the best and most simple account of the means of giving tone or strength to debilitated persons, without the aid of Peruvian bark, wine, or foreign medicines, shall be awarded twenty acres.

And he who will write the best and most simple account of the substitutes for foreign cathartics found in this country, with the means of preserving and exhibiting them, shall have ten acres.[20]

Not only was the country as a whole growing rapidly but Pennsylvania especially was in the van of the general prosperity:

Under these circumstances [Brown queried], and as the welfare of agriculture and commerce mutually depend on each other, and as there is a competition between the states of New York and Maryland for a participation in the trade of Pennsylvania, would it not be good policy in our citizens to endeavor to promote an union of town and country capital, for the improvement of water carriage and roads generally?[21]

Good roads, Brown insisted, were the country's greatest need in the development of an expanding and healthy economy.  Not only do good roads make good neighbors: they make good citizens of the inhabitants of widely separate portions of our country.  In discussing the feasi-

[18] "Literary, Philosophical, Commercial, and Agricultural Intelligence," *Literary Magazine*, VIII (Oct., 1807), 150-151.

[19] *Ibid.*, p. 98.  The Custis mentioned is probably George W. Parke Custis (1781-1857), stepson of George Washington.  He organized an annual convention in 1803 for the promotion of the wool industry.  "Colonel Humphreys" is David Humphreys, of Connecticut Wits fame.  He imported merinos from Spain and Portugal in order to improve the quality of New England wool.

[20] "Literary and Philosophical Intelligence," *Literary Magazine*, VII (June, 1807), 460.

[21] "Remarkable Occurrences," *Literary Magazine*, I (Oct., 1803), 66.

bility of a road from Philadelphia to Pittsburgh, Brown was among the first who perceived the close tie between geography and economics. Channels of distribution he recognized as elements of prime importance in a country's prosperity.

To enlarge on the high importance of cementing the union of our citizens on the western waters with those of the Atlantic states would be unnecessary. Politicians have generally agreed that rivers unite the interests and promote the friendship of those who inhabit their banks; while mountains, on the contrary, tend to the disunion and estrangement of those who are separated by them. In the present case, to make the crooked ways straight and the rough ways smooth will in effect remove the intervening mountains, and, by facilitating the intercourse of our western brethren with those on the Atlantic, essentially unite them *in interest*, which is the most effectual means of uniting the human race.[22]

In politics Brown as usual maintained a policy of neutrality on all controversial political subjects, reminding both readers and contributors of his self-imposed nonpartisanship. When someone submitted an article that violated this policy, Brown mildly but firmly refused it:

It is with great reluctance that he reminds his correspondent of that political neutrality to which he has condemned himself, and which obliges him to decline the introduction of the favors sent him. No one can be more sensible than he is of the merit of the performances alluded to, as specimens of eloquence; and he would willingly adorn his pages with the whole or part of them, if he were not under a moral necessity of silence.[23]

In sketching the nature of Volume VIII of the magazine, he found it necessary to repeat that

It shall be the study of the editor, as it always has been, on all occasions to avoid meddling with politics; convinced that the rancorous passions engendered by party rage tend more to obstruct than facilitate the progress of literature, it shall be his endeavor to allay and soothe them by turning the attention of his readers to more pleasing objects; and though this course may draw on him the censure of zealots, it cannot fail ultimately to give general satisfaction.[24]

Only once, it seems, did he permit himself to become facetious about political matters:

There is something ominous in this social disposition of our feathered visitants—Quails that invaded Philadelphia in great numbers. Some very good sort of people, but of temperaments a little prone to hypochondria, are extremely apprehensive that this phenomenon indicates the triumph of *democracy* in the state. . . . or at least in the city! Others suppose they may

[22] "Abstract of a Report on American Roads," *Literary Magazine*, V (Jan., 1806), 24.

[23] "To Correspondents," *Literary Magazine*, II (July, 1804), 320.

[24] *Literary Magazine*, VII (June, 1807), 472.

be on their way to Pennsylvania, with a view to obtain certificates of citizenship preparatory to the next presidential election.[25]

In a series of biographical sketches on the political views of Adams, Jefferson, and Hamilton, he characteristically refused to commit himself even while praising their achievements. After a temperate and factual sketch of John Adams's life, he closed with these words:

We purposely avoid entering into an exhibition of the public character of Mr. Adams, because political zeal has long since enlisted all men in the number of his friends or enemies, and we are desirous of avoiding, on this occasion, to offend any.[26]

In his sketch of Jefferson he said:

The biography of such a man as Thomas Jefferson can only be drawn up by his own hand, and a true judgment of his merits can only be formed by future generations. When the animosities of the present age have been laid asleep by time, his character and actions may rise to the view in their native and proper colors, and the meed of blame or of praise will be conferred on him in the degree to which he is justly entitled to it. . . . In this state of things, it would be highly absurd, in a publication like the present, to enter into investigations of the character and conduct of this eminent personage. It would be equally impossible to escape the indignation of his friends or enemies, and nobody is neutral in this controversy, or to destroy that bias in the writer's own mind, which, whether favorable or unpropitious to the person in view, is necessarily adverse and destructive to candor and truth.[27]

About Alexander Hamilton he permitted himself to be more enthusiastic, partly, perhaps, because of his personal acquaintance with Hamilton and partly because of the statesman's recent death; but as usual Brown refrained from outright partisanship:

The political and literary interests of this country have suffered a great loss in the death of General Alexander Hamilton. In every region of investigation into which this man entered, he discovered a burning and intrepid genius. Our hearts bleed at the recollection of the manner in which he died; and most bitterly do we deplore that such a man has fallen in such a manner. . . .[28]

In preceding sketches Brown had already written feelingly but discriminatingly of the lamented Hamilton:

As a member of a free community, he was of course enrolled in one of those parties in which such a community can never fail to be divided. Hence, while all admire his genius and his knowledge, and the purity of his motives,

[25] "Remarkable Occurrences," *Literary Magazine*, I (Nov., 1803), 154-155.
[26] "Biographical Sketch of John Adams," *Literary Magazine*, II (Aug., 1804), 332.
[27] "Thomas Jefferson," *Literary Magazine*, II (Sept., 1804), 413-414.
[28] "Notices of American Writers and Publications," *Literary Magazine*, II (Aug., 1804), 345.

a part only acknowledge the force of his reasonings, the truth of his opinions, and the wisdom of his conduct. . . . The next twenty years may be expected to teem with great events and revolutions in our country. Had Hamilton lived, his genius would have towered high, if it had not actually presided in the storms of the state. A mysterious fate had drawn away his genius and intelligence to another sphere, and who shall venture to call in question the rectitude of this decree?[29]

Brown steadfastly but dispassionately defended the Constitution, declaring that even though it was not perfect (having been drawn up by mortal men), it was at least an effort to promote "the wealth, the peace, and the happiness of the whole." He held Jefferson's opinion that in a representative government the "natural aristocracy" of the country should be in control:

No representative legislature can ever be respectable or secure unless it contain within itself a great proportion of those who form the natural aristocracy of the country, and are able as individuals to influence the conduct and opinions of the greater part of its inhabitants. Unless the power, and weight, and authority of the assembly, in short, be really made up of the power and weight and authority of the individuals who compose it, the factitious dignity they may derive from their situation can never be of long endurance; and the dangerous power with which they may be invested will become the subject of scrambling and contention among the factions of the metropolis and be employed for any purpose but the general good of the community. . . . The difference between a free government and a tyrannical one consists entirely in the different proportions of the people that are influenced by their *opinion,* or subjugated by *force.* In a large society, opinions can only be re-united by means of representation; and the natural representative is the individual whose example and authority can influence the opinions of the greater part of those in whose behalf he is delegated. This is the natural aristocracy of a civilized nation; and its legislature is then best modeled, when it is in the hands of those who answer to that description. The whole people are governed by the laws, exactly as each clan or district would have been by the patriarchal authority of an elective and unarmed chieftain; and the lawgivers are not only secure of their places while they can maintain their influence over the people but are withheld from any rash or injurious measure, by the consciousness and feelings of their dependence on this voluntary deference and submission.[30]

Brown freely acknowledged that our form of government had its drawbacks, but maintained that free men could endure no other. In the passage below, Brown wrote courageously and even daringly, but astutely and wisely, propounding political maxims that are sound if not especially penetrating:

[29] "Alexander Hamilton," *Literary Magazine,* II (Oct., 1804), 492.
[30] "Of the French Revolution," *Literary Magazine,* VI (Nov., 1806), 355-357.

We estimate the felicity of ages and nations by the seeming tranquillity and peace they enjoy; or believe them to be wretched under the agitations and troubles which sometimes attend the possession of liberty itself. The forms of legislature which imply numerous assemblies, whether collective or representative, have been often censured as exposing men to all the inconveniences of faction or party division; but, if these inconveniences are to be dreaded, they nevertheless may be fairly hazarded for the sake of the end to be obtained in free governments, the safety of the people, and the scope which is given to all the noble faculties of the human mind.

If I mistake not the interests of human nature, they consist more in the exercise of freedom and the indulgence of a liberal and beneficent temper than in the possession of mere tranquillity, or what is termed exemption from trouble. The trials of ability which men mutually afford to one another in the collisions of free society are the lessons of a school which Providence has opened for mankind and are well known to forward instead of impeding their progress in any valuable art, whether commercial or elegant.[31]

### BROWN AND THE SLAVERY QUESTION

A subject which, as Brown several times noted, carried political as well as humanitarian implications was the problem of Negro slavery. Like most thoughtful men of his day, the Quakers in particular, Brown abhorred slavery and staunchly advocated its abolition. He held the environmentalists' view that the Negroes in the West Indies had been degraded by circumstances and not by God, and that if they were freed and educated they might some day be capable of self-government. This position was a daring one for that early day, and the editor quite probably received many a vigorous protest from irate readers. Brown was among our earliest prophets to foresee that the slavery question would eventually lead to serious civil strife in our own country, for the great number of slaves in the South and West were already affecting representation in the national government. Brown saw national tempers rise, and he sensed very clearly that the crux of the matter was representation. In a carefully thought-out article, "How Far Do Slaves Influence Political Representation in America?" he presented figures to show that the inclusion of slaves in the basic population figures gave the slave holding states a disproportionate number of representatives. The rapid increase of population, both slave and free, in these states would make the proportion increasingly unjust.

The day is not far when the southern and western states will have more representatives in congress and electors of president, for slaves only, than the northern will have for all their free people.[32]

[31] "On Free and Despotic Governments," *Literary Magazine*, III (March, 1805), 80.

[32] *Literary Magazine*, IV (Dec., 1805), 30.

## BROWN AND FOREIGN AFFAIRS

Brown's endeavor not to offend the political sensibilities of his readers did not extend to refraining from the free discussion of foreign affairs. In the first number of his magazine he had stated his willingness to "speculate freely on foreign transactions." Although he had hailed the French Revolution in its early stages, he now admitted that much harm had followed in its wake. In an article of some pretension he gave voice to his disapproval of the course of the Revolution. His position was that taken by the more conservative elements in England and in America; to one who has followed Charles Brockden Brown's course of thinking it comes with no great surprise. The pattern of change was that made familiar by Edmund Burke, and for similar reasons. Editorial responsibility had to a deplorable extent solidified and solemnized Brown's thinking—had indeed so channeled his thought-processes that he seemed peculiarly unaware of the great changes for the betterment of mankind which flowed directly from the Revolution. That Brown could write vigorously, challengingly, penetratingly, and yet shortsightedly about the failures of the Revolution can be seen in the following passage:

Among the many evils which the French revolution has inflicted on mankind, the most deplorable, perhaps, both in extent and duration, consists in the injury which it has done to the cause of rational freedom and the discredit in which it has involved the principles of political philosophy. The warnings derived from the misfortunes of that country and the lessons which may still be read in the tragical consequences of her temerity are memorable, no doubt, and important; but they are such as are presented to us by the history of every period of the world; and the emotions by which they have been impressed are in this case too violent to let their import and application be properly distinguished. From the miscarriage of a scheme of frantic innovation, we conceive an unreasonable and undiscriminating dread of all change or reform. The failure of an attempt to make government perfect reconciles us to imperfections that might easily be removed; and the miserable consequences of treating everything as prejudice and injustice which could not be reconciled to a system of fantastic equality has given strength to prejudices and sanction to abuses which were gradually wearing away before the progress of reason and philosophy. The French revolution has thrown us back half a century in the course of political improvement and driven us to cling once more, with superstitious terror, at the feet of those idols from which we had been nearly reclaimed by the lessons of a milder philosophy. . . . On a review of the whole matter, it seems impossible to acquit those of the revolutionary patriots whose intentions are admitted to be pure, of great precipitation, presumption, and imprudence. Apologies may be found for them, perhaps, in the inexperience which was incident to their situation; in their constant apprehension of being separated before their task was accomplished; in the exasperation which was excited by the injudicious proceedings of the cabinet; and in the intoxication which naturally resulted from the magnitude of their early triumph and the noise and resounding of their popularity. But the errors into which they fell were inexcusable in politicians of the eighteenth century; and while we pity their sufferings and admire their genius, we cannot feel any respect for their wisdom, or any surprise at their miscarriage.[33]

Brown showed a lively interest not only in the underlying principles of the Revolution but also in the events in the course of its daily progress. In "Summary of Politics," for instance, he discussed the possibilities of a French invasion of England, dismissing it as impracticable at a time when Wordsworth and Coleridge from their nearer view were convinced of its possibility and alarmed at its prospects. He could not understand the surrender of Hanover to Napoleon's army, putting it down to internal disaffection. He made pungent remarks on other events as they occurred.

### BROWN'S INTEREST IN AMERICAN HISTORY

For his own country's history Brown always displayed the deepest concern. Every historical work that showed promise he eagerly welcomed, particularly if the author had made use of original documentary sources. In a review of *The History of Virginia*, by John Burk, he applauded the author's gathering of facts from sources that were rapidly disappearing. Another book, *A View of South Carolina* (1802), by John Drayton, attracted his interest especially because it was more nearly a natural history or geographical treatise than a political history, and because its general account of the discovery and settlement of that state employed primary sources. In acclaiming its significance he wrote:

We have great pleasure in meeting with a work of this kind. At present, the geographical and statistical condition of the United States is very little known; and it can only be known by the compilation of works like the present. The District of Maine, the States of Vermont and New Hampshire are the only portions of our country which have been made the subjects of particular histories or descriptions, before the present undertaking; and we now add the name of Drayton to those of Williams and Belknap as the literary benefactors of their country.[34]

Brown showed strong enthusiasm for our growing nationalism, not only by encouraging a native literature but by welcoming any work that shed light on the early life in our country, and particularly on "antiquities" of all kinds, from Indian arrowheads to colonial bedspreads.

*American antiquities,* if any such things there be, chiefly relate to monuments of those nations who occupied America before the European discoveries. The most permanent, conspicuous, and remarkable of these are undoubtedly

[33] "Of the French Revolution," *Literary Magazine,* VI (Nov., 1806), 351, 359.
[34] *Literary Magazine,* I (Oct., 1803), 30.

the mounds of ramparts scattered over the western country. These have two qualities to recommend them, in the highest degree, to curiosity, and that is the remoteness of their origin and the mysteriousness of their design. Other monuments consist of the weapons and domestic utensils, which are made of durable materials, and will probably continue to be found, or to be preserved, some thousands of years hence.

The spirit of curiosity is exactly in proportion to the remoteness and the mysteriousness (and the latter is one of the consequences of the former) of the object; so that the relics of Indian manners will go on acquiring value from age to age; a greater number will be busy in collecting and describing them; and a stone, tobacco-pipe, or arrowhead, will in time become of much more value than its weight in gold.

Time will produce another species of antiques, in the relics of those generations which have passed away since the colonization of America. Two centuries have almost elapsed since our ancestors began to migrate hither, and this period will admit of a succession of ten generations at least. There are a great number of books, and of domestic utensils, which were manufactured in Europe and were brought hither for their immediate accommodation, by the early colonists. These are greatly prized by their descendants. This city [Philadelphia], which was the earliest settlement of the English in this state, contains a great number of these relics and the antiquarian spirit glows very strongly in some bosoms.[35]

### FREE EDUCATION AND DEMOCRACY

Brown, being himself a scholar, was naturally interested in education—not only for gentlemen's sons but for everyone. We have seen in an earlier chapter that he advocated education for women as well as men. At the risk of being called "radical" or socialistic, Brown printed a plea for "the establishment of schools throughout the state of Pennsylvania, in such a manner that the poor may be taught gratis."[36] If all children were given schooling at public expense, the article continued, the promotion of literature would be greatly facilitated, and our religious and civil liberty would be assured by "perpetuating our happy form of government." In that day education for all our citizens at the expense of all through general taxation met the same selfish and narrow-minded opposition, and from the same sources, which socialized or state medicine is meeting in our day. The one was as inevitable in that day as, for better or worse, the other is in ours, for that is the democratic way. From Brown's day to our own, democracy has met the strongest opposition from the very quarters where it should least be expected. Indeed, Brown saw quite clearly that the success of the democratic way of life depends upon an educated citizenry. The "pressure boys" of Brown's day tried to run the government for their own aggrandizement just as their twentieth-century counterparts, the cartelists and the lobby-

---

[35] *Ibid.* (Jan., 1804), p. 246.
[36] *Literary Magazine*, III (June, 1805), 385-386.

ists, are striving to do.[37]   In his firm belief that widespread education was the *sine qua non* of a living democracy, Brown never forsook his early radical position that education must be free and general for both sexes.   Remembering the argument in *Alcuin,* Brown did not demur when the author of the "Olio" maintained that:

Nothing tends so much, except real religion, to the guidance of the heart, and consequently to the true elevation of the sex, as an enlightened education.[38]

His idea of a suitable education for women would hardly answer to the demands of our own day, but it represented advanced thinking for the early nineteenth century.   In addition to the usual deeds of charity, lessons in painting, drawing, music, and needlework, Brown advocated the study of philosophy and religion:

That immovable anchor of the soul, religion, is the best safeguard against the impulses of the passions, against the delusions and miseries of life.   But even in religion beware of enthusiasm on one hand and dull conformity on the other; for that religion which springs not from a regenerated heart can never be acceptable to an all-wise and perfect creator.[39]

### BROWN'S PLEA FOR A NATIVE ART

Another phase of American culture in which Brown showed his nationalism was art.   He gave wholehearted encouragement to painting and sculpture.   He urged the young nation to awaken to the desirability of encouraging sculpture and pictorial art.   No wonder that he exulted over the establishment of the Pennsylvania Academy of Fine Arts:

This design is highly honorable to the spirit of those who have adopted it.   Our country is generally considered as a youthful, or rather, in some respects, an infantile country, whose imbecile and growing state requires corporal nutriment and exercise rather than intellectual; but the success of this project is a proof that we are not altogether occupied in these coarser cravings. . . .   Whatever justice there may be in the contempt with which the literary and scientific spirit of America is regarded by Europeans, we are surely remarkably distinguished for our genius for the arts.   Notwithstanding the want of examples and incitements, America had hitherto produced the greatest painters of the age, and this preeminence they have established, not only in spite of the want of all the customary motives to diligence and emulation but in defiance of numerous discouragements and obstacles to which the artists of other nations have not been exposed.[40]

[37] For convincing details see Kenneth Gale Crawford, *The Pressure Boys* (New York, 1939).

[38] *Literary Magazine,* VIII (July, 1807), 3-4.

[39] *Ibid.,* p. 5.

[40] "Pennsylvania Academy of Fine Arts," *Literary Magazine,* IV (Aug., 1805), 129.

But an academy was not enough: he urged the establishment of a national gallery for furthering interest in art. European models could be thus housed, thereby giving practical aid to the young artists and scholars of America. Our artists, then, when they went to Europe to study would already be familiar with famous pieces. They could then pass on to more advanced stages without loss of time. After they had returned to America they could refresh their memories by studying the models again. Besides, wealthy people in the United States would probably want copies and thus furnish employment for young artists. Scholars who could not afford a trip to Europe could familiarize themselves with these works of art and "would hence find daily opportunities of benefiting and crediting their country . . . by their erudite remarks on monuments that relate entirely to classic ground."[41]

Although this somewhat naïve article gives no indication of the recognition that we should develop our own distinctive art, Brown was not entirely without the consciousness that in painting as well as in literature we needed to cultivate individuality. In a report on some new pictures lent by Robert Fulton to the Philadelphia Academy of Fine Arts, he singled out for special notice two by Benjamin West, who had already won fame abroad. These paintings were not only important as works of art but significant in reflecting "great honor on the genius of our country . . . of themselves a basis for forming a good taste in our new school of art."[42]

Brown considered that Americans owed it to their country to take an abiding interest in its native culture. "It must not be urged," he said, "that this country is too young or too poor for anything like encouragement of the fine arts. . . . The Americans have, within a few years, made a rapid progress" in other fields. Certainly our backwardness had not been due to lack of genius. Had we not already produced Copley, Trumbull, and West? People of wealth would greatly benefit their country by buying works of art for their homes. Besides, Brown added slyly, these pictures would increase in value and therefore be good investments.[43] But he realized the difficulties under which all the arts struggled:

That the arts are not encouraged in America is a fact which cannot be disputed. The cause of it forms a subject of curious speculation. That it arises from nothing inherent in the physical or moral constitution of the people, in their climate or form of government, is evident. That it does not arise from their poverty is no less clear, for where can be found a more flourishing and prosperous nation?[44]

[41] "A Plan for the Improvement and Diffusion of the Arts Adapted to the United States," *Literary Magazine*, III (March, 1805), 181-183.

[42] News item, *Literary Magazine*, VIII (Nov., 1807), 263-264.

[43] "On Collections of Paintings," *Literary Magazine*, III (May, 1805), 374-375.

[44] "Why the Arts Are Discouraged in America," *Literary Magazine*, VI (July, 1806), 76-77.

Since there were no Americans possessed of great fortunes and comparatively few interested in the arts, America must patiently await a fairer day, but her gifted sons and daughters must not cease to strive. Brown clearly saw that wealth and leisure and social stability were prime essentials for attainment of the higher cultural goals, and America did not possess these. But his faith in the inherent artistic greatness of the American people never flagged:

A people must secure a provision of absolute necessaries before they think of conveniences; and must enjoy conveniences before they can indulge in the agreeable arts of life. Long exercise of the indispensable arts will stock them with useful things, which, if their institutions be wholesome, will make them in general easy and even rich as a people without supposing enormous possessions in individual hands, and the attendant misery of others. The Americans began with loghouses, and are now in the progress to brick and stone, convenience and elegance; their attentions observe the like progress and expand with the ability of attainment. When agriculture—with its attendant arts—and commerce have rendered them comfortable in all respects, they will then naturally aspire to and encourage works of ingenuity and polite arts, which, though as yet unsuitable and beyond their views, will then evince their prosperity instead of their decay.[45]

### BROWN AND CREATIVE WRITING

It is surprising that such a devout nationalist as Brown could fail to stress literary activity in America in this purposively literary magazine; but as a matter of fact less emphasis is given to it than in his earlier journal. As we have seen, even reviews of American books were not so numerous as in the *Monthly Magazine*. Besides the usual essays on the classics he wrote such general articles as "The Distinction between Poetry and Prose,"[46] in which he maintained, consonant with the new romantic theory of poetry, that poetry does not necessarily have to be clothed in verse form, but that it must contain emotional fervor and striking imagery. Echoing the recent but well-known distinctions set forth by Wordsworth and Coleridge, Brown would prefer to correlate the terms "verse" and "prose"; "poetry" and "philosophy."

In another essay[47] he discussed the popularity of fiction, suggesting that many people, finding life dull, sought excitement in novel-reading. As a result they preferred novels of the Gothic type, full of "a certain proportion of murders, ghosts, clanking chains, dead bodies, skeletons, old castles, and damp dungeons." In this condemnation (1807) of the Gothic type of novel Brown was consistent with his earlier vigorous protest. However, between 1804 and 1807 there came a curious

[45] *Ibid.*, p. 77.
[46] *Literary Magazine*, III (Nov., 1804), 583-586.
[47] "On the Cause of the Popularity of Novels," *Literary Magazine*, VII (June, 1807), 410-412.

change in his attitude toward novels. In 1804—about the time of his last novel—he had defended novels against the charges commonly being made against them:

They who prate about the influence of novels to unfit us for solid and useful reading are guilty of a double error; for in the first place, a just and powerful picture of human life in which the connection between vice and misery and between felicity and virtue is vividly portrayed is the most solid and useful reading that a moral being (exclusive of particular cases and professional engagements) can read; and in the second place, the most trivial and trite of these performances are to readers of certain ages and intellects the only books they will read. If they were not thus employed, they would be employed in a way still more trivial or pernicious.[48]

Of course, he admitted, some novels were merely silly, like the "terrific novels" of the Radcliffe imitators, but there were enough good ones to supply the most fastidious.

In the 1807 article previously alluded to, the critic was concerned with the general tenor of modern novels. He posed, but did not answer, the following question:

Why are works entirely composed of murders considered as most certain of being perused? The answer to this question I shall leave to my readers, and content myself with hoping that the present fashion, like all departures from nature and common sense, will have but a short reign.[49]

The deleterious effects of such works, he continued, lay in the possibility that younger readers would neglect other types of reading and would absorb false views of life. This position is strikingly at variance with that of the enthusiastic young writer of *Wieland* and with the Declaration of American literary independence found in the Preface to *Edgar Huntly* (1799). Had the gravity of the editorship of a thought-molding, fact-crammed magazine changed him or had it only matured and broadened his outlook on life? Had the tyranny of facts laid its cold, dead hand on him or had he "just learned things"? The following observation answers those questions though only in part:

An attentive observation of the scenes around us will store the mind with reflections of an indefinite variety and far greater utility than are to be derived from the wild narratives of the imagination, and we shall soon be enabled to conclude, upon the surest grounds, that he to whom real life appears dull must himself be a man of dull capacity.[50]

[48] "Novel Reading," from "A Student's Diary," *Literary Magazine*, I (March, 1804), 405.
[49] "On the Cause of the Popularity of Novels," *Literary Magazine*, VII (June, 1807), 412.
[50] *Ibid.* p. 412.

For this defection from his former faith in creative writing he may have been trying to justify himself in an article entitled "Alliance between Poverty and Genius":

Besides, though the rich are seldom authors, there are other methods of displaying a literary spirit besides that of writing books. To read, reflect, inquire, by deduction or experiment, is the occupation of vast numbers who are free from the vanity of book-making. They know that there are books enough in the world, and their modesty forbids them to imagine that they can beneficially add to the number.[51]

It must be admitted that this does little to dispel our bewilderment. While he denied that money was the sole incentive to creative writing, his failure to earn a comfortable living from it must have acted powerfully in changing his attitude. It is very evident that Brown was forsaking creative literature for the more mundane but equally important fields of history, politics, and science. This fact became palpable in the years immediately following.

This attitude seems to have been part of his discouragement over the meagerness and the meanness of American literature. True, he sometimes found occasion to rejoice in anticipation over an American literary achievement, for example Barlow's *Columbiad:*

There will soon be published in Philadelphia a new and interesting work entitled *"the Columbiad,* a poem, in ten books, by Joel Barlow." This work will be ornamented with twelve engravings, which have been done in England by the most eminent artists, and at great expense. They are in the first style of elegance. The typographical part, wholly American, is executed in a manner highly creditable to the several artists employed. . . . A work like this, on a great national subject, must excite a high degree of interest. In the present instance, we are confident that the public expectation will not be disappointed; and while the *Columbiad* will be cited as a monument of American genius, the publishers are determined that this edition shall do equal honor to our arts.[52]

Brown freely admitted the justice of the censure of foreign writers upon our indifference toward some of America's outstanding literary personages. The following remark about our neglect of Franklin shows Brown's humiliation:

Nothing, says this writer, can show more clearly the singular want of literary enterprize or activity in America than that no one has yet been found in that flourishing republic to collect and publish the works of their only philosopher.[53]

From this lack of literary activity one is not to infer that Americans

[51] *Literary Magazine,* III (May, 1805), 333.

[52] "Literary, Philosophical, Commercial, and Agricultural Intelligence," *Literary Magazine,* VIII (Oct., 1807), 204-205.

[53] "Character of Dr. Franklin," *Literary Magazine,* VI (Nov., 1806), 367.

did not read. Besides the novels mentioned they consumed, to Brown's evident disgust, great quantities of newspapers:

> In the United States, the number of newspapers can scarcely fall short of two hundred, though the population is only half that of England. Indeed, in no country in the world are newspapers more read than with us.
>
> What inferences must be drawn from these facts as to the comparative state of the three nations? The circulation of newspapers has by some been deemed a test of the literature of the country. But if newspapers are chiefly confined, as with us, to traders' notices, foreign and domestic politics, and remarkable events, and pay little or no regard to literary or scientific topics and inquiries, their currency is rather a proof of the low than of the high state of knowledge among us. They will clearly prove that in no nation is the knowledge of the political state of transactions of our own and of foreign countries so widely diffused as among us.[54]

The *Literary Magazine* lacks the note of optimism apparent in Brown's earlier journalistic adventure. His countrymen were still under the spell of Europe, he complained. When a writer succeeded in producing a creditable piece of creative or scholarly writing, American readers should be proud of him instead of automatically ranking his production below European works of perhaps inferior worth.[55] Only when American writers and artists became famous in Europe were their countrymen willing to do them honor. Europeans themselves were slow to recognize American genius. "Our literary and political achievements are either despised, or, what is still more humiliating, they are totally overlooked...."[56] He still fretted over the lack of poetry, maintaining that our country ought to be a paradise of poets:

> The muse seems at present to slumber in a country eminently calculated to awaken her exertions. We have skies which give us the varied and kind return of seasons; we have winds which one would think would blow the spark of genius into flame; we have waters, which should allure to their banks the vagrant foot of enthusiasm; and we have mountains which furnish us with all that is grand and elevating in prospect.... We could indeed give a list of poets whose works are entitled to a considerable portion of praise; but we complain of the smallness of the number, and we wish to see some effort which shall go beyond any that has yet appeared.[57]

This examination of the *Literary Magazine* leads to the conclusion that Brown possessed outstanding ability as editor of a purely literary journal. Literary historians in concentrating almost entirely on his

[54] "Circulation of Newspapers," *Literary Magazine*, IV (July, 1805), 33-34; reprinted from *Monthly Magazine*, III.

[55] *Literary Magazine*, I (Oct., 1803), 44.

[56] "Commercial Reputation of the United States," *Literary Magazine*, II (Aug., 1804), 280.

[57] "Notices of American Writers and Publications," Item 8, *Literary Magazine*, II (Aug., 1804), 345.

novels have done him a disservice. Professor Mott, however, stands
out among them as recognizing the importance of his magazines,[58]
and Pattee also wrote with appreciation of this phase of Brown's
labors:

> No man ever worked harder than he to raise the level of American litera-
> ture with his magazines, and no one was ever more unsparing of himself or
> his time. . . . Brown did his best. With twice the energy of Dennie, with
> none of Dennie's procrastination and conviviality, he put his whole soul into
> his editing. Peculiarly was he fitted for such work. Like Poe in later years,
> he believed that the future of American literature was with the magazines.[59]

Though the magazines were not original in type or subject matter,
they indicate their editor's sound judgment and catholicity of taste.
The original selections were, of course, determined by his correspondents' contributions as well as by what he himself could produce. In
the reviews (more fully evaluated in another chapter) Brown revealed his desire to further American literature, though not at the
sacrifice of sound literary standards.

In evaluating Brown as a writer we must accordingly remember
that for the first quarter century of our national life he was not only
America's leading novelist and critic but also, as editor of three distinguished magazines, her outstanding journalist.

[58] Frank Luther Mott, *The History of American Magazines*, I, 124.
[59] Fred Lewis Pattee, *The First Century of American Literature*, pp. 190-191.

# IX

# BROWN AS A LITERARY CRITIC

### GENERAL ATTITUDES AND OPINIONS

As A REVIEWER Brown was well equipped; his classical education, his knowledge of French and Italian literatures, and, what was more rare, of German literature, his own work as a writer of fiction, and the Quaker honesty and high seriousness that were so much a part of him —all these, combined with a conscious endeavor to create and foster a native literature in which all Americans could take pride, marked Brown as the greatest critic in America before Edgar Allan Poe.

We have seen that in the prefaces to his novels and in his magazines, Brown made several specific statements concerning the nature of the writer's art and the function of the critic. The novelist, he maintained, must be a realist and assume the role of instructor, painting life as it is and eschewing the fanciful in scene and situation. The novelist must show "depth of view into human nature," and penetrate and reveal "the moral construction of man." Since the world is governed by men of soaring passion and intellectual energy, the novelist must avoid commonplace characters and situations except as contrasts to the supermen and their realm of activity. In brief, Brown aligned himself with Godwin, Bage, Holcroft, and others in creating the novel of purpose. The prevailing philosophy of benevolence and perfectibility, in fact, left almost no other course open to the young American novelist. In his choice of subject matter as in his attitude toward the function of the novelist Brown was a romanticist, although in his tendency to sentimental moralizing he had much of the neoclassic about him.

It is the purpose of this chapter to point out Brown's general literary opinions and indicate his attitude to contemporary writers, both English and American. Since Brown left no formal treatise on the principles of criticism, as did his great contemporaries—Wordsworth, Coleridge, and Shelley—we must draw our conclusions from many scattered and occasional remarks.

### HIS PRINCIPLES OF CRITICISM

Although we have already noted how literary criticism progressively waned in each of Brown's successive periodicals—giving way to the historical treatise—he never completely lost his interest in aesthetics. In his insistence upon broad, objective principles of literary criticism and in his fearlessness in upholding those principles, Brown set a high standard of achievement. As a reviewer he had only one rival—Joseph Dennie of the *Port Folio*. If Brown had a wider outlook and was on the whole more reliable in his judgments, his friend of the *Port Folio* was perhaps more brilliant. Dennie, for instance, at once saw the merits and the shortcomings of the *Lyrical Ballads*,[1] while Brown hesitated and could not exactly make up his mind about that revolutionary volume.

Under the new romantic impulse objective literary standards were giving way to subjective judgment and to the dangerous conclusion that that which satisfied one's taste was "good" and that the literary judgment of one person was apparently as good as that of another person. While Brown could not bring himself to accept the theory of subjective criticism, in the following paragraph he came very near to acknowledging its validity:

Critical opinions are so much biassed and modified by the personal habits and prejudices of the critic that they are seldom of any use to readers in general. No man who is interested in the author or subject of a book will be satisfied with the sentence of another. This sentence, indeed, considering the materials which must necessarily compose a professed critic, can hardly ever conform to the standard of abstract justice, but this conformity, even when it does take place, can be rarely of any practical utility. Each man reads what his own judgment, right or wrong, disposes him to approve, and what his own curiosity, formed and guided by accidents peculiar to himself, and generally, in some respects, different from that of all other men, renders interesting and important in his own eyes.[2]

When he did write criticism, however, Brown was unwilling, despite his growing distrust of its ultimate value, to compromise standards by which he determined his literary judgments. For the most part his personal literary opinions, as we have already suggested, were expressed only in his formal reviews, in prefaces to his novels, and in occasional comments; yet in one article of considerable length[3] he summed up in a negative way his ideas of good literary taste. While the essay is couched in general terms and does not take up the details of literary standards, still it is valuable as an endeavor to set up reasonably universal rules of literary excellence. Differences of judgment, said Brown, occur not so much in pronouncements on the works of established writers as on those newer authors whose reputation is not yet fixed. There are three sources of error in judgment, stated negatively. Lack of feeling of sensibility—"the inability to enjoy

---

[1] Harold Milton Ellis, *Joseph Dennie and His Circle*, p. 104.
[2] "Review of Literature," *American Register*, I (1806-1807), 154.
[3] "On Standards of Taste," *Literary Magazine*, VI (Oct., 1806), 291-295.

... the pleasures of the imagination''—is perhaps the most important. If one does not really enjoy poetry, for instance, how can he judge of its excellence? Lack of knowledge of critical rules—he means neo-classical rules—is a second source of error. Unless one understands both universal and arbitrary rules and has a good background of both life and literature, he is likely to err in his opinion. This same lack of knowledge often leads to hasty decisions. The third source of error is prejudice. A person fearing that hesitation may indicate ignorance makes snap judgments. Not possessing sufficient knowledge, he has little basis for reflection; sentence is therefore passed on grounds of prejudice or temporary feeling. Brown continued in some detail:

Of these three sources of critical error, want of sensibility most naturally leads men to dispraise what is good; and want of knowledge, to praise what is indifferent. This is, however, nothing like a general rule. Some are afraid to censure what they cannot relish; and a great many condemn what they cannot judge of. . . .

The remedy for error in criticism is precisely the same as for error of any other kind: a diligent inquiry into truth. Criticism is a science, and taste can only be rendered accurate by much study and attention. As astronomy is not learned by casting our eyes on the heavens, so a taste in poetry cannot be acquired by lightly running over poems. . . .

The principles of the fine arts are founded partly on general nature and partly on arbitrary rules. But to judge of general nature requires much attention and experience. Whether, for instance, the character of Achilles in Homer is justly and naturally delineated cannot be decided by every one. We meet with no such men in the streets. We must previously form notions of human nature, as general as possible, dropping all local and individual characteristics. We must enlarge our views of it by the study of ancient manners, and of its state in countries remote from our own. Arbitrary rules, it is still more evident, must be understood before we can know whether they are preserved. . . .

The laws of taste are partly natural and partly arbitrary. Under the former class fall, in poetry and eloquence, whatever suggests associations generally delightful and interesting, or awakens sympathies which the constitution of mankind leads them to feel. . . . Under the latter may be reckoned what is called style in writing; and the observance of those rules with which critics are conversant in the other arts.

Men are also influenced by accidental associations. They take a liking to something without analyzing the reason. In fact, Brown observed, emotion rather than ''so cold an arbitress as reason'' too often rules one's literary judgment entirely; ''the state of our spirits and temper will make a mighty difference: a new poem is the worse for an east wind; and a good critic may execrate a good actor, when he found nothing but standing-room to hear him.''

Despite his acknowledgment of the validity of the subjective element in evaluating a work of art, Brown strongly insisted upon objectivity as far as humanly possible. He tried to separate subject matter and style in his literary judgments. Each must inhere in a work of art, both separately and allied. Depth of content and charm of style Brown demanded in a literary work of art:

We trust none will accuse us of placing polish of language and beauty of phrase at the head of the list in recounting the attributes of good composition. We are sensible everything of this kind ought to be viewed, and is viewed by discerning readers, as a subordinate consideration. It ought not to be forgotten, however, by writers at the present day that the taste of the age, with respect to style, is fastidious and that it is the duty of whose who wish to be read to make their *manner* as attractive as possible.[4]

Elusive charm is demanded of the truly great artist, not merely felicity of phrase but the inevitable wedding of thought and form if the artist would seize the imagination of his reader. As an illustration, here is Brown's pronouncement upon a volume of Samuel Low's poems:[5]

But in short occasional compositions, like those of the present volume, we expect almost uniformity of excellence; at all events, neatness and elegance are indispensable; destitute of these qualities, they will never be favored with a second perusal. Some of the pieces are correct, without point or strength; but none of them conspicuous for originality of idea, beauty of simile, ingenuity of description, or harmony of verse.

While Brown liked "classical purity and severity" of style, he insisted upon the value of emotional content. Regarding Nathan Strong's *Sermons*, he complained in severely balanced phrases that

There is much force; but oftentimes, a want of smoothness; much seriousness and solemnity, but a deficiency of the pathetic and persuasive; much sensible reasoning, but perhaps, too little of the warmth and force of the orator.[6]

The writer must not, however, go to the opposite extreme and allow the emotions to lead him into that undisciplined and uncharted freedom which is the mark of the untutored mind and unbridled imagination. Brown found this a common fault in the elegies on Washington:

On the present occasion, there is danger lest the imagination of the orator, so powerfully impressed with the magnitude and grandeur of his subject, should lead him astray from the path of a just and manly eloquence. Too

---

[4] Article LIV, *Monthly Magazine*, III (Dec., 1800), 425.

[5] Samuel Low (1765?-?) was well known at least in New York for his odes and anthems, many of which were sung or recited at St. Paul's and Trinity Churches. The subscription list to the *Poems* which Brown reviewed contained many distinguished names, including John Jacob Astor, William Dunlap, Dr. Peter Irving, and Philip Hone. Low also wrote a drama, "The Politician Outwitted," which was probably never acted. For further information see Montrose J. Moses, *Representative Plays by American Dramatists*. The selection is from Article IV, *Monthly Magazine*, III (July, 1800), 58.

[6] Article III, *Monthly Magazine*, I (April, 1799), 49.

many of those who have attempted to eulogize the father of our country have indulged an undisciplined and lawless fancy . . . they have wholly lost sight of the noble simplicity and true dignity of that great man whom they wish to honor and immortalize by their matchless strains. His productions would have furnished them with models of a pure and correct style, replete with the lessons of wisdom and truth, the result of a keen penetration and just discrimination, long exercised on the characters and conduct of men.[7]

Manner, Brown maintained, was by no means the more important factor in determining the excellence of a piece of writing; matter after all is that which gives dignity and power to a work of art. Although Benjamin Trumbull in his *History of Connecticut* had failed to pay enough attention to organization and style, he had gathered his facts with commendable care "from the most respectable sources."

But though Dr. T. does not paint with the hand of a master, he does what is much more important: he aims and in the main, we think, with success to give just and definite coloring. Though he had not completed a structure with that exquisite symmetry and alluring polish which modern readers are apt, perhaps unreasonably, to insist on, he has laid together a substantial and most valuable edifice, which succeeding artists may modify at their pleasure.[8]

Form without substance is like a nut without the kernel: it does not satisfy. For an adequate if not complete idea of Brown's conception of what constitutes poetry, listen to his judgment on Charles Caldwell's *Elegiac Poem on the Death of George Washington:*

The performance before us is of a very singular kind. We have seldom met with a production in which all the *apparatus* of poetry is diplayed in a more correct, polished, and splendid condition. We have seldom met with numbers more flowing and melodious. Syllables and pauses are adjusted according to the most perfect standard. The rhymes, with a few exceptions, are accurate and proper. No thoughtless omissions, no distressful hiatus, no jarring combinations, no misplaced emphasis, anywhere occur. "The march is, everywhere, majestic, and the energy of *numbers* divine"; and, were we called upon to produce a specimen of musical, correct, and polished versification, we should not hesitate to offer this performance as such a one.

The value of numbers and phraseology will be differently estimated by different observers. The value is surely not small; but there are none who will maintain either that the metre and the phrase are all that are of any value in a poem, or that they are not subordinate to imagery and sentiment. Just and powerful conceptions will delight, even when divorced from elegance and harmony; but harmonious elegance may justly please, even when associated with trite or injudicious sentiments. . . .

It is with sincere regret that we find ourselves obliged to limit our praise of this elegy to the style and the measure. . . .

[7] Article XV, *Monthly Magazine,* II (Feb., 1800), 131.
[8] Article I, *Monthly Magazine,* I (April, 1799), 46.

The fancy that dictated this poem is not barren. His store of images is large, but he culls from it without taste; and his reason stands aloof, from an erroneous belief that reasoning is incompatible with poetry. . . .

In fine, if to take from the great storehouse of language none but words authorized by poetical usage and to arrange these in well-balanced and musical numbers make a poet, this fraternity must be admitted; but if just thoughts and congruous images be deemed requisites, we are afraid that he would run imminent risk of being black-balled.[9]

Although substance must take precedence over style, the average author who neglects the latter will come to grief. In reviewing Alexander Hamilton's *Letter Concerning the Public Conduct and, Character of John Adams, Esq., President of the United States,* Brown expressed admiration for Hamilton's sentiments, but deplored his involved and diffuse style:

Many passages display strong views and luminous conceptions; but the style is not always equal to the sentiment. Terms are often selected with too little discrimination and with an apparent haste that occasions the needless multiplication of words. Sentences may be found prolix and circuitous and destitute of that *precision* which is the result of an intimate knowledge of the properties and powers of the English language.[10]

That Brown had long held these ideas is evidenced by his letter to "J. D——n" (if "J. D——n" means Brown's friend John Davidson, a member of the Belles Lettres Club, the letter must have been written before Brown's twentieth year), extracts from which are in Chapter II (pp. 49-50). In them will be found Brown's early philosophy of composition in his treatment of the relative claims of matter and of manner upon the writer.

That Brown followed the formula described in this letter of "thinking accurately and reasoning justly," and thereby achieving a "style with many valuable though simple qualities" is clearly seen in the minute realistic style of his novels and in the power of his historical and critical essays. His insistence upon purity of style and nobility of thought places him, despite the many and distinct elements of the new romantic ideals, among the neoclassicists. Living in an age of transition, Brown is not easily classified. We do know, however, whether classicist or romanticist, he was essentially a realist and a moralist.

His most elaborate discussion of realistic technique is found in a letter to Henrietta,[11] in which he asserted his belief that the account of any person's life might be made more fascinating than fiction; that, one need not travel widely to learn about life, but could merely look about him and find the raw materials ready to his hand:

[9] Article XIX, *Monthly Magazine,* II (March, 1800), 217-219.
[10] Article XLIV, *Monthly Magazine,* III (Nov., 1800), 369.
[11] See chap. iii, section 60.

The book of nature, like every other volume, is useful to the reader exactly in proportion to his sagacity and to the attention with which he peruses it, but what advantage can he derive from it, whose rapid and unsteady glances can produce none but general and indeterminate ideas, who dwells not on a single object long enough to know its properties? Nothing is more common than this inattentive and unobserving disposition, and those circumstances which though continually passing in our sight we wanted either power, time, or inclination to remark will, when depicted in words and set before us in a light so [clear] and forcible that they cannot fail of arresting our attention, be viewed with singular satisfaction and advantage.

Sometimes for practice he described a domestic incident in minute detail, recording every act and every word, and describing the setting and the characters as meticulously as if he were an artist depicting the scene.

Being a child of his age, Brown believed that literature should instruct as well as entertain—should actually point a moral. On this score he commended Cowper (a favorite among his British contemporaries) :

The moral tendency of his poetry . . . the elevation of his motives in writing above everything sordid or humiliating place him in the noblest rank of those who have employed their lives in purifying the hearts and delighting the imagination of mankind.[12]

In a little essay entitled "A Modern Socrates" Brown was careful to indicate that his magazine had a loftier purpose than the mere imparting of information:

If you cannot transform him [the reader] to angel or philosopher, you may somewhat influence his taste, character, and manners. If you cannot highly or lastingly benefit, you may innocently entertain, you may gain an occasional hearing, at least; you may rouse his curiosity, and by a skilful use of familiar illustrations, by the *lucky* dexterity of invention and wit, blend his pleasure with his benefit and accomplish by the same means more ends than one.[13]

Strongly reminding us of the long and heated debate between Wordsworth and Coleridge concerning the respective functions of prose and poetry, Brown contended that prose was a better vehicle than poetry for conveying instruction:

The selection of a theme truly important, adorning it with the lustre of eloquence, supplying, with judicious hand, the deficiencies of history, in the statement of motives and the enumeration of circumstances; . . . suggesting to the reader beneficial truths is the sublimest province that can be assigned

[12] "The Life and Posthumous Writings of William Cowper, Esq.," *Literary Magazine*, I (Feb., 1804), 345.
[13] *Monthly Magazine*, II (May, 1800), 328. This article is unsigned, but it may with fair certainty be assigned to Brown.

to man. It is questionable whether verse be a more advantageous garb of such a theme than prose. . . . All that constitutes the genuine and lasting excellence of narratives; all the subtilties of ratiocination, the energies and ornaments of rhetoric, and the colors of description are compatible with prose. Numbers are an equivocal, or at least not an essential, attribute of a moral and useful tale.[14]

A natural result of this insistence on "moral tendency" was Brown's reaction against the sensuality characterizing many of the ancient classics—a fact we have noted in an earlier chapter. A modern critic remarks:

It is characteristic of his [Brown's] period, which saw the rise of a middle class morality, that the classics, hitherto accepted in their entirety by an aristocratic society, without any cavil at their frank animality, should be reweighed in moral scales.[15]

Although, like all educated young men of his time, Brown had received thorough training in the classics, he shared the moralistic view that they were as a whole unfit for readers of fastidious tastes. It will be recalled that he tried to dissuade Henrietta from learning Latin and Greek because her moral sensibility would be offended by much of what she read; and he printed in his magazine several articles deploring the mixture of beauty and lasciviousness in the ancients:

How much are mankind misled by names. Lycaeus and Aphrodite, Bacchus and Venus, the mirth and love of Anacreon and Horace shall be listened to with reverence and regarded as something like divinities, and yet reduced into plain English and stripped of metaphor, they are nothing but drunkenness and lewdness. Anacreon is neither more nor less than a hoary debauchee and reveller, whose vicious and beastly habits are only strengthened by age, and whose understanding is so depraved that he glories in that which should constitute his shame, which at any age, is hostile to true joy and true dignity, but which is peculiarly shameful and detestable in grey hairs.[16]

In reviewing Southey's *Joan of Arc* Brown regretted that Southey, like countless others, should have imitated Homer, who was defective and superstitious. As for the *Aeneid*, an attempt to supply Rome with a noble past, it was sheer folly.[17] This is essentially what Shelley was to say two years later.

### BROWN AND CONTEMPORARY BRITISH POETRY

It will, perhaps, clarify our conception of Brown's philosophy of composition should we note what use he made of his literary ideas in his judgment of his contemporaries.

[14] Article IX, *Monthly Magazine*, I (June, 1799), 226-227.
[15] Ernest Marchand, "Literary Opinions of Charles Brockden Brown," *Studies in Philology*, XXXI (Oct., 1934), 562.
[16] "A Student's Diary," *Literary Magazine*, I (Dec., 1803), 165.
[17] Article IX, *Monthly Magazine*, I (June, 1799), 226.

Brown realized that "The lovers of poetry in America still look for the gratification of their taste to the production of the British bards."[18]  Although his purpose, especially in the *Monthly Magazine,* was to review the works of American authors, his occasional reviews and incidental remarks on British writers give us an idea of his interests.  He had, of course, admiration for the older writers, although he suggested, strange as it may seem, the modernizing of Spenser's *Faerie Queene* in order that more people could enjoy it:

The dialect of Chaucer and Spenser may augment the value of their compositions to a few, but doubtless it creates an insuperable obstacle to the study of them in the minds of the many.  These writers are pretty much in the situation of writers in a foreign language, and as much require translation as Virgil, Klopstock, or Racine, to make them intelligible and agreeable to the ears of their posterity.  Indeed this modernizing system is nothing but a species of translations, susceptible of the same license, and subject to the same laws.

What Chaucer's appearance is in modern language, we see in the specimens given us by Pope and Dryden.  Of Spenser we have hitherto had no opportunity of judging in this way.  Yet Spenser possesses all the excellencies of the poet in a degree unspeakably superior to Chaucer.  We may form some notion of the transcendent charms which this poet, if his lines were new modelled by a skilful hand, would acquire, by reading the late translation of Wieland's *Oberon,* a poem written in the genuine Spenserian manner.  What an inestimable banquet would the translator of Wieland provide for us by taking the *Fairy Queen* in hand, and bestowing the same bewitching numbers and style upon a poet who deserves them, at least as much as Wieland.

The scruples of the classical antiquarian could not be offended by a proceeding of this kind.  The poet, in his native and pristine dress, would still remain, and they would have the same opportunities as formerly of delving in this mine of English undefiled.[19]

Of contemporary English writers he reviewed or commented on Campbell, Young, Thomson, Goldsmith, Johnson, Cowper, Southey, Scott, Burns, and others.  He named Gray, Goldsmith, and Campbell as stiff competitors among aspiring young poets.  As one critic writes: "The names which recur, and the tenor of the remarks, lead to the conclusion that the established writers of the eighteenth century were most in his eye."[20]  In fact Brown's poetic taste was molded essentially by the classical or pseudo-classical writers of the eighteenth century, and his own poetic effusions were usually stiff and colorless imitations of classical models.

[18] Article VII, *Monthly Magazine,* I (May, 1799), 135-137.  Brown may not have been the author of this review, but he several times expressed similar sentiments.

[19] "Spenser's Fairy Queen Modernized," *Literary Magazine,* III (June, 1805), 424-425.

[20] Marchand, *op. cit.,* p. 554.

Brown probably shared his brother-in-law's opinion of the *Lyrical Ballads*, expressed in a scathing review in the *Literary Magazine*.[21] In this respect he was in good company, for the rising school of English romanticism received but scant praise from his pen or from any other critic's pen in America, or for that matter in England.[22]

Brown's review of Cowper's works,[23] and his essay on Goldsmith and Johnson[24] are interesting as revealing American literary taste at the time and as closely paralleling the modern view of these writers: "Johnson's attempts at portraying life and manners as they existed around him," he said, "were remarkably unfortunate. His Eastern tales have all the merit compatible with plans so wild, grotesque, and unnatural; but no man of just taste in morals or in composition can hesitate a moment in preferring not only the moral spirit but the taste and genius which display themselves in Goldsmith's simple and natural tales to those which animate the pompous and gloomy fictions of Johnson. Their essays breathe a temper and spirit nearly the reverse of each other, and Goldsmith is, in this particular, as benign, cheerful, and agreeable as Johnson is morose and melancholy."

Strange as it may seem, Brown had a high regard for the poetry of Robert Burns, as evidenced by an essay in which he compared the Scottish poet with Cowper. As this essay gives us insight into Brown the critic as well as Brown the man, and as it also reveals the literary tastes of America in the early national period, I shall quote at length from it:

The genius of Burns was more sublime than that of Cowper. Both excelled in the familiar; but yet the latter was by nature as well as education more gentle, more easy, and delicate; he had also more of tenuity, while Burns was more concise, more bold, and energetic. They both also abounded in humor, which possessed the same characteristics in each; one mild, serene, and smiling; the other daring and powerful, full of fire and imagery. The poems of one fill the heart and the fancy with the soft pleasures of domestic privacy, with the calm and innocent occupations of rural solitude, the pensive musings of the moralist, and the chastised indignation of pure and simple virtue; the poems of the other breathe by turns grief, love, joy, melancholy, despair, and terror; plunge us in the vortex of passion, and hurry us away on the wings of unrestrained and undirected fancy.

Cowper could paint the scenery of nature and the simple emotions of the heart with exquisite simplicity and truth. Burns could array the morning, the noon, and the evening in new colors; could add new graces to female beauty, and new tenderness to the voice of love. In every situation in which he was placed, his mind seized upon the most striking circumstances, and combining them anew and dressing them with all the fairy trappings of his

[21] "Critical Notices, " IV, *Literary Magazine*, I (Feb., 1804), 336-341.
[22] *Ibid.*, pp. 336-341.
[23] Review of William Hayley's "Life and Posthumous Writings of William Cowper, Esq.," *ibid.*, p. 345.
[24] "Goldsmith and Johnson," *Literary Magazine*, III (June, 1805), 403-404.

imagination, he produced visions such as none but "poets dream." Wherever he went, in whatever he was employed, he saw everything with a poet's eye and clothed it with a poet's tints. . . .

There is a relative claim to superiority on the side of Burns on which I cannot lay so much stress as many are inclined to do. I mean his want of education, while the other enjoyed all the discipline and all the advantages of a great public school. . . .

But it seems to me vain and idle to speculate upon education and outward circumstances as the causes or promoters of poetical genius. It is the inspiring breath of Nature alone which gives the powers of the genuine bard and creates a ruling propensity and a peculiar cast of character, which will rise above every impediment, but can be substituted by neither art nor labor. To write mellifluous verses in language which may seem to the eye and the ear adorned with both imagery and elegance may be a faculty neither unattainable nor even uncommon. But to give that soul, that predominance of thought, that illuminated tone of a living spirit which spring in so inexplicable a manner from the chords of the real lyre, is beyond the reach of mere human arrangement, without the innate and very rare gift of the muse. That gift has regard neither to rank, station, nor riches. It shone over the cradles of Surrey and Buckhurst, amid the splendor of palaces, and the lustre of coronets; it shone over those of Milton, and Cowley, and Dryden, and Gray, and Collins, amid scenes of frugal and unostentatious competence and mediocrity; it shone over that of Burns, in the thatched hovel, the chill abode of comfortless penury, humble labor.[25]

In regard to Southey's poems Brown put his finger on the weak spot, a weakness not necessarily born of the new school of poetry. That Brown had a catholicity of taste in poetry and that he did not scorn the romantic poets as a group, his appraisals of Southey[26] and Scott[27] will attest.

### BROWN AND CONTEMPORARY AMERICAN WRITERS

Naturally Brown devoted a good deal of attention to contemporary American writers. As we have seen, he was quick to espy the best literary work that was then being done in America, and he pointed it out with precision and unerring judgment. He felt that encouragement was needed, and he realized that the best encouragement and stimulus for a healthy native literature would surely be a wise and sympathetic criticism of that literature. He evaluated most of the contemporary American writers, with the exception of Hopkinson, Brackenridge, and Freneau—the last of whom he probably ignored in accordance with his editorial policy to shun works of controversial nature. He devoted a great deal of space to sermons and orations, for which he apologized in the following terms:

[25] "Character of Burns," *Literary Magazine*, I (June, 1799), 429-438.

[26] Article IX, *Monthly Magazine*, I (June, 1799), 225-229.

[27] *Literary Magazine*, IV (Aug., 1805), 99-102. This article is unsigned, but may with some certainty be assigned to Brown.

We have thus given the leading features of this oration [by John Lowell], on which we have bestowed more attention than many of our readers may think due to its magnitude or importance.  But productions of this nature form so considerable a portion of the literary harvest of our country that we may be excused for conferring on them a degree of attention unsuitable to their intrinsic worth, and which, amidst a frequency of more valuable and lasting works, would be wholly disproportionate and misplaced.

When beings of a larger growth and more durable existence do not present themselves, the curious and deliberate inquirer may be allowed to regard, with more protracted observation, the qualities of the fleeting insects of a day.[28]

Although Brown admired Richard Alsop's poem on the death of George Washington, he tactfully pointed out that it was pleasing but by no means inspired:

There is no great boldness of design displayed, nor much of that fine frenzy, that magic power which leads the imagination captive, awakens and irresistibly sways all the feelings of the soul. . . . The thoughts are just and appropriate, and the author appears to have been satisfied with clothing them in a poetical dress, without exerting the utmost powers of art and imagination.  If his fancy soar not on eagle-wings, under the guidance of a chaste and correct judgment it bears him on his way with dignity and ease. . . . The composition has all the advantages of thought, of numbers, full, flowing, and harmonious, and a versification, with few exceptions, smooth and elegant.  While he bestows praise on these essential and valuable ingredients of style, the lover of genuine poetry may, perhaps, require something more— rich and splendid imagery, and an eloquence fervid, pathetic, and transporting, which at pleasure awakens and subdues every emotion of the heart, filling it with sensations of wonder and delight.[29]

He gave generous praise to William Clifton—or Clifton (1778-1796), a young man who had written some vigorous satire in prose and in verse, defending the policies of the Federalists.  On the occasion of the publication of a volume of his poetry, Brown remarked:

It is impossible to dismiss this little volume without a sigh of regret for the untimely fate of the juvenile bard.  We venture to assert that a poet of superior genius has not yet arisen among us.  For originality of ideas, combined with precision, strength, and elegance of expression, he is inferior to none of his countrymen; but for a union of these with genuine wit and sublime fancy, he is perhaps unrivalled in our land.[30]

[28] Article XXIII, *Monthly Magazine*, I (Aug., 1799), 375.
[29] Article, XXXIII, *Monthly Magazine*, II (April, 1800), 309.
[30] Article LV, *Monthly Magazine*, III (Dec., 1800), 433.  See *Magazine of History*, vol. XXIII, no. 4, extra no. 92, for a reprint of Cliffton's ''The Group,'' taken from the 1800 edition of his poems.  Regarding the worth of Cliffton's poetry, the editor of *Magazine of History* writes: ''Had his life been prolonged to the usual period, he would no doubt have attained a very respectable rank among our poets.''

He esteemed this young poet at least as highly as he did any of the Hartford Wits, who were generally considered the leading poets of the time.  But for some unknown reason Brown almost completely ignored them in his reviews.  He did call to his readers' attention Trumbull's *M'Fingal*, rather satirically remarking that, since the Revolution was "an obscure and antiquated story" to the younger set, the poem would probably not move them.[31]  He gave a good deal of attention, indeed, to Joel Barlow's *Columbiad*,[32] finding occasion for rejoicing in its nationalism, as expressed by a contributor:

This title announces a work of the highest interest in a literary view that the present age has produced, especially as it regards our country, to which the subject is national.  And, from a hasty perusal of a proof-sheet copy, we do not hesitate to pronounce the poem to be every way worthy of the subject.  Greater praise than this could not well be expressed in a single phrase; as no subject within the compass of human actions can be more important or more affecting to a mind susceptible of great ideas.

Finally, in the *American Register* for 1807, Brown announced the publication of the *Columbiad:*

In the department of the fine arts, we meet with a work which, in extent and value, cannot be expected to present itself very often.  *The Vision of Columbus,* by Joel Barlow, has been altered, revised, and much enlarged, and has reappeared, with much typographical splendor, under the new name of *The Columbiad.*

A production that received most attention was Noah Webster's *A Brief History of Epidemic and Pestilential Diseases.*[33]  The review is dignified, judicious, and discriminating, and is worthy of Jeffrey and the *Edinburgh.*  In thirty pages the critic pointed out that both the nature of the subject and the manner of its treatment would claim an uncommon portion of attention.  In the first place, the author was not a physician and had no technical knowledge of his subject, but in a popular discussion technical precision is not necessary.  Webster's remarks on travelers and historians and the trust he puts in them were superfluous, and suggested the spirit which students too often display—that of depreciating every object of pursuit but their own.  Brown questioned Webster's premise that since the pestilences described in the Old Testament corresponded to modern plagues, the authenticity of the Scriptures as inspired was proved.  Did not infidels, he reminded the reader, use the same argument to prove these writings merely ancient history?  If, as some people still hold, plagues

---

[31] "Trumbull's 'M'Fingal,'" *Literary Magazine,* VI (July, 1806), 57.

[32] *Literary Magazine,* VII (Oct., 1807), 204-205; *American Register,* I (1806-1807), 215-220; *American Register,* II (1807), 159.

[33] Articles VII, XVII, XXVII, *Monthly Magazine,* II (1800), 30-36, 108-115, 208-213, 289-296, respectively.

and storms are instruments of divine judgment, would it not be sinful to attempt any remedy?

Brown laments that such a volumnious work should lack an index, and he marvels that one who set himself up as an authority on the English language could be so negligent of his style:

Though mere expression be subordinate to reasoning and sentiment, it should never be despised or neglected. Somewhat depends upon the selection and arrangement of proper and significant terms, as well as on laborious searches, and accurate conclusions. Mr. W. will incur some censure in this respect, for while he is always and minutely careful to cut off a vowel from the end of some of his words which ordinary writers retain, he is unreasonably negligent in more important matters, and has failed to make his sentences coalesce fully with each other, or to harmonize with themselves. This negligence, together with a new scheme of quotation, gives the first part of his work the air, less of a scientific treatise, than of a crude mass of memorandums, a transcript of marginal notes, where, for the sake of brevity, particles and pronouns are dropped and the meaning conveyed by the use of disconnected nouns and verbs.

In a peculiarly significant way Brown was a product of his time: for the most part he held, in true eighteenth-century fashion, to objective, universal standards rather than to the subjective ideal that was just beginning to develop with the strengthening romantic current; he insisted on a polished, elegant style and "purity" of language, employing mid-eighteenth-century literary usage as his standard. Brown did not, however, put form above content: it was, rather, coequal and indispensable; manner should fit matter as a glove the hand. To warm a subject into vitality there must be emotional content, but it must always be under the control of reason. Realistic details, he insisted, will help the writer to achieve a vital, vivid, living literary product.

And what was the function of literary productions? Entertainment of course, but also instruction—the true classical, Horatian ideal. The logical outgrowth of this ideal, tempered by the Puritan moral sense and the social conscience of the Anglo-Saxon middle class, was the insistence on austerity and purity of thought and expression and the consequent disapprobation of much classical material long taken for granted. Indeed, Brown was not alone in his condemnation of the indecencies and vulgarities of ancient writers: he was merely running with the tide. In both England and America there was a revolt against the reading of the classics in our schools; it was not a mere coincidence that Thomas Bowdler (1754-1825) lived at this period and prepared his *Family Shakespeare* and bowdlerized Gibbon's *Decline and Fall*.

If Brown held too rigidly to late eighteenth-century standards of literary criticism, his name as an important American critic is not therefore to be disparaged. If the test of a great critic is just evaluation of his contemporaries, Brown will take a high rank. Since he rendered a just account of the few writers that America produced during this barren period, one wonders what heights he would have attained in an age of great literary activity. To say that he would have been a profound critic would be presumptuous, but there can be little doubt that he would have distinguished himself. He was a critic both by nature and by education.

# X

# BROWN TURNS HISTORIAN

POLITICAL PAMPHLETS, *AMERICAN REGISTER*, CLOSING DAYS

CHARLES BROCKDEN BROWN's early interest in historical writings has already been mentioned. Before 1800 he had planned extensive historical fictions in *Carsol* and the *Carills and Ormes*. In his magazines essays of a historical nature grew more numerous than stories, and greater emphasis in the review sections began to fall on historical works. National life and manners and real men and women began to interest him more than imaginary persons of "soaring passions." History had indeed triumphed over fiction, and instruction over entertainment.

### FOUR POLITICAL PAMPHLETS

During the years 1803-1809 four important historical-political pamphlets, generally ascribed to Brockden Brown, were published in Philadelphia. In the order of publication they were: *Address to the Government of the United States on the Cession of Louisiana to the French; and on the Late Breach of Treaty by the Spaniards, including the translation of a memorial, on the War of St. Domingo, and the Cession of the Mississippi to France, drawn up by a Counsellor of State* (1803), running to ninety-two pages; *Monroe's Embassy, or the Conduct of the Government in Relation to our Claims to the Navigation of the Mississippi* (1803), consisting of fifty-seven pages, and signed *Poplicola;* the *British Treaty*, without a date or name of publisher, a pamphlet of eighty-six pages; and fourth, *An Address to the Congress of the United States on the Utility and Justice of Restrictions upon Foreign Commerce, with Reflections on Foreign Trade in general and the Future Prospects of America* (1809), consisting of five and a half pages of Introduction and ninety-seven pages of text.

The treatment of Brown as political pamphleteer and historian calls for frequent quotation from the pamphlets themselves. A mere paraphrase or summary would not make apparent, for example, Brown's considerable ability to write persuasively for the early nineteenth-century American public. His methods of gaining emotional response by effective use of synonyms, by delaying the point of a sentence with parallel introductory conditional clauses, by a repetition of catchwords and phrases, by calling national traits their common names, and by painting a realistically alarming picture of the future, can be made clear and forcible only in excerpts from the pamphlets themselves. Furthermore, the objectivity which Brown displays in his analysis of the national as well as the international problems of his day deserves especial attention. His cool discriminating reasoning—largely an analysis of the principles of commerce and benefits derived therefrom—against the Embargo Act, for example, marks a milepost in early American historical writing. Similarly, his treatment of the foreign policy of Jefferson is singularly keen. There is a contemporaneous appeal, too, in the discussion of his country's relations with China, for today those problems remain virtually the same. The heights which Brown reaches as a pamphleteer and as a historian can be fully seen only through his writings.

### THE BRITISH TREATY

Of the four pamphlets, three—the first, the second, and the fourth—were by Brown. The third, the *British Treaty,* ascribed to Brown by Dunlap, and generally so ascribed, was almost certainly not Brown's. This conclusion is based upon the following facts: first, its insulting dedication *To Those Members of Congress who have the Sense to Perceive and the Spirit to Pursue the True Interests of Their Country;* second, a statement in the Preface by the author that he knew Madison when the latter was a youth—clearly impossible if Brown were the author; and third, an ascription in a contemporary hand—perhaps that of Oliver Wolcott (1760-1833), whose name appears on the pamphlet as owner—which reads: "By Gouv. Morris, Esq."

### AN ADDRESS TO THE GOVERNMENT

*An Address to the Government* on the cession of Louisiana was undoubtedly Brown's. Its leading ideas Brown had already expressed elsewhere, and its central thesis he was soon to present in his magazine. Though Brown loved the ways of peace, and though he was true to his Quaker upbringing in his frowning on war in any form for any purpose, yet he could, as we shall later see, countenance a defensive war to preserve the national honor and the nation's existence when all pacific means had failed.

The occasion for the *Address* was the intense feeling aroused over Spain's transfer to France of the vast Louisiana territory by the secret treaty of San Ildefonso, October 1, 1800. It was not until May, 1801, that President Jefferson secretly learned of the treaty and of Napoleon's plan to put down the rebellion of Toussaint L'Ouverture and the Santo Domingoans and to occupy New Orleans. This prospect so aroused Jefferson that, apparently without consulting his cabinet and conveniently forgetting his isolationism, he wrote on April 18, 1802, that historic letter to our minister in Paris, saying, "the day that France takes possession of New Orleans . . . we must marry ourselves to the British fleet and Nation." Toward the end of the year the Spanish Intendant in the Louisiana territory withdrew certain privileges of American traders at New Orleans. When the news of this event reached the public, a storm of protest broke over Jefferson's head. His opponents, to embarrass him, clamored for war, but Jefferson in his annual message in December adopted a policy of watchful waiting.

The American public, after the news broke in December, 1802, was aroused as at no previous period in its national history. Our western people along the Ohio and the Mississippi would have been absolutely ruined if some powerful and hostile force sat astride the Mississippi at New Orleans; the Southern states by their proximity to this foreign power would have been always threatened; and the commercial East would have found its trade with the West Indies curtailed, if not actually destroyed, by France's control of the island routes of trade.

In March, 1803, Jefferson sent James Monroe as plenipotentiary to France to assist our resident minister, Robert Livingston, to negotiate the purchase of New Orleans and the Floridas. The eventual outcome of Monroe's embassy was the purchase, April 30, 1803, of the vast Louisiana territory for a mere pittance.

It was during this period of excitement and national peril that Brockden Brown conceived a unique plan for influencing public opinion for the immediate acquisition of the Louisiana territory. He began his pamphlet by denying any desire for personal gain and by minimizing his own competency in argument; but, he said, a powerful secret document had recently been entrusted to him, a document which contained persuasive and unanswerable arguments drawn up by a French Counselor of State during the lull in the European War—following the peace of Amiens in 1802—to present to the First Consul, then "rusting" on his laurels and casting about for more worlds to conquer. The Counselor urged upon Napoleon the necessity for France to establish a powerful empire to rival her deadly enemy, England. Cleverly he showed that Napoleon should waste no more French lives and property by trying to subdue Santo Domingo. Then very cunningly he suggested that the newly acquired Louisiana would be a more attractive morsel. Once established in Louisiana, France would be the most powerful empire in the world. French soldiers, he urged, must be settled somewhere. Where? In Santo Domingo? No, the climate was forbidding and soldiers would refuse to go. With equal cleverness the Counselor dismissed the suggestion that France colonize New Holland and push out the Dutch and English.

Then follows a glowing picture of Louisiana over against a correspondingly gloomy picture of America. France will have the opportunity and the bounden duty "to propagate a new race of intellectual beings'' in the New World. Luxuries like coffee, sugar, and tobacco, which so captivate the Frenchman's taste, will thrive there in abundance!

The Counselor now stops to comment on the secret of good government, setting forth an essentially Physiocratic philosophy:

In every civilized nation, there must be a certain proportion of wretchedness and poverty; of men whom the pressure of distress compels to great and anxious efforts to improve their condition. To favor these efforts is the end of all good government; to promote equality without detriment to order is the great political secret. The obvious and most eligible means for effecting this is not by agrarian schemes subversive of established property but by appropriating new ground and distributing it among the needy. Nor ought this distribution to be by the direct and entire agency of government.

With their hands already full, England and Spain, the ''Frenchman'' maintains, will hardly take steps to prevent the French from developing Louisiana. But what about the Americans? Here Brown's remarks are calculated to arouse his countrymen to fever heat and bring the warring factions among them to their senses. Brown's deep and abiding patriotism was in no wise diminished by his acknowledgment of his country's many shortcomings. As only a sincere friend can tell a person of his faults, so only a genuine patriot can point out his country's mistakes. Brown here courageously and unerringly lays bare our national traits and our well-known weaknesses—many of which haunt us to this day. This American Jeremiah, clothed in the robes of a French Counselor of State, writes vigorously. As these pamphlets are practically inaccessible, and as the disturbed state of the world at that time bears so many parallels to the present national and international turmoil, extensive excerpts will be quoted:

If there be any truth in the picture heretofore drawn of the value of this province to France, it must be, in a still greater proportion, of value to the American States. If the Powers of this rising nation were intrusted to the hands of one wise man . . . if the founder of the nation was still its *supreme magistrate,* and he had no wills to consult but his own, the French most probably would never be allowed to set their foot on that shore; but the truth, the desirable truth is that opposition is the least to be dreaded from those who have most reason to oppose us. They whose interests are most manifest may be most easily deceived; whose danger is most imminent may most easily be lulled into security. They whose vicinity to the scene of action puts it most in their power to enact their own safety; whose military force might be most easily assembled and directed to this end, we shall have the least trouble, in dividing, intimidating, and disarming.

I come now to the last difficulty which the most scrupulous objector has discovered: and this difficulty will be dissipated with more ease than the rest. On what foundation does it repose but the visionary notion that the conduct of nations is governed by enlightened views of their own, and they are gained by the gratification of these private views. The more individuals there are that govern and the more various their conditions and their character, the more dissimilar are their interests, and the more repugnant these interests to those of each other and the interests of the whole.

Was there ever a people who exhibited so motley a character, who have vested a more limited and precarious authority in their rulers; who have multiplied so much the numbers of those that govern; who have dispersed themselves over so wide a space; and have been led by this local dispersion to create so many clashing jurisdictions and jarring interests, as the States of America.

They call themselves *free,* yet a fifth of their number are slaves. That proportion of the whole people are ground by a yoke more dreadful and debasing than the predial servitude of Poland and Russia. They call themselves *one,* yet all languages are native to their citizens: all countries have contributed their outcasts and refuse to make them a people. Even the race of Africa, a race not above, or only just above the beasts, are scattered every where among them, and in some of the districts of their empire are nearly a moiety of the whole. Already there are near twenty states, each of which is governed by a law of its own; which have formed a common union, on voluntary and mutable principles; and a general constitution, whose end is to secure their utmost efficacy to popular passions, and to prevent the scattered members from coalescing into one symmetrical and useful body. They are a people of yesterday. Their institutions have just received birth. Hence their characters and views are void of all stability. Their prejudices are all discordant. Their government is destitute of that veneration which an ancient date and of that distinctness and certainty in its operations and departments which long experience confers. Their people are the slaves of hostile interests; blown in all directions by forward passions; divided by inveterate factions, and the dupes and partisans of all the elder nations by turns. . . .

This is a nation of pedlars and shopkeepers. Money engrosses all their passions and pursuits. For this they will brave all the dangers of land and water; they will scour the remotest seas and penetrate the rudest nations. Their ruling passion being money, no sense of personal or national dignity must stand in the way of its gratification. These are an easy sacrifice to the lust of gain, and the insults and oppressions of foreigners are cheerfully borne, provided there is a recompense of a pecuniary nature. Insults and injuries that affect not the purse affect no sense that they possess; and such is the seemingly inconsistent influence of the mercenary passion that the pillage of their property, while it produces infinite discontent and clamor, urges them to no revenge. The dictates of a generous nature, which prefers honor to riches and will hazard property and life itself in the assertion of its own or its country's wrongs, are strangers to their breasts. When the counsel is war, they prudently reckon the expense and determine rather to keep what is left them than to risk it in endeavoring to regain that of which they have been robbed. . . .

Since this period they have grown in wealth and numbers and have been busily employed in bringing their disjointed members into some sort of combination; in building up and pulling down their separate constitutions; in quelling tumults excited by attempts to levy taxes on a liquid poison called Whiskey, in supplicating France and England that they would be good enough to repay the value of the plunder committed by these nations on their commerce, and Spain that she would be pleased to let them pass up and down the Mississippi; and in the most furious and disgraceful animosities of party, fomented by the two great rivals in Europe and convertible at will into more successful engines of conquest than armies and fleets. Instead of providing for their own defense against foreign and domestic foes, by armed ships and disciplined troops, they have relied on the power of entreaty and a rabble of militia. Instead of asserting their natural claim to the continent of North America, they have left all their southern districts and the mouth of their most useful river in the hands of a nation, despicable and defence-less—whose claims are groundless and ridiculously asserted by themselves, but formidable and fatal when transferred to others. . . .

But the great weakness of these States arises from their form of govern-ment and condition and habits of the people. Their form of government and the state of the country is a hot-bed for faction and sedition. The utmost force of all the wisdom they possess is exerted in keeping the hostile parts together. These parts are unlike each other, and each one has the individual-izing prejudices of a separate state; all the puerile jealousies of the great-ness of others; all the petty animosities which make neighbors quarrel with each other without cause. How slight an additional infusion is requisite to set this heterogeneous mass into commotion, to make the different parts in-cline different ways, on the great question of war? . . .

The peculiar color of their factions is, also, extremely favorable to the designs of a powerful and artful neighbor. They quarrel about forms of government. These forms are not subtile threads, and scarcely visible, drawn from the bowels of their own invention, but are the gross and clumsy models taken from European examples. The rivalship between France and England has extended to the speculations of this people, and by natural consequence, a prejudice is thus created which makes one faction friendly to France and the other to England.

. . . . . . . . . . . . .

This party [Jefferson's Republican or Anti-Federalist], always formidable in its spirit and numbers, has lately gotten the mastery. The majority of the people and their present rulers are pliant clay fittest for our use. From these we may exact neutrality to all our schemes. They will take pains to shut their eyes against future evils. They will be remarkably quick sighted to the dangers of a rupture with us. Their scruples against the violations of treaties and against offensive war will be wonderfully strong. . . .

Devoted to the worst miseries is the nation which harbors in its bosom a foreign race, brought by fraud and rapine from their native land, who are bereaved of all the blessings of humanity; whom a cruel servitude inspires with all the vices of brutes and all the passions of demons; whose injuries have been so great that the law of self-preservation obliges the State to deny to the citizen the power of making his slave free; whose indelible distinctions of form, color, and perhaps of organization will forever prevent them from blending with their tyrants into one people; who foster an eternal resentment at oppression, and whose sweetest hour would be that which buried them and their lords in a common and immeasurable ruin. . . . An example is before their eyes of the consequences of a servile war. Their country is full of exiles from the scene of such a warfare. Their travellers, their daily papers supply them with the picture, in all its circumstantial horrors. They are shaken by panics on this very account already, and no consideration would have a stronger influence on their conduct than this.

There is still another rein, however, by which the fury of the States may be held in at pleasure . . . by an enemy placed on their western frontiers. The only aliens and enemies within their borders are not the blacks. They indeed are the most inveterate in their enmity; but the INDIANS are, in many respects, more dangerous inmates. Their savage ignorance, their undisciplined passions, their restless and war-like habits, their notions of ancient right make them the fittest tools imaginable for disturbing the states.

After Brown has presented the "Frenchman's" argument, he follows up with his own observations. Cleverly Brown comments upon the Counselor's criticism of America, but the reader will have no difficulty in divining his true position and his real purpose. Fearing that he has overdrawn the picture, the author proceeds now to fill in a few low lights, and here again his psychological purpose is patent. With almost poetic fervor Brown appeals to his countrymen to disprove the Frenchman's charges of weakness:

This writer has given such a portrait of us as was most suitable to his views. Our national pride will induce us to deny, perhaps, the truth of the picture; and surely we are not quite so fluctuating and distracted in our counsels, so irreconcilable in our interests; so inveterate in our factions as he thinks proper to paint us. With all our faults, are we, indeed, incapable of vengeance for unmerited wrong? Is our country, its rights, its honors, its prosperity, no dearer to us than any foreign land? Do the people of the coast regard as aliens and enemies those beyond the mountains? Those of the northern states, however distant in place and dissimilar in manners, do they regard with no paternal emotions the happiness or misery of their Southern countrymen? Is our government a tottering fabric which the breath of foreign emissaries can blow down at their pleasure? Has corruptions made such strides among us that the purse-holders of France can purchase our forbearance, when our nearest interests, our most manifest honor are assailed?

No. The American war supplies us with an eternal confutation of the slander. It was then evident that the ploughman and mechanic at either end of the continent could recognize a common interest with each other; could sacrifice their ease, their fortunes, their lives, to secure a remote and general benefit; that the passion for gain could not deter us from repelling encroachments on our liberty, at the cost of every personal advantage. . . . Mutinous slaves in the heart of our country; hostile garrisons and fortresses on one side; numerous and tumultuous savages around us; the ocean scoured by the fleets of our enemy; our sea ports open to their inroads; a revenue to create out of paper; the force of an established government . . . all these affrighted not the men of that day from the pursuit of an end most abstracted from personal ends; from the vulgar objects of gain; an end which only a generous spirit, a mind that makes the good of posterity and distant neighbors its own, that prefers liberty and all its hardships to servitude, that hugs her chain in pomp . . . could have loved with ardor and pursued with perseverance.

And what change has twenty years made that should make us doubt the display of equal spirit on the same occasion?—Has this period added nothing to our numbers and wealth? Has the enjoyment of independence only weakened our affection for it? Is it easier to fetter the full grown man than to keep the child from bursting his bonds? Has a national government, and twelve years of its benign influence, done nothing towards the union and coherence of the states? Surely the force of the nation; the power of directing it to common ends; the wisdom and foresight of its rulers; the jealousy of foreigners are not lessened by the progress of time; the increase of wealth, numbers, and harmony, and the contemplation of European scenes. . . .

But let us not indulge a prejudice as far beyond the truth as that of the Frenchman falls short of it. Let us not overrate our own force or underrate that of France. It cannot be denied that our intestine disputes, though no more than are incident to *human nature,* under popular forms of government, and though less unruly and ferocious than the popular commotions of other states have led to national preferences too favorable to the arts of intriguers. It is plain that our division into numerous states tends to the production of hostile sentiments and promotes the success of those who wish to conquer by disarming, to resist by dividing us; the blacks are a bane in our vitals, the most deadly that ever a nation was infested with. . . .

We have a right to the possession. The interests of the human race demand from us the exertion of this right. These interests demand that the reign of peace and concord should be diffused as widely and prolonged as much as possible. By unity of manners, laws, and government is concord preserved, and this unity will be maintained, with as little danger of interruption as the nature of human affairs will permit by the gradual extension of our own settlements, by erecting new communities as fast as the increase of these settlements requires it, and by sheltering them all under the pacific wing of a federal government.

To introduce a foreign nation, all on fire to extend their own power; fresh from pernicious conquests; equipped with all the engines of war and violence; measuring their won success by the ruin of their neighbors; eager to divert into channels of their own the trade and revenue which have hitherto been ours; raising an insuperable mound to our future progress; spreading among us, with fatal diligence, the seeds of faction and rebellion. . . . What more terrible evil can befall us? What more fatal wound to the future population, happiness, and concord of this new world? The friend of his country and of mankind must regard it with the deepest horror. . . .

Such is the melancholy strain which the conduct of the States has hitherto but too well justified. We have looked on with stupid apathy, while European powers toss about among themselves the property which God and Nature have made ours.

Far be it from me to sanctify the claim of conquest. America is OURS, not only as the interest of the greater number and of future generations, is the paramount and present interest; and therefore Louisiana is ours, even if to make it so, we should be obliged to treat its present inhabitants as vassals; but it is ours, because the interests of that people and of ourselves are common. . . .

To these pleas, however, our rulers have been hitherto deaf; and fortune, as if to put our discretion to the hardest test, as if to take away from our conduct every possible excuse, has, at last, thrown the golden apple at our feet. It now lies before us, and we need only to stoop to take it up. . . .

Were the heads of our government endowed with the French subtlety, we should incline to suspect a concert on this great occasion between them and the Spanish officers. . . . Or is this breach of treaty committed in pursuance of the mandate of Bonaparte, who disdains to take the gift, clogged with any troublesome or disagreeable conditions? Or is it the blunder of a well-meaning man, *dressed in a little brief authority,* who interprets the treaty in this manner?

The government must not hesitate. The western people will not be trifled with. They will not bear that injuries to their dearest rights should excite no emotion in that government whose claim to their regard is founded on the equality and efficacy of its protection. There never was a time when this government might gain the hearts of that important portion of its citizens more effectually than now. To let the opportunity pass unimproved will be a deadly wound to its popularity. It will probably be followed by some immediate act of rebellion. The loss of the affections of the western states will be the certain consequence. And what inexplicable evils will ensue should the French be enabled, by this delay, to take possession? . . .

FROM YOU, assembled Representatives, do we demand that you would seize the happy moment for securing the possession of America to our posterity; for ensuring the harmony and union of these States; for removing all obstacles to the future progress of our settlements; for excluding from our vitals the most active and dangerous enemy that ever before threatened us; for gaining the affections of your western citizens by enforcing their rights; by rescuing their property from ruin. Give us not room to question your courage in a case where courage is truly a virtue; to doubt your wisdom, when the motives to decide your conduct are so obvious and forcible. *The iron is now hot;* command us to rise as one man, and STRIKE!

That Brown's cleverly executed design of arousing the Congress and his countrymen to action had some effect may be inferred from the fact that the pamphlet had a considerable vogue. A new edition, revised, corrected, and "improved," issued from the press on February 18, 1803. There was reprinted at Martinsburg, Virginia, by John Alburtis, later in 1803, a review of Brown's *Address* which had appeared in the New York *Herald.* The review consists of forty-eight pages, made up largely of quotations from the original work.

### MONROE'S EMBASSY

Close on the heels of *An Address to the Government* upon the cession of Louisiana came a second pamphlet more urgent and vigorous, pleading for immediate seizure of the Louisiana territory. In this work Brown, almost completely forgetting his Quaker principles of peace and good will among men, urged a course of action that would undoubtedly have led to war with Spain and France. While cause for action was palpable and genuine, the reason set forth by Brown—the closing by the Spanish Intendant of the port of New Orleans to our western trade—was not the real cause. Brown was moved primarily by wholesome patriotism—the desire to see his country expand from ocean to ocean. He believed that it was America's manifest destiny to spread westward to "the South Seas." When Jefferson adopted his policy of watchful waiting and peaceful negotiations, and in March, 1803, sent James Monroe to Paris and Madrid to try to argue those powers into honoring their treaty obligations, Brown could stand it no longer—the result: *Monroe's Embassy*. In it he repeated much of the argument which had appeared in *An Address*, but in a more urgent, insistent tone. Jefferson, he argued, had let the nation down. So concerned was Brown that America should act at once—before the French had time to send their seasoned soldiers to our shores—that he openly denounced the dilatory tactics of Jefferson and his party and called upon our hardy men of the West to take action themselves and not wait for the government. The peaceful Quaker had almost turned into a warmonger. And yet, if his premise be granted, that immediate action would prevent war rather than cause it, one would have to soften his judgment. Then, too, the author might have maintained that his denunciation of the President was really not a criticism of Jefferson as a weakling, but of his party, whose leaders held him in leash, and of our clumsy governmental setup, in which the Senate could block the President's action in foreign affairs.

A detailed analysis of the contents of the pamphlet is unnecessary, since it repeats in essence the arguments of *An Address;* a few paragraphs will give sufficient insight into the tone and style of the document. The writer's portrait of President Jefferson is clear-cut and revealing:

Who, for instance, could have ventured even to guess that the drama of Louisiana would have concluded in an embassy? Not the opponents of the present government. It is true the First Magistrate stands not at a very illustrious height in their esteem. They never dreamed that fortitude and magnanimity were in the list of his virtues. To see a great way before him; to decide promptly and resolutely; to prefer the arbitrament of swords to the contest of wits; to discover that seasonable war is frequently the surest means of peace, and the most effectual way to prevent bloodshed were never thought to belong to him. In ordinary cases, therefore, what else could we expect but that the President would hesitate; pause; shrink; tremble at the sound of war. What else could be expected by those who regard him as a weak visionary, timorous and irresolute; whose hand is well enough qualified for the nice adjustment of quadrants and telescopes, but far too feeble and unsteady for managing the helm of government.

But what is the supreme magistrate in a new government like ours? . . . His conduct is seldom, or never, entirely dictated by his own mind. It must be modeled by what he foresees to be the will of his party, or it will be nugatory. . . . What is in some degree true of all Presidents, by virtue of constitutional limits, is in a remarkable degree true of the present. His character, in the eyes of his political opponents, while it inclines him to cowardly and dilatory measures, in cases where a decision must be made by himself, disposes him to lean upon the aid and counsel of those who surround him; to study the interest and pleasure of his party, and to do, not what is intrinsically right to be done, but what the upholders of his throne will approve. If an embassy, therefore, had been the mere offspring of the President's brain, his enemies would not have wondered at the monster. . . .

If the French, therefore, should be willing to sell the province for a sum far inferior to the cost of invading and preserving it, that man is a silly calculator, as to the value either of money or of honor, who should think the purchase cheaper than the seizure. I will not affirm that the purchase cannot be made. It is clear that we cannot offer a consideration that is adequate. . . .

But the government has been insensible, alike, to every spur and every allurement. They have trifled not only with the safety of the state, but, what is far more wonderful, with their own popularity. They have committed the unity and independence of the nation to the hands of France; they have devoted the fortunes of the Western people to immediate and irretrievable destruction, and have transferred their future allegiance and affection to a foreign power.

Fate has manifestly decreed that America must belong to the English name and race.

The very last paragraph of this document closes on a hopeless note not characteristic of Brown:

But the prospect is too mournful. My pen will not proceed further. To depict evils which cannot be averted; which those who only have the power to avert regard with stupid indifference or incredulity is only adding to the evil when it comes the torment of anticipation. Our only refuge is in that SOVEREIGN PROVIDENCE, which has hitherto preserved us, in spite of ourselves. Under THAT protection, the folly of our rulers fights against us in vain.

### AN ADDRESS TO THE CONGRESS

Whatever merit Brown's plan of immediate action may have had, Jefferson's course of watchful waiting and finally of outright purchase of the territory of Louisiana proved the wiser.

If the great event in Jefferson's first term in office was the Louisiana Purchase, that of his second was the Embargo Act, which in many of its aspects was more immediately fateful to the nation than the Purchase. It aroused infinitely more partisan politics than that which gathered around the Louisiana question. The Embargo brought squarely before the country for the first time since the days of the great debate over the formation and adoption of the Constitution the all-important question of whether our government was to be a democracy, or an oligarchy ruled by wealth and privilege. But unlike the tense days of constitution-making, action, bold and decisive, was now demanded. Jefferson however, hesitated, convinced that in the current crisis any action which he might pursue would lead to war, either with France or with England, or with both.

The circumstances which placed Jefferson in this historic dilemma were involved and of long standing, but they may be summarized, without violence to the main issues, as follows: France, the traditional rival of England and the staunch friend of America in the darkest days of the Revolution, was now at war with England. The country was pretty sharply aligned into two groups: the first, the mass of the American people, who sympathized with France and showed whatever sympathy they could for her in her struggle for freedom against almost the whole world; and second, English sympathizers, found chiefly among the wealthy and privileged, principally in New England and New York. The first group was led by Jefferson, the second by Hamilton and his party. This political alignment must be held firmly in mind in endeavoring to understand the political strife which clouded Jefferson's second administration. Against this tense background the following facts must be judged, and Jefferson's final course of action explained. Gratified over the successful outcome of the Louisiana dispute and his wise course of peace steered between the warring European nations and his frugal government at home, his countrymen in 1804 returned Mr. Jefferson to the presidency with an overwhelming majority. Thereupon he set about to fulfil this mandate from the people. But it should be remembered that his task was infinitely more difficult than that of Washington or Adams in their administrations. They had but one European belligerent to face at a time: Jefferson confronted both England and France at once, and had neither army nor navy with which to bargain.

Near the end of Jefferson's first term the European war was renewed; with ever increasing fury it went its way, sucking in nearly all the neutral nations. England took drastic steps to meet Napoleon's new tactics for crushing her. To build up her navy, her first line of defense, she resorted to impressing her own countrymen into the naval service. Since many of her merchant seamen had deserted and had joined American ships—both merchant and naval—England insisted on the right of searching American vessels and seizing her own subjects. As it was not always possible to determine whether a seaman on an American vessel was American or English, many unavoidable mistakes were made. The administration, long harassed over questions of contraband and in continual diplomatic maneuvers with the British, had prided itself on driving a narrow, but peaceful and honorable, course between the two mighty and ruthless belligerents. But on January 7, 1807, a British Order in Council, tightening its already strangling grip on American commerce, brought the two nations to the verge of a shooting war. The die seemed cast, when on June 22 an English man-of-war fired upon the American naval vessel, the ''Chesapeake,'' wounding twenty of her men. The nation was aflame with anger, and for once Jefferson had the whole country, including the deepest-dyed Federalist, behind him. But the peace-loving Jefferson like Wilson one hundred years later, adopted, or rather continued, his policy of watchful waiting. He ordered Monroe, in London, to demand an apology and reparations, and the Congress voted money for naval vessels.

The President now conceived the idea of an embargo, and on December 22, 1807, the Congress passed the Embargo Act forbidding American or other merchant vessels to clear American ports. Thus almost overnight our lucrative merchant trade with foreign nations came to a standstill. In a real sense the Embargo was futile, for between the British Orders in Council and Napoleon's Berlin decree, American ships would of necessity be forbidden to trade.

The Embargo Act was Jefferson's undoing: it brought the whole Federalist phalanx against him, it split his own party asunder, and it brought the country to the point of civil war. New England and New York in particular were disaffected. But worst of all, perhaps, the Embargo, which was to have been for his second administration what the Louisiana Purchase had been to his first, was admittedly a mistake not only in domestic affairs but more significantly a complete failure in foreign affairs: it failed to aid American merchants, it failed to stop Britain, it failed to halt France in her determined course. So violent was the protest that the Embargo Act was repealed on March 1, 1809, and three days later, his second term ended, Jefferson repaired to Monticello, without disgrace but without glory.

This was the unhappy state of affairs when in January, 1809, Brockden Brown took up his pen once again for his country and indited the strongest of his three political pamphlets: *An Address to the Congress.* On this occasion Brown appealed for action, not to the President but to the Congress. The pamphlet is a tersely written, if not powerful, document against the Embargo.

As Brown's own Introduction to this work furnishes a comprehensive outline of the entire essay as well as insight into the author's political and social philosophy, and exemplifies his fair-mindedness and integrity as a historian and his realistic understanding of the motives governing nations, we shall quote significant passages from it. His message is as applicable to the world's present deplorable condition as it was in 1809. Listen to this daring and honest Quaker:

I HAVE endeavored, in the following pages, to trace the present differences between Europe and America to their true source and to place the controversy between them on its true basis. I have examined the question concerning the policy or justice of the Embargo, as it stood when the law was first passed. I have explained the state of the controversy at the present moment. I have given some reflections to the scheme, which some have imputed to the government, of destroying the commercial intercourse between this nation and foreign ones; and have endeavored to show that all restrictions upon foreign commerce, whether as a precaution against the future violences of foreign states; or as a mode of revenge and punishment for those already committed; or as a method of dissolving our connection with them altogether are not warranted by justice, policy, or honor. . . .

There are others who will pass me by as a visionary; and some, observing the city where I thus make my appearance, may think my pacific doctrine, my system of rational forbearance and forgiveness carried to a pitch of Quaker extravagance. The truth is, I am no better than an outcast of that unwarlike sect, but cannot rid myself of reverence for most of its practical political maxims. I feel a strong inclination to admit to an equality of rights and merits men of all nations and religions; to pass the same sentence on the same conduct, even though the men who practice it bear, at one time, the name of French, at another of English, and at another of American; sometimes that of federalists and sometimes that of republicans.

If any think it of moment to enquire to what party I belong, I answer confidently, that I pertain to NONE. As I believe in the justice and policy of peace and unrestricted trade in our present circumstances, I can claim no kindred with one party. As I believe that the merits and demerits of Great Britain and France, in relation to us, are exactly equal, and that the conduct of both is dictated by no principle but ambition, and measured by no rule but power, I must be excluded from the others. As I believe our own conduct to flow purely from the same principles; that our right to navigate the ocean and the right of England to exclude us from it are rights precisely of the same nature, sources, and validity; that the claims of the two nations are merely grounded in the interest, exclusive and incompatible of each, and which each is bound by the principles of human nature to regard to the clashing interests, or even, to the actual detriment of the other, I expect to be, with equal indignation, renounced by both parties.

If there be any class of readers whose affection for their country is not clouded and distorted by groundless hatreds and insane attachments to foreign states and whose endeavors for its solid and permanent advantage are not shackled or precipitated by zeal for imaginary rights, or revenge for chimerical wrongs, I may hope for a refuge in their ranks and should rejoice to know that their ranks had, in any degree, been augmented by my means.

Brown was equally concerned over the ever-increasing and unenviable reputation of Americans as a nation of mere traders and peddlers. Turning from an exposure of American weakness Brown drew up a ringing indictment of international morals:

It may be said that our ultimate end was to restore the blessings of a free trade to all these nations, which end was a laudable and beneficent one. . . . Indeed! I was then greatly mistaken. Our aim, I thought, was to force from the sufferings of France and her allies a recall of those edicts which prohibited, and merely in name prohibited, our trade with England. . . . Our aim was likewise to force from the sufferings of England, permission to trade with the French empire, and, in both cases, the glorious end was to profit ourselves. If any of them were in want of bread and had nothing to give for it, I am afraid we should not be very anxious to supply their wants. If a famine rages among them, we shall hurry, indeed, to their ports, but merely to profit by the high prices which the famine produces. The evil of others is our good. Their sufferings are our enjoyments: gladly do we hear of their calamities, when they can put anything into our purses. Great is our joy if they want what we have got, because they will then pay us the more for it.

This view of the subject will be called visionary. We are bound, it will be said, to think only of ourselves. . . . The examples of all ages and nations justify us in preferring the smallest good of our own to the greatest of other states, in establishing our rights and extending our gains by means which we are to choose or reject, merely from their capacity of doing this.

All this is very true. Europe, Britain, has done this: and alas! those who fancied that the spirit of Europe was regenerated or improved by crossing the Atlantic are woefully mistaken. It was indeed quite ridiculous to think that this branch of the European body was exempted from any of the vices of those. How should it happen? What is there in our intellectual constitution that should make us wiser or better than our kinsmen beyond the sea? If any proof were wanting that our system of political justice is as narrow, selfish, depraved, unfeeling as that of European states, we have only to consider the purpose of the Embargo, the intention of imposing it; the effects on foreign nations which some of us rejoiced that it would, and which the rest of us lamented that it would not, produce. . . .

We have carefully imitated them in selecting ends with no view but to our profit and aggrandizement; we have had as little regard to those who are no parties in the business, in selecting our means. . . .

France thought it her interest to divide, and therefore weakened her rival. She assisted, therefore, the colony in shaking off the yoke of the mother country, and this was as gross a breach of national or public law as any writer on it can imagine; yet we, for now we were a nation and bound to regard things not in their abstract nature but in their relation to our separate interest, found this conduct to be truly heroic and magnanimous. The ally was now great and good, though twenty years before fighting against us in a war strictly defensive on his side, each individual Frenchman was worse than an hundred devils. But history is nothing more than a tissue of such cases, and we have done our all, though hitherto our all has been but little, to make some figure in this catalogue. If we have been somewhat more harmless than others, consider we are, nationally, but children. We shall be more conspicuous as we grow older and stronger. Meanwhile the motives and ends of the Embargo may serve to show what we shall do when we are able.

The real law of nations; the sole law which all of them recognize is that they must enrich and aggrandize themselves by all the means in their power. The neutral, therefore, will not lose any part of a profitable trade with a belligerent, if he can help it. A belligerent will deprive his enemy of all the benefits he is able to seize. What they actually do in all cases is proportioned to their power. The belligerent encroaches as for as he can with safety. The neutral resists as far as he can with success. To keep what he has, or to gain more, he goes to war, if he hopes to succeed by that means. If war will not answer the purpose, he yields just as far as necessity obliges him.

After a detailed and scrupulously impartial exposition of the nature and probable effects of the Embargo upon England, France, and America, the author observes:

A year has passed away since our Embargo was imposed. It has done nothing but evil. The good we expected, always in the opinion of some unattainable, must now be hopeless to all. This is some cause of disappointment and humiliation. That all our sufferings should have been incurred for nothing; that the species of warfare which the distance of one of our enemies and the irresistible power of another allow us to employ is wholly ineffectual. They are as proud, insolent, refractory as ever.

Neither England nor France had been materially impaired by the Embargo; only America had suffered. The reader will note in the paragraphs to follow that Brown never let slip a chance to make rapier thrusts at the money-changers in our temples. In this realistic way Brown built up to the climax of his argument, the tone of the calm and unperturbed reasoner changing now to a sarcastic and now to an impassioned appeal to his countrymen to defend their nation's rights:

Embargoes and interdicts are then either useless to us or pernicious; but what can we do? Does it become us to relinquish our rights without a struggle? Meanly and tamely to submit to their injustice? What paltry, what unmeaning declamations are these? *Relinquish!* You are called upon to relinquish nothing. Your enemies have taken away your rights, as you call them, without asking you to loosen your hold. Your power to navigate the ocean is at an end. If it be not at an end, your business is to enjoy it. With regard to the British dominions, there is no let or hindrance in your way. Your power is the same as ever. With regard to the other countries, if you have the power to trade with them, exert it. But you know you have not the power. You acknowledge it. But your honor will not allow you to submit. Why surely that perturbed spirit, called honor, has no option, has no room to play its pranks, to domineer and fret, in this case. It surely does not require you to sting and torment yourselves to no purpose. If it enjoin any thing, it must be open war; a fearless attempt to regain by force what force had deprived you of; does honor require you to aim a stabbing blow at your enemy under your cloak, with one hand, while with the other you doff the hat and assure him that you mean him no harm at all? And does honor sanction the motives of this artifice which are to elude his resentment and inflict your wound in such a way that while it penetrates his vitals, he shall want a pretext to retort the blow. This versatile, this pliant thing called honor, will allow you to forbear open war, because that will do you more harm than good. Your enemy is too much for you in fair regular fight. Honor does not forbid you to submit to that necessity. But you try the covert, the safer way of an embargo. That fails: you are called upon to give it up, exactly for the same reason you had previously declined open war. Because, it answers not the end; because it hurts yourself, but does not bring your enemy to your feet, either because it benefits your enemy, or because he values not the hurt it does him. But here your honor becomes all of a sudden very refractory. Those reasons which bowed and bent it before have no influence upon it now.

But we have rights to defend; for which we ought cheerfully to lay down our lives. The right to navigate the ocean, the great highway of nations; the common property of mankind. Does it avail nothing to remind you that the right you speak of is founded upon usage?

Brown then flayed our diplomats for their lack of common sense in reasoning about the rights of blockade. A nation has no rights, he maintained, which it has no power to defend. Dropping this dangerous if not entirely spurious doctrine of might makes right, Brown turns to a consideration of the nature of wealth and the source of a nation's happiness. Our modern isolationists could profitably study his arguments for internationalism as the apologists of an economy of scarcity should listen to his pleas for an economy of abundance. Brown's picture of the interdependence of all nations and of the inherent internationalism of trade appeals to our heads as to our hearts:

Exactly in proportion as the interdict fulfills the conditions of a genuine and legitimate blockade, by the completeness with which it is enforced, are we enraged at its injustice and indignity. For England to place her ships in such a manner that all trade with her enemies is effectually destroyed is no injustice. . . . These quiddities are suitable enough for disputation among jurists and secretaries, but is the conduct of nations that would be thought to be enlightened to be guided by such logic? Is their blood to flow; their houses to burn; their practicable commerce to be abjured in defence of these metaphysical phantoms?

*Remember:* I am not the advocate of foreign powers; I am not the preacher of devout submission to their claims as rightful. Their conduct flows from a single principle: the promotion of their own advantage; and is regulated by a single circumstance: their power to promote it. But neither am I so blind as not to see that our claims, our conduct has no other foundation. That equity, justice, right, though in the mouths of all, equally disclaim alliance with all. Our rights to the sea are measured by no standard but its conductiveness to our advantage; our means to enforce it by no scale but their efficacy; our conduct should originate in no fantastic illusion; no chimerical puerile distinctions; in no desire but the sole advantage of the nation; to be sought for by no means but the practicable. . . .

The business before you is a calculation of national advantage. The trade you are deprived of you should seek, if it be profitable to the nation. As to the right, that is to be adjusted by a standard of general utility and without personal or national preferences, which to your patriotic ears would be jargon and impertinence. If you consider your national good as the only test of justice, you will at least be in no danger of injuring yourselves for the sake of sounds and phantoms. On that ground, war—open or covert—expeditions to Canada, privateering voyages, embargoes, and suspended intercourse are all to be judged of alike by their efficacy; all of them are alike absurd, unreasonable, and inexpedient.

However, you pretend not that the trade with some parts of the world is unusually dangerous; that its gains are directly or indirectly hurtful to the nation; but only that by prohibiting your citizens from the free trade, you will either force your enemies to make all free, or punish them for obstinately fettering it. The goodness of this end and the wisdom of this means, we have already discussed; and any attempt to show that the authority to impose general embargoes is a shred, a fragment of that barbarism in which your European ancestors were once involved, and which, like many shreds of a cruel, contradictory, pernicious, and disjointed policy is the chief political inheritance they have left you would be unworthy of a good citizen. This power you have exerted, and you will exert; the people will elude your power, by secret fraud and by partial violence, but God forbid that your councils should generate a foreign war, not merely because the evils it directly produces are enormous, and incurred without adequate motives, but because of the eminent peril to which a foreign war, in a case like this and in the present circumstances of the nation, will expose our internal and domestic peace. If foreign war must come, those who labored most to avert it ought by inculcating submission and promoting unanimity to save us from its worse evils.

In a country which has hitherto depended so extensively for clothing, ornaments, food, tools, furniture, and all the apparatus of civilized life on importation; which has hitherto exported in value, at least, one-third of all the produce of its land and labor, a total and sudden cessation of this import and export must needs produce a vast and wide spread revolution.

Ought we to be all foreign traders? All farmers? Or partly traders and farmers and foreign traders? Or partly farmers and partly manufacturers, without foreign traders? If the whole society be made heartily to agree in one of these opinions, no one finds it easier on that account to change the path in which destiny has placed him. The merchant, the artificer, and the farmer, has been such before he begins to reason on these subjects. Is there a magic in a mere opinion of this kind, which will supersede the influence of habit; supply the want of education; and create a farmer, where there is no room for him; an artisan where all the custom is already engrossed; a merchant, where all the current business is already done by others. He must continue in the track, he must acquire a living, and raise a fortune in the way in which he is fixed by the complex and motley system of a great and civilized society, and may amuse himself with theories and visions, as to a better order of things, with his book and his closet, if he has the time and the taste.

When we reflect on the perpetual jealousies and bickerings, the hardships and oppressions, the frauds and cruelties to which an extensive foreign trade necessarily exposes a state; on the gigantic evils of war, to which the clashing interests of our own and of other nations make us liable; on the intestine broils and factions which derive their existence and their venom from this source; on the seeming necessity there is of protecting trade, if we have it, by frigates and by squadrons; on the enormous and insupportable expense which any efforts of this kind require; on the utter hopelessness of affording adequate protection to it in the present state of the world; on the mortification and shame of submitting to injustice and oppression, when we cannot avenge or repel it; on the absolute misery which this injustice and oppression diffuses through a part of the community and which arises from the fluctuations of war and peace among foreign powers: When we think on our helpless dependence for the comforts and decencies of life upon nations three thousand miles off, we may, without a crime, be disposed to wish that all intercourse of this kind were at an end; that we should sit, quiet spectators of the storms that shake the rest of the world, secure in our solitude and in the waste that rolls between them and us, employing all our vigor in building up an empire here in the West and in cementing the members of our vast and growing nation into one body.

There is something charming too in the picture of a world within ourselves; of bringing within our limits all the sources of comfort and subsistence; of supplying all our wants with our own hands; of gaining all the functions, occupations, and relations of a polished nation; of being a potent political body, complete in all its members and organs, and in which no chasm or defect can be found. We catch likewise an imperfect notion that we should be richer and more populous by this means. We should go on multiplying persons and towns and cottages faster; and thus become much greater and more wealthy, if all our surplus products were consumed by mouths at home, and not abroad; if the millions who now weave and sow and hammer and file for us were members of our own body, swelling by their gains and their expenses the tide of circulation in our own community.

With regard to the beauty of the spectacle afforded by a nation in which all the departments of human society are filled up by its own citizens; whose farmers feed and furnish its citizens and traders only, and whose artisans and traders supply each other and those farmers only, little need be said. It is in reality commended by nothing but a certain shape of order and completeness, adverse and not friendly to the dignity and happiness of mankind. Human society is a complex body, the members of which are not equal in use or value, in their faculties of self-enjoyment; in the power they exert over the commonweal; in the immediate benefits which, as individuals, they derive from their employments. There must be some to till the ground and raise bread, but they must produce more than they can consume, otherwise they can merely eat. They demand clothes, shelter, and domestic accommodation. Tools and machines to till the ground, even for their own use, they must necessarily have; and to procure these, they must raise a surplus produce and give it to the artisan, who makes and the merchant who fetches and carries. Artisans must be numerous in proportion as the farmer's taste and habits require much accommodation, and as his surplus produce is great. They must be divided into numerous classes, in proportion to the refinement which the arts have attained. As their numbers are greater, they are obliged to work for lower wages and with more industry. The fruit of their work is cheaper, and those whom they supply get better things, and more of them for the same quantity of produce, or money which represents it; but the subsistence of the artisan is more precarious, his enjoyments fewer, his drudgery more painful, all the causes of human misery and distress operate more cruelly upon him, as his wages are scantier. And thus the condition of the artisan is worse, as the produce of his labor is cheaper, and of consequence the ease and luxury of those who buy that produce greater.

Now what is our present condition? We are a nation of farmers, traders, and artisans, but our wants are not entirely supplied by our artisans. The produce of manufacturing labor which is annually consumed is immense, but a vast proportion is produced by the labor of distant nations. We are clothed, and adorned, and supplied with tools, in a great degree, by artisans beyond the ocean. Our principal employment is to catch fish, to cut timber, to reap corn, to feed cattle, and to carry what we do not consume of these away in exchange for the viands of foreign climates, or those articles of foreign manufacture which they will buy, and which we want. From circumstances peculiar to the countries that supply these, their workmen are many; they are obliged, therefore, to work cheap; powerful machines are in use which do more than human hands at a less cost. Hence, the misery and want of the artisans of these countries; hence the cheapness and abundance of their work to us; and hence more than half of the population of these countries are cooped up in towns; while only one-fourth or one-fifth of our population is thus cooped up. . . .

Thus embarrassed and qualified are all reasonings and comparisons about the eligibility of different callings and conditions in human life. There may be a solid ground at bottom, and we might possibly find it, were it our present business to search for it; but this would lead us into volumes, and is not to our present purpose. We are at present a community of merchants, artificers, and farmers. Some of our artificers even work for exportation. If things are left to their own course, the period will inevitably arrive when most of our own wants will be supplied by our own hands, except such as peculiarities of soil and climate deny us. But we shall not stop here. We shall become the manufacturers of other nations. Such we are, even now, to a certain degree, but our manufacturers will multiply in a larger proportion than our husbandmen. Less and less of the produce of mere handicraft will be imported from abroad, and more and more will be exported. The latter will depend, in some measure, on the state of foreign nations; but the former will be chiefly influenced by internal and domestic causes. It will even be our lot to import the raw materials of our manufactures, even for our own consumption, nor can anything but the real state of foreign countries prevent us, in fine, from importing bread and meat itself. All this will come. Eternal and immutable causes will bring us finally to this point, without the aid of government to push us forward, and in spite of all its efforts to hold us back; but the impossibility of any internal regulation to suspend our commercial intercourse with foreigners will be as evident when that intercourse consists in carrying cloths and fetching flour and cotton, as now when it consists in carrying cotton and fetching cloths. This is a point not susceptible of serious argument.

That intercourse among men is useful is a self-evident maxim. Alone, I am helpless, forlorn, wretched, and must perish. Give me another man to assist and commune with me, my condition is greatly improved; add to the number of my associates and you add to the common benefit. Commerce, or the intercourse of buying and selling, is itself manifestly beneficial, and necessarily implies and creates all the more liberal kinds of intercourse. Extend the sphere of this intercourse, or the number that uphold it, and a proportionable benefit results. Render this intercourse frequent and thorough by bringing them nearer, and by smoothing, shortening, and multiplying roads between them, and the augmented benefit keeps pace with these improvements.

Let us not be surprised that even at the beginning of the nineteenth century Brown clearly saw the advantages accruing to the peoples of the world from political and commercial consolidation as well as the dangers to the nations in a short-sighted policy of isolationism and national self-sufficiency. Brockden Brown, in other words, saw all too clearly at the beginning of the nineteenth century what even now in the twentieth only advanced thinkers admit as true: that this is one world and each inhabitant thereof is his brother's keeper as truly as if he were neighbor Smith around the corner. Were Brockden Brown living at present, he would be a staunch and indefatigable defender of the United Nations Organization. But let the author speak for himself:

One of the consequences of extended empire is to pull down those barriers which separate mankind from each other; to enlarge that circle which each man calls his country; to take away the grounds of dissension and rivalship; to create one nation out of many; to blend into one system of friendly, and especially of commercial intercourse, tribes that formerly looked upon each other as natural and hereditary enemies. Curious examples of this consolidation are to be found in the history of Europe; one memorable one is afforded by the history of Asia, but the most magnificent of all will be given to posterity in the history of North America.

The Romans combined into one people all the southern and western parts of Europe, the western part of Asia, and the northern region of Africa; all the Turkish empire, real or nominal; all the piratical states of Barbary, with Egypt and Morocco; all European territories within the Rhine and Danube. These were cemented into one nation as much as in after times the dissolution of the Heptarchy and the conquest of Wales cemented the people of South Britain into one people. The Mediterranean was the medium of their commercial intercourse, which, immense and wide spread as it was, was still nothing more than domestic trade. A commerce between the same parts must now take the name of foreign trade, and as such be burthened with restraints and thwarted by violences wholly unknown to them when they trafficked together as Romans. An hundred and fifty millions of people, dispersed over a great variety of soil and through great diversity of climate, and various in their arts and products, strongly endued with the spirit of traffic and adventure, and befriended by a lenient and enlightened government, with a thoroughfare so convenient and comprehensive as the Mediterranean, must have exhibited a scene of stupendous activity and bustle.

This wonderful body was broken by incessant blows, repeated for three or four centuries, into innumerable fragments, which as soon as they had reached their minutest divisions, began again to reunite. By the operation of the laws of inheritance and marriage, and by fraud and violence, conducted exactly on the principles which have produced the changes of the present time, one state was subjected to another; time and habit converted the subjection into incorporation; parts hostile and dissimilar, finally coalesced, and eight or ten nations rose from the parcelling combinations of five hundred. What new advances to unity the next age will witness, we connot conjecture. There seems to be no reason why they should stop where they are at present, more than at any former period. On the contrary, there is a cause in the present state of navigation by which armies and messengers can cross half the globe, with more facility than they could formerly cross a forest or a desert, for believing that the empire of a single European state may, in time, comprehend the world; but this is too copious a theme and leads us from the review we intended of mankind, under the influence of commerce, and of the true distinction between foreign trade and home trade.

The Chinese nation are remarkable for living in seclusion from the rest of mankind. They allow of little intercourse with foreigners; that little only at a single port; and only in foreign ships. Such an instance of dreary solitude, of sullen reserve, is no where else to be found, and yet what is really the extent of commercial intercourse enjoyed by this nation. To know this, we have only to imagine China struck out of the world's map, and all the other inhabitants of the globe, in both hemispheres, in every climate, so modeled that a boundless commercial intercourse prevails among them, without jealous interferences, without those bars which diversity of language and antipathy, religious or political, would produce. This surely would be a marvellous picture. IMPOSSIBILITY seems written upon it. And yet this is short of the picture actually displayed by China. To complete the parallel, we must imagine all the rest of the globe improved in the arts of civilized life; at least, in all the arts of domestic accommodation, as much as France and England. Then we shall have China and Chinese commerce before us, with this important diversity: that a number of civilized men, equal to all the rest of mankind together, are brought into one compact mass of contiguous provinces traversed by roads, canals, and rivers, and blended into one system of convenient and unrestricted intercourse. If trade has any influence on human society, if this influence depends upon the numbers whom it binds in its golden chain, the state of China must read us important lessons, since it operates on a scale of magnitude altogether stupendous and hitherto unexampled. To talk of the want of foreign trade in China and to draw grave inferences from that want is strange, since all the trade, foreign or domestic, which any other nation enjoys, or can bestow is to the extent of the Chinese internal trade, as one to an hundred.

I dwell thus upon China, not only from its extraordinary situation and the prevalent errors concerning it, but because North America is destined to afford a similar example of internal wealth and population in the coming age. Our actual territory has about the same area. It lies in the same beneficent climates. It is almost equally compact. The surface is far more level and fertile. It is occupied by one language; one people; one mode of general government; one system of salutary laws. Its population is small at present, but our progress to a more than Chinese abundance of product and people is no contingent event; it is one of those future appearances, of which the certainty is just as great as of any things past. Barring deluges, almost general, and pestilences that extinguish mankind; or the untimely destruction of the globe itself, this, and, indeed, a great deal more than this, must happen, because the present limits of our territory are not immutable. They must stretch with our wants. The South Sea only can bound us on one side; the Mexican gulf on the other; the polar ices on the third; but time, instead of diminishing our intercourse and dissolving our connection with foreigners, will only augment and strengthen them. The other states in the Western hemisphere, we shall, of course, approach more nearly and mix with them more intimately. The gaps of unpeopled waste which now sever them and us will disappear. Our limits will touch. As to the nations of Europe, as they conquered and peopled this hemisphere, they are destined to conquer and possess and people what remains to be peopled of the Eastern World. Hence our mere local proximity will continually increase. Our commercial intercourse will make rapid advances, but its particular relations or conditions must change. It will assume new forms and while its actual extent will increase, its extent relative to our numbers may, possibly, with regard to Europe at least, be diminished.

These may appear to some minds wholly occupied with the passing scene as silly and unseasonable dreams. Yet those who meditate on the present state of things and find no comfort may thank him who snatches them away to the future. How little will the errors of the present moment, with all their brood of mischiefs, appear to those who think of that progress to greatness, to which the worst of these errors can create but momentary obstacles. We have, however, a much nearer consolation. The causes of our present difficulties are in themselves fugitive and transient. They spring entirely from a war in Europe, which must come to an end. This end is proved by indisputable tokens to be not very remote. The reign of maritime peace in Europe is at hand, and when it arrives, all our embargoes will vanish of themselves; all our fortresses moulder and crumble. The ports of the Eastern World will again be open. Ships of war will no longer overspread the ocean. The great highway will no longer be cut across with dykes, be thrown up into ramparts, or be edged with batteries. All again, for a season at least, will be level, and commodious, and those who choose to pass may pass.

Thus ends a significant document. The advanced nature of his thinking and the persuasiveness of his rhetoric would be a credit to any author, in any age. Brown evidently felt his power in this kind of writing, for by 1806 he had definitely made up his mind to conduct an historical magazine.

### THE AMERICAN REGISTER

In the January (1807) number of the *Literary Magazine*, Brown announced that proposals for a semiannual work, to be known as the *American Register*, would appear in the next number. No proposals appeared, but in November the magazine reported that the first volume of *The American Register, or General Repository of History, Politics, and Science*, for 1806-1807 had been published. With the *American Register* well launched, Brown dropped the *Literary Magazine* and devoted all his time to the historical register. Although Professor Mott passes lightly over the *American Register,* dismissing it as "hackwork,"[1] Professor Pattee recognizes it in his evaluation of Brown's talents as an historian:

More and more in this later period Brown became interested in historical composition and political propaganda. . . . His historical surveys in *The Register,* done with thoroughness and accuracy and literary skill, would fill a large volume. They make Brown unquestionably the pioneer American historian in the modern manner, just as earlier he had been the pioneer American novelist.[2]

"This work," wrote Brown, "is a work previously unattempted in America . . . particularly designed to be a repository of American history and politics."[3]

We have seen how in the *Literary Magazine* Brown recognized the importance of documentary materials for the historian. Hearsay and mere personal impressions, he insisted, must be scrutinized before being credited. The editor proposed to write:

An impartial and well-digested history of American affairs, and of foreign transactions, so far as they illustrate and are connected with those of our native country, will be given in this work. Public documents are the only legitimate bases of history. These, in our times, are so copious, so circumstantial, and so authentic, that they almost supersede the business of the historian, and will ever obtain, with all judicious inquirers into history, their principal attention. In this work the original materials are inserted, and the facts, authenticated by them, methodized and illustrated in a regular narration. . . .

*The Register* includes a comprehensive abstract of all the laws passed by the general government. This is not introduced for the benefit of the lawyer, to whom the originals only are of any service, but as the most important historical documents. The laws of the United States, from the nature of the government, relate almost wholly to the levying and collection of a revenue; to the formation, distribution, and maintenance of a military force by land and by sea; to the modeling and government of frontier territories; to the public intercourse with the Indian tribes; and to modes of conduct with regard to foreign nations. Regulations on these points are closely connected with the current history of the nation and are absolutely necessary to be known by those who would be acquainted, not with the municipal law but the political condition of their own country.[4]

Adhering closely to his plan, he devoted most of the space to copies and abstracts of laws and historical documents. In general, the semi-annual volumes followed a fairly regular pattern. "Annals of Europe and America," appearing in every volume, was Brown's own narra-

[1] Frank Luther Mott, *History of American Magazines,* I, 222.
[2] *Wieland,* ed., Fred L. Pattee, Introduction, p. xxiv.
[3] Preface, *American Register,* V (1809), iii.
[4] *Ibid.,* pp. iii-iv.

tive of current foreign and domestic events, a narrative remarkable for its moderation and impartiality as well as its choice of significant current events. He was determined to steer an even course between two rival party factions:

The writer is sensible how little hope of present popularity can be reasonably entertained by him who does not enlist under the banners of a faction, and set out on a systematic plan of praising or condemning public measures, merely on account of the persons who perform them; of assigning to one political party all manner of wisdom and excellence, and to the other the simple and unmixed mead of wickedness and folly. He is sensible that this spirit extends to the transactions of foreign nations, even between themselves; that almost every reader is the warm and zealous advocate of either France or England. What indulgence, therefore, can be hoped for a work which bestows censure and praise without respect to persons or nations; which considers political events merely in relation to justice and truth, and distributes blame sometimes to the other, and sometimes to both in the same page? Who, in writing the history of a war between France and England, never forgets that he is neither Frenchman nor Englishman, nor is bound to shut his eyes upon the faults or merits of either?

Brown early realized what it has taken many people long years to understand: that America's welfare is closely bound up with European affairs and that whatever disturbs the peace of Europe will affect the peace of America. Isolationism, he vowed, was a chimera of narrow and selfish minds. His keen and cosmopolitan mind saw quite clearly that trade and commerce transcend national boundaries and limit the destinies of all nations.

An American observer who proposes to give an account of passing events immediately perceives that the field before him naturally divides itself into foreign and domestic. It may seem, at first sight, that his concern is only with the latter; but a little reflection convinces him that the destiny of his own country is intimately connected with the situations and transactions of European nations. As trade is the principal employment of the American people; as their trade is chiefly with the nations of Europe, or their colonies; and as the present state of navigation renders the whole globe a theatre of commerce to more than one people, our situation is deeply influenced through the medium of traffic, by the domestic condition and mutual operations of European states. If they are at war among themselves, those wants which in peaceable times were supplied by one another, must now find a supply elsewhere, and whatever influences their manufactures and produce which feeds it, on the other, is deeply interesting to a country like our own, which has both the inclination and power to extend and dilate its commercial dealings almost without limit. Trade and navigation likewise have the wonderful power of annihilating, in its usual and natural effects, even space itself. They bring into contact nations separated by half the diameter of the globe, and supply them with occasions and incentives for rivalship, jealousy, and war: two maritime and trading nations encounter and interfere with each other in every corner of the globe that is accessible by water. With France, Spain, and England, America has not only the relations incident to trading nations, but, by means of their colonies, she is in some respects directly or indirectly the territorial neighbor of all of them; and with all of them, therefore, she is liable to those disputes which flow from clashing interests and irritated passions, both on land and water.[5]

While trade binds, he believes political differences and ambitions divide nations.

"The Annals of America," occupying increasingly more space in each succeeding number of the *Register*, is particularly interesting to the student of American history. The aftermath of the Louisiana Purchase, the trouble with Spain, the Aaron Burr conspiracy—all come to life and gain new significance in these vivid contemporary accounts.

Seeing that our nation was becoming strong and mighty in its unity of thought and purpose, Brown rejoiced that

The evils of internal dissension and rebellion, instead of approaching nearer, are every day removed to a greater distance; the gulf which divides the master and the slave is becoming gradually narrower, and the ties which bind together the various members of the nation multiply and strengthen by time.[6]

In common with other patriots of the period, dizzied by the remarkable growth of the country, Brown at times allowed his enthusiasm to exceed its usual bounds of moderation:

During this period, the American nation has increased in numbers and opulence, in a degree far beyond any known example. This increase, indeed, is the natural consequence of their local circumstances; but those who were unacquainted with any previous instance of increase on so large a scale could not have imagined anything resembling that which the present age has witnessed in America. That an infant colony, settling in a fertile and wholesome country, previously unoccupied, would increase from fifty to a hundred persons, in twenty years, could be easily conceived by one that lived in the seventeenth century; but that, in the same circumstances, five millions should increase, in the same time, to ten millions, is equally certain, yet the imagination of such an observer would be startled and rendered incredulous merely by the magnitude of the event. Though this rate of increase cannot be eternally progressive, yet, considering the condition of the people with regard to arts, manners, and government, and the actual extent of territory inland, it is not easy to set the due limits on it. We can discover no material obstacle to the continual extension of our settlements to the Pacific Ocean, nor can the increase be less than double in every twenty years, till the whole be occupied, in the proportion of at least a hundred to a square mile. Supposing, therefore, that there is only three millions of square miles of good land, connected

[5] Preface, *American Register*, II (1807), iii-iv.
[6] "Annals of Europe and America," chap. i, *American Register*, I (1806-1807), 3-4.

with good climate, on both sides of the Mississippi, our numbers, in a hundred and ten years hence (little more than the life of some men), must be *three hundred millions*. Two hundred millions would people this space only in the small proportion of sixty-six to a square mile. Mighty and gigantic as this increase is, the reader must remember that the increase that has actually taken place would equally have startled a follower of William Penn, or a member of the Plymouth company. Twenty-two years of prosperity have increased the population of the country from three millions to six millions. Each individual of the present generation is richer, is surrounded with more luxuries and comforts, than his ancestor. The increase, therefore, in money, stock, public and private revenue, and trade is augmented in more than a double proportion.[7]

In the following year, however, the vexing Western question, intensified by the rapid settlement of the new country, gave him cause for uneasiness. The reader will recall from our introductory chapter that even before the adoption of the Constitution, the Western frontiersmen, overwhelmingly democratic and agrarian, had resented domination by the older seaboard section. Now, in their rapidly growing strength and wealth, and struggling with problems peculiar to their section, many Westerners felt it might be advisable to set up their own government and be free of the central government at Washington. The growing bitterness between the democratic West and the aristocratic East, Brown looked upon as inevitable but nonetheless unfortunate:

As the western regions form the grand theatre of emigration and settlement, their population and culture are daily and rapidly increasing. Their relations to the maritime districts consequently undergo incessant variations. Ideas of separate interest and individual importance continually multiply and strengthen. The national metropolis being placed in the maritime country, and the scale, as to wealth and numbers, hitherto declining on that side, wherever the interests of the two districts interefere, the preference will naturally be given to that of the maritime country, and thus are opened new sources of jealousy and faction, and new topics are supplied to those who recommend a political separation of the two districts.[8]

Thus we see foreshadowed the great sectional struggle which to this day continues to wield a measure of its disruptive influence.

The editor was deeply shocked by the Burr-Hamilton duel. Now in the far more serious affair of the apparent betrayal of his own country by Burr, Brown took a dispassionate attitude. His account of the incident has stood the test of modern scholarship.[9] In spite of

[7] Appendix, *American Register*, IV (1808), 31-48.

[8] "Annals of America," chap. x, *American Register*, I (1806-1807), 66.

[9] W. F. McCaleb, in his Introduction to the scholarly and interesting biography of Aaron Burr by Wandell and Minnigerode, rises to an impassioned and somewhat biased defense of this misunderstood man. He attributes most of Burr's misfortunes to the political enmity of Jefferson:

the passions aroused by the trial, Brown refused to be swept away by either admiration or condemnation of Burr, for he was bent on a just and historically accurate report. Too long to reproduce here, it is a model of disinterested reporting and stands in the front rank of contemporary accounts.

Besides the "Annals, Laws, and Acts," the section on "Foreign and American State Papers," primarily a record of state papers, bulked large in each volume. Of most concern to the student of Brown's literary interests were "Poetry" and the "Review of Literature" sections. He prefaced the first with this observation:

> Good poetry is the most scarce of all literary commodities, though poetry, or matter that, by courtesy, bears the name, is sufficiently abundant. There has not lately been published in America any poetical *volume* of much value. We are therefore obliged to have recourse to the daily, weekly, and monthly periodical works for materials. The above pieces have most of them been carefully selected from these, and will probably be allowed to possess merit, at least, above mediocrity.

The poetry section, which appeared in three of the volumes, varied in length. The most significant single piece was Brown's long autobiographical poem, "Devotion: An Epistle," reprinted herein as Appendix A. Dated 1794, it was first published in the *American Register*. Regarding this poem, we might repeat that Professor Pattee considers it proof of a genuine poetic strain in Brown. He ranks certain passages with the best writing being produced in England at the time.[10]

In three issues appeared the important "Review of Literature," divided into British and American. Although his hope for the future of American literature had somewhat languished, his interest in good literature from whatever clime had nowise flagged. Brown had come to see the English language and literature as essentially one with the American, and he justified his extensive interest in English publications as follows:

> English literature, beyond that of any other nation, may be represented as that of the whole world. The curiosity of that nation is such that no

---

"Then it was he came to issue with Jefferson, when, quite unexpectedly, the two were tied in the Electoral College for the office of President of the United States. Had Burr been a trickster he might easily have been chosen Chief Executive; but he was playing the game squarely; however, he did not save himself from the jealous, suspicious Jefferson, who at once saw that he had to reckon with a leader of men, and from that day forward Burr was marked for destruction.

The climax of Jefferson's persecution was reached in the trial of Burr for treason, one of the most deliberate persecutions that history records. The President left nothing undone to convict Burr. He pardoned some of the accused; he bribed Eaton, a plain liar, with public funds; and saved Wilkinson, a dastardly wretch, from public condemnation—all to no avail. The results of that trial might be offered as a biting corollary to the Bill of Rights, which Jefferson himself is credited with writing—a choice bit of irony out of the ages" (pp. xix-xxi).

[10] *Wieland*, ed., Fred L. Pattee, Introduction, p. xv.

work of general importance can make its appearance in any part of the civilized world without being speedily translated into English, and even the literature of our native country becomes English by the republication of all important and valuable productions in Great Britain.

All publications have an absolute as well as relative value. Many of them, in all countries, relate to local occasions and temporary topics, and the interest they are calculated to excite, and the instruction they are adapted to convey is small in one place, exactly in proportion as they are great in another. *We* are so intimately united with Great Britain in language, manners, law, religion, and commerce, that, in a literary point of view, we may justly be regarded as members of the same society, as a portion of the same people. Many English publications which may be described as strictly local and temporary excite as much curiosity in America as in Scotland or Ireland; and the whole annual produce of the British press being regularly transported to our shores, and furnishing almost the whole employment of our readers, British literature may truly be considered, so far as books are the property of their readers as well as of their writers, as likewise American.

In Volume I appeared "A Sketch of American Literature," Brown's last significant essay on the literature of his country. As we have seen, he began his editorial career optimistic for the future of American literature. Gradually, as he sensed the hopelessness of the situation, he said less and less about his cherished dream for American letters. Into this article he distilled all his disappointments as he reviewed the fruitless labor he had expended on his attempts to establish a distinctive American literature. He was not bitter or angry; his tone was rather one of regret and of hopelessness. Was the country too poor, or too illiterate, or too indifferent to support the profession of letters? Were there no writers with genius? His answer was: Bookmaking does not pay in America, because there is no financial reward or copyright protection for author or publisher. As the essay gives the fullest account of the literary status of our country at the beginning of the nineteenth century, large sections of it deserve quotation:

Let us suppose a stranger to be merely informed that the American states composed a nation of five or six millions of persons, enjoying all the ordinary benefits of civilization and refinement, unattended with that poverty and ignorance in the lower classes, and with that sloth, pride, and luxury in the upper ranks, commonly met with in other nations, and as generally enlightened by an elementary and useful education, as the people of the European states. Such an observer would probably conclude that there was annually a considerable harvest of original literary and scientific productions among us. He would imagine that in so large and thriving a community, a few hundreds of persons would be found, to whom the industry of their fathers had secured a decent competence, and whom a liberal education or inquisitive temper would lead to employ their leisure in some favorite course of study. The habit of writing is so natural and serviceable to the studious, and the vanity so general that leads us to publish what we write, that it might naturally be suspected that a few of this class would publish their learned and ingenious labors. There are some propensities too, so strong, that neither want will extinguish, nor drudgery divert the mind from them. Of this kind is a poetical spirit, and a stranger might suppose that, among a people so numerous and enlightened, the lapse of ten or twenty years would produce a few poets, sufficiently ambitious and popular to produce a few annual volumes. As necessity, however, is the strongest impulse to literary as well as all other kinds of invention and industry, it might be supposed that bookmaking would in some few cases be pursued merely as a trade, as a method of subsistence and that some few original works might be produced. . . .

Our republications, in general, however, are confined to professional books and to the fashionable poetry and novels of the day. Among other works, the chief demand, especially in the Eastern states, is for the writings of Junius and Edmund Burke. Of these, new editions are continually issuing from the press. Lindley Murray's school books have an unbounded circulation here as in England, and Shakespeare has passed through several editions among us. The standard English historians, Hume, Robertson, and Gibbon, are occasionally republished, and widely circulated. Yet we may venture to pronounce that any original work from an American pen, however well written, on any branch of European biography or history, upwards of fifty years old, would find nobody to publish it at their own risk. . . .

In investigating the state of book-making, in any country, and the causes that encourage or depress it, we are apt in general to refine too much and to seek the causes of appearances rather in the constitutional genius of the people than in the common and obvious circumstances on which the fruits of literary genius and industry, like all other commodities, depend for their abundance and scarcity. Authors will, in fact, be always found, and books be written, where there is a pecuniary recompense for authors and a ready sale for books, but where any circumstance denies them this reward, or reduces the sale of books, there will necessarily be few authors. . . .

Ill-informed persons might draw many erroneous inferences from the scarcity of original books among us. In the first place, it might be hastily supposed that we were very imperfectly supplied with books, and that we wanted either the faculty, the inclination, or the opportunities to read; and yet this is by no means true. America is probably as great a mart for printed publications as any country in the world; the proportion of readers is probably not exceeded even in Germany or England. The press is nowhere more extensively employed, nor knowledge more widely and equably diffused. Nay, paradoxical as it may seem, though there are few *books* of original speculation among us, there is an enormous quantity of original *publication*. A vast number of pens are constantly busy, but circumstances oblige them or incline them to be satisfied with brief essays, in daily newspapers and gazettes.

The source of the difficulty was, then, not a lack of either interest or talent, but the deplorable publishing situation. No international copyright law yet existed to protect the author or his bookseller. Because of the high price of English books, due to heavy taxation and duties, American booksellers found it cheaper to reprint popular works without paying royalty.  Unfortunately they found this pirating more profitable than buying the products of American writers:

In America, a considerable impediment to authorship is removed by the security of literary property granted by the Federal government, but there are other obstacles of more importance, arising from the connection which subsists between Great Britain and America.  An American bookseller has always a plentiful supply of books from the old continent.  In framing his orders, he is at liberty to consider what books are likely to be most saleable, and in this he is guided by his own experience with regard to old books and by the tide of present popularity in England with regard to new ones. . . .

When the American student has completed a laborious work, he carries it to the bookseller, and offers it for sale.  He puts a price upon it somewhat equivalent to the time employed in writing it, but the offer is very properly and prudently rejected by the bookseller, for says he, here I have a choice of books from England, the popularity and sale of which is fixed and certain, and which will cost me nothing but the mere expenses of publication; whereas, from you I must purchase the privilege of printing what I may, after all, be unable to dispose of and which therefore may saddle me with the double loss of the original price and the subsequent expenses.  If the disappointed author abates in his demand, and even finally is willing to make a present of his work to the publisher, the uncertainty of the sale still remains and renders the project a hazardous and precarious one.  His reluctance increases in proportion as it is extensive and voluminous.  This will probably be found to be the true cause why original works are so rare in America.  There are very few in any country who write books without any prospect of pecuniary recompense, or, when their books are written, can afford to publish them at their own expense.  The ingenious, therefore, are obliged to spend their time in desultory reading, or to turn their attention to the walks of plodding but lucrative business. . . .  The capital of booksellers is at present fully employed in importing and publishing.  If more of their manufacture were of domestic materials, an equivalent diminution must take place in the materials of foreign growth, and upon the whole we are more likely to be well supplied as things are at present.  At any rate, the evil, if it be one, seems to be irremediable.  As long as England, France, and Germany continue to produce books, and America is at liberty to choose among them what she will import and what she will republish, it will always be most prudent to pursue a great and certain, in preference to a small and precarious, gain.  Thus, we see at present an American bookseller undertake to republish a work in twenty volumes quarto, and demanding a capital of an hundred thousand dollars, who will refuse to give fifty dollars for a pamphlet written by his neighbor, or even to publish at his own expense, from the risk of loss which attends it; and this caution it is impossible for an impartial man to censure, though he may applaud the generosity which of its own accord will put something to hazard, or voluntarily abridge its own gains for the sake of cherishing or relieving genius in despair, or learning in beggary.

Brown's lament for the sad state of literature in his beloved country and his plea for a wiser course went unheeded in his day.  Almost another century passed before the copyright law gave ease to harrassed author and publisher.

## BROWN'S CLOSING DAYS

With the ever-mounting duties of two arduous trades and the burdens and obligations of an increasing family, Brown could not be expected to live long. His physical health, always frail and uncertain, finally gave way under the stress and strain of his heavy duties. During the early part of 1809 symptoms of tuberculosis showed themselves in failing physical strength and inability to apply himself to work of any kind for long periods of time. He sought relief in short vacations in New York and New Jersey, returning with renewed confidence, but with a little less strength each time.

The signal honor which came to him in 1809 when, along with such notables as Noah Webster and Timothy Dwight, he was elected to honorary membership in the New-York Historical Society, cheered him but could not check his declining health and his flagging spirits.

In the summer of 1809 Brown made a journey through New York and New Jersey in search of health. From Hoboken he wrote to Mary Linn that instead of his enjoying the landscape his thoughts were hovering over the images of his wife and children and his sisters. He was lonely, and unhappy because his mind had grown less curious and less active.

Of the closing years of Brown's life, his poor health, and his final demise, Dunlap wrote the most inspired portions of his biography.

On the tenth of November, 1809, he was attacked by a violent pain in his side, for which he was bled, and retired to his chamber to be nursed as he thought for a few days. From this time to the twenty-second of February he was confined to his room; his sufferings were then relieved by death. During this long confinement he scarcely ever enjoyed ease, and sometimes suffered greatly, yet he never uttered a murmur or impatient exclamation, and scarcely a complaint. . . .

On the morning of the nineteenth of February, 1810, it was observed that a change for the worse had taken place. He thought himself dying, and desired to see all his family, and spoke to each in the tenderest and most affectionate manner. He, however, remained in this dying state until the twenty-second, frequently conversing with his friends with perfect possession of his faculties to the last.

Thus at the age of thirty-nine, died Charles Brockden Brown, taken from the world at a time when the mass of knowledge which he had acquired by unwearied but desultory reading, and by acute and accurate observation, being preserved by a strong memory and marshalled by an uncommonly vigorous understanding, was fitted with the aid of his perseverance and zeal in the cause of virtue to have conferred the most important benefits upon his fellowmen.

Brown was buried in the Friends Burial Ground in Philadelphia, a fact that inclines one to the supposition that he had become reconciled with the church of his boyhood, or at least that for the sake of his family he was allowed to rest in the old cemetery of the Society.

His friends and family left sincere tributes to Brown's character. Dunlap concluded his biography with an encomium on Brown as a man of uncommon acquirements, amiable manners, and exalted virtues. He dwelt particularly on Brown's generosity to the members of his family and on his ability to converse fluently on a wide variety of topics.

Poulson's *American Daily Advertiser* carried the following obituary on February 27, 1810:

Died in this city . . . Charles Brockden Brown, editor of the semi-annual *Register,* and well-known to the literary world as the author of several other productions of genius and merit. In this afflicting dispensation, it will be the source of consolation to his distant friends to know that he died in the enjoyment of his mental faculties, a Christian, full of the hope of immortality, at peace with himself and with all mankind.

The manners of the deceased were mild and unaffected, his attachment to his friends ardent and sincere, his knowledge extensive, and his criticisms were generally admitted to be acute, liberal, and profound, and if in early life he indulged in speculative theories and opinions, it was to be ascribed to the versatile exuberance of a brilliant imagination—the unwearied inquisitiveness of a rich and active mind—and to that never failing propensity to scrutiny and investigation, consequent on a disposition to admit nothing on trust when in search of truth. He was blessed by nature with the most facile capacity for the acquirement of knowledge, and having received a liberal education, which he greatly improved by study and research, and possessing at the same time a laudable but modest ambition for the acquirement of literary fame, together with the most copious command of language, he seemed destined to become one of the brightest ornaments of this country. He lived in innocent but not inactive seclusion from the world, being wholly devoted to literary pursuits, to a beloved family, and to the society of a few select friends, to whom he endeared himself by the most amiable and disinterested attentions, by his overflowing affability and by the instructiveness of his unassuming conversations.

The following information and beautifully written obituary notice was found among Brown's papers in the handwriting, perhaps, of Elizabeth Linn Brown, but it was probably not entirely her composition. Although the manuscript shows by the many cancellations of words, phrases, and entire sentences, that its author carefully weighed every statement, a curious, but—under the strained circumstances and at the beginning of a new year—quite understandable error has crept in in giving the year 1809 instead of 1810. The "constitutional imbecility" referred to means, of course, physical weakness.

On the 22nd of February, 1809, fell a victim to the consumption Charles B. Brown, the editor of the *Register.* His health had for a long time held by a precarious tenure, inheriting from nature a delicate frame of body which a sedentary life, rendered indispensable by his literary pursuits, tended to augment. Early in life he aspired to the love of letters, with an ardor which constitutional imbecility rather served to heighten than abate. He found in his own mind rich resources; his attention was so powerfully abstracted and engrossed by his studies as to render him almost unconscious of bodily pain and insensible of its exercise. Ever on the alert in quest of information, he patiently inquired, he read, reflected, examined, and compared opposing facts and arguments, and the result was a judgment luminous, consistent, and just. This habit of investigation and research became at last so familiar to him that it almost formed a part of his nature. The most trivial incident which to an ordinary eye would be passed without observation was often with him a subject of ardent curiosity and was so appropriated as to lead to the illustration of matters more important in literature, politics, or morals. It is difficult to conceive what acquisition a mind thus constituted possesses above ordinary men. Those hours devoted by the generality of the world to colloquial amusement, and which the memory afterward retains no vestige of, were to him all subordinate to the grand purpose of his life, the acquisition of knowledge. Study and investigation lost the character of painful drudgery and assumed that of pastime and recreation. In early life he delighted to indulge in the visions of fancy, and the productions of his juvenile pen bear the stamp of that character. The world has already witnessed the success of his reiterated attempts, and his tales of artificial distress have extorted tears of sympathy from our eyes. For the last five years of his life he abandoned the regions of fancy, and devoted himself exclusively to more solid and severe pursuits. He undertook the difficult and arduous office of an annalist, and the *American Register* is decisive evidence of his skill and talents in that responsible department of letters. The habits of analysis for which he was so peculiar and characteristic were now applied to an object that above all others requires the exercise of such talents. Added to this, there was another trait in his character that peculiarly fitted him for the office of an annalist, the philosophic candor he maintained in his record of political events. As an annalist inaccessible to the biases of party, he seemed more to write in the style of an historian of past ages than the recorder of those passing occurrences that tincture our public councils and embitter the charities of domestic life. We do but echo the opinion of the public when we pronounce this *Register* under his superintendence to have put all competition at defiance. The merits of this eminent writer were rivalled by the virtues of his private life. His friends in his society and converse felt none of that reserve and uneasiness that great intellect naturally inspires. His mild and unassuming manner, so rarely associated with superior talents, and his hospitable heart rendered him the delight and ornament of friendship. It was in the endearing recesses of domestic life where the heart, warmed with confidence, expands and unfolds, that the character of the deceased shone with its loveliest lustre. It was in the cultivation of those domestic endearments indescribable but by appealing to the bosom of the friend, the parent, and the husband, and which Thomson so beautifully expresses by the general terms "fireside enjoyments, homeborn happiness," that he delighted to participate. Benevolence was not with him a sudden impulse of passion that subsides with its cause but a steady rule and systematic principle of action. He had been so wont to consider the happiness of a friend as forming an integral part of his own that he labored with the same zeal and perseverance to promote it that others do from selfish motives alone.  We may be well assured that characters of this kind were not formed to amass wealth or to catch the fleeting and evanescent popularity of the day; it may be said without the slightest trespass upon truth that they are above the exercise of those arts that secure the possession of both.  They are formed for higher rewards, the approbation of those who know how to estimate worth, and a self-approving conscience.  Some may regard this as a portrait drawn from fancy, and would to heaven that it was!  We should not then be compelled to cite the sympathies of bereaved friendship and the tears of the widow and the relatives as melancholy vouchers of the fact.  While the literary world has lost a member whose genius amused, delighted, and instructed, the circle of his private friendship has been bereaved of its brightest ornament; and both will confess that this is no panegyric on the memory of Brown.

At this juncture it would be profane to add anything to this honest, sincere, and eminently just evaluation of the life and the character and the work of Charles Brockden Brown.

# XI

# TIME THE ASSESSOR

IT IS THE PURPOSE of this chapter to give a fairly complete record of the reputation of Charles Brockden Brown in England and in America during the century and a half since his death. Brown's popularity in France and Germany was considerable; his novels were translated into both French and German and apparently influenced writers of both countries; Brown has been the subject of many a tedious German dissertation and of a few brief French brochures. But the reader will find no refutation of Richard Garnett's fanciful biography in the ninth edition of the *Encyclopaedia Britannica* (1878) which refers to Brown as the greatest American novelist *since* Hawthorne and which repeats Peacock's unfortified story of Shelley's fascination with Brown's novels. There will be no detailed notice of Sir Walter Scott's interest in Brown nor of Godwin's tribute to him nor of Mrs. Shelley's probable debt to *Carwin* in her novel *The Last Man*.

## BROWN'S REPUTATION IN ENGLAND

Like many other American writers Charles Brockden Brown was recognized in Europe before he attracted any considerable notice in his own country. It was his friend John Davis who in his *Travels of Four Years and a Half in the United States of America* (1803) gave the fullest recognition to Brown's work. Davis, an Englishman who spent some time in Philadelphia and New York, contributed substantially to Brown's *Monthly Magazine*. In his *Travels* Davis characterized Brown's style as "chastized" and "scrupulously pure" but devoid of humor.[1] To Davis we are also indebted for two lively and revealing contemporary portraits of Brown at work and in society: he described Brown wearing the typical dress of an author, "a great coat and shoes run down at the heel," and making his pen fly before him; in Brown's living quarters Davis saw a "dismal room in a dismal street"; being asked if he could not write with more facility were his window to command the prospect of Lake Geneva, Brown answered, "Good pens, thick paper, and ink well diluted would facilitate my composition more than the broadest expanse of water, or mountains

[1] John Davis, *Travels*, pp. 151-152.

rising above the clouds." Later Davis recalled seeing Brown in Philadelphia ingratiating himself in the favor of the ladies by writing a new novel.[2] At social gatherings Davis found that Brown was lost in meditation, his creative fancy conjuring up scenes to spin out the thread of a new novel.[3]

Another British visitor favorably impressed by Brown as a man and as a writer was John Bernard, popular actor and theatrical manager. In his autobiography, *Retrospections of America* (1887), Bernard wrote a description of Brown's physical appearance and gave an extended analysis of his place as a writer. He called Brown the most agreeable acquaintance he formed in Philadelphia, the first and for many years the only novelist America produced; few men, he said, had united talent and worth in such a large proportion or had been more clearly marked by equanimity; his powerful mind bespoke an active and speculative life, engendering contentment for the best and respect for the weakest of the world's admixture. Bernard saw Brown as a writer who styled his work after the illustrious modern thinker Mr. Godwin; like Godwin he was an explorer of the inner world of man, not a painter of its external habits; he was no recorder of the artificial conventionalities of human conduct, but a diver into its depths and a delineator of the source; seeing Brown as unequal to his prototype, Bernard nevertheless expressed an appreciation for the simplicity with which Brown's stories evolved and for his ability to sustain the reader's interest and press the moral or argument with great force. Despite his ill health and straitened circumstances, Brown enjoyed life and was a cheerful if not an entertaining companion. Bernard, struck with Brown's geniality in society and the somberness of his writings, was told by the author that he was conscious of a double mental existence: his imagination and his social being. "In my literary moods," Brown said, "I am aiming at making the world something better than I find it; in my social ones I am content to take it as it is." Bernard was amazed at the facility with which Brown wrote; once the subject presented itself to him he walked about, fermenting the thought, the feeling, and the purpose in his mind; then when he sat down, all the material came as rapidly as he could write. As a proof, *Arthur Mervyn* was written in three weeks and *Edgar Huntly* in little more. When asked, Brown admitted that he had suffered disappointment over the literary tastes of his countrymen, but to him writing had been a matter of both physical and mental necessity; when he put two ideas together he had an immediate craving to invent; he admitted a desire, certainly, for fame, but had he been exiled, he was sure that he would have been impelled to write as a mental necessity and would have found his highest enjoyment in composition.[4]

[2] *Ibid.*, pp. 163, 222.
[3] *Ibid.*, p. 122.
[4] John Bernard, *Retrospections of America*, pp. 250-254.

British magazines were at first not disposed to recognize Brown as possessing any high qualities as a writer. In 1811 a reviewer in the *Monthly Review* (London) wrote disparagingly of *Wieland:* he thought that as the story was founded on the tricks of ventriloquism and the outrages of madness it failed to excite interest or to instruct the mind.[5]

By 1820, however, Brown's fame in Britain had increased considerably. The *New Monthly Magazine and Universal Register* (London) carried a long, laudatory review, insisting that Brown's novels, though in every circulating library in England, had not received the attention they deserved. He said that if *Wieland* or *Arthur Mervyn* or *Edgar Huntly* had been written "by the author of Waverley," he doubted not that every reader would have been in raptures with their beauties and every "babbling critic lending his tributory stream of the shallow admiration of the writer's power."[6]    The reviewer predicted that as discerning readers came to know Brown they would do him the justice of recognizing his real worth; he also compared Brown's work to Godwin's, noticing particularly their common use of suspense as the mainspring of action. He suggested that Godwin's peculiarities formed a complete key to the prevailing style and manner of the novels of Brown. Although Brown's subject matter was different, the same modes of chaining down the reader's attention and harassing him with every passion was so much like Godwin's that the spirit and accuracy looked more like identity than imitation. "But," he continued, "what renders Brown the most singular and original of imitators is that, notwithstanding his pertinacious predilection for the phraseology and manner of another, he has in no instance betrayed any disposition to adopt that person's speculative views of human affairs." In addition the critic maintained that Brown's exploitation of American materials lent particular interest to his works. In the final summing up of Brown's merits as a writer the critic pointed out that

There is want of skill in plots and variety in the personages and event; they contain no sentimental raptures—no fascinating pictures of love and gallantry; they have neither heroines nor heroes, properly so called—no sublime marauders; they have few allusions, political, historical, religious, or literary; and, finally, they, as far as we can discover, are absolutely without a moral; but with all these deficiencies, they are the first fruits of a young and powerful mind; they are full of life and freshness and enterprise—those vital signs by which works of genius will ever be distinguished.

One of the critics most favorable to Brown was *Blackwood's (Edinburgh) Magazine.* In 1820 a critic charged that America had shame-

[5] *Monthly Review*, CXLV (Jan., 1811), 96.
[6] "On the Writings of Charles Brown, The American Novelist," *New Monthly Magazine and Universal Register* (London), XIV (Dec., 1820), 609-617.

fully neglected both Brown and Irving: though Brown's novels were widely read, and notwithstanding commendations they had received, they had never been "mentioned," according to the critic, "among the classical or standard works of that species of composition."[7]  This reviewer, like most others, compared Brown with Godwin, pointing out his "dark, mysterious power of imagination" and his knowledge of the human heart.

Several notices appeared in 1822.  The *Monthly Review* (London) carried an evaluation of the Allen-Dunlap *Life of Charles Brockden Brown*.[8]  The reviewer of *Carwin and Other Tales* also commented on the *Life*.  He acknowledged the presence of a sort of morbid genius and commented on Brown's wide reputation in Great Britain; he concluded by expressing a "mingled feeling of pleasure and regret— of pleasure at beholding portrayed the splendid progress of that Western star to the summit of knowledge and literary honors, and regrets at knowing that it had scarcely attained that height ere its rays . . . were quenched in everlasting darkness; of pleasure at being made acquainted with a character so truly amiable . . . of regret that the life of so good a man should have been rendered miserable by ill health and pecuniary difficulties."[9]

During the same year the *New Monthly Magazine* (London) contained two reviews equally laudatory and appreciative.  In the first article (April, 1822) the critic pointed out the powerful descriptions and the striking situations in *Wieland, Ormond, Arthur Mervyn,* and *Edgar Huntly.*  Brown, he declared, was original, "grand, yet simple, moral, and affecting."  He made the usual and not unfounded charge that Americans neglected their geniuses; "but the Americans are beginning slowly to find out that taste and literature may be subjects of pride, as well as steamboats."  The May issue contained a review of *Carwin and Other American Tales,* just published in London, which the critic pronounced exciting and dramatic, particularly admiring the "curious self-analyzation which forms one of the greatest attractions in this writer's productions."

*Blackwood's,* always kindly disposed toward Brown though not toward American writers generally, published a series of articles on American authors, in one of which Brown's life, personality, and ability as a writer were censoriously and contradictorily analyzed. In the article the critic—probably the American-born John Neal— breezily announced his aversion to mere accuracy, saying that "there is nothing so insupportable . . . as unnecessary precision."  He substantiated his point by launching forth into an amusingly fantastic,

---

[7] "On the Writings of Charles Brockden Brown and Washington Irving," *Blackwood's (Edinburgh) Magazine,* VI (Feb., 1820), 554-561.

[8] "Dunlap's Memoirs of Charles Brockden Brown, the American Novelist," *Monthly Review,* CLXXX (Oct., 1822), 151-157.

[9] *Gentleman's Magazine,* XCII, Pt. 2 (1822), 622.

inaccurate account of Brown's life and struggle for existence. This is what the great *Blackwood's* fed its readers: Brown had gained no recognition from his countrymen and moreover lived and died "miserably poor and went into the grave with a broken heart." Then the critic recounted the yellow fever plague of 1798, from which Brown had no escape; he paid tribute to Brown's wife as "a very superior and interesting woman" and mentioned (of course, inaccurately) his "several children—daughters." By great good luck, surprising perseverance, and patronage uncommonly munificent by American standards poor Brown succeeded "in burying all his friends and outliving all confidence in himself." He bemoaned the fact that there were no second editions of Brown and yet people would talk of their native literature. Then the critic wrote:

Some years ago, we took up Charles Brockden Brown; disinterred him; embalmed him; did him up decently; and put him back again—(that is—one of us did so.) Since then, poor Brown has had no peace, for his countrymen. We opened upon the North American creature, making him break cover; and riding after him as if he were worth our while. Then, but never till then (we were the first) did they give tongue, on the other side of the Atlantic. We puffed him a little. They have blown him up—"sky high." We went up to him, reverently; they, head-over-heels. We flattered him somewhat—for he deserved it and was atrociously neglected. But they have laid it on with a trowel. He would never have been heard of, but for us. They are determined, now, that we shall never hear of anything else. . . .

Then came the proposal for a handsome edition of the novels of this "Scott" of America, but none was brought out. To the critic *Clara Howard* and *Jane Talbot* were mere newspaper novels, "sleepy, dull, common-sense, very absolute prose," but *Arthur Mervyn* was better, especially the character Welbeck, whom Brown never later equaled; of *Edgar Huntly, Ormond,* and *Wieland*—they were "unfinished, irregular, surprising affairs." All were remarkable for vividness, circumstantiality, and startling disclosures; yet all were full of perplexity, incoherence, and contradiction. The author was critical of Brown's paucity of material, saying that he always clung "to one or two favorite ideas—the ventriloquist and the yellow fever." With all of his disparaging comments, he somewhat redeemed himself when he concluded that Brown was "the Godwin of America," that had he lived anywhere but in America, he would have been one of the most capital story-tellers, in a serious way, that ever lived, and that "it would be well for his countrymen to profit by his example. We want once more, before we die, to look upon the face of a real North American. God send that we may!"

Another critic called Brown "a good fellow, a sound hearty specimen of trans-Atlantic stuff, the American backbone—without knowing it." He was again called the imitator of Godwin. "He had no poetry; no pathos; no wit; no humor; no pleasantry; no playfulness; no passion; little or no eloquence; no imagination—and except where panthers were concerned, a most penurious and bony invention." But with all these things lacking, Brown had been able according to this critic to secure the attention of extraordinary men. Here is the heart of his interpretation:

His language was downright prose—the natural diction of the man himself—earnest, full of substantial good sense, clearness, and simplicity, very sober and very plain, so as to leave only the meaning upon the mind. Nobody ever remembered the words of Charles Brockden Brown; nobody ever thought of the arrangement; yet nobody ever forgot what they conveyed; you feel, after he has described a thing and you have just been poring over the description, not as if you had been reading about it, but as if you had just parted with a man who had seen it—a man whose word had never been doubted and who had been telling you of it—with his face flushed. He wrote in this peculiar style, not from choice, not because he understood the value or beauty of it, when seriously and wisely employed, but from necessity. He wrote after his peculiar fashion, because he was unable to write otherwise. There was no self-denial in it; no strong judgment; no sense of propriety; no perception of what is the true source of dramatic power (distinctness—vividness.)[10]

In the course of the article the critic pointed out various instances in which other writers had borrowed from Brown. Irving, he averred, took the description of the murderer's head from *Wieland;* Neal and Cooper stole his "catamounts and played the devil with his Indians." And that is what one leading British journal knew about Charles Brockden Brown.

In 1829 William Hazlitt, in a review of William Ellery Channing's *Sermons and Tracts,* made mention of Brown as one of the few American writers well known in England. While he admired Brown's defiance of petty criticism, Hazlitt deplored the "convulsive throes" and "banquet of horrors" presented to the reader; he described Brown as a man of genius, strong passion, and active fancy. But he was critical of Brown's ghosts, for such had never appeared in North America; "the night of ignorance and superstition which favors their appearance was long past before the United States lifted up their head." Compared with the novels of Scott, Brown's lacked ease and strength; the map of America is not historical, and works of fiction do not take root in it; for if fiction is to be good, it "must not be in the author's mind, but belong to the age or country in which he lives. The genius of America is essentially mechanical and modern."[11]

In 1858 a reviewer noticed the resemblance between Poe and Brown:

[10] *Blackwood's (Edinburgh) Magazine,* XVI (Oct., 1824), 415-428.
[11] *Edinburgh Review,* L (Oct., 1829), 125.

We are disposed to think that we can trace his [Poe's] inspiration in a great measure to the writings of Godwin and Charles Brockden Brown. There is in each the same love of the morbid and improbable; the same frequent straining of the interest; the same tracing, step by step, logically as it were and elaborately, through all its complicated relations, a terrible mystery to its source. These authors pursue events through all their possible involutions, but seldom deal with character. There is indeed a singular want of the dramatic faculty in all these eminent persons.[12]

Perhaps the most thorough analysis of Brown as a writer ever to appear in a British journal was an article by George Barnett Smith in the *Fortnightly Review* (1878). He began by saying that Charles Brockden Brown was an unfamiliar American literary critic, known only "by those who have an habitual curiosity about everything literary, and a becoming pride in all good writing which appears amongst ourselves (Americans)." He believed the almost unknown works of Brown should be recognized by a public then so liberally admiring Hawthorne. The works of Brockden Brown came second to those of Hoffman in the literature of the weird, and at the same time they surpassed Hoffman because of Brown's psychological subtlety in spiritual analysis. The author concluded his general estimate with these penetrating words:

To a daring imagination—the most singular and flexible, perhaps, yet witnessed amongst American writers—Charles Brockden Brown united a placid temperament and a contemplative intellect. Such a combination of seemingly discordant, and yet sharply defined qualities, is almost unique. Deep-rooted melancholy and the pathos of an apparently disordered mind distinguish the works of this author, and yet few men were happier in their lives, or more profoundly enjoyed the simple fact of existence; he coveted no complex pleasures or recreations; his greatest solace was Nature; and he extracted happiness from those commonplace pursuits which by most men of genius would have been deemed monotonous and insupportable. His creations are dire, astounding, terrible—his life was sedate, tranquil, serene.

Then followed a just analysis of the novels. Some of his observations are well worth attention as embodying a high appreciation of Brown's good qualities as well as a candid acknowledgment of his weaknesses; in fact, Smith's criticism is so thorough and so just in its discernment of the essential qualities of Brown's style that it has not been superseded to this day. The abiding impression left after a perusal of Brown's novels, the critic said, is that "of a singular and abnormal imagination," there being nothing else like them; the fulness and spontaneity of eloquence is matched only by Shelley's in poetry. Then he pointed to the many similarities and differences between Brown and Godwin—Brown being the reverse of Godwin's cold, calculating, precise, and diplomatic approach; Brown surpassed God-

12 "Edgar Allan Poe," *Edinburgh Review*, CVII (April, 1858), 419-426.

win in his soft, childlike disposition and his high moments of poetic exaltation.  He admitted that Brown overstepped the bounds of reality in such incidents as that of spontaneous combustion of the elder Wieland, but as an imaginary instance of that phenomenon the narration is at once "graphic and enthralling."  He observed that although there was some objection to "the exceptional manifestations of Nature" as legitimate material for the purpose of fiction, nevertheless Brown "conveyed an indelible lesson against all superstition":

Man is rebuked for his proneness to believe that he is worked upon by supernatural powers, and the crimes of Wieland are a protest against those hysterical religious feelings which may not always result in such dire calamities, but which—when cherished and brooded over—inevitably lead to the dethronement of reason.  In the hands of a tiro, the materials of which *Wieland* is composed would have resulted in a melodrama of the commonest and most pinchbeck order; but being infused by the spirit and power of genius, they are transformed into a gloomy and awful tragedy, in which the reader forgets for a time the incredibility of the incidents and the impossibility of the situations.

After a detailed analysis of Brown's leading novels, Smith concluded that they abounded in improbabilities and contradictions almost impossible to trace; that many episodes were wholly irrelevant; that certain passages were unsurpassed in beauty, eloquence, and dramatic effect; that his descriptions were graphic and picturesque—the account of the plague ranking with that of Boccaccio's plague of Florence and Defoe's plague of London; that except for Constantia Dudley, Brown's characters were stereotypes; that his work was devoid of humor; and that his plot construction had many deficiencies.
Yet the critic's final estimate was that

in Brown we not only behold a pioneer in the world of fiction, but one of the earliest of those writers who have endeavored to give a native tone and character to American literature. . . .  Like the great nation of which he formed a part, he was struggling with a youth of noble potentialities.  Hawthorne, Cooper, and others have since done more perfect work, but in none was there evidence of precisely the same latent original power.  He was the intellectual product of a people as yet in its nonage, and which stepped forth amidst the nations of the world with all the hope and elasticity of youth, yet lacking the stronger fibre of manhood.[13]

With but few reservations it might be successfully maintained that this interpretation by the Englishman has stood the test of time.  The discriminating and heartening reception in England was not paralleled in America for more than one hundred years.  It is the familiar story of the prophet in his own country.

[13] "Brockden Brown," *Fortnightly Review*, XXX (Sept., 1878), 399-421.

Only slowly, then, did Brown's countrymen come to appreciate or even understand his great gifts. In the *Port Folio* of his friend Joseph Dennie notices appeared from time to time with an occasional laudatory review of a novel, lamenting that more attention was given in England to American productions than at home, that critics in general treated American literature with delicacy and respect, and expressing deep regret at the gross misrepresentation in many of our "vulgar papers."[14] Dennie was appreciative of the fact that in "a very respectable British magazine for January, 1804," Brockden Brown had received honorable mention.[15] He expressed his pleasure that at that time Brown's "scrupulous purity of style, industrious habits, and knowledge of French idiom render him fully adequate to the task" of translating *Tableau du climat et du sol des États-Unis*.[16] Dennie was especially pleased with Brown's *American Register*, whose purpose it was to "preserve all valuable historical, state, and miscellaneous papers, to which every year gives birth. . . . This portion of his performance is entirely original; it is modelled after Burke's historical introduction, and it is written with great ability, and in a temper of utmost moderation."[17] At the time of Brown's death an unsigned poetic panegyric in the *Port Folio*[18] indicated the high esteem in which Brown was held by his countrymen. In the same periodical for July, 1811, appeared "a critique on the writings of Charles Brockden Brown," signed A. R.—one of the earliest critical articles to appear in an American journal on Brown's work as a whole; the author lauded Brown's novels and pointed out one fact that has been commonly ignored by critics even today: that his style, at first diffuse and awkward, gradually became vigorous and strong.

For almost a decade following his death little attention was paid to Brown's works. The Allen-Dunlap *Life* (1815) caused little stir, though in 1819 G. C. Verplanck seized the opportunity in reviewing the *Life* to write for the *North American Review* an appreciative criticism of Brown himself. The biography, he thought, was poor, for the authors failed to trace out the growth of Brown's mind or to set forth the merits and defects of his art. Verplanck began by saying that Brown owed his reputation to his novels, for unfinished and artistically crude as they were, they did show the character of the author's mind. Brown's lack of recognition sprang, no doubt, from his careless habit of composition as well as from the fact "that his subjects were too monstrous or too extraordinary for common sympathy." It is amusing to us today to read the frequent complaint that

[14] Joseph Dennie, *Port Folio*, III (June 4, 1803), 181.
[15] *Ibid.*, (April 28, 1804), p. 134.
[16] *Ibid.* (Aug. 25, 1804), p. 269.
[17] *Port Folio*, IV new series (Nov., 1807), 279.
[18] *Port Folio*, IV second new series (July, 1810), 287-290.

eighteenth-century America was no place for the setting of a romantic novel: there were no ruins, it was maintained, no dark mysterious "corners in the cities"; the people were normal, frank human beings, with little class consciousness; they did not even commit exciting crimes! How Brown, incorrigibly romantic, but determined to write novels about America, overcame these difficulties, Verplanck attempted to explain. Even though he had the courage to lay the scenes of his stories at home, he had not attempted to draw a peculiar American character, rarely depicting common life or ordinary events. "His power was usually of a moral kind; he established an inquisition to put the mind to torture; looks, tones, persuasions, threats, and dark insinuations are his instruments." Our interest is not in the event, he said, nor does the reader think of accustomed modes of living or ordinary experiences; but we "are held captive by the force of character, the intensity of intellectual suffering, the unrelenting perseverance of a spirit disappointed. . . . He selects minds that are strangely gifted or influenced, as if for the pleasure of exploring some secret principles of our nature, disclosing new motives of conduct, or old ones operating in a new direction." Sometimes, Verplanck added, Brown carried this minute mental analysis to the point of irksomeness, allowing the reader little opportunity to reach his own conclusions. When at last he plunged his characters into action, he exhausted both reader and actor by the intensity and terror of his descriptions of highly excited states of feeling. In Verplanck's opinion Brown was not an experienced observer of mankind; he did not see life steadily or see it whole. He saw only the tragic and the unusual, his views being of a singular kind only, and showing that he thought more than he observed. He believed that Brown's style, "clear, simple, and nervous," was unconscious in manner, the thought, not the form, being important to him. "There is no attempt at what is too vaguely called fine writing; no needless ornament, no sacrifice of spirit and energy from a weak ambition of harmony or finish, no use of a strictly poetical term to excite the imagination, when another and a simpler one will convey the meaning more definitely."[19]

In 1827 the *United States Review* carried an article that was laudatory of Brown's virtues and overcritical of his faults. Like the British reviewer, the author scolded America for insufficient appreciation of her young native writers, for letting twenty-odd years pass before even an imperfect edition of the works of our "long unrivalled novelist is given to the public." Although he called Dunlap's *Life* a "bulky work," he admitted that to it we are indebted for all that is known of Brown's life. Brown's melancholy tone and somewhat narrow range were not, the author contended, signs of deficiency; they merely sharpened the impact on the reader. The fact that Brown

[19] *North American Review,* IX (June, 1819), 58-77.

produced his work when most speculative minds were bent on pursuit of riches, or party politics, or the achievement of material success in other professions—when making writing a profession was held little better than being a drone—shows clearly the power of genius over circumstance. So strong was the melancholy cast of his mind, and so single was it in its purpose, "that of all men of imagination we know of none who appear from their writings to have looked so little at nature, or to have been so little open to its influences." In spite of this deficiency in Brown's genius, this want of variety, this narrowness of aim, the reader becomes somewhat reconciled to the improbabilities and the careless style and forgets that he is not reading some serious matter of fact. The critic again noted the similarity to Godwin, whom Brown surpassed in depicting characters; he dwelt on the mystical, the gloomy, the sorrowful, the melancholy, and the humorless quality of Brown's style. The reviewer criticized Brown's occasional lack of propriety, accusing him of recording unnecessarily realistic details; his heroines often displayed alarming frankness in declaring their love or receiving midnight callers, though acting in all innocence. Perhaps Brown was himself so frank and innocent that he was unaware of the temptations to which he was exposing his characters. Brown's use of realistic details was, however, a source of strength in giving verisimilitude. His minute descriptions, his tracing of the reason behind every act, even one as simple as lighting a lamp, produced a powerful impression of reality. His style, however! *That*, protested the critic, was almost too much, for Brown never used an Anglo-Saxon word if he could think of a Latin one—a statement that the facts do not warrant.[20]

Besides figuring in full-length articles, Brown was frequently mentioned in connection with other writers, especially Irving and Cooper. One critic credited Cooper with laying the foundation of American romantic novels; for Brown, who was gaining distinction both at home and abroad, never produced an American novel.[21] Another a few years later decided that Brown had made at least one "characteristically American" contribution. His pictures of Indians and Indian life had never been equaled even by Cooper, and probably never would be.[22] Again, in connection with Irving, Brown was called "a powerful and original writer" whose works have increased in fame since his death.[23] Another critic, noting that the popularity of Brown's novels had dropped in the circulating libraries, said they were not popular with the masses but with "the cultivated and reflecting classes of society." He predicted that "Brown will afford a mental

[20] Richard Henry Dana, Sr., "The Novels of Charles Brockden Brown," *United States Review and Literary Gazette*, II (Aug., 1827), 321-333.

[21] *North American Review*, XV (July, 1822), 281-282.

[22] *North American Review*, XXVII (July, 1828), 144.

[23] *North American Review*, XXVIII (Jan., 1829), 108-109.

repast, rich and noble, which can be excelled by none with which we are acquainted, in the whole regions of fictitious literature."[24] Admitting that Brown probably got the idea of his philosophical novels from Godwin, the critic said that Brown had carried them to new heights, creating "a school of romance highly magnificent and instructive." Recognizing Brown's very considerable skill as editor one author reiterated that Brown's fame was acquired by his novels, but he established several important magazines "with most praiseworthy industry, distinguished and various talent, and a very sober, enlightened, and generous spirit."[25]

In the *American Whig Review* of March, 1848, appeared an article, "Charles Brockden Brown," in which the author expressed his appreciation for the influence of Brown on him personally; he was sure that Brown's reputation abroad had paved the way for the transatlantic fame which many others had so abundantly enjoyed; he lamented the fact that Americans let Brown's works fall into neglect; he appreciated Brown's defiance of convention in giving chief place to passions other than love; in the truest sense Brown was original. Brown had an unusual knowledge of men, but "His chief power lay in tracing out from the deep hidden springs of the human soul—from the region of motives, and impulses, and purposes—a connected and consistent series of actions and events moving on to momentous issues"; in *Wieland* the critic saw "very plainly the working of a genius kindred to that which gave birth to the tragedy of Macbeth, and to the wild, frantic energies of the Moor of Venice"; however, despite his great admiration for Brown, this critic underestimated the value of the place he was to occupy in the history of literature.

But magazine writers were not the only critics who took note of Charles Brockden Brown's work. H. T. Tuckerman, in the *Sketch of American Literature* (1852), in crediting Brown with being the first American writer of romantic fiction, declared his novels to be eminently psychological; when the disadvantages under which they were written were considered, they deserved to be ranked among the "wonderful productions of the human mind. . . . Had his works been as artistically constructed as they were profoundly conceived and ingeniously executed, they would have become standard."[27] In his *Mental Portraits* (1853), Tuckerman, classifying Brown as "the Supernaturalist," discussed him as a psychologist and lover of the marvelous achieved by natural means. He stressed also the unfulfilled promise of Brown's immature writings. "We perceive in his writings," he said, "germs which under more cherishing influences would

---

[24] "The Novels of Charles Brockden Brown," *American Quarterly Review*, VIII (Dec., 1830), 312-337.

[25] *North American Review*, XXXIX (Oct., 1834), 295.

[26] *American Whig Review* VII, (March, 1848), 260-274.

[27] Appended to T. B. Shaw's *Outlines of English Literature*.

have expanded into glorious fruits . . . the pledge and the promise, as well as the partial realization of original intellectual achievement. . . . If we examine the writings of Brown, it is evident that they only rise to high individuality in the analysis of emotion, and the description of the states of mind.''[28]  Tuckerman was careful to note Brown's combination of the highly imaginative writing of his novels and the more practical, disciplined style of his journalistic and political works. Although practical people often have a love for mystery and the supernatural, they seldom write in both practical and imaginative fields. Brown's strongest point, the critic felt, was his power of psychological analysis.[29]

By way of summary of the first fifty years of American criticism of Brown we note much disparity of opinion.  It is significant that Brown's contemporaries considered his style elegant, pure, and unaffected, while later generations, with some exceptions, condemned it as Latinized, overscholarly, artificial, and melodramatic.  The ''elegant'' style of his novels was falling into disfavor even as he wrote, and most critics, unfamiliar with his later work, failed to note the gradual change in his journalistic writing to a more vigorous, unadorned style.  Reviewers have agreed, however, that his work was marred by haste and failure to revise, and they have felt that his writing showed more promise than attainment.  They have agreed that the major novels, with all their faults, possessed undeniable fascination and produced the feelings of despair and terror intended by their author.  Opinion has varied as to whether they were primarily motivated by a desire to philosophize or by a love of action.  Some maintained that Brown was an excellent psychologist and observer of people; others, that he did not know people sufficiently well to make the actions of his characters convincing.  Some admired his minute analysis of character and action, while others felt that he carried it to the point of tediousness.

The question of the native American quality of his novels was not discussed so much by American as by English critics, many American reviewers denying that even the scenery was typically American.  The characters, they have insisted, were not really American: they did not talk like Americans (or anyone else off the stage of melodrama); and the scenery was often so changed by his somber pencil as to be unrecognizable.  On the other hand, many—and among them the most astute—warmly praised him for his effective presentation of Indian life and native scenery, both urban and rural.

During the next fifty years, a dearth of Brown criticism is noted. Interest had shifted from the intrinsic value of his works to an interest in them as monuments of literary history and of patriotic pride.  In

[28] *Mental Portraits*, pp. 272, 281.
[29] *Ibid.*, p. 285.

1898 Professor George Edward Woodberry in the *Atlantic Monthly*[30] declared that Brown's novels possessed only historical interest, which lay in his reflection of the moods and ideas of eighteenth-century thinkers. Brown was ahead of his time, Woodberry observed, in trying to include local color, but his choice of subject matter precluded his producing truly realistic works. However, his idea of substituting the pseudo-scientific for the supernatural was a step forward. But Brown was "still under the shadow of the old castle" in his presentation of characters, action, and dialogue. Professor Woodberry perceived the "Byronic" element in Brown's novels, but it was the critic's perception of Brown's kinship with Shelley that has remained consistent with that of most Shelley scholars. It is one of Brown's distinctions that he advocated the rights of women to equal education and to a position of equal dignity intellectually with men. On the imaginative side Brown also touched the marrow, for he and Shelley alike were "extravagantly romantic." Therefore, said Professor Woodberry, "as a social philosopher, a romancer, and a dealer with curious quasi-scientific phenomena, Brown had a threefold interest to his youthful admirer." In concluding, Professor Woodberry indicates how completely out of sympathy he was with the earlier romantic novel, and how harshly he judged the realism which was fully exhibited in Brown's novels:

He was a romancer of the old kind, although he made efforts in the direction of realism; he has no art; he is awkward, long-winded, and melodramatic, interested almost wholly in adventure, and save for the accident of coming first and being a Philadelphian would be without note.

This unsympathetic attitude was not shared by all. Whittier, as already noted in an earlier chapter, gave high praise to *Wieland;* in discussing the dire effect of religious fanaticism on Wieland, Whittier commented on the terrible strength of the scene in which he heard a voice bidding him kill his wife, declaring that "in the entire range of English literature there is no more thrilling passage than that which describes the execution of this baleful suggestion. . . . The masters of Greek tragedy have scarcely exceeded the sublime horror of this scene."[31] Whittier felt that though the book possessed great strength and power, but no beauty, "its defects were compensated for by the strong moral—a warning to religious zealots."

### RENEWED INTEREST IN BROWN

The twentieth century has seen a revival of interest in Brown. The movement was initiated in 1904 by Martin S. Vilas in *Charles*

[30] George E. Woodberry, "Charles Brockden Brown," LXI (May, 1888), 710-714.

[31] *Writings*, VII, 393.

*Brockden Brown, A Study of Early American Fiction.* Besides analyzing the novels with some care the author made a scholarly attempt to examine Brown's literary background and his possible indebtedness to other writers and that of others to him. Brief articles and notices appeared sporadically thereafter. By 1920 the revived interest in Brown extended to practically every field of scholarship—history, politics, culture, literature. Indeed the early American author is at last being granted his rightful position as an outstanding pioneer of American culture. An examination into recent Brown scholarship will reveal a renewed interest in Brown not only as a pioneer but also as a literary figure of continuing significance. Scholarly editions of his works, learned articles on his sources and influence, biography, numerous theses and dissertations in our universities, and the increasing space devoted to Brown in recent literary histories and anthologies establish beyond a doubt Brown's high and secure place among American writers. An examination of the general bibliography in this text will show the truth of this statement. From a glance at all of these evidences of recognition it is obvious, then, that the interest in Brown is based not merely on his historical position but on the intrinsic worth of his writings and the wide appeal of his ideas. Brown is indeed not merely an ancestor: he is a figure firmly fixed on the literary horizon —a challenge to the present and an inspiration to the future.

# XII

# THE SUMMING UP

WE BEGAN THIS biography by declaring that Brown was primarily a philosopher concerned with interpreting to his countrymen the main currents of the social, political, and literary thought and ideals of his age. It has been the purpose of this biography not only to trace the course of his life but also to explain his life in terms of his thought.

The path of Brown's thinking was not smooth and broad like a modern highway, but was often narrow and tortuous. Yet despite the windings and false legends along the way, Brown moved relentlessly on to a goal which apparently he alone envisioned. To many of his contemporaries he seemed to be "voyaging through strange seas of thought alone." However, much of the seeming confusion was bound up with the many conflicting and divergent interests of the times. Brown suffered the fate of any pioneer in a changing world: there was hesitation and doubt on the one hand, and zeal and confidence on the other. To his everlasting credit Brown for the most part took a middle course. Early a disciple of the French Enlightenment and later a follower of the Godwins, Brown was firmly convinced that the source of social injustice and religious intolerance was to be found not in the original nature of men but in their social institutions—the church and the state. These two positive institutions were encrusted with the evils of selfish men and women who, firmly entrenched behind their hoary institutions, had waxed fat and strong and now refused to abdicate in the general interest or to surrender one iota of their power or privilege. But the new philosophy of democracy demanded abdication or surrender of at least a portion of that power and privilege. From the beginning Brown ranged himself definitely on the side of the people, and maintained that the democratic way of life could be realized if only man's acquisitive instincts and his selfish impulses could be directed into worthier channels. Education democratically shared, Brown argued in *Alcuin*, would change the very nature of man's social and religious outlook. Since the criminal is not criminal by nature but by reason of inheritance and environment, Brown maintained that it is logical if not inevitable that education could cure criminality and any other antisocial tendency. Parrington saw the picture in this light:

To an ardent young American like Brockden Brown, with the Hamiltonian struggle for power before his eyes, such a philosophy must have come with immense appeal. America confronted a future unmortgaged to the past; why should it repeat the old follies and mistakes that had reduced Europe to its present level? Here the pressure of vicious institutions was light as yet. Here the appeal to reason and justice was less hampered by selfish pre-emptions. Let social commendation be bestowed on the uncorrupted heart, on generous impulses, on native integrity of character. Let education be a natural unfolding of humane instincts, not a sharpening of wits to over-reach one's fellows. Let rewards go to frank, outspoken truth, rather than to chicanery and deceit. Inspired by such sentiments, Brockden Brown proposed to make fiction serve social ends.[1]

We seek to emphasize Brown's services to his country as a pioneer voice in behalf of the rights of women in the new nation, as a pioneer historian in the modern manner, as a pioneer in internationalism, as a pioneer social philosopher, as a pioneer literary critic, and finally as a pioneer professional man of letters.

Throughout these many activities Brown was essentially an interpreter. He interpreted America to herself and to the world, and the world to America; he held the mirror up to nature and showed his countrymen their comely or their horrid features. As editor of three successful magazines, as historian of some of the most momentous events in his country's history, as small businessman, as literary critic, and as novelist, Brown had a unique opportunity to see his country steadily and see it whole. He sensed the national genius, encouraging here and deploring there, as few men of his time did. His well-stored mind, his sense of historical development, and the salutary restraints born of Quaker honesty and respect for facts bred in him a dispassionate and disinterested attitude toward the great social, political, and religious movements of his day. With few notable exceptions Brown never allowed his personal sentiments or preconceptions to stand between him and his forthright expression of the truth as his mind gave him to see the truth. His advice, for instance, to his countrymen to take the Louisiana territory by force, if need be, cut squarely across his Quaker antipathy to war. To permit this vast territory to fall into hostile hands would be in the long run, he argued, a greater calamity than war. Again, liberal as Brown was at heart, he saw that a compromise between the liberal and conservative forces in the nation had to be effected for the general good. A handful of wilful men, he insisted, must never be permitted to get their hands on the governmental and educational helm and steer the nation into dangerous waters; nor must it be turned over entirely to the fickle will of the people. But his fundamental principles Brown would never compromise. He stood like a wall, as we have seen, against family and friends when his deeper convictions were challenged.

[1] *Main Currents in American Thought*, II, 189.

As a pioneer voice of the social and political trends in his country, Brown was farsighted. Like Jefferson he visualized America as extending from the Atlantic to the South Seas and embracing within her boundaries 300,000,000 souls by 1900. This same America, he declared, would eventually lead the world in the output of forge and loom as she would in the products of the soil. He predicted great strides in the nation's commerce and prophetically saw that it was precisely through the dominant role which trade would play that the world was destined to become One World. In this prediction Brown was more than one hundred and fifty years in advance of his time. As interpreter of the social and religious trends of his day, he was severely critical of the outmoded customs and manners transplanted by our forefathers to the New World, as he was keenly alive and receptive to the emergent new. Geopolitical as he was in thinking, Brown argued that new climate, new soil, and a heterogeneous citizenry had effected significant changes in the old patterns of thought and was transmuting itself into something rich and strange—a new civilization. He saw that the aristocratic concepts and social taboos of the Old World could not thrive in the open spaces and free atmosphere of the New. His advanced views on religion, for instance, helped to break down the medieval notion that it was sinful to marry outside one's own faith, just as his condemnation of religious fanaticism, in *Wieland,* was a powerful appeal to the common sense of his reader. Indeed, Brown was alarmed not so much at the breakdown of rational systems of religion as at the growth of highly emotional sects based upon merely individual religious experiences and finding their alleged sanction in the theology of St. Paul or St. Augustine, as manifested in such movements as Pietism in Germany and Methodism in England and America.

Brown saw that the new physical conditions and many other diverse influences in the New World called for democratic thinking and living. In a country in which the ordinary man might possess his own land and home and means of livelihood, where there was no cringing or genuflecting before the lord of the manor, a person could naturally breathe more freely and feel himself an equal among equals. There were as yet no sharecroppers and other economic slaves to disgrace his country before the world.

In vigorous and forthright terms Brown argued for the social, political, and economic emancipation of women. In this Brown was truly a pioneering voice in America demanding the application of democratic principles without regard to race or sex. Women must, he pleaded, be given equal education with their brothers so that they might become better citizens, wives, and mothers, and so that they might if they desired take their places in the professional life of the nation as teachers, as lawyers, as doctors, or even as preachers—an ideal which to this day has not been fully realized.

In his capacity as political observer and historian Brown was a pioneer voice in insisting upon primary sources and original documents as the sole basis of valid historical writings. This insistence characterized Brown as an historian in the best modern tradition. He pioneered in examining and weighing data before drawing conclusions, in sifting the evidence mercilessly before theorizing. His training in the law and his Quaker heritage had begotten in him respect for truth and candor in judging his fellow-men. His account of the conduct of Aaron Burr, for instance, is a superb piece of objective reporting on a subject surcharged with deep personal and national feeling. Notable, too, is the fact that Brown's style in his historical works is surprisingly simple and direct for one whose early essays and novels were characterized by verbosity, Latinity, and involved sentence structure. In his maturity Brown had in fact developed a prose style at once simple and appealing, direct and discursive, and though not so light as that of Addison or Steele, yet not so heavy as Gibbon's or Johnson's.

Brown was certainly the pioneer literary critic in the new nation, and he still stands in the front ranks of his country's literary interpreters. We have seen that he set his standards high and that he exacted both from himself and from others a severe observance of those standards. Mediocrity found no sympathy in his pen. Brown as the pioneer voice of literary criticism in America has until recently received too little attention from both his detractors and his disciples, but he is now coming into his own. One modern student comments:

His reviews in the magazines of which he was editor are often informative and penetrating. The writing of fiction was to him no haphazard matter despite the fact that he wrote always too rapidly and always without revision. He brought to his novels a surprisingly full knowledge of literary technique: from his various reviews one might gather a small treatise on the nature and art of fiction.[2]

That Brown took seriously his function as literary critic may be seen from the following excerpt:

The selection of a theme truly important, adorning it with the lustre of eloquence, supplying, with judicious hand, the deficiencies of history, in the statements of motives and the enumeration of circumstances; fashioning falsehood by the most rigid standard of probability, and suggesting to the readers beneficial truths, is the sublimest province that can be assigned to man. It is questionable whether verse be a more advantageous garb of such a theme than prose; but whatever superiority we ascribe to verse, this superiority is small. All that constitutes the genuine and lasting excellence of narratives; all the subtilties of ratiocination, the energies and ornaments of rhetoric, and

[2] *Wieland*, ed. F. L. Pattee, Introduction, p. xxvi.

the colors of description, are compatible with prose.  Numbers are an equivocal, or, at least, not an essential attribute of a moral and useful tale.[3]

But after all, Brown's work as critic was only ancillary to his role as America's first professional man of letters—as essayist, short-story writer, and novelist.  It is upon his work as novelist that Brown's fame has almost entirely rested.  Brown's claim to the title of father of American literature needs no defense.  His position likewise as a pioneer literary ancestor no one has risen to challenge.  To him as America's first professional writer must go the honor of having proclaimed the American declaration of literary independence, as also to him by virtue of his talents and his persistence will go the signal honor of having made good that declaration.

But Brown did not win his spurs easily: he had to work hard. Like Ibsen and Shaw after him, Brown had to fight valiantly to establish the "respectability" of his profession.  Feeling called upon to disarm the lingering prejudice against novel-reading, Brown offered the following defense of his profession:

My fancy has received more delight, my heart more humanity, and my understanding more instruction from a few novels I could name than from any other works.[4]

Brown did not need to apologize for his pioneering in the use in fiction of purely native material—American scenes and characters— for in this he enlisted the patriotic pride of all his countrymen.  In choosing to contrast the decadent civilization of Europe with that of the new nation he only added to that pride.  To effect this contrast Brown chose European criminals, usually Irishmen, and placed them in the society, commonly in the home, of innocent, unsophisticated Americans to work their mischief.  Brown's heroes were men of soaring passions and intellectual energy, who as a rule were in the service of a secret order, like the Masons or the Illuminati, and bent upon carrying forward a program of reform.  Brown foreshadowed the Nietzschean superman who considers himself beyond good and evil. To Brown good and evil were purely relative terms.  To the Newtonian concept of a moral universe governed by laws as inviolable as those in the physical world Brown was never a convert despite occasional evidence to the contrary.  In this respect he was not a child of the orderly eighteenth century but rather a child of the individualistic, democratic nineteenth—a romanticist.  Whatever their faults, however indistinct they may be, Brown's characters are individuals— not mere types—and the novels in which they move are, in a limited way, tracts for their time.  Though not objectionably didactic, his

---

[3] Article 9, Monthly Magazine I (June, 1799), 226-227.

[4] "Novel Reading," from "A Student's Diary," *Literary Magazine*, I (March, 1804), 405.

novels were assuredly works with a thesis. While the power of Brown's novels lies primarily in his consummate ability to create gripping plots and stirring scenes, this moral tendency cannot be overlooked, for it was by virtue of this tendency that his novels for the first hundred years after their publication made the strongest impression upon their readers.

Brown's method of approach in his novels is the method of the analyst. He piles up detail on detail, scene on scene; he explains motive, lays bare the soul, analyzes every action with a Defoe-like verisimilitude that holds the reader spellbound. In sheer power of gripping plots and masterful climaxes Brown has few superiors. His weakness, on the other hand, lies in his inability to resolve his plots and scenes into their realizable effects. His narratives are never straightforward: irrelevant details of all kinds are allowed to obtrude upon the reader's main interest. These defects are due in the main to haste, for it was Brown's habit to have more than one novel under way at once and to send parts of each to the printer before he had clearly thought out the various sequences. His work is characterized by an unfortunate mingling of crudeness and strength. However various the subject matter of Brown's novels, virtue in distress, virtue in the hands of a cruel and inexorable fate, is the central theme of each. Calvinism had spread its gloom and laid its deadening hand upon all human activity, and became the guiding impulse with Brown's characters.

As a pioneer voice in a revolutionary age, Brown was then a challenge to the future and a prophet of the America of the nineteenth and twentieth centuries. For his services as pioneer in American thought and ideals, in the advocacy of equal rights for women, in his argument for the abolition of Negro slavery, for his historical writings, for leadership in early national magazines, as literary critic, and finally as the father of the American novel, Brown has not received his full meed of praise. As Pattee expressed it:

Brown has been underestimated: he had powers that approached genius. It has been the commonplace to rate him as the strongest man in a feeble age, one who seemed brilliant because of the utter crudeness of the American wilderness into which his life had been cast. But Brown would have been a notable figure in any country and in any age. Had he been born in England and had the encouragement and the advice and the literary atmosphere that he needed he could not have failed even there to be a leading figure in his age. He had a creative imagination. He possessed the power, rare in any epoch, to originate new literary effects. . . . He had, more than this, the power to project his reader into the inner life of his characters; he was able to analyze and to dissect the springs of action; he had poetic vision that cast life into images of beauty; and he had that narrative enthusiasm, rare indeed, that seizes the reader at the start and hurries him despite himself breathless to the end of the tale.[5]

Charles Brockden Brown's place in American life and literature is secure. He was not a lonely figure in a barren period; his contemporaries were many and outstanding. Brown, however, was a star of a greater magnitude, whose light, though dim, still shines. Editor, literary critic, historian, and novelist, Brown firmly established himself as a worthy ancestor—as the pioneer voice of America.

[5] Pattee, *op. cit.*, p. xiv.

# APPENDICES

A. *DEVOTION: AN EPISTLE*

B. *AN INVENTORY OF THE PROPERTY OF
CHARLES BROCKDEN BROWN*

# APPENDIX A

## DEVOTION: AN EPISTLE

TO CALISTA

Thee, my Acasto, with her rarest gifts
Has Fortune Crown'd; to thee the bliss belongs
Which only Wisdom, of celestial birth,
Brings in her train; Wisdom, the daughter fair
Of God, all-wise and good, his eldest born,
Native of highest heaven, sojourned here
On earth with thee; for thee Devotion mild
Hath nightly visited, the noisy world
Aloof or slumbering, Heaven's all-seeing eye
Only awake; thy secret chamber she
Is used to visit oft; to raise thy hopes
And raptures to a pure seraphic height.
    The Muse, whom hymns devout and heavenly strains,
Meet for inspired lips and hallow'd ears,
Only delights; she whose resounding song
The world primeval heard, and those who dwelt
In bright abodes, ere the primeval world
Arose from Chaos; her benign regards
On thee hath shed, and upward led thy steps
To brighter worlds, where to thy eyes is given
Freedom to range abroad, and amplitude
The wide survey to comprehend, and send
Their steadfast glance to bounds where nature stands
Check'd by the dreary void, or mount to heights
Above all height, and inaccessible
By all of earthly kin, to all but thee,
And those of lot as happy, whom the voice
Divine, the herald of supernal grace,
Hath called; to whom the spirit devout and pure
Imparts her fiery energies, and gives
Infernal foes to vanquish, and to drag
In triumph at their chariot wheels, and raise
Illustrious trophies, sacred to the fame
Earn'd in hard conflict with the host of ills
That throng this mortal scene.
                O thou! what name
Befits the best, for not thy name is known,
Thy heavenly name; there are indeed, who know
Thy sacred footsteps, and (the mild behests

Oft by supernal grace consigned to thee)
Have witness'd thy approach at solemn hours.
Friend of devotion! dictatress of praise!
Mistress of heavenly minstrelsy! that rul'st
The choral symphony, when angels join,
On Heaven's high altars, their unclouded flame
To kindle, whence harmonious incense rolls,
Be just! thy hand be lavish still to pour
Thy bounties on Acasto; but to one
Confine not thy beneficence, but shed
On me thy inspiration; deign to hear
Another supplicant; nor turn away
Indignant, should he urge an equal claim
To gifts from thee, thy succor, when he lifts
In solitude his tuneful prayer.
                                    The youths
Whom sympathy of souls, consenting wills
Unite; alike by fortune scorn'd; to fame
Alike unknown; whom some prevailing power
Hath guided to the self-same path, and doom'd
Their cups to overflow with kindred ills;
Youths whom an equal fate condemns to waste
In dull obscurity their joyless days;
Victims of dark oblivion ere the prime
Of life ascend, ere the refulgent morn,
That rose so fair, yield to expecting noon
Her sway, noon that, alas! shall ne'er arrive.
Yet not to them their ruling fate denies,
Blest antidote of ill, the cure of all,
The solace, dearer to their hearts, than all
The splendor of renown, the pomp of power,
Or wealth drawn from o'erflowing mines, the boast
Of Cochin or Peru; their humble fate
Not hopeless, while a smiling ray serene
Illumes their dubious steps and paths obscure;
While Friendship, from her native seats descending,
Of holy rest, this lower scene for them
Her transient dwelling deigns to make: to those
Whom common griefs betide, one star malign,
O let thy precious gifts be common too!
    Thine are melodious breathings; thou canst call
Sounds of ineffable import, seraphic airs,
From harps, else mute, harps, unattun'd, unstrung,
And voiceless if unvisited by thee.
    Or if the harp be wanting, thou canst call
From energies unwarbled, strings untouch'd,
And viewless, nigh though far, though loud unheard,
A music fairer than the fairest child
Of voice and hand; than vocal ecstasies

More sweet, majestic more, and worthiest thee,
And thy impassioned votarist, who stands,
In sacred silence wrapt, adoring still.
    For twangling wires, loquacious, thrill the ear,
And shed a sweet intoxication round;
But thou and thy unwarbled raptures, cloth'd
In sanctity of silence, sweep along
On plumes of darkness o'er the untroubled waves
Of midnight air; thou lift'st to heights denied
To earth-born ministrelsy, in her best mood,
At her best hour, obsequious Night attending,
Adorn'd with all her stars, or with the moon
In peerless majesty, or star of Eve,
The bridal lamp, in modest pomp arrayed;
While, with the vocal lapse of streams, that chide
The busy resonance of sandy shores,
The solemn grove her stilly murmurs mingles,
And pipes, and strings, and voices sweet unite
To form the spell; but she of earthly mould
And mortal mother is, earth-born, earth-doom'd;
But thou, enshrin'd in starry tabernacle,
Of heavenly origin, the darling art
Of dread eternity! what wonder then
"Thy notes the soul, hers only charm the ear?"
    Thou standest at the door of Bliss, and guard'st
The holy vestibule from all profane
Intrusion: me, no wayward thought conducts,
Of pride and vain imagination bred;
No curious eye that in its boundless range
Must needs look in and see what strange or new
Religion's house contains; and whether those
Of elder times speak true, who hither call
Each way-farer, and urge his tardy step
By hanging in his view the token high
Of hospitable invitation fair,
With golden characters inscrib'd, that all
May read who list. "Lo! the abode
"Of Happiness; whoe'er is wise will knock;
"The porter ready stands to open; all
"Who ask will find."
            There is, who joys to find,
What, e'er he look'd, he was resolv'd to find,
The hope that leads to heaven, a flitting dream,
A meteor of the intellectual night;
A wild phantasm, child of a feverish brain,
Nursling of Ignorance, the gilded toy
Of doting Age, Age faltering and aghast,
That eyes the oblivious night, which lours at hand,
As children, fancy-struck, look on the void

Of cheerless dark, with thousand spectres throng'd.
Full freighted with discoveries, back he hies;
Of monkish dreams talks loud, and priestly craft;
Of miracles which none believ'd who saw;
Of mystic prophecies, a knotted maze,
Inextricate, obscure, inscrutable,
That must be first fulfilled, ere understood;
Of Fate, that made a world, and Fate that rules.

Not madly thus, and impiously, do I
Beyond the sphere of sense extend my view.
Without thee, mild Devotion, what on earth
Can give me aught but momentary ease?

The studious path have I not tried, and found
Joys bright, indeed, in prospect, but, alas!
Tasteless or bitter found, when to my lips
I fondly lifted the enchanted cup?
In Fancy's fairy land, my steps have long
Been wont to stray, where Schuylkill pours her tide
Twixt unaspiring banks, lowbrow'd, and rich
In naught but waving rushes, sight deform'd
And indelectable; o'er downs that stretch
On either hand, for many a weary mile,
By many an ox and many a ranging steed
Depastur'd, scenes that sober thought abhors;
Scenes unakin to beauty, health estrang'd,
But deck'd with orient charms, when Fancy wav'd
Her wand, and rent the veil which hides
Her soft retreats from vulgar gaze, and op'd,
In genial hues array'd, a prospect wide,
And scenes dear only to poetic eyes.

Not unattempted too th' historic page
Fraught with the spoils of hoary Time, and with
Th' accumulated lore of ages fraught.
Oft have I ranged the spacious round, and long,
In wonder wrapt, have listen'd to the tale
Of other times; of kings and heroes fam'd
For virtue, warlike or pacific; great
In fighting fields, or bickering senates, arm'd
In panoply of eloquence or steel;
The checker'd narrative of life and death
Political; the pedigree of states,
Trac'd high, and branching out a thousand fold;
Of cradled Greece, and Rome's infantile years;
Or when, the noon of life attain'd, she look'd
Proudly from her hill-top, and upward threw,
Exulting loud, her all-subduing arms;
Or rushing down the deep descent, when Time
The signal gave, th' abyss of death at last
Receiv'd her and her cumbrous train, a world.

Plain Nature, in her flowr'y paths, has long
Detain'd me, lost in her enchanting maze
Awhile; anon, delighted more to trace
The footsteps of Linnean guide, and out
Of such sweet prison wind me, by the clue,
Spun by Upsalian hands, conducted safe
Through pleasant paths: and long has been the march
And weary, through the thorny tracts that lead
To nothing in the metaphysic wilderness.
To trace the secrets of mysterious mind;
To tame the offspring, frolicsome and wild,
Of Fancy, in unwonted fetters bound,
And captive to the analytic power,
And fleeting Memory's capricious train;
Or thoughts, of dubious stock, and stubborn kind
(Link'd and unlink'd at random, starting now
A thousand leagues awry; eluding long
The yoke; which to impose my task enjoined;)
To teach to range, in firm phalanx, and form
The mystic dance spontaneous, and to move
Their files in beauteous order, quick to spy
Error, their lurking foe, or ardent wield,
In war with Sophistry, indignant arms;
To beat, with indefatigable heels,
Th' highway which Reason's oracle directs
The traveller to tread, who meditates
A journey from his own to other worlds,
Has oft been mine; nor have I fail'd to march
Newtonian banners under, war to wage
With Prejudice, intrench'd behind the mound
Of old Opinion, arm'd
With subtilties, whose force is known to all
And which a thousand victories attest.
At length, grown weary of the task, I left
Old Mathesis, his problems, and his scales,
To those who list, and sped to scenes of gay
And wild exuberance, where Fancy sports
At freedoom, doting on the specious worlds
That (mimicking Omnipotence) she builds,
Strengthens, embellishes, admires; anon,
Diverted by a newer freak, o'erturns
With headlong haste what she with equal haste
Had built; prone to abolish as create.
'Twas then I linger'd in the bright retreats
Where forms august or beautiful advance,
Called by the pencil's magic from the bounds
Remote of an ideal universe.
Oft in poetic I stray'd, and pluck'd,
With wanton hand, wreathes that disdain'd a date

Less than immortal; wreathes, by Phrenzy deem'd
(What less than Phrenzy could?) reserv'd for me.
Such is the fond delusive dream that haunts
The dream of youthful poet, far too prone
To banquet on futurity, and gild
His twilight with the splendor of renown,
And slow the glittering honors to resign,
Though snatch'd to decorate more worthy brows,
For his unfit.
           Oft has Achaia's tower'd pride
And Roman grandeurs fill'd my eager eye.
The dome that, rear'd aloft, repos'd in air
Sublime as Heaven's high arch, in tranquil state,
Majestic as a slumbering deity;
Or, springing upward, seemed averse to yield
Obedience to the power that check'd his flight
Audacious, and confin'd his foot to earth.
    How while I gaz'd aloft has wonder crept,
Slowly at first, with stealthy pace, along
My bosom, till, anon, the rapture rose
To dizzy heights: the eye too narrow seem'd
To grasp the vast design, the brain too small
To harbor the gigantic thought, that grows
At every glance; till, starting from my dream
Of ecstasy, the beatific dream,
Child of Vitruvian, and Paladian art,
The boast of ancient days, I hie me straight
To classic fields, where many a nodding tower
And crumbling arch remain to tell the tale
Of empires, time-engulf'd, and grandeurs fall'n,
The prey of barbarous rage, remain to charm
Th' enthusiastic eye. To Tedmor's wild
I bend my way, to ponder, where the hills
Hide in their mighty bosoms forms of old
Creation; such as giant arms have built;
Or, as the rover of the desert dreams,
The work of more than mortal hands; of sage
Enchanters, destin'd to survive the wreck
Of nations, and to stand while nature stands;
Proof against every shock but that which sounds
The signal of the general doom, the shock
That into primitive confusion hurls
This beauteous world. Here strayed I, while my soul
Revolv'd the mutable and transient state
Of things made up of mortal elements.
    The witcheries of music too, have oft,
Too oft, in chains of sweet enchantment led
My captive soul, too wise to spurn the yoke,
But with such thraldom pleas'd, while, far aloof,

The thoughts that brooded o'er disastrous scenes
Obeyed the melting voice and fled away;
Or ghastly Reminiscence ceas'd to haunt
My footsteps, sure to shun the forthright path.
　　But what avails it now to court the vain
Expedients, once indeed of force to lead
My thoughts astray from anguish, potent once
To charm the weariness of pilgrim steps?
But now the spell has lost its power; no more
Fancy breeds wings to reach celestial heights.
Supernal spirit, thou must show the way;
Withheld be not thy succor, else shall Hope
Desert me; she already shakes her plumes,
Prepared for flight. Dark, desolate, and void,
And dreary is the temple of my soul:
Dispenser of the good I crave! descend,
This void replenish, and dispel this dark.
　　Fair friend, for friend to every good thou art
And blameless plan; thou, where thy Maker leads
Wilt follow swift; thy guide is he who loves
Each sign of meek repentance, and whose ear,
Propitious to the good, is bent to catch
Th' aspirings of a soul devoutly raised;
The voice of trembling hope to heaven, and Him
That there inhabits, highest, holiest, best,
That God, whom, in all else, the pattern pure
Thou deemest, and high example, safest guide
Of erring man (beacon, whose sacred lamp
Darts through this drear expanse of stormy waves
A ray serene, propitious to detect
Encircling perils, and disclose the sands
Insidious, and the hostile shore, and rocks,
Whose thundering echoes menace high, and send,
Aided by ruffian blasts, defiance far);
Thou to the good will prove, like Him, a friend:
If but a spark appear to glimmer there,
Where, ere the spark was kindled, single night
Prevail'd, and thou canst foster it, and raise
A flame that points to heaven, thy aid will not
Be wanting; O! to me impart that aid!
　　If gentle intercourse, benign regards,
The interchange of words that know no guile;
Such words as Friendship in her glowing mood
Will furnish to the lips and eyes of those
That own her righteous sway; if these avail
To lift the eye to virtue, and dislodge
Ill thoughts from their strong holds, where long they held
The sceptre, and maintain'd disast'rous sway,
And kept their gloomy court, wilt thou withhold

The succor sought? for know'st thou not the force
Contagious of a fair example, set
By Virtue femininely cloth'd, and deck'd
With charms that hover only round the shrine
Of lovely woman, loveliest, when, amidst
Her radiant sphere, by mystic notes and high
Led on, the muses and the graces meet,
To mingle energies and mingle charms;
When in her train are seen, in heavenly guise,
Impassion'd Innocence, with Candor link'd,
That never smiles, but thousand hearts are touch'd
With glowing adoration and sweet awe,
Resistless yoke imposing? Know'st thou not
The potency of precepts, dropped from lips
Rever'd and lov'd? By Virtue's charms enthrall'd,
To beauteous sanctity no stranger I
Ere long will be, if fondest Hope deceive
This heart no more; if thou, fair maid, appear,
Soft advocate, yet irresistible
In Virtue's cause; if thou, preceptress mild,
Wilt deign a pupil in Devotion's school
To prompt; his erring steps to check; his right
To urge; when, by Temptation led astray,
The warning voice, that whispers still "Beware,"
The inward oracle, whose "still, small voice"
Wafts to the hallow'd ear divine behests
And speaks in vain, unheard or disobey'd,
And would though thunders spoke: be thou at hand
To hurl rebuke from thy indignant eye.

But when, observant of the track prescrib'd,
Heaven smiles, to deeds of men a witness high
And holy, a mysterious judge unseen,
Be thou a witness too, and also smile,
Approving; let the music of thy praise
Be heard: how sweetly will its murmurs flow,
How sweetly sink into his ravish'd ears!

And, O! too highly honor'd will he deem
His lot; yet stronger plum'd his hope will soar,
And nearer heaven's high threshold take her stand,
If thou, fair maid, a higher claim admit
Than humble pupilage, should add to these
A privilege more sweet, yet blameless; ties
Of dearer kindred, yet austere and chaste;
Bonds that, in blest equality unite
Consenting minds; the death-surviving bonds
Of amity, *unwedded, passionless.*

Accept in recompense, if aught can be
A not unworthy recompense; accept
A thousand grateful fervors, and what else

(Its savageness subdu'd, and call'd, though late,
To blest fertility, by balmy dews,
Shed by propitious Friendship) forth may throw,
Accounted not of thy accepting hand
Unworthy: slender is indeed the boon
Of Nature's sparing hand, wise to dispense,
Frugal and circumspect, what, when bestow'd,
She knows not whether or to good or ill
May furnish arms. Her eyes abated naught
Of rigorous regard, and cold, but scoul'd
A cheerless glance, and louring, when on me,
New cradl'd, and, as yet, unvisited
By light of Reason's morn, their orbs were turn'd.
    Oft o'er the margin of thy natal stream
I stray'd of late, the moon my lamp; and oft
Beneath the shady copse that skirts her shore
Found refuge from the noon-tide's fiercer ray:
A haunt to musing sacred, dear to those
Who meet, in solitude, a friend that opes
The door to solemn thoughts, and lifts the veil
That to the pensive votarist denies
Communion with his own sad heart; a scene
By its own charms endear'd to those who seek
No dwelling more delightsome than the green
Abodes of Nature, unmolested yet
By Art. To those retreats, it was but late
That Chance my steps conducted; if to Chance
I owe the boon; not rather to the hand
Of some aerial guardian, wise and good,
Supernal friend. For shall I not adore
The hand unseen, that led to these retreats
A wanderer I, and reckless which the track,
If, friendly to forgetfulness, it gave
To meddling thoughts a respite, or deceiv'd
A moment of its customary freight
Of dark repinings; when the only bliss
Was not to feel; since the distracted mind
Immanael'd by some infernal spell,
A vassal to some necromantic power,
Could 'scape not from the mirror, which upheld
Before her startl'd eye, and show'd her naught
But her own image, ghastly and deform'd
By many a boisterous passion, prone to ill;
Flagitious, by a sable troop beset
Of bad intents.
              O! shall I not adore
The guidance which, with radiant finger, points
To these divine abodes, where troublous waves
The chiding of the torrent stream, that leap'd
From rock to rock, and clamor'd as in rage,

Assail no more the shatter'd bark, so long
By temptest tost, but, opening to the view
　Of eyes devout the happy isle at last!
Night's shady curtain rising, death achiev'd,
The grave in triumph past, the happy isle
Is seen, the haven of eternal rest,
Where ministers of ill molest no more
The good, and weary Virtue finds repose.

　Not hither unobserv'd of Heaven I came;
Of some bright habitant of starry worlds,
My patroness and friend; for such there be,
Or much I err, by parent Heaven decreed
To each immortal mind, enclos'd in clay:
A gentle Deity, of mild intents
And charitable, one whose lot, assign'd
By wisest Providence, is only good
To foster, and to screen from guilt the soul
Her sacred charge, against infernal arms
To shield the conscious pupil, if aright
He use the proffer'd bounty, nor reject
The whisper'd admonition sent to save.

　'Twas here that first my eyes beheld
My mystic guide, my genius, my divine
Instructress, better angel, heavenly friend,
Ethereal messenger, with Heaven's behests
Encharg'd; my heart and fancy's queen, my muse;
A mortal shape assuming, here she stept
Forth from an azure cloud, in flowing vest
Arrayed, of dazzling hues, with locks that play'd,
Though in bright circlet bound, and threw around
A fragrance, overtasking mortal sense:
Light from above her harbinger, her train
Melodious airs, with every symbol deck'd,
Of beatific power: she came, she stood
Before me, visibly; these wakeful eyes
Beheld her, in her borrow'd shape how fair!

　Or, haply, I but dream'd; for, o'er the world
Meek Twilight, stealing from her western cave,
With progress unobserv'd, dumb steps and slow,
Had thrown her sober mantle; Nature slept;
And hush'd was all the air: but Silence breathes
A more resistless spell, when leagu'd with sounds
That haunt the leafy covert, sounds unown'd
By earth or air; sounds that await the beck
Of Echo, who delights in fostering glooms,
And bowers canopied by intertwin'd
And verdant branches; and, abhorring rest,
Will bandy hollow noises with herself,
If other work be wanting: shrouded here,
May better prove than barren thanks the soil

She caught the floating murmur most akin
To silence, winding through the rocky maze:
That for its wave no rest was found, was heard,
But heard afar.
                    In this recess I sat
And saw, or dream'd I saw, an airy shape,
And heard aerial notes, a voice that far
Outwarbled dulcet breath that whispers love
At bridal hours; outtalk'd impassioned strings
Kiss'd by enamor'd fingers, or by airs
Æolian kiss'd, it sung, and this the song:—
But whither would thy steps, advent'rous youth,
Lead thee? Who told thee that Calista's ear
Would deem the accents of thy friendship sweet?
Nor dress her eye in terrors, when thou com'st
Before her in this questionable shape?
      Thou knowest not whether to thy strains she lend
Benign attention, and, dispos'd to hear
The dictates of thy inoffensive muse,
Smil'st on thy artless efforts; nor withhold'st
Her hand, if, from thy unexhausted store,
Hereafter thou select a tribute new
For her, the incense of a guileless heart,
And fancy touch'd by no polluted flame.
Whether, in Decorum's mounds entrench'd,
Suspicions guard the door, and wary watch
Keep, that no lurking foe have entrance there
To trouble their enchanted queen, that sits
In dreary state, with icy fetters bound
Of cold punctilio; scornful she reject
Thy humble lay, and blast the infant hope
Erewhile so blithesome. Here, oh, most rever'd
And gentlest of thy sex! Oh, most belov'd!
Though with such love as angels smile to see
In those whom sex distinguish not, the love
That boasts participation with divine
Existences; soul thraldom; reason leagu'd
With reason, to improve the structure fair
Of knowledge; heart with heart allied to nurse
The plants, whose golden fruits, transplanted when
To heavenly ground, shall smile with orient hue,
And shed eternal fragrance. Here thy friend
(For such himself will deem whate'er decree
Thy sternness shall pronounce), thy pupil here,
In not untremulous suspense shall stand,
Till thou, in thy own time, transmit the pledge
Of peace, or enmity: nor leave thou him
Bewilder'd long in doubtful maze, and lost
In fears, that his audacious lay has come
Too soon, or late, and no acceptance found.

# APPENDIX B

## AN INVENTORY OF THE PROPERTY OF
## CHARLES BROCKDEN BROWN

Among the private papers of Charles Brockden Brown is an inventory of Brown's property at the time of his death, drawn up by Elizabeth Linn Brown and Elijah Brown as administrators of the estate. They gave bond for $10,000, and Mrs. Brown testified that the total property of her husband did not exceed $5,000. The inventory shows that there was the sum of $451.83 in the bank and that the remaining property amounted to $1187.50, consisting largely of household goods. What the value of the dollar was in 1800 in terms of present-day currency cannot be accurately determined, but it was likely considerably greater. Circumstantial evidence would seem to indicate that only a small portion of this property was derived from his mercantile business. Apparently Brown owned no real estate.

Contrary to generally received opinion, Brown was not a failure financially as America's first professional man of letters. Even a hasty glance at the inventory would show that Brown provided a comfortable living for his family; in fact many of his household effects were comparatively sumptuous.

But what is more important, a study of the various items gives an intimate picture of Brown's household. Reading down the list, one can almost imagine himself a guest in the home. Can't you see yourself stopping before that twenty-five dollar "pair of window curtains" or pausing to get the "feel" of that forty dollar "sopha," or gaming around one of those expensive card tables? Is that six-dollar bust the likeness of his beloved Milton? You wonder why *one* breakfast table and *two* dining tables, and conclude that the Brown family did nothing but eat! Can't you imagine yourself gazing at one of Brown's "powdering tubs"? And why, you say, those two dozen *empty* bottles in the home of a teetotaler!

### [Living room and Dining room]

| | |
|---|---:|
| 1 Ingrain carpet .........................................$ | 20.00 |
| 1 Looking glass ........................................... | 15.00 |
| 8 Rough Bottom chairs .................................... | 10.00 |
| 1 Sopha .................................................. | 40.00 |
| 2 Mahogany card tables ................................... | 18.00 |
| 1 picture ................................................. | 10.00 |
| 1 pair andirons, shovel, and tongs ......................... | 10.00 |
| 1 wire fender ............................................ | 3.00 |
| 1 fire rug ................................................ | 3.00 |
| 1 plated lamp ............................................ | 3.00 |
| 1 pair window curtains and cornices ........................ | 25.00 |
| 2 coquelicot waiters ...................................... | 4.00 |
| 1 foot-bench ............................................. | 5.00 |

1 small medal ............................................... .50
1 bust ..................................................... 6.00
1 pair snuffers and tray ................................... 5.25
1 ingrain carpet .......................................... 10.00
1 looking glass ............................................ 5.00
1 side board .............................................. 25.00
1 breakfast table .......................................... 7.00
1 mahogany stand .......................................... 4.00
5 Windsor chairs .......................................... 10.00
3 Venetian blinds ......................................... 12.00
1 tea chest ............................................... 3.50
4 common Japan waiters .................................... 2.00
1 pair andirons and shovel and tongs ...................... 5.00
1 pair plated candlesticks................................. 3.00
1 pair snuffers and tray .................................. .75
1 bellows ................................................. .50
2 dining tables ........................................... 14.00
1 entry and 1 stair carpet ................................ 4.00
1 entry lamp .............................................. 3.00
3 tin cannisters and 1 demijohn ........................... 3.50
1 pair green baize ........................................ 1.50
1 large writing desk ...................................... 15.00
1 portable desk and table ................................. 4.00
1 Rees's Cyclopedia (ten volumes in calf) ................. 66.00
200 other books ........................................... 165.00
5 maps ................................................... 15.00

### [Master Bedroom]

1 carpet ................................................. 6.00
2 dressing glasses ........................................ 6.00
2 bureaus ................................................ 24.00
1 high post mahogany bedstead ............................. 12.00
1 suite of bed curtains ................................... 15.00
3 window curtains ......................................... 15.00
1 pair andirons and shovel and tongs ...................... 3.00
1 crib and bed ............................................ 5.00
1 low post bedstead ....................................... 3.50
3 paper window curtains ................................... .30
1 cradle ................................................. 3.00
2 feather-beds, bolster, and pillows ...................... 32.00
6 chairs ................................................. 4.50
1 wash stand and water kettle ............................. .50
2 rocking chairs .......................................... 1.00
5 children's chairs ....................................... 2.00
1 low bedstead ............................................ 3.00
1 carpet ................................................. 3.00
6 Windsor chairs .......................................... 4.00
1 Field bedstead .......................................... 4.00
1 feather bed and bolster ................................. 10.00

| | |
|---|---:|
| 1 washstand and water kettle | 1.50 |
| 1 pair andirons shovel and tongs | 3.00 |
| 1 bureau | 4.00 |
| 1 stone bog-log | 1.00 |
| 1 wooden table | .25 |

### [Children's Bedroom]

| | |
|---|---:|
| 1 baize carpet | 1.00 |
| 1 bureau | 12.00 |
| 1 dressing glass | 1.50 |
| 1 Field bedstead | 8.00 |
| 4 rough bottom chairs | 3.00 |
| 2 toilette tables | 1.00 |
| 1 Patient wool mattress | 5.00 |
| 1 single feather bed | 10.00 |
| 1 cot | 1.00 |
| 1 wash stand and pitcher | 2.00 |
| 3 crib covers | 2.00 |
| 13 pair sheets | 20.00 |
| 10 pair pillow cases | 5.00 |

### [Furnishings, etc.]

| | |
|---|---:|
| 5 pair blankets | 15.00 |
| 12 napkins | 3.00 |
| 12 common towels | 1.00 |
| 10 bedcovers | 18.00 |
| 1 gold watch | 40.00 |
| 1 pair castors | 3.00 |
| 42 ounces of silver | 52.00 |
| plate ware | 30.00 |
| china and glass | 16.00 |
| 1 library share [Brown was a member of the Library Company] | 30.00 |
| 1 large trunk | 2.00 |
| 1 small trunk | 1.00 |
| 1 portmanteau | 1.00 |
| 1 pair window curtains | 3.00 |
| 12 table cloths | 12.00 |
| 2 pair bureau covers | 1.00 |
| 1 rag carpet | 2.00 |
| 1 large drawing table | 1.50 |
| 1 small table | .75 |

### [Kitchen]

| | |
|---|---:|
| 5 iron pots | 2.00 |
| 1 wash kettle | 2.00 |
| 17 articles of tin ware | 3.00 |
| 2 pairs flat irons | 1.00 |
| 5 candlesticks | 2.00 |
| 1 coffee and pepper mill | .50 |
| 2 grid-irons | .50 |

| | | |
|---|---|---:|
| 1 | bake oven | .75 |
| 1 | frying pan | .50 |
| 4 | pot-hooks | .35 |
| 1 | pair andirons and shovel and tongs | 2.00 |
| 5 | tubs | 2.00 |
| 2 | buckets and 1 pail | .50 |
| 2 | powdering tubs | 2.00 |
| 1 | bake iron | .50 |
| 2 | clothes horses | 1.00 |
| 1 | clothes line | .10 |
| 1 | rolling pin | .10 |
| 1 | clothes basket | .50 |
| 1 | market basket | .25 |
| 1 | chopping knife | .15 |
| 1 | toaster | .10 |
| 1 | bench | .10 |
| 2 | chopping dishes | .30 |
| 1 | warming pan | 1.00 |
| 2 | dozen empty bottles | 1.00 |
| 1 | Japan tray | .10 |
| 1 | knife | .10 |
| 2 | dozen knives and forks | 1.50 |
| 1 | broom | .20 |
| | crockery | 3.00 |
| 6 | chairs | 4.00 |
| 1 | wheelbarrow | 1.00 |
| ½ | cord of wood | 2.50 |
| | wearing apparel | 124.00 |
| | Funds in bank | 451.83 |
| | **Total** | **$1,641.33** |

# SELECTED BIBLIOGRAPHY

WORKS OF CHARLES BROCKDEN BROWN

*Manuscripts* (all the manuscripts listed below are being edited for immediate publication):

A. Unpublished Brown manuscripts, now in the possession of Mrs. Emilie B. Reiff of Philadelphia:

1. "Don Manuel," 32 pp., 8 x 10, being a part of a novel.
2. Henrietta Letters, 68 pp., 7 x 9, being letters to and from Henrietta G., copied into a notebook or journal.
3. "Journal," 32 pp., 7 x 8, of a philosophical nature and on a variety of subjects including the Ellendale Letters.
4. "Journal" or "Notebook," 29 pp., containing essays on diet, music, poetry, physical exercise, progress of knowledge, together with a large number of architectural drawings, and mathematical calculations.
5. Brown's Letters to Elizabeth Linn, 95 pp., 5 x 7¾. There are 38 letters, many of them in journal form—there being separately dated portions of a single letter.
6. Brown-Wilkins Correspondence. Letters from William Wood Wilkins, 50 pp., 7 x 8. There are 14 letters in this group. They shed much light on Brown's early formative years. Brown's Letters to Wilkins, 12 pp., 7 x 8. There are 3 letters (important). Note: Nos. 2, 3, and 4 are in a single notebook, in minute handwriting. Part of this correspondence was published in the University of Texas *Studies in English*, XXVII, No. 1 (June, 1948), 75-107.

B. Other manuscripts in the William Linn Brown Collection:

1. "Contract for Publishing a Geography," 3 pp., 6 x 12.
2. "Contract for Publishing Life of Brown," 1 p., 10 x 12.
3. "Agreement with Paul Allen for Completing Geography."
4. "Rough Notes of Travels," 26 pp., 11 x 18. Long thought to be the Geography, but not Brown's.
5. "Obituary Notice," probably in Mrs. Brown's handwriting.
6. "Deed to Land in Virginia," in French, 4 pp., 10 x 15. This item I translated and published in the *Virginia Magazine of History and Biography*, LIII (April, 1945), 127-131.
   Note: Among the above manuscripts is a printed circular, "Proposals for Printing the Life of Charles B. Brown."

C. Other Brown Manuscripts:

1. In the Library of the Pennsylvania Historical Society:
   a. "Medwaye," 2 pp., portion of an early draft of *Jane Talbot*.
   b. Letters:
      (a) Brown to William Johnson, 1794.
      (b) Brown to Dunlap, 1798.
      (c) Brown to Mrs. Brown, 1806.

2. In Haverford College—Letters:
   a. Brown to James E. Hall, May 8, 1801, concerning *Jane Talbot*.
   b. Brown to James E. Hall, 1806, concerning contributions to the *Literary Magazine*.
3. In the Library of the Library Company of Philadelphia—Letter: Brown to his brother James Brown, Oct. 25, 1796.

D. Related Manuscripts:
1. William Dunlap's "Diary":
   a. In Yale Library.
   b. In New-York Historical Society.
   Note: Of the thirty-odd volumes of the Dunlap Diaries, the whereabouts of only eleven are known; of these, six are in the Yale Library and five in the Library of the New-York Historical Society. The eleven volumes were published in 1930 by the New-York Historical Society. For full details, see the Introduction to this publication.
2. The Elijah Brown notebooks in the Pennsylvania Historical Society.
3. Elihu Hubbard Smith's unpublished Diaries (1794-1798), at one time on deposit in the Yale Library, are now in the possession of Miss Francis G. Colt.
4. Norris and Shippen manuscripts in Pennsylvania Historical Society Library, Philadelphia.

*Editions: Fiction*

A. Published:
1. *Wieland; or The Transformation*, New York, T. & J. Swords, for H. Caritat, 1798.
2. *The Man at Home* (serialized in the *Weekly Magazine*, Philadelphia, 1798; never published in book form).
3. *Ormond; or The Secret Witness*, New York, 1798, 1799.
4. *Arthur Mervyn; or Memoirs of the Year 1793*, Philadelphia, 1798. In two parts, as separate novels.
5. *Edgar Huntly, or The Memoirs of a Sleepwalker*, Philadelphia, 1799.
6. *Clara Howard; or The Enthusiasm of Love*, Philadelphia, 1801. Published in England as *Philip Stanley*.
7. *Jane Talbot*, Philadelphia, 1801.
8. *Memoirs of Carwin, the Biloquist, and Other American Tales and Pieces*, London, 1822.

B. Unpublished:
1. "Skywalk," now lost, but parts of it were used in other novels.
2. "Don Manuel."

C. Fragments (published in Dunlap's *Life*, 1815):
1. "Thessalonica: A Roman Story."
2. "The Scribbler."
3. "Stephen Calvert."
4. "Jessica."
5. "Adini."
6. "Sketches of the History of Carsol."
7. "Sketches of the History of the Carrils and Ormes." Note: Nos. 2, 3,

and 4 were included in *Memoirs of Carwin,* London, 1822; the others were published in Dunlap's *Life* (1815).

*Miscellaneous Works:*

A. *Alcuin; a Dialogue on the Rights of Women,* New York, 1798.
B. *Monroe's Embassy . . . or The Conduct of the Government in Relation to our Claims to the Navigation of the Mississippi Considered,* Philadelphia, 1803. Signed "Poplicola."
C. *An Address to the Government of the United States, on the Cession of Louisiana to the French* . . . Philadelphia, 1803 (Anon.). Corrected, revised, London, 1803.
D. *The British Treaty,* Philadelphia, 1807. (Anon., probably not Brown's.)
E. *An Address to the Congress of the United States on the Utility and Justice of Restrictions upon Foreign Commerce,* Philadelphia, 1809.
F. "Sketch of the Life and character of John Blair Linn," first published as the Introduction to an edition of Linn's *Valerian, a Narrative Poem,* Philadelphia, 1805; republished in the *Port Folio,* Jan.-March, 1809, 21-29, 129-134, 195-203.

*Translation:*

A *View of the Soil and Climate of the United States of America with Supplementary Remarks upon Florida, on the French Colonies of the Mississippi and Ohio and in Canada; and on the aboriginal tribes of America;* by Comte de Volney. Translation and Notes by C. B. Brown, Philadelphia, 1804.

*Collected Editions:*

A. *The Novels of C. B. Brown,* Boston, 1827. With a Memoir of the author.
B. *The Novels of Charles Brockden Brown,* Philadelphia, 1857. With a Memoir of the author.
C. *Complete Edition of the Novels of C. B. Brown,* by David McKay. Philadelphia, 1887. With a memoir of the author.

## Magazines

(Of which Brown was the editor and to which he was the chief contributor.)

A. *The Monthly Magazine and American Review,* New York, Vols. I-III, April, 1799-December, 1800.
B. *The Literary Magazine and American Register,* Philadelphia, Vols. I-VIII, 1803-1807.
C. *The American Register, or General Repository of History, Politics, and Science,* Philadelphia, Vols. I-VII, 1806-1810.

## BIOGRAPHY

A. Clark, David Lee. "Charles Brockden Brown, A Critical Biography," a privately published abstract of an unpublished Columbia University dissertation, Austin, Texas, 1923.
B. Dunlap, William. *The Life of Charles Brockden Brown;* together with Selections from the Rarest of his Printed Works, from his Original Letters, and from his Manuscripts before Unpublished. 2 vols. Philadelphia, 1815.

Note: Paul Allen began the *Life* and William Dunlap completed it.

C. Prescott, W. H. *Life of Charles Brockden Brown* ("American Biography," Vol. I, ed. Jared Sparks). Boston, 1857.

D. Warfel, Harry R. *Charles Brockden Brown, American Gothic Novelist*. Gainesville, Fla., 1949.

### CRITICISM

Adams, James Truslow. *The Epic of America*. Boston, 1932.

Allen, James S., ed. *Selections from Thomas Paine*. New York, 1937(?).

"American Pioneer of the New Psychic Romance," *Current Opinion*, LXIV (April, 1918), 278.

"American Writers," *Blackwood's Edinburgh Magazine*, XVI (October, 1824), 415-428.

Beard, Charles A. and Mary R. *A Basic History of the United States*. New York, 1944.

Bernard, John. *Retrospections of America, 1797-1811*, ed. Brander Matthews. New York, 1887.

Blake, Warren B. "Brockden Brown and the Novel," *Sewanee Review*, XVIII (October, 1810), 431-443.

Blankenship, Russell. *Amercian Literature as an Expression of the National Mind*. New York, 1931, pp. 241-242.

Boykin, Edward, ed. *The Wisdom of Thomas Jefferson*. New York, 1941.

Boynton, Percy H. *A History of American Literature*. New York, 1919, 100-109.

――――. *Literature and American Life for Students of American Literature*. New York, 1936, 198-203.

Brinton, Howard H., *Quaker Education in Theory and Practice*. Wellingford, Pa., 1940.

Brown, Herbert Ross. *The Sentimental Novel in America*. Durham, N. C., 1940.

Calverton, V. F. *The Liberation of American Literature*. New York, 1932, pp. 94, 210, 221.

"Carwin and Other American Tales," *New Monthly Magazine and Literary Journal*, VI (May, 1822), 222.

"Carwin and Other Tales," *Gentleman's Magazine*, XCII (1822), 622.

"Charles Brockden Brown," *American Whig Review*, VII (March, 1848), 260-274.

Clark, David Lee. "Brockden Brown and the Rights of Women," *University of Texas Bulletin*, No. 2212 (March 22, 1922).

――――. "Brockden Brown's First Attempt at Journalism," University of Texas *Studies in English*, No. 7, 1927, 155-174.

――――. Introduction to an Edition of *Edgar Huntly*. New York, 1928.

――――. "Sources of Poe's 'The Pit and the Pendulum,'" *Modern Language Notes, XLIV* (June, 1929), 349-356.

――――. "Unpublished Letters of Charles Brockden Brown and W. W. Wilkins," University of Texas *Studies in English*, XXVII, No. 1 (June, 1948), 75-107.

Clark, Harry H. *Poems of Freneau*. New York, 1929.

Cox, Samuel Hanson. *Quakerism not Christianity*. 1833.

Curti, Merle. "The Great Mr. Locke, America's Philosopher 1765-1865," Huntington Library *Bulletin*, XI (April, 1937), 107-151.

Dana, Richard Henry, Sr. "The Novels of Charles Brockden Brown," *The United States Review and Literary Gazette*, II (August, 1827), 321-333.

Davis, John. *Travels of Four Years and a Half in the United States of America, during 1798, 1799, 1800, 1801, and 1802.* New York, 1909.

Dennie, Joseph. *The Port Folio*, III (June 4, 1803), 181.

"Dunlap's Memoirs of Charles Brockden Brown, the American Novelist," *Monthly Review*, CLXXX (October, 1822), 151-157.

"Edgar Allan Poe," *Edinburgh Review*, CVII (April, 1858), 419-426.

Ellis, H. M. Joseph Dennie and His Circle," University of Texas *Studies in English*, No. 40 (1915).

Ellis, Milton. "The Author of the First American Novel," *American Literature*, IV (January, 1933), 359-368.

Erskine, John. *Leading American Novelists.* New York, 1910, pp. 3-49.

Fisher, Sidney B. *The Quaker Colonies.* New Haven, 1919.

Goodrich, Carter, and Sol Davison. "The Wage-Earner in the Westward Movement," *Political Science Quarterly*, L (1935), 161-185; LI (1936), 61-116.

Greene, Evart Boutell. *The Revolutionary Generation.* New York, 1943.

Griswold, Rufus Wilmot. *Prose Writers of America.* Philadelphia, 1870, pp. 107-111. (First appeared in 1846.)

Haviland, Thomas P. "Preciosité Crosses the Atlantic," *Publications of the Modern Language Association*, LIX (March, 1944), 131-141.

Hazlitt, William. "William Ellery Channing's Sermons and Tracts," *Edinburgh Review*, L (October, 1829), 125.

Hendrickson, J. C. "A Note on *Wieland*," *American Literature*, VII (November, 1936), 305-306.

Holbach, Baron, *Système de la Nature.* Trans. H. D. Robinson (2 vols.). Boston, 1877.

Johnson, Merle. "American First Editions," *Publishers' Weekly*, CXXI (June 18, 1932), 2422.

Jones, Frank Pierce, "The Role of the Classics in the Emancipation of Women," *Classical Journal*, XXXIX (March, 1944), 326-342.

Jones, Howard Mumford, "European Ideas in American," *American Literature*, VII (Nov., 1935), 253-254.

Keiser, Albert. *The Indian in American Literature.* London, 1933, pp. 33-37.

Kimball, Leroy Elwood. Introduction to *Alcuin; A Dialogue* (Type-facsimile Reprint of the First Edition Printed in 1798), New Haven, 1935.

Leary, Lewis. *That Rascal Freneau.* New Brunswick, N. J., 1941.

"Literary Notices," *Graham's Magazine*, L (March and May, 1857), 277, 468; LI (July, 1857), 86.

Loshe, Lillie D. *Early American Novels.* New York, 1907, pp. 29-58.

Marble, Annie Russell. "The Centenary of America's First Novelist," *The Dial*, XLVIII (February 16, 1910), 109-110.

———. *Heralds of American Literature.* Chicago, 1907.

Marchand, Ernest. Introduction to an edition of *Ormond.* New York, 1937.

———. "The Literary Opinions of Charles Brockden Brown," *Studies in Philology*, XXXI (October, 1934), 541-566.

McDowell, Tremaine. "Scott on Cooper and Brockden Brown," *Modern Language Notes*, XLV (January, 1930), 18-20.

"Memoirs of Charles Brockden Brown, the American Novelist," *New Monthly Magazine*, VI (April, 1822).

Miller, P. G., and T. H. Johnson. *The Puritans*. New York, 1938.

Morris, Mabel. "Charles Brockden Brown and the American Indian," *American Literature*, XVIII (November, 1946), 244-247.

Morse, James Herbert. "The Native Element in American Fiction," *Century Illustrated Monthly Magazine*, XXVI (May, 1883), 288-298.

Mott, Frank Luther. *A History of American Magazines, I: 1741-1850*. New York, 1930 pp. 124, 150, 190, 218-222.

Oberholtzer, Ellis Paxson. "The First American Novelist," *Journal of American History*, I (April, 1907), 236-240.

"On the Writings of Charles Brockden Brown, the American Novelist," *New Monthly Magazine and Universal Register*, XIV (December, 1820), 609-617.

"On the Writings of Charles Brockden Brown and Washington Irving," *Blackwood's Edinburgh Magazine*, VI (February, 1820), 554-561.

Parrington, Vernon Lewis. *The Connecticut Wits*. New York, 1926.

————. *Main Currents in American Thought*. New York, 1930, I, 180-182, 190-193, 368-381; II, 188-190.

Pattee, Fred Lewis. Introduction to *Wieland*. New York, 1926.

————. *The First Century of American Literature, 1770-1870*. New York, 1935, pp. 96-106, 190-193.

Peden, William. "Thomas Jefferson and Charles Brockden Brown," *Maryland Quarterly*, II (Spring, 1944), 65-68.

"Periodical Literature of the United States," *North American Review*, XXXIX (October, 1834), 295.

Prescott, F. C. "Wieland and Frankenstein," *American Literature*, II (May, 1930), 172-173.

Prospectus, *Port Folio*, I (1801), i.

Quinn, Arthur Hobson. *American Fiction, an Historical and Critical Survey*. New York, 1936, pp. 25-39.

Randall, John Herman, Jr. *The Making of the Modern Mind*. Boston, 1940.

Rodell, Fred. "The Law Is the Bunk," *Prose Annual*, No. 3, ed. Gay, Boatright, and Wycoff. Boston, 1942.

Shafer, Joseph. "Some Facts Bearing on the Safety Valve Theory," *Wisconsin Magazine of History*, XX (1936), 216-232.

Sickels, Eleanor. "Shelley and Charles Brockden Brown," *Publications of the Modern Language Association*, XLV (December, 1930), 1116-1128.

Smith, George Barnett. "Brockden Brown," *Fortnightly Review*, XXX (September, 1878), 399-432.

Snell, George. "Charles Brockden Brown: Apocalypticalist," *University of Kansas City Review*, IV (Winter, 1944), 131-138.

Solve, Melvin T. "Shelley and the Novels of Brown," in the *Fred Newton Scott Anniversary Papers*. Chicago, 1929, pp. 141-156.

Stearns, Bertha M. "A Speculation Concerning Charles Brockden Brown," *Pennsylvania Magazine of History and Biography*, LIX (April, 1933), 99-105.

"Supplement to the Guide to the Manuscript Collection in the Historical Society of Pennsylvania," *Pennsylvania Magazine of History and Biography,* LXVIII (January, 1944), 99.

Tassin, Algernon. *The Magazine in America.* New York, 1916, pp. 109-112.

Trent, W. P., and John Erskine. *Great American Writers.* New York, 1912, pp. 12-20.

Tuckerman, H. T. *Mental Portraits.* London, 1853, pp. 146-156.

———. "Sketch of American Literature," in T. B. Shaw's *Outlines of English Literature.* Philadelphia, 1852.

Van Doren, Carl. *The American Novel.* New York, 1921, 10-15.

———. *Benjamin Franklin.* New York, 1938.

———. "Early American Realism," *Nation,* XCIX (November 12, 1914), 577-578.

———. "Minor Tales of Brockden Brown," *Nation,* C (January 14, 1915), 46-47.

———, ed. *Selections from Benjamin Franklin and Jonathan Edwards.* New York, 1920.

Verplanck, G. C. "Dunlap's Life of Charles Brockden Brown," *North American Review,* IX (June, 1819), 58-77.

Vilas, Martin S. *Charles Brockden Brown, A Study of Early American Fiction.* Burlington, Vt. 1904.

Warfel, Harry R. "Charles Brockden Brown's First Published Poem," *American Notes and Queries,* I (April, 1941), 19-20.

———. "Charles Brockden Brown's German Sources," *Modern Language Quarterly,* I (September, 1940), 357-363.

———. Introduction to an edition of *The Rhapsodist, and Other Uncollected Writings.* New York, 1943.

Wharton, Anne H. "Philadelphia in Literature," *The Critic,* XLVII (September, 1905), 224-231.

Whittier, J. G. "Fanaticism," in *Writings.* Riverside Edition. Boston and New York, 1889, VII, 391-395.

Woodberry, George E. "Charles Brockden Brown," *Atlantic Monthly,* LXI (May, 1888), 710-714.

———. *Literary Memoirs of the Nineteenth Century.* New York, 1921, pp. 275-282.

Woody, Thomas. *Early Quaker Education in Pennsylvania.* New York, 1920.

———. *Quaker Education in the Colony and State of New Jersey.* Philadelphia, 1923.

## ANTHOLOGIES

(Arranged chronologically)

*A Book of American Literature,* eds. Franklyn B. Snyder and Edward D. Snyder, New York, 1928, pp. 230-236.

*Century Readings in American Literature,* ed. Fred Lewis Pattee, New York (4th edition), 1932, pp. 152-159.

*American Poetry and Prose,* ed. Norman Foerster, Boston and New York, 1934, pp. 259-271.

*American Life in Literature,* ed. Jay B. Hubbell, New York, 1936, pp. 215-225.

*The American Mind,* eds. Harry R. Warfel, Ralph H. Gabriel, and Stanley T. Williams, New York, 1937, I, 320-327.

*The Literature of America,* eds., A. H. Quinn, A. C. Baugh, and W. D. Howe, New York, 1938, I, 431-433.

*American Issues,* eds., Willard Thorp, Merle Curti, and Carlos Baker, Philadelphia, 1941, I, 150-156.

*American Literature,* eds., Joe Lee Davis, John T. Frederick, and Frank Luther Mott, New York, 1948, I, 231-240.

## BACKGROUND MATERIALS

Babbitt, Irving. *Masters of Modern French Criticism.* Boston, 1912.

Bailey, Marcia Edgerton. *A Lesser Hartford Wit: Dr. Elihu Hubbard Smith. Maine Bulletin,* XXX, No. 15 (1928).

Berkeley, George. *The Works of George Berkeley, ed.* Alexander Campbell Fraser. Edinburgh, 1881.

Boykin, Edward, ed. *The Wisdom of Thomas Jefferson.* New York, 1941.

Cobbett, William. *Selections from Cobbett's Political Works.* London, 1835.

Dunlap, William. *History of the American Theater,* Vol. I. New York, 1832.

Fénelon, François. *De l'Education des filles.* Paris, 1687.

Francis, John Wakefield. *Old New York.* New York, 1866.

Godwin, William. *Political Justice.* 2nd ed. London, 1796.

Howard, George Elliott. *A History of Matrimonial Institutions.* Chicago, 1904.

Johnson, William, ed. *Memorial of the Life and Character of John Wells.* 1874.

Kellog, Thelma Louise. *The Life and Works of John David. Maine Bulletin* XXVI, No. 8 (June, 1924).

Kelly, Howard A., and Walter L. Burrage. *American Medical Biographies,* Vol. I. Baltimore, 1920.

Lamb, Martha J. *History of the City of New York,* Vol. I. New York, c. 1877-1880.

Miller, Dr. Edward. *The Medical Works of Dr. Edward Miller,* Vol. I. Ed. Samuel Miller. 1814.

Miller, Samuel. *Life of Samuel L. Miller.* Philadelphia, 1869.

*New York Mirror,* I, 265-266.

Poulain de la Barre, François. *De l'Egaliti des deux sexes.* Paris, 1673.

Stanwood, Edward. *A History of the Presidency,* Vol. I. Boston, 1898.

Trumbull, John. *The Progress of Dulness.* 1772-1773.

Turner, E. R., "Woman Suffrage in New Jersey: 1790-1807," Smith College, *Studies in History,* I (1916), 165-187.

Wendell, Barrett, and C. N. Grennough. *A History of Literature in America.* New York, 1904.

Wilson, James Grant. *Memorial History of the City of New York,* Vol. IV. New York, 1892-1893.

# GENERAL INDEX

*(Items under* CHARLES BROCKDEN BROWN *are separately indexed under the following headings:* LIFE, *pp. 356 ff.;* NOVELIST, EDITOR, AND CRITIC, *pp. 358 ff.; and* ATTITUDES AND OPINIONS, *pp. 361 ff.)*

# CHARLES BROCKDEN BROWN

## I. LIFE

Albany, CBB visits, 217
Ancestry, 13-14

Belles Lettres Club, 42-49; membership, 42; formation, 42-43; type of writing, 42; object of club, 42; deciding factor in early life of CBB, 43; CBB gives keynote address, 43-45; CBB's fear of democracy, 44 n.
Birth, 13
Blackstone, CBB's aversion to, 38
Boyhood interests, 17-18
Bringhurst, Joseph, and William Wood Wilkins, friendship with, 23-49
*British Treaty*, 261; wrongly ascribed to CBB, 261
Brockden, Charles, CBB named for, 14 n.
Brown, Elijah, father of CBB, 13; brothers and sisters of, 14; character of, 14; marriage to Mary Armitt, 14; children of, see *Family Tree*, 15; conveyancer, 17, 108; landbroker, 17, 108; clerk in U. S. Treasury, 108
Brown, Elizabeth Linn: CBB falls in love with, 197; character of, 197-198; excerpts from unpublished letters from CBB to, 198-213; jealousy of sister Susan, 199; obituary, 292-294
Brown family, attitude toward CBB, 34; unambitious as businessmen, 109; not active in state, municipal, or religious affairs, 109
Brown-Henrietta correspondence, 55-107; subject of the letters, 54-55; personality of CBB, 56; skill in composition, 56-57; on immortality, 57-58; idealization of Henrietta G., 58-59, 63, 82-85, 94; romantic sensibility, 59; long walks, 59, 90-93; sentimental heroine, 61, 77-78; romantic despair, 61; Wertherism, 62-63; extent of his knowledge, 63-64; educated women, 64; Henrietta's desire to learn classical languages, 65; Henrietta's uncle, 66; women and cul-

tural pursuits, 66-67; opinion of Italian, 67-68; knowledge of French, 68-69; turns from reading to writing, 69; evaluation of classical literature, 69-71; importance of studying English language and literature, 71; knowledge of the classics, 72, 72 n.; romantic melancholy, 72-73; hindrances to marriage with Henrietta G., 72-73, 85-86, 107; Neoplatonic love, 73-74; plays the flute, 74-75; Henrietta's admiration for his talents, 75-76; pleads with Henrietta to marry him, 86; complex personality, 87-89; first meeting with Henrietta G., 87-89; Henrietta plays the harpsichord, 88; minds of women, 93-94, 93 n.; ideal home-site, 96-97; power of the imagination, 96-97; description of the Brown-Wilkins lodge, 97-98; self-analysis, 100-101; unhappiness with family, 101-102; on the changing nature of man, 103-104; opinion of women's talents, 104; influence of Henrietta on CBB, 104-105
Brown, Joseph, invites CBB to go into mercantile business, 109
Brown-Wilkins correspondence, 24-40
Burial in Friends Burial Ground in Philadelphia, 291-292

*Carrils and the Ormes*, preparation of, 41-42
Children born to CBB and Elizabeth Linn, 216
College education, attitude toward, 21-22
Composition, theory of, 49-52
Cuilli Pays de Vaud, letter written from, 28-31

Death, 291
Decision to become an author by profession, 52
Dennie, Joseph, appraisal of CBB, 303
Desire for authorship, 37-38

## II. NOVELIST, EDITOR, AND CRITIC

## III. Attitudes and Opinions